Re-viewing English

edited by
Wayne Sawyer
Ken Watson
and
Eva Gold

St Clair Press
Sydney 1998

Re-Viewing English

Acknowledgements

The editors would like to express their gratitude
for permission to use the following:

The photograph from *Dolly* magazine in Chapter
14, courtesy of Simon Lekias and *Dolly* magazine.

"Night Sowing" by David Campbell from his
Selected Poems, (1986, Angus and Robertson)
courtesy of Harper Collins, Australia.

Additionally, we have sought permission
for the use of "Slow" by Gundy Graham.

© St Clair Press
Sydney 1998

ISBN 0 949898 84 8

St Clair Press Pty Ltd ACN 003 829 043
PO Box 287
Rozelle NSW 2039 Australia
Phone: 02 9818 1942
Fax: 02 9418 1923
e-mail: stclair@australis.net.au

Cover Design: Tony Jas, 15 Hawkins Street, Artarmon 2064, Phone: 02 9904 8043
Illustrations: Prudence Sawyer
Photography: John Stephens
Typesetting: Propaganda/goose, PO Box 161, Glebe 2037
Phone: 02 9660 0037, Fax: 02 9552 1714
Printing: Alken Press Pty Ltd, 128 Long Street, Smithfield 2164
Phone: 02 9604 7999, Fax: 02 9604 0708

Contents

Section IV: Writing Texts

Section V: Oracy and Drama

Section VI: Aspects of Language

Section VII: Assessment

Section VIII: Aboriginal Perspectives

Dedication

During the time this book was being written, the world lost a number of great English educators. We would like to dedicate *Re-Viewing English* to the memory of:
Mike Hayhoe ◆ James Moffett ◆ Bob Shafer ◆ Syd Smyth.
All English teachers also owe a debt to:
Garth Boomer ◆ James Britton ◆ Andrew Wilkinson
each of whom has died in the last few years.

Editors' Preface

Re-Viewing English has two aims, which we see as complementary. The first is to invite English teachers to look again at some of the major advances in English teaching that took place in the two decades following the Dartmouth Seminar of 1966, and to reflect on their relevance as we approach 2001. The second is to explore some of the more recent developments in our subject and its pedagogy.

Often it seems that English teaching, like the Red Queen in *Through the Looking-Glass*, takes one step backward for every two taken forward. Not only are some of the best teaching ideas of the period from 1966 to 1986 in danger of being forgotten, but attempts are being made to re-write the history of education in general, and of English teaching in particular, during this period. As this preface is being written, a professor from the University of New South Wales is talking of the 1960s and 1970s as a period of "anarchic progressivism" in education. Yet a most comprehensive survey of New South Wales English Departments carried out in the mid 1970s identified only a handful of departments to which the adjective 'progressive' could property be applied, and only one high school where 'progressive' ideas were being put into practice across subject boundaries. Incidentally, this school's Higher School Certificate results, when considered in relation to its intake, were probably the best in the State.

Another myth about this period is that English teachers neglected the study of language. This claim is made despite the fact that the most widely used textbook series contained an immense amount of traditional grammar, and that the survey referred to above found that a great deal of language study – some of it, to be sure, misguided in its emphasis on 'dummy-run' exercises – was occurring in English lessons. Claims of a decline in standards of written expression similarly lack supporting evidence.

English teachers, more than any others, need to be on guard against having the content and methods of their subject defined and circumscribed by outsiders with their own agendas. This can be done only if teachers have a sound understanding of their subject and have developed a clear rationale to guide their teaching practice. We hope that this book will make a positive contribution to those ends.

Wayne Sawyer, Ken Watson, Eva Gold

Watson, Ken (1978) *The New English in Secondary Schools: A Study of the Origins and Implementation of the 1971 English Syllabus (Years 7-10)*, Unpublished M Ed thesis, University of Sydney.

Introduction

Graham Little

I t is an honour to be invited to write an introduction to these papers, which give an impressive overview of professional thinking about English teaching in Australia at the end of the century. It seems appropriate to consider major developments since the beginning of the century as a way of assessing how far we have come. In doing so I attempt to place English teaching in the context of education and the politics of education, using New South Wales as a case study in the knowledge that developments in other States have not been dissimilar. As suggested by the editors, I attempt to flesh out some of the references to earlier periods with my own recollections.

Framework

The table below follows Simon Marginson's *Educating Australia: Government, Economy and Citizen Since 1960* (1998) in identifying three periods in the history of Australian education:
+ a period of relative stasis under the state bureaucracies;
+ liberalisation under state and federal co-operation since about 1960;
+ an attempt at reassertion of bureaucratic control since 1975.
Within each period, note is taken of . . .
+ economics and politics;
+ education and curriculum in general;
+ English teaching in particular.
For curriculum, reference is made to the standard Tyler model of curriculum development, *Aims and Objectives* -> *Content* -> *Learning Processes* -> *Evaluation*. This helps to identify variations in emphasis.

Overview

1880s-1910s	The Colonial Education acts: elementary schooling in Basic Skills. ✳ State systems of secondary education. ✳ Curriculum as content for assessment by public examinations. ✳ The long reign of 'tripod' English: grammar, composition, ✳ literature.

1960s	✳ ✳ ✳ ✳ ✳ ✳	Economic boom. Strains in state systems alleviated by federal-state co-operation in expansion and liberalisation: The Karmel Report. Curriculum seen more in terms of learning processes, with increased school-based curriculum development and assessment.
1975- 1997	✳ ✳ ✳	Campaigns about declining Basic Skills due to 'progressivism' in a context of recession and economic rationalism: economy and efficiency, user pays, restructuring, downsizing, the bottom line. Attempts at control through evaluation of outcomes: Basic Skills Tests, National Curriculum Statements, Profiles, Benchmarks. 'Post-modern' models of English teaching.
1998		Review of literacy through the century: retrospective studies by The Australian Language and Literacy Council and the Australian Census Bureau, shedding light on the history of Basic Skills.

Basic Skills

I begin with this topic as a key issue throughout the century, which needs to be addressed before any others.

Origins

I have written before (Little, 1977) about confusions underlying the coining of the expression *standards of literacy* in the nineteenth century. The original context was the establishment of mass schooling in Britain and her colonies, as advocated by political economists on the model designed by the leading jurist and utilitarian philosopher Jeremy Bentham. The links between this movement and contemporary economic rationalism in politics and education are not accidental.

Bentham was a major influence in shaping the idea of "economic man" [sic] as a sort of automaton: a bundle of sense organs responding to the elements of light, sound, heat, pleasure, pain and so on. This automaton had but one motive: to maximise sensory pleasure while minimising sensory pain. It had but one way of processing information – to associate pleasure with things leading to pleasure and associate pain with things leading to pain. To Bentham, words such as *mind, justice* and *rights* were nonsense. If rulers were wise to all this, they would maintain their power in the manner of Napoleon, through clear and logically-consistent laws, vigilant surveillance and consistent use of stick and carrot, with mass schooling as a major instrument of policy.

Bentham stated that a good school would be run like a monastery, an army, a factory, a workhouse, a hospital or a prison, under the eye of all-seeing supervisors who were under the eye of **their** all-seeing supervisors in an unbroken chain of command right up to the top. The children would be taken off the streets to be trained by repetitive drills in basic skills useful to commerce, industry and the state.

For literacy, Bentham said that all that was needed was systematic and sequential drill in letter-sound associations leading to the recognition, pronunciation and writing of words, their classification into parts of speech, and the rules for combining them into sentences. Diligently pursued, a systematic and sequential program of this kind would infallibly produce the ability to read and write for any subject, purpose and audience, without wasting time on reading literature or practising composition.

Bentham also said that as his system was based on perfect knowledge of cause and effect, any failures would obviously be due to teachers not following their instructions to the letter. As teaching was simply a matter of following simple instructions, unpaid pupils (pupil-teachers) could be effectively used, motivated by the carrot of later employment. The paid teacher's life would be one of monotonous drudgery, motivated solely by fear of instant dismissal for departing from orders.

Parliament adopted the system and before long it was installed in the colonies. It was satirised by Dickens in *Hard Times*, and publicly attacked by Matthew Arnold, the first of Her Majesty's Inspectors of Schools. Arnold rejected the idea of education as instilling mechanical habits, when anything resembling genuine education meant the free play of mind upon such habits. He also testified that the 'standards' were so poorly defined that no two inspectors could agree on their application.

What has been learned about language and learning since those days has given many further reasons for refuting Bentham, as indicated in this collection of papers, together with such encyclopaedic works as those of Crystal (1995, 1997) and Pinker (1994, 1997).

The fact remains that Australian education was founded upon Bentham's model, albeit not as severely implemented as he would have wished. Nevertheless the notions of literacy as mechanical drills which would work perfectly if teachers were not slack gained an uncanny hold on Australian folklore.

Declining Standards

I have been hearing and reading this expression as long as I can remember. There was an outburst on the subject in my first year of teaching at Broken Hill High School in 1952, but I did not believe it for two reasons. First, I recalled that in my own rather ordinary Australian family and neighbourhood the older people were generally very basically literate thanks to their elementary schooling, but the more recent generations had more facility because of more opportunity to participate in formal education. Second, I observed, as the keeper of an attendance roll, that parental notes generally showed less facility with writing than did the composition books of the children approaching the school leaving age of 15.

It was around 1975 that the Declining Standards Theory, in the form that attributed the decline to 'progressive education', became the theme of an international campaign, as documented by Marginson (1997). It involved:

✦ The Back to Basics movement in the USA, linked to the Cold War through the Sputnik scare in the 1950s, and taken up in subsequent liaisons among various groups on the New Right, cultural conservatives, religious fundamentalists and advocates of Reaganomics.

✦ The culturally conservative *Black Papers on Education* in the UK, feeding into Thatcherism and resulting in the remarkable campaign slogan, *Educashun isn't wirking.*

✦ ACES, the self-appointed Australian Council for Educational Standards, which quoted freely from the overseas sources and vigorously developed its own variations of the general theme.

As Marginson points out, the Australian debate was, like the others, scarcely a debate at all. The campaigners were:

> . . . a select group of institutional heads, university experts, industry leaders and politicians led by the culturally conservative educators in the Australian Council for Educational Standards . . . citing media reports of each other's statements as evidence and authority.

As in 1952, I did not believe such claims. By then I had researched the issue and worked in schools in the UK and the USA as well as Australia, and failed to uncover any convincing evidence of either declining standards or a triumph of progressive education. (Little 1978)

In debating decline theorists face to face on several occasions, I noted how agile their minds were. When confronted with evidence they did not like, they would say it was not 'hard' evidence. If it was a little hard for them to refute on the spot, they would say that even if that evidence was valid, there was a great deal of **other** evidence to the contrary. When they couldn't readily produce any, they would shift ground to say that whether past standards were higher or lower was not really the point; the fact was that standards were not good enough now and that in any case it was obvious that here was an impending decline in need of being arrested.

Hard Evidence at Last?

The most extensive evidence on standards of literacy over time was published by The Commonwealth of Australia in 1997: The Australian Language and Literacy Council's *Australian Literacies*, a thorough study of all previous evidence, and The Australian Census Bureau's new evidence, gathered in a generational survey.

The following statement from the preface of *Australian Literacies* may well be the most important ever made on the subject. (Emphasis as in the original.)

> From the very outset it is important to state unambiguously that there is **no general literacy crisis in Australia**. There is, however, systematic under-performance in English literacy by some groups and many individuals.

The evidence from all sources was that older people have more problems than younger, and unsurprisingly this is systematically associated with increasing opportunity through the generations to participate in formal education. Apart from this, six categories of persons were nominated as particularly likely to have literacy problems:

1. children and adults who are socio-economically and educationally disadvantaged;
2. some children and adults of non-English-speaking backgrounds;
3. some groups of both urban and rural Aborigines and Torres Strait Islanders;
4. older Australians with interrupted or disrupted schooling;
5. some Australians who live in remote or isolated areas;
6. some groups who are disabled, physically, emotionally or intellectually.

While we may agree with Marginson that the Decline Theory is too strongly entrenched in some minds to be negated by surveys or logic, it can be reasonably agreed that as there is no decline, we do not need to seek a cause of the decline, such as 'progressive education' or developments in English teaching since the 1960s. Therefore we do not have to seek a cure for the decline such as putting the clock back. What matters is to get on with the job of trying to do better and better for all Australians.

Meanwhile it remains a duty to disseminate these findings as widely as we can, for the media and the politicians have not taken much notice of them. After all, it is shock-horror that sells papers and wins votes.

Comments on Three Periods of English teaching

Foundations to About 1960

Upon Federation, education remained a state matter. In a run of patriotic enthusiasm about being a new nation in a competitive world, the states somewhat liberalised primary education and set up secondary education systems. Despite (or was it because of?) war, depression, war and post-war reconstruction, the systems were thereafter steered steady as she goes.

What was it like to be schooled in this period? I come into the story in the 1930s as Kegworth Public School, Leichhardt. On Basic Skills I report that I don't know when or how I learned to read, but do remember skipping first grade after Miss Lamont found me reading under the desk instead of attending to her phonics lessons. I also remember accompanying the keen readers in my family in regular visits to the public library, and reading at least three books a week from a very early age. I found primary English enjoyable but I recall being surprised when there was a sudden fad for reading around the class in sixth grade that there were a number of boys who could scarcely read. There was not much Benthamite teaching, except in arithmetic, when some of us used to go to pieces when a finger was poked into our faces with a shout of "Seven nines".

At the Primary Final examination, I not unexpectedly made it to a selective high school. As indicated in the table, the curriculum consisted of subject-matter knowledge assessed by public examinations, which in New South Wales were held at the ends of Years 9 and 11. 'Tripod' English was taught under the syllabus of 1911, which was not amended until 1943, and then only slightly.

When I occasionally meet old friends from high school, we reminisce about our main English teacher, dear old Mr Fisher-Webster, who specialised in mysterious Spanish proverbs. We liked them, and when we realised he was making them up on the spur of the moment, we liked them all the more. This reminds me of the French proverb: *What teachers teach is themselves*, and that leads me to make up my own anti-Benthamite proverb: *Systems may prescribe what they prescribe, but teachers will teach what they teach, and learners will learn what they learn.*

As for the official curriculum, Mr Fisher-Webster taught grammar twice a week by dictating notes from memory, but tended to forget what topic he was up to. When he asked us, we always said "Nouns, Sir" and he usually went on with nouns. In these sessions, he tended to doze off in mid-sentence, especially after lunch. It was a point of honour never to disturb him. What grammar we needed to know for English examinations we got from foreign languages taught on the grammar-and-translation model, which taught me to speak French as haltingly as some of my friends and neighbours speak English, having been taught by the same method.

Composition. In Mr Fisher-Webster's class we did not write compositions except for half-yearly examinations. These efforts showed that we could all write a glib piece on a conventional topic 'out of the blue', so what else was there to do? In my case it was writing to a relative away at the war and for the Argonauts' Club on ABC radio, and getting encouraging feedback from no less a personage than A D Hope disguised as a centaur.

Literature. In Mr Fisher-Webster's lessons the high point was his raconteurship. The challenge for us students was to ask him questions which used the text as a pretext for getting him to reminisce about being a pilot in World War 1, and to talk about his travels and books he found interesting. This, together with the standard method of one lesson per week on a section of each text, meant that we never 'finished' a book other than a Shakespeare play by the end of the year. This did not matter, because we could all read and write and were well practised in taking examinations.

I kept on reading my own way through novels, non-fiction and drama, and was eventually told by my teachers' college principal that I had topped the state in English Honours, and that was why I was awarded a scholarship to be an English teacher. And so I continued to read my own way through a degree, with some attention to lectures, and did the same in my Diploma of Education. And thus I joined the generations of English teachers who returned to schools to teach under the same official curriculum they were supposed to have been taught.

I began to learn in my first appointment to Broken Hill in 1952 that many of my unconscious assumptions about students and English teaching, based on my own secondary education, were irrelevant to the point of culture-shock. Except for some congenial relationships with some classes, I was not teaching well and neither was the school as a whole. The official curriculum was still irrelevant to what was actually going on, but now it mattered in ways that could not be glossed over by the gentlemanly games of my old school. I also began to realise that the NSW and other state systems were in deep crisis not only because of rapid increase in the sheer number of students, but in the variety of their backgrounds.

Economic Boom and Educational Reform 1960-75

This became a period of unprecedented federal-state co-operation on education policy supported by both sides of politics. High points were the Karmel Report and the setting up of the Schools Commission. Even the previously unthinkable idea of government aid for private schools became a reality.

In English, the period was marked by the emergence of new thinking, both local and in the form of the influential post-Dartmouth books disseminated by the newly-formed English Teachers' Associations and their federation into the Australian Association for the Teaching of English. English teaching began to change, although not rapidly, if only because education systems are like aircraft carriers, and are not easy to turn around – something that current politicians and bureaucrats seem not to understand.

The 1971 Year 7-10 English Syllabus for NSW

The articles which follow take up the story of developments in thinking about English teaching in the post-Dartmouth period, but there may be some value in a short case-study of the first state syllabus to attempt to institutionalise 'The New English' in Australia: The NSW Year 7-10 English Syllabus of 1971, of which I was Chair.

Change was in the air. The trigger was an administrative problem of four syllabuses brought out over time to cater for Advanced, Credit, Ordinary and Modified Levels. Through the English Teachers' Association, of which I was Chair, teachers asked for a single syllabus, on the grounds that English was not a subject that could be carved up into discrete areas like Algebra and Trigonometry in Mathematics. The system agreed, and appointed me, as an Inspector of Schools and Chair of the Syllabus Committee, to undertake a revision. It then announced that henceforth all syllabuses would be in the form of a statement of aims and objectives.

A major issue was how to interpret the ambiguous Aims and Objectives model of curriculum development. At what level of detail were objectives to be prescribed and by whom? The committee decided that objectives should be prescribed at a fairly high level of generality as exemplified by an example of an objective in third-year French: *Read the Paris dailies with understanding.* That sort of objective would give acceptable directions to schools, but not put them in straitjackets.

We saw our task in terms of framing proposals for widespread consultation before adoption or amendment. We found no ready-made models to suit our brief, and began to try out various possibilities. We came to think of English as a complex whole that should be considered from complementary points of view, rather than as a set of discrete building-blocks. The headings for the syllabus gradually emerged as:

AIM		
The utmost possible competence in understanding and using language		

LANGUAGE	SCOPE IN USE	IN CONTEXT
Vocabulary	Listening	Everyday communication
Usage	Speaking	Media
Structure	Reading	Literature
Style	Writing	Personal expression

KEY QUESTIONS
Meaning: What is said?
Form: How is it said?
Values: What is the value to self and others
of its being said, and said in the particular way?

Looking at English from the point of view of aims, we came to the view that there was one aim, which Chomsky was calling competence: capacity to do a range of things with language. In that sense, valid assessment of a student's competence would be a generalisation based on a fair sample of work of various agreed kinds: in short, a portfolio.

We agreed that the basic content of English was **texts**. This was paraphrased as **language in use in context**, under the heading *Scope* to suggest a set of points of view. This approach provided headings for three aspects of language use that were always features of texts: forms of language, modes of use and contexts of use. We made it explicit in Notes to the Syllabus that there was little value in discussing form without reference to meaning, or either without regard to context.

That was clearly not all there was to it. We also knew that a 'discipline' is defined not merely by its content, but by the sorts of questions it asks. For example, texts can provide the raw materials of acoustics or law and so on, but the questions asked about the texts in those disciplines are not the ones we wanted to be emphasised in English for Years 7-10. We reflected on common questions asked about texts and entertained for a while a communications model using the Wh-questions: *Who is saying what to whom? When, where why and how? With what effects?* We came to see this as valid up to a point, but limited because it did not raise the vital question of values.

It was then that we thought of the three Key Questions which seemed to be characteristic of lively discussion in good English classrooms: questions of meaning, and of form in relation to meaning and of values in relation to both. Like Matthew Arnold, we saw the free play of mind upon such questions as the hallmark of education as opposed to Benthamite indoctrination. And if there were no absolute right answers, so that at the end of a discussion people might agree to differ while recognising that others have a right to different views, so much the better for education in a democracy.

We wrote a small number of objectives for each of the items in the middle section of the table above, and thought we were beginning to get it right when there seemed no more to say without going into excessive detail.

The Syllabus was overwhelmingly endorsed by the reference groups and the huge majority of those who attended meetings in all regions of the state, and made written submissions, and the Draft Syllabus was adopted by the Board.

After its release, Decline theorists came out of the woodwork to express outrage at the (non-existent) 'banning' of grammar and Shakespeare while making the uncritical viewing of crass TV shows compulsory. On grammar it may be worth recording that Notes recommended continued use of the common terms for the parts of speech along with 'phrase', 'clause', 'sentence' and 'paragraph'. What they did make clear was that exercises in parsing and analysis (exercises on form without reference to meaning or value) would no longer be compulsory in public examinations. Teachers could still teach them if they liked.

Obviously there would be a need for inservice teacher education for the sharing of ways of implementing the approach, and this began to take place through the Inspectorate, the appointment of English Consultants, and the English Teachers' Association. It gave us some satisfaction to learn that when the syllabus was revised a decade later it was basically re-endorsed, and that the later National Statement of English bears a fairly close family resemblance to it.

Recession and Contraction After 1975

As indicated above, this period has been marked by the campaign by the Right about declining standards, cutbacks related to recession, and the 'economic rationalist' cult of economy and efficiency, and renewed attempts at centralised control. (Saul, 1997) Meanwhile the dialogue within English teaching has continued, to include further issues discussed in this collection of papers, such as genre theory, 'critical literacy' and systemic-functional linguistics, with its interests in relationships between language and power. And why not?

The changing economic and political climate has not been propitious for optimistic discussions because of the rise of 'economic rationalism' in the governance of education: 'restructuring' in the interests of 'more for less', and a shift from 'management by objectives' to management by centralised prescription of 'outcomes', with little regard for inputs and processes.

A major model of such an approach has proved to be that of Mrs Thatcher's administration in the UK. Its *Education Reform Act* can be seen as a sort of Benthamite counter-reformation of the reforms of the previous period: making cutbacks, putting more power over education and curriculum into the hands of central government, and – especially – authorising bureaucratic processes for setting up a national curriculum together with performance targets for K-12, with 'league tables' to identify under-performing schools.

In New South Wales, an education act of the same general tenor, with the same name, was implemented by the Coalition Government, and has not been amended by the ensuing Labor administration. State and Federal co-operation involving both sides of politics has continued, with schemes for national curriculum and assessment on the Thatcher model.

I have written about these developments in *The Value-Added Child* (Little, 1992). It would seem that in curriculum, as distinct from funding, these supposedly fast-track reforms have so far failed to meet success on their own terms. Mrs Thatcher's national curriculum and assessment schemes collapsed under their own weight before her administration was replaced by that of Mr Blair. There seem to have been many reasons for this, including a proposed assessment system for English which provided lists of criteria too numerous to be practicable and too incoherent to be valid. Underlying all this is the attempt to impose these things on schools without due consultation and advice.

In Australia, the proposed National Profiles in English have failed to attain consensus for the same underlying reason, and have been sent back 'for more work'. The attempt to establish national 'benchmarks' for literacy (Australian Language and Literacy Council, 1997) has resulted in a stand-off over rival versions. But various 'Basic Skills Tests' are proliferating among the states, so far with concentration on Years 3, 5 and 9 or 10. Again, there is the tendency to impose such things without due consultation.

So the old argument between Bentham and Arnold has been revived in our times. I agree with Marginson and Saul that we should see ourselves and our students as citizens of a civil society, not just parts of an economy, and be willing to stand up and be counted on the issue.

References
Australian Bureau of Statistics (1997) *Survey of Adult Literacy.*
Australian Council for Educational Research (1997) *Literacy Standards in Australia*, Canberra: Commonwealth of Australia.
Australian Language and Literacy Council (1997) *Australian Literacies*, Canberra: Commmonwealth of Australia.
Crystal, D (1995) *The Cambridge Encyclopedia of the English Language.* Cambridge: Cambridge University Press.
Crystal, D (second edition, 1997). *The Cambridge Encyclopedia of Language*, Cambridge: Cambridge University Press.
Little, G (1977) "Meaning and Maturation in English Curriculum" in K D Watson and R D Eagleson (eds) *English in Secondary Schools Today and Tomorrow*, Sydney: English Teachers Association of NSW.
Little, G (1978) "Standards", *English in Australia* 40.
Little, G (1992) "The Value-added Child" in Wayne Sawyer (ed) *Outcomes and Incomes*, Sydney: Australian Education Network.
Marginson, S (1997) *Educating Australia: Government Education and Citizen Since 1960*, Cambridge: University Press.
Pinker, S (1994) *The Language Instinct*, Melbourne: Harper Collins.
Pinker, S (1994) *How the Mind Works*, Harmondsworth: Penguin.
Saul, J R (1997) *The Unconscious Civilisation*, Harmondsworth: Penguin.

Graham Little was President of the NSW English Teachers Association during the formation of the Australian Association for the Teaching of English, and Chairperson of the Committee which produced the innovative Year 7-10 English Syllabus of 1971. He subsequently became Principal Lecturer in Curriculum Studies at the Canberra College of Advanced Education, and is currently Director of the Australian Education Network Co-operative Assessment Project, a six-year study of criterion-referenced assessment of writing across the curriculum in a New South Wales primary school.

Section 1: Looking Back

1 Post-Dartmouth Developments in English Teaching in Australia

Jack Thomson

Preliminary Notes

1. In my title I include "in Australia" very deliberately. The reason for this
    is that I believe that Australian English teachers have been far from slow
    in dealing with the practical implications of contemporary cultural and
    curriculum theory. There is plenty of evidence from publications on
    English teaching in England, the United States and Australia, to suggest
    that Australia is at the leading edge of significant research, curriculum
    theorising, and practical classroom application of recent sociolinguistic,
    cultural, literary and learning theory. Further, Australians appear to
    read the professional publications of other countries, whereas the
    parochialism of (particularly) American luminaries is all too evident in
    the way the texts they write exclude, silence, or at best marginalise
    Australian voices. For example, Kathleen McCormick's *The Culture of
    Reading and the Teaching of English* (1994) completely ignores the work
    of people like Wendy Morgan, Ian Reid, Peter Adams, Garth Boomer,
    Bill Green, Bronwyn Mellor, Brian Moon, Pam Gilbert, John Stephens
    and Ken Watson, which would undoubtedly have provided some
    enlightenment for the pretty bleak American English teaching scene she
    describes.
2. In the list below all the points are inter-related. A diagram that showed
    the nature of these inter-connections would be more circular – or even
    spiral – in shape than linear, so the numerical ordering of the issues
    below is probably an inappropriate form in which to present them,
    implying as it does a sequential and incremental logic of development
    of ideas rather than a complex dialectic.

I realise, however, that if I were asked to draw such a diagram I would find it very difficult to produce anything clear, coherent or illuminating, and the value of the exercise would be in what the process of doing it achieved for my own understanding rather than in what the product could possibly communicate to anyone else. (This problem is caused partly by my own personal limitations of understanding and communication, and partly by the limitations of the (English) language of my culture and the way my thinking is linguistically constructed and circumscribed.)

3. All of the classroom activities mentioned in the outline below can be either agents of literacy growth and empowerment for students or meaningless routines of industrious futility merely filling the daily time available for work in English. They are inevitably the latter when they are introduced rigidly and formulaically into the classroom rather than in contexts in which students understand the point of doing them. When any activity hardens into a routine system it becomes meaningless. Two examples of this, I believe, are:

   i. process-conference writing when every piece of writing students do is required to go through a series of drafts to finished product regardless of the purposes of that writing; and

   ii. the writing of reading journals (or learning logs) when students respond to all books they read in exactly the same way: for example, by answering the same questions on each text. Perhaps this could be summarised by saying that all student activities in English are less than useful when they are not continually reflected on, and evaluated, by both students and teachers.

Developments In English Teaching 1968-1996

1: Learning Processes

We now have a deeper understanding of many of the processes of human learning, so that we know that all human beings who are not severely brain-damaged can learn literacy skills. These processes include cognitive development, emotional-intellectual growth (intelligence of feeling), the role of language in learning, language development, and the development of writing and reading abilities and skills. These processes are all inter-connected, so that the work of Piaget, Vygotsky and Bruner on cognitive development and the relationship between language and thought links with Britton's work on language as a tool of learning (Britton, 1970); with Barnes' work on talking in small groups and the relationship between language form and function (Barnes, 1976); with different models of language functions (including Halliday's, 1973); with the work of Britton et al on the development of writing abilities across a range of writing functions at developing incremental levels of conceptualisation (1975); and with work by people like the Goodmans, Frank Smith, Robert Scholes (1985) and others on the development of reading abilities.

One of the important more recent findings linking all of the above developments in our understanding of learning, thinking and languaging processes is **the importance of metacognition – of students reflecting on their learning** to make explicit to themselves both what they have learned from particular activities and how they have learned it; and going on to reflect further on their reflections to achieve higher level self-reflexive understanding of their own – and their culture's – preferred ways of learning. The incremental order of metacognitive conceptualisation is, therefore, from "what I have learned", through "how I learned that", to "how I best learn different kinds of knowledge/understanding/skill in different contexts", with increasing understanding of the particular contributions of languaging processes (talking and writing of various kinds, performing and presenting in various ways) to different kinds of learning in different learning situations.

2: Relationship Between Theory and Practice

We now have a much clearer and deeper understanding of the intricate dialectic relationship between theory and practice, for too long (and still often by many teachers) conceived of as binary opposites. We now know that there is no such thing as practice without theory. We know that every teacher in a classroom, in every teaching activity, is implementing a theory of learning whether that teacher is conscious of this simple fact or not. Therefore, we recognise **the importance of teachers theorising their own practice.** The first step to pedagogic improvement for all of us is to come to understand, and to be able to articulate clearly, exactly what is our present (often covertly held) theory of learning that underpins our present practice.

After reaching this kind of understanding and articulation, teachers are in a position to be able to look for answers to identified pedagogic problems by reading more theory and research, and to go on to apply what they find as relevant aspects of it in their teaching. The model I have in mind here is of a spiral progression from present practice; through developing – and intentionally explored – theoretical understanding of how people best learn; to a higher level of consciously chosen/constructed practice underpinned by a fully developed theoretical rationale. On this point, I think it is interesting to note that F R Leavis, who condemned theory as an intrusive abstraction that got between the reader and the 'concrete experience' of the text, and who thought his preferred way of responding to literature was 'natural', 'logical' and unproblematical, became irritable when he found that only a few cherished private souls like himself were capable of reading the way he taught. What he lacked, and needed most, was a theory of reading and learning!

3: Language as a Tool of Learning

The classroom implication of the finding that we not only learn language by using it but that, far more importantly, **we learn by using language,** is that there should be constant encouragement of students to use informal, comfortable language ("expressive" language, to use Britton's term) in talk and writing as a way of coming to sort out and understand new ideas and (to share) different interpretations of texts. Examples of such "expressive" uses of language in the classroom are:

i.   **talking informally in small groups** to solve problems and sort out ideas co-operatively, before, for example, reporting back to the full class more formally.

ii.   **writing expressively** in the form of:
  - **notes** (to use as a basis for small group discussion, or further writing, for example);
  - **initial response statements** to literature and other texts to be explored;
  - **reading journals and learning logs,** including self-reflexive metacognitive explorations.

The insight that language is a tool of learning has progressively developed from the first phase called **"language and learning"**, based on the work of Britton (1970) and Wilkinson (1971 and 1975), through a second phase called **"language across the curriculum"** based on the work of Douglas Barnes (1976), to the present phase called **"negotiating the curriculum"** initiated by Garth Boomer (1982). The major pedagogic moves in this development involve a move to a higher level of theoretical generality – from emphasising language and language processes to emphasising learning and learning processes – and a recognition of the central importance of **passing on the secrets of the curriculum to students**; that is, making explicit to students the point or purpose of all that we ask them to do.

4: Learning Language: Brian Cambourne's Seven Conditions of Language Learning (Cambourne, 1987)

Brian Cambourne's research identified seven conditions relevant to all kinds of language learning: **immersion, demonstration, expectation, responsibility, approximation, employment and feedback.** Cambourne says that teachers should try to replicate these conditions in the classroom so that students engage in language activities that are what James Britton calls "real operations" as opposed to artificial "dummy runs" (Britton, 1970).

Cambourne describes his preferred ways of teaching language development as the "natural" way to learn. Others have strongly criticised Cambourne's use of the term "natural" here, claiming that while this way of learning might be more relevant, logical and meaningful to learners in that it uses the methods intelligent, knowledgeable and thoughtful parents use in teaching their children to talk and develop a sense of story, it is not really a "natural" way of learning but a culturally acquired one. I think this criticism of Cambourne is a bit pedantic. Perhaps it would be more accurate to describe his method as the most sensible, logical and obvious for teaching children growing up in a culture like ours that requires the mastery of verbal and literacy skills. In the most usual senses of the word, this method is "natural" in the context of our culture.

5: Learning About Language: The Contribution of Linguistics

i. Language variation: the insight that **language difference is not language deficit**; that although social and regional dialects differ from the dominant form, Standard English, in such surface features as grammar, syntax, lexis and phonology, such dialects are just as capable of generating and explicating the highest levels of thinking as is the Standard form. The significant pedagogical implication of this is that instead of trying to change – or eradicate – the dialects of non-dominant social groups we should accept them and positively encourage their use in the classroom, while at the same time teaching such students the way to master the Standard dialect, in the context of making it clear to them why they need such mastery. In this way, speakers of less dominant dialects don't have their cultural identity denigrated and they come to understand the need to expand their linguistic repertoires – to give them access to the wider culture and the ability to operate with more choice and power in it.

ii. **Language Functions**: The work on language functions by Michael Halliday (1973), and by James Britton et al (1975) (particularly on levels of the transactional function in writing), shows the range of functions we use language for and the different purposes language serves. This work emphasises **the importance of organising language activities in the classroom so that students develop competence in all functions and to the highest levels of performance.** This means that many students from disadvantaged backgrounds, for example, will gain experience in using the speculative function of language, a function crucial to the development of higher level conceptualisation and one often denied them in their home and culture.

iii. **The Conscious Exploration of Language in the Classroom – Textuality**: The work of Doughty, Pearce and Thornton for the Schools Council in England in the 1970's (Doughty, Pearce and Thornton, 1973) produced some excellent materials for students to use in exploring, and developing competence in, the social uses of language. These explorations involved, for example, coming to understand and be able to use appropriately and purposefully different genres, discourses, registers and functions of language. This approach was further developed by Leslie Stratta, Andrew Wilkinson and John Dixon in *Patterns of Language* as activities for **"the conscious understanding of language in the classroom"** (Chapter 4: "Language and Experience", in *Patterns of Language*, 1973). This aspect of linguistic pedagogy has more lately further developed into **classroom work on textuality** where students learn the processes of construction of genres and discourses and texts of different kinds, as well as how to deconstruct and reconstruct such texts for their own transactive purposes (see points 8 and 9 below). This also links with Richard Andrews' new "rhetorical" model of English teaching (item 12 below). It also links with the recent work on **critical literacy** by people like Hilary Janks (*Critical Language Awareness* series, 1993) and Wendy Morgan (1996) and Colin Lankshear (1994) (item 6 below).

6: The Development of a Deeper Understanding of the Relationship Between Language and Power

Hilary Janks calls this attempt to *raise students' awareness of the ways in which language can be used, and is used, both to maintain and to challenge existing forms of power*, "critical language awareness" (Janks,1993). She says "What makes CLA 'critical' is its concern with the politics of meaning: the ways in which dominant meanings are maintained, challenged and changed" (page iii).

7: The Development of Wider Definitions of Literature and New Ways of Teaching It

Whereas in the past the term "literature" implied imaginative writing of canonical status which students were bidden to learn to admire in what was a "portrait-gallery model" of teaching, now the definition of literature has widened so that the term, more democratically, describes forms of writing rather than achieved status within those forms, so that it includes imaginative writings of students in *a "workshop model" of teaching*, to use Ian Reid's apposite descriptions (Reid, 1984). *In this model of literature teaching, students write as well as read literature.* This writing includes re-writing texts, or parts of texts, in other media: for example, turning a short story into a radio play, or a poem into a news report on television or in a newspaper. It also includes imaginative explorations of alternative possibilities of texts students have read, whereby they might rewrite an ending of a novel to resist the positioning ideology of the original, or rewrite some events from the point of view of marginalised, silent or absent voices (Stratta, et al, 1973). Peter Adams calls this kind of writing "dependent authorship", meaning that in using the structures, narrative methods and/or styles of published authors, students learn the rhetorics of literature as apprentices to master writers (Adams, 1996; and Adams in Thomson, 1992).

8: A Developing Understanding of Contemporary Cultural and Literary Theory and its Profound Implications for the Teaching of Reading, Writing and Textuality

This takes the definition of texts to be read – and written – much further still, so that "textual study" or "textuality" involves reading not just different kinds of literature, and not just, as well, reading different kinds of what Britton called "transactional" or non-fictional texts, but also *reading all the sign systems of our culture* from the poems of John Milton to the lyrics and music of Elton John, from the news constructed by television and the print media to the representations and constructions of gender, ethnicity and class in printed, visual, sound and multi-media texts.

Those who object to the apparent cultural relativism of an approach which seems to assume that all texts, from Shakespeare's tragedies to menus in fast-food restaurants, are of equal value, need to recognise that *a (not "the") literary canon is itself a cultural formation serving the specific aims and interests of the groups who constructed it in the first place.* The important questions to ask here are, "Whose canon is it?" "Who constructed it, and for what purposes?" and "Whose interests does it serve?" I think it is important, however, not to go too far the other way and deny the importance or validity of making value judgments about texts. Speaking personally (and culturally), *I would want my students to value Shakespeare's plays more than an advertisement for Kentucky Fried Chicken* both in terms of language, style and discourse, and in terms of their (relative) contributions to our understanding of human behaviour and the human condition (See comments on the "Rhetorical model" of English teaching in item 12 below).

Shakespeare's tragedies and advertisements for fast foods are not equally valuable, but both demand attention and analysis by our students. We, as teachers and citizens, have to make value judgments daily about which texts we deem worthy of our attention and for what purposes. It would be less than responsible not to help our students to make such judgments for themselves, as long as we don't impose our judgments on them, and as long as we give them the tools for understanding the values implicit in the choices and judgments they make. However, to argue that a close reading of the eighteenth century poems of William Cowper and James Thomson for aesthetic purposes is more valuable and useful for students than a deconstructive analysis of advertisements for a McDonald's breakfast is the kind of nonsense we get from those with a vested interest in socialising students in compliance with prevailing consumerist patterns of thought. The massive profits of the health-degenerating fast-food industry is evidence of the need for deconstructive work on a McDonald's breakfast!

Our teaching now aims to give students a mastery of the skills and conventions of reading and writing rather than authoritative explications of specific texts. As Robert Scholes says, "Our job is not to produce 'readings' for our students but to give them the tools for producing their own." (Scholes, 1985)

The understanding that texts, readers and reading practices are culturally constructed and ideological has led to new ways of teaching reading so that students learn the processes by which texts are constructed, the ways texts are interwoven of competing discourses, all of which have designs on readers and which are inevitably ideological. *In unravelling the discourses of textual construction, students move from deconstructing texts to reconstructing texts and writing new texts of their own with their newly expanded repertoire of rhetorics.* In this kind of teaching, reading and writing are not seen as binary opposites – the one a matter of (passive) reception and the other a matter of (active) production, but two sides of the same active process, whereby every reading is a re-writing and every writing a re-reading. Students learn to read texts from a writer's point of view and write texts from a reader's point of view. In both reading and writing they also come to understand the extent and limits of their freedom to make new meanings as readers and writers. They are free to the extent that readers make their own meanings from their repertoires of personal experience, cultural knowledge and values and beliefs, and they are constrained by their own cultural shaping and by the ideologically saturated genres and discourses of their culture out of which all texts are constructed. They realise that what a text means is ultimately dependent on the reading practices they employ, and they realise they can choose to read a text in many different ways.

One way of helping students to become masters of the genres and discourses of their culture rather than their servants is to encourage them to write generically promiscuous texts, because those who can create new genres, or who can use traditional genres in situations in which they aren't normally used, are listened to and read with more attention than is normally accorded.

9: Questions for Readers and Stages of Reading Development

i.   Questions for readers: Because there is no final, objective, determinate meaning in any text, as all meanings are infinitely deferred along a chain of signifiers (even to look up the meaning of any word in a dictionary leads to finding strings of other words whose meanings one has to chase further), *the important question for student readers becomes not "What does this text mean?" but "What is it that I am bringing to this text that causes me to respond to/interpret/construct it as I do?"*

In these circumstances, metacognition reaches another dimension of powerful self-knowledge, having progressed from "What have I learned from this activity?"; through "How did I learn it?" and "What were the processes of my learning?" and "How do I learn best?"; to "What do I know about texts as linguistically, culturally and ideologically constructed communications?" and "What do I know about myself as a linguistically, culturally and ideologically constructed subjectivity?"

ii.   **Stages of reading development**: To use Robert Scholes' terms, students' *reading development, at best, is a progression from the stage of "Reading" where readers submit to the power of the text, through the stage of "Interpretation" where they share power with the text, to the stage of "Criticism" where they have developed power over the text* (Scholes, 1985:18-73).

Scholes' "reading" is a "submission to the power of the text", a largely unconscious activity, and requires "as much knowledge as it does skill". The knowledge required to "construct characters, situations and a world out of words" is of the "codes" or conventions "that were operative in the composition of the text and the historical situation in which it was composed" (21). "Interpretation" involves considering the significance of textual events; and "criticism" is "a critique of the themes developed in a text, or a critique of the codes out of which a text has been constructed" (23); that is, the reader criticises the text by exerting his or her own power against the text to resist its representation of the world and/or the ideology underpinning it:

> In working through the stages of reading, interpretation, and criticism, we move from a submission to textual authority in reading, through a sharing of textual power in interpretation, toward an assertion of power through opposition in criticism (39).

As teachers, Scholes says, "our job is **not** to intimidate students with our own superior textual production; it is to show them the codes upon which all textual production depends, and to encourage their own textual practice" (24-5).

Reading:
Coming to understand our own "reading" involves being able to answer questions like "What makes a story a story?" and "How does a writer construct a character?"

Interpretation:
Interpretation depends on understanding the cultural codes "implicated" in any text. How do we get our students to make the move from characters and events to generalised themes and values? We can use the structuralist insights into repetitions and oppositions, similarities and differences, parallels and contrasts and consider what they represent. This is a matter of "making connections between a particular verbal text and its larger cultural text" (33).

Criticism:
"How can we honestly encourage our students to be critical – to produce

text against text?" asks Scholes (35). One way of helping students to move from "interpretation" to "criticism" is to ask them where their sympathies are in a text and where they think the author's sympathies are. If their sympathies as readers are the same as what they see to be the sympathies of the implied author, they can be further asked whether they think it is possible that they are being manipulated by the text. This produces really penetrating discussion and enlightenment.

Finally, other useful teaching ideas for helping students to criticise texts and unpackage their concealed ideologies include transposing their elements (Hollindale,1988: 3-22). Changes of gender, race, nationality, class and age can be both entertaining and revealing. For example, in Joseph Conrad's novel *Heart of Darkness*, imagine Miss Marlow as black, African, working class, female and young! Further, change the setting and have the Company headquarters in London rather than Brussels and the "great river" in the United States, not Africa. Further still, modernise the details; for example, have the "big river" as the Mekong 1960, rather than the Congo in the nineteenth century, and turn Marlow into an educated middle class black American senator on a fact-finding mission to Vietnam. Textual silences and contradictions start to open up pretty widely for students when they are engaged in this kind of deconstructive re-creation.

See also Jack Thomson's "Developmental Levels of Response to Literature" identifying six levels of response from "1. Unreflective interest in action" to "6. Consciously considered relationship with the text, recognition of textual ideology and understanding of one's own reading processes", with specific reading strategies associated with each level. (Thomson, 1987)

10: Developing Understanding of Multimedia Technology and Increasing Mastery in Using It

Students are increasingly able to read, interpret and criticise a range of multimedia technologies and use them to construct texts of their own. These include accessing information and constructing texts on computers (reading, writing, using visual and graphic tools, data bases, CD Rom, and the Internet), reading, viewing and constructing films, videos (soap operas etc.) and video games.

11: An Increasingly Powerful Range of Assessment and Evaluation Procedures

In the best English classrooms *students' work is now being assessed by themselves and their peers, as well as by the class teacher, and by larger groups beyond the classroom* (when performances, presentations and larger audiences are involved). The teacher's assessment itself is more meaningful to students because it now takes place in a context of negotiation in which students are fully conversant with the teacher's assessment criteria which have been made explicit to them in advance.

Further, students are required to reflect on and thus evaluate their own learning and performance in each unit of work, as well as the activities they have negotiated with their teachers. This enables them not only to understand the processes of their own learning, but develops the practice of questioning what is happening in their classroom and gives them an active role in shaping what happens in it.

Further still, the assessment and evaluation activities go beyond individual performance to take into account students' contributions towards co-operative projects working in groups. (One of the major criticisms by industry of secondary school graduates in recent years has been their inability to work together co-operatively to solve problems in teams or groups.)

12: New Models of English Teaching

When students can read, write and present in all genres, using all of the discourses of their culture, and all of the language functions at all levels, and can improvise on such genres and discourses so as to use them freshly and unconventionally (as well as conventionally) for their own transactive purposes, they become masters and re-makers of their culture rather than servants or victims of it. They are not only able to make conscious choices about the way they read and write texts and their lives, but they also understand the ethical and value-laden implications of such choices, while, at the same time, being fully aware of both the freedom of, and constraints on, self-expression and the (partial) constructedness of subjectivity.

In these circumstances, an education in English might incorporate all of the older models of English teaching, but go beyond them. The older models incorporated into the new would include the following:

✦ *the cultural heritage model*, as students still need to be aware of the way their cultural history has positioned them, but now without being unconsciously indoctrinated and controlled by it. Students do need to be aware of their cultural heritage in so far as this means both historical/cultural knowledge and, more importantly, an understanding of the history that has shaped the culture in which they live. For example, current apathetic and supportive responses in Australia to the Liberal/National Party coalition government's proposed industrial relations policies indicate that many Australian workers have little understanding – or appreciation – of the role of trade unions or of their historical struggles and development. In a postmodern society such history might now be seen as problematic, as a multiple discourse full of gaps, silences and contradictions, but it is nevertheless a history whose narratives need to be known.

✦ *the language skills model*, as students still need to master all of the language skills, but now not for the purposes of being mere ciphers of the commercial interests which see the transmission of such skills as the only – or most important – justification of education. At its worst the skills model in the hands of the supporters of the so-called "back-to-basics" movement means the teaching of individual and unrelated skills outside of any context in which they might make sense or have any real purpose. At its best, in the work of the Schools Council "Language in Use" team (Doughty et al, 1973), and in the critical literacy work of Hilary Janks (1993) and Wendy Morgan (1996), it means teaching such language skills in a meaningful social and cultural context, so that students develop control of all of the functions of language, genres and discourses of their culture.

✦ *the personal growth model* (see John Dixon, 1967), as personal growth and development is still crucial, including pleasure and enjoyment in reading and the values of beauty and ethical understanding. Now personal growth is extended by a deeper understanding of the historical, cultural and political/ideological contexts in which such growth takes place, so that the personal and the social aspects of life are seen to be inter-dependent and dialectic in their relationship.

✦ *the 'cultural studies' or 'textuality' model,* in which English as a subject is placed in a wider cultural context to incorporate a greatly enlarged definition of 'literature' and a greatly enlarged range of texts considered appropriate for students to read and write. (See, for examples, McCormick, 1994 and Peel 1994.) Students no longer read only canonical literature and restrict their writing to the transactional function: they (re)read and (re)write all of the texts – or social practices – of their culture. Such texts range from poems and novels to multimedia texts, popular entertainment, political speeches and classroom seating patterns; in other words, all of the sign systems of high, popular and mass culture that can be read for their social purposes.

A new model, then, might well be called a "rhetorical" and ethical model, or even a Rhetorical, Ethical, Socio-Cultural, Political Model, as it is a RESPonsible model, on behalf of, or REPresenting human agency: Richard Andrews uses the term "rhetorical", by which he means that students should learn to use all of the rhetorics of their culture with some expertise to operate in – and on – their world as choice-making human beings (Andrews, 1994 and 1995) . I would add to Andrews' comments an additional emphasis on helping students to understand the values involved in all aspects of their work in English, and the need, when making choices, to understand the ethical implications and consequences of such choices.

Such a rhetorical/ethical model involves personal growth as well as a full awareness of the relationship between language and power, a familiarity with social practices and their discourses, and an understanding of the political and ideological formation of texts and of matters of values and ethics.

In considering the issue of values and ethics, my approved model of English teaching, unlike the "cultural studies" or "textuality" model, recognises that some texts are more complex and profound than others, even more humane and "life-promoting" – to use F R Leavis's term, without endorsing the rest of his program. Ultimately, I believe we need to help our students to develop the skills and understandings to be able to make hierarchical value judgments that some texts are linguistically, stylistically, aesthetically, psychologically and/or philosophically more significant – and better – than others, while recognising that such judgments are partially culturally constructed. I would emphasise the point that in helping students to develop the literary – and literacy – abilities to make such judgments, we want such judgments to be made by students themselves and not imposed on them by teachers (or by media commentators, politicians or other community leaders). In such circumstances there will be many different, even conflicting, value judgments made in any classroom.

Further, the more students know about the linguistic, historical and cultural construction of reality and subjectivity, the less they are likely to be fully determined human beings. As Pam Gilbert says, "By fostering in our students a genuinely critical stance towards language and its discursive formations, we foster 'producers' not 'consumers': active participants rather than passive recipients" (Gilbert, 1987, p249).

Obvious examples of ethical practices for teachers are to make sure they:

✦ don't teach one reading practice as if it were the only way to read (as happened to my generation at Sydney University, when New Criticism was in vogue, and assumed to be not so much the preferred model of reading as the only one);

✦ don't impose their own value judgments on students, but are honest about their preferences, when asked (in other words, they shouldn't replace any traditional canon with one of their own);

✦ do teach students all of the reading practices available in the community, so that the same student can read the same text in multiple ways, and choose a preferred reading, in the full knowledge that what is chosen is partial and relative, and constructed from one's own experience, cultural knowledge, value system and historical-cultural positioning;

✦ do help students to recognise and respect the point of view of other readers whose preferred interpretations arise from different repertoires (of experience, cultural knowledge, values and historical-cultural positioning), so that all come to understand sympathetically the perspectives offered from different cultural positionings;

◆ do help students to understand that cultural difference is to be respected – in language use as well as in (inevitably ideological) reading practices – and that such differences are not hierarchical or to be treated as deficits.

In a rhetorical/ethical model, which sets a critical approach to the reading and writing of texts in a political context, students are invited to start to challenge and question their world. In order to take an active role in shaping their future world they need to develop rhetorical skills; to become active producers of their own knowledge and skills; to learn to take responsibility for their own learning; to come to understand themselves in relation to others; to learn to co-operate with other people to solve problems; to make choices about what they do; to make decisions; and to understand and make informed, responsible and tolerant judgments about issues of values and ethics.

A new model of English teaching that supports egalitarianism and ethical responsibility rather than social division and competitive materialism is urgently needed in Australia at this moment as the fissures in the social fabric grow wider and multiply. Recent research shows the gulf between rich and poor, the haves and have-nots, of Australia's largest city is rapidly increasing (Macken, 1996). Phil Raskall, a social economist, who until recently headed the Social Policy Research Centre at the University of N.S.W., has shown that the social enclaves on either side of a skewered east-west dividing line (that runs from Castle Hill in the north to the Sydney Airport on Botany Bay) are "two armies confronting each other":

> . . . the gentrification of the inner city, the broader polarisation of society, greater competition for government resources and seismic economic forces have built an international city at the core and a rust belt on the rim.   (Macken p2)

Exacerbating the widening social division is the Federal Government's recent decision to encourage further the rapid growth of private schools by both abolishing previous restrictions on their establishment, growth and public funding and funding this expansion itself by taking money out of the public school system. In the *Sydney Morning Herald* of Saturday, 5 October 1996, Adele Horin reported that " for every new student who moves into a private school from January 1997, the Federal Government will cut its funds for four government school students" (Horin, 1996).

A rhetorical/ethical model is designed to give students from disadvantaged groups a powerful literacy and access to mainstream culture, with all of the choices that such access entails. It is also designed to ensure that the socially advantaged and culturally dominant groups develop the same powerful literacy and choices as their social location would lead them to assume as their normal life expectation. It is a model which involves all students in learning to work together co-operatively to solve problems and in coming to understand other people and their beliefs, while at the same time developing an understanding of the social origins of such beliefs. It is a model designed to help all students to live ethically in a plural but increasingly tolerant society, where difference is respected and valued. It is a model designed to problematise the current theory of 'economic rationalism' (itself a contradictory text in a liberal-humanist society) driving the political and economic policies of Australian Governments for the past 10-15 years – a theory which assumes that people need increasing material rewards to work conscientiously; and a theory which assumes a view of human behaviour as being inherently motivated by greed, selfishness and fear.

References

Adams, Peter (1996) *At the Far Reach of Their Capacities: Case Studies in Dependent Authorship*, Norwood, South Australia: Australian Association for the Teaching of English.
Andrews, Richard (1994) "Towards a New Model: a Rhetorical Perspective" in Ken Watson (ed) *English Teaching in Perspective: in the Context of the 1990s*. Sydney: St Clair Press.
Andrews, Richard (ed) (1995) *Rebirth of Rhetoric*, London: Routledge.
Barnes, Douglas (1976) *From Communication to Curriculum*, Harmondsworth: Penguin.
Boomer, Garth (1982) *Negotiating the Curriculum*, Sydney: Ashton Scholastic.
Boomer, Garth (1985) *Fair Dinkum Teaching and Learning: Reflections on Literacy and Power*, Upper Montclair, New Jersey: Boynton/Cook.
Britton, James (1970) *Language and Learning*, Harmondsworth: Penguin.
Britton, James et al. (1975) *The Development of Writing Abilities (11-18)*, London: Macmillan.
Cambourne, Brian (1987) *Natural Learning and Literacy Education*, Sydney: Ashton Scholastic.
Dixon, John (1967) *Growth Through English*, Huddersfield: OUP and National Association for the Teaching of English.
Doughty, Peter, Pearce, John; and Thornton, Geoffrey (1973) *Language in Use*, London: Edward Arnold.
Gilbert, Pam (1987) "Post Reader-Response: The Deconstructive Critique", in Bill Corcoran and Emrys Evans (eds) *Readers, Texts, Teachers*. Upper Montclair, New Jersey: Boynton/Cook.
Gilbert, Pam (1989) *Writing, Schooling and Deconstruction: From Voice to Text in the Classroom*, London: Routledge.
Green, Bill (ed) (1988) *Metaphors and Meanings: Essays on English Teaching by Garth Boomer*, Norwood, South Australia: Australian Association for the Teaching of English.
Halliday, Michael (1973) "Relevant Models of Language" in *Explorations in the Functions of Language*, London: Edward Arnold.
Hollindale, Peter (1988) "Ideology and the Children's Book", *Signal*, 55.
Horin, Adele, "Schools Are Being Quietly Privatised", in *The Sydney Morning Herald*, Saturday, October 5, "Spectrum" Section, p2.
Janks, Hilary (1993) *Language, Identity and Power*, Johannesburg: Hodder and Stoughton.
Lankshear, Colin (1994) *Critical Literacy*, Occasional Paper No 3, Australian Curriculum Studies Association, Belconnen ACT.
McCormick, Kathleen (1994) *The Culture of Reading and the Teaching of English*, Manchester: Manchester University Press.
Macken, Deirdre: "A City Divided", in *The Sydney Morning Herald*, Saturday, October 5, "Spectrum" Section, pp 1, 6.
Mellor, Bronwyn (1989) *Reading Hamlet*, Scarborough, WA: Chalkface Press.
Mellor, Bronwyn, O'Neill, Marnie and Patterson, Annette:
(1987) *Reading Stories*, Scarborough, WA: Chalkface Press.
(1991) *Reading Fictions*. Scarborough, WA: Chalkface Press
(1996) *Investigating Texts*, Scarborough, WA: Chalkface Press.
Moon, Brian (1990) *Studying Literature*, Scarborough, WA: Chalkface Press.
Moon, Brian (1992) *Literary Terms: A Practical Glossary*, Scarborough, W.A: Chalkface Press.

Morgan, Wendy (1987) *Border Territory: An anthology of Unorthodox Australian Writing*, Melbourne: Nelson.

Morgan, Wendy (1992) *A Post-Structuralist English Classroom: The Example of Ned Kelly*, Carlton: Victorian Association for the Teaching of English.

Morgan, Wendy (1996) *Critical Literacy: Readings and Resources*, Norwood, South Australia: Australian Association for the Teaching of English.

Peel, Robin (1994) "The 'Cultural Studies' or 'Textual Studies' Model of English" in Ken Watson (ed) *English Teaching in Perspective: in the context of the 1990s*, Sydney: St. Clair Press.

Reid, Ian (1984) *The Making of Literature: Texts, Contexts and Classroom Practices*, Australian Norwood, South Australia: Association for the Teaching of English.

Scholes, Robert (1985) *Textual Power: Literary Theory and the Teaching of English*, New Haven: Yale University Press.

Stephens, John (1992) *Language and Ideology in Children's Fiction*, Harlow: Longman.

Stephens, John and Watson, Ken (eds) (1994) *From Picture Book to Literary Theory*, Sydney: St. Clair Press.

Stratta, Leslie, Dixon, John and Wilkinson, Andrew (1973) *Patterns of Language: Explorations in the Teaching of English*, London: Heinemann.

Thomson, Jack (1987, 1990, 1992) *Understanding Teenagers' Reading: Reading Processes and the Teaching of English*, Ryde: Methuen and Australian Association for the Teaching of English.

Thomson, Jack (ed) (1992) *Reconstructing Literature Teaching*, Norwood, South Australia: Australian Association for the Teaching of English.

Watson, Ken (1992) *Ways of Telling: A Short Story Workshop*, Sydney: St. Clair Press.

Watson, Ken (1994) *English Teaching in Perspective: in the Context of the 1990s*, Sydney: St. Clair Press.

Wilkinson, Andrew (1971) *The Foundations of Language*, London: Oxford University Press.

Wilkinson, Andrew (1975) *Language and Education*, London: Oxford University Press.

2 Seminal Books

I n the 1960s and early 1970s a number of books on aspects of English teaching, most of them published in the United Kingdom, began to stimulate a rethinking of English teaching amongst Australian teachers.

These books included the *Reflections* series of Clements, Dixon and Stratta (1963), Alec Clegg's *The Excitement of Writing* (1964), Frank Whitehead's *The Disappearing Dais* (1966), and Fred Flower's *Language in Education* (1966). But probably the most influential were David Holbrook's *English for the Rejected* (1964), John Dixon's report of the Dartmouth Seminar, *Growth Through English* (1967), *Language, the Learner and the School* by Barnes, Britton and Rosen (1969), James Britton's *Language and Learning* (1970) and the products of the Schools Council Project on Linguistics and English Teaching. At the same time from the United States came James Moffett's *Teaching the Universe of Discourse* (1968). Given the significance of these last-named titles, we have chosen to revisit them from the perspective of the '90s.

"That's what I no": Revisiting David Holbrook's *English for the Rejected*

Margaret Gill

Why pick Holbrook? Today his name features only in histories of English, a citation to illustrate 'progressivism', 'romanticism', 'liberal individualism': another false prophet fallen by the wayside as subject English continues the unending quest for the ultimate re-definition, re-vision, re-making, re-viewing, re-theorising of itself. Why revisit him thirty years on?

Holbrook's writing on the teaching of English belongs to another era. He wrote out of the experience of post World War Two England and of an education system which sorted children into grammar school students ('bright') and secondary modern school students ('dull'). Holbrook ·even refers to a type of child called the 'secondary modern child'. The intellectually disabled he referred to simply as 'backward'. And though he wrote prolifically, it was from startlingly limited experience of English classrooms. In the 1960s he produced ten books for teachers of English on the basis of less than one year's full-time teaching, or, as Hansen (1967, p5) puts it "one book for every five weeks... of secondary teaching experience". Further, in his case studies of children and his commentaries on their writing, he casts himself as an amateur psychoanalyst, drawing uncritically on the work of Melanie Klein and W H Winnecott, extrapolating from the children's writing to the furthest reaches of their psyches.

Did these things matter? Not to the many English teachers who read his books in the 1960s. Nor did they matter to the Council of the Victorian Association for the Teaching of English which, in Holbrook's memorable words, "tried for two years to lure me to the Antipodes" (Holbrook, 1973, pi) and which, in 1970, hosted his visit to Australia – and with some consternation read his subsequent account of Australian English teaching where the syllabuses were "antiquated and unrelated to the modern world" and the schooling system was "barbarous, grim, hopeless and derelict". (Holbrook, 1973, pp xii-xiii)

So why include him in the group of writers who have had an important influence on English teaching?

English for the Rejected is Holbrook's passionate defence of the capabilities of the 'backward' child. It is an extraordinary account of his efforts "to make these children literate" (p8). The core of the book is a collection of nineteen case studies of intellectually disabled students taught by Holbrook for one day a week during a year and a half's part-time teaching in a village secondary modern school in Cambridgeshire. Holbrook scrutinises the writing of a class of 'C stream' students, providing an idiosyncratic commentary which blends over-the-top, Kleinian exegesis with accounts of his pedagogical approaches which generated writing of surprising vigour and confidence, defying the current wisdom that would have confined such children to individual word exercises. He then reflects on his experiences, generalising and formalising them into a detailed pedagogy and curriculum for other similar classrooms.

Holbrook refused to write off those children "least endowed with intellectual capacities". Anticipating Gardner (1983), he recognises the child's "capacity to explore and perceive, to come to terms with, speak of, and deal with experience by *the exercise of the whole mind and all kinds of apprehensions, not only intellectual ones.*" (p10, his italics). He insists on the importance of the 'poetic function', that is, the role of the aesthetic and the imaginative as central to the study of English. Though pre-dating Freire, he sets up a classroom where these marginalised children were encouraged to find their own 'voice', to articulate and affirm their thoughts and experiences, real and imagined. Holbrook accepts this as a self-evident good; he is not distracted by problematic issues of 'empowerment' or institutional regulation. His attention is focused on the potential capabilities of the children – something he refuses to doubt – and the necessity of building a relationship of sympathy and trust if these capabilities are to have the chance to develop.

In his view, free imaginative work, together with a demanding reading and oral language program, constituted "a stern, life-promoting, vigorous discipline" for English (p243), a far cry from the wilder shores of the 'creative writing movement' often associated with his name. And yet part of the fascination of the book lies in his attempt to come to terms with the wilder shores on which the children's frequently violent, pornographic and surreal writing beached him. He had landed himself in a paradox.

Even in the 1960s Holbrook could be described, for want of a better phrase, as an old-fashioned gentleman. He believed in "the human inclination to strive for good" (p30). He believed in good manners. He believed in moral training and 'discipline' in the classroom. He believed in "the civilising value of imaginative writing" (p59). He wanted his classroom to be a haven of freedom and creativity for abused and disturbed children. A truly pastoral pedagogue. Yet the realities of his classroom were much more complicated than even he anticipated. He found himself struggling to reconcile his commitment to nurturing the children's spontaneity with the requirement to accept the aberrant forms it took. He repeatedly tells the reader that "creative activity is a constructive quest for a sense of meaning in experience" (p210), yet the written and graphic evidence provided by the children reveals themes of murder, mutilation, rape. Perhaps it is not surprising that psychoanalysis provided the escape route which allowed him to preserve his maxim of "endless and unflagging encouragement" (p207) in the face of work which, on every count, affronted his moral and aesthetic sensibilities.

He struggles too with pedagogical contradictions. He discovers that the only context in which he can encourage student freedom of choice and creativity is through the imposition of a prescriptive syllabus, close surveillance of the students and an interventionist pedagogy which he glosses as "paternal benignity" (p206). He is remarkably open in his acceptance of this paradox, one so often fudged in the writing of later progressivists. His syllabus and teaching strategies (pp 202-203, 233-236, 241-243) are intelligent and resourceful. Most would sit comfortably amongst the curriculum materials which accompany the current state curriculum and standards frameworks. In the classroom he juggles spur-of-the-moment opportunism with tightly orchestrated routines. At different times he worries about correcting spelling or not correcting it. Notwithstanding his advocacy of the 'poetic function', a substantial amount of the children's oral and written work is directed to 'practical English'. Holbrook attempts to reconcile these discontinuities by defining the English teacher as 'teacher-artist' and English teaching as an 'art', foreshadowing the complex role of the teacher which Boomer (1988) captured definitively in his account of 'Mrs Bell'.

More broadly, the book is a passionate defence of English teaching. Holbrook moves beyond his classroom to affirm the authority of teachers and the prestige due to the profession of school teaching. He launches a polemic against "our society and its system of education [that] at the moment imply inevitably and often mercilessly that children who do badly in intelligence tests are inferior creatures" (p7). He rails against the tyranny of external examinations and "textbook mills", the absence of specialist provision for students with special needs, the lack of specialist teachers, the lack of training for such teachers, the prevalence of large classes. He argues the importance of professional development for all teachers. He could be writing now.

Yet – a final paradox – his passionate engagement with professional issues comes, not from any professional training, but from his background as a poet and a writer. He is a maverick educationist, redeemed by his determination to speak *for* the disenfranchised and *to* the teaching profession. He belongs to a tradition of radical educators (for example, Ashton-Warner, 1963; Holt, 1964; Dennison, 1969; Freire, 1970; Rose, 1989; Edelsky, 1991) who have taken up the cause of the socially marginalised and, in the process, changed literacy practices and our understanding of those practices. Much current writing on literacy treats it as a grand sociocultural abstraction, and literacy theorists run the risk of appearing, more and more, to be talking only amongst themselves. Like other radical educators, Holbrook spoke directly to the profession. In the process, he offered a savage critique of government instrumentalities and their policies and funding for education. Perhaps we need a Holbrook today.

References

Ashton-Warner, S (1963) *Teacher*, London: Secker and Warburg.

Boomer, G (1988) *Metaphors and Meanings: Essays on English Teaching by Garth Boomer*, Melbourne Australia: Australian Association for the Teaching of English.

Dennison, G (1969) *The Lives of Children: The Story of the First Street School*, New York: Vintage Books.

Edelsky, C (1991) *With Literacy and Justice for All: Rethinking the Social in Language and Education*, London: Falmer Press.

Freire, P (1970) *Pedagogy of the Oppressed*, New York: Seabury Press.

Gardner, Howard (1983) *Frames of Mind: The Theory of Multiple Intelligences*, London: Heinemann.

Hansen, I V (1967) "The Teacher of English as Poet", *VATE Journal*, February.

Holbook, David (1964) *English for the Rejected: Training Literacy in the Lower Streams of the Secondary School*, Cambridge: CUP.

Holbook, David (1973) *English in Australia Now*, Cambridge: CUP.

Holt, J (1964) *How Children Fail*, Harmondsworth: Penguin.

Rose, M (1989) *Lives on the Boundary: The Struggles and Achievements of America's Underprepared*, New York: Penguin.

Growth Through English

Wayne Sawyer

First published in 1967, John Dixon's *Growth Through English** remains one of the most influential books on English teaching ever written. A report on the seminal Anglo-American Dartmouth Conference of the previous year, it popularised the central tenets of what was to become the growth model of English.

Skills/Cultural Heritage/Growth

Dixon argues in *Growth Through English* that the history of English can be conceived of as reflecting three main curriculum models, which he characterises as:

a) *skills*: This model emphasised drills in aspects of language and literacy and issued from an era demanding initial literacy.

b) *cultural heritage*: This model stressed the 'given-ness' of 'high' culture, which it was the teacher's job to pass down to his/her students. With its roots in Arnold and Newbolt, such a view grew out of a belief in the need for a civilising and culturally unifying content.

c) *personal growth*: Dixon's favoured model focused on re-examining learning processes and the meaning for the individual student of what was being covered in English lessons. The revolution brought about by this model was in re-defining English not in terms of curriculum content, but in terms of processes. English became defined as activity. Central activities were talking and writing and the ordering of experience that these involved. Dixon's description of the rationale for this model linked very closely to Britton's description of the value of "spectator role" language (Britton, 1970), which in turn linked to a constructivist view of learning:

> at the level of language . . . we make for ourselves a representational world . . . making it afresh, reshaping it, and bringing into new relationships all the old elements.
>
> (Dixon, 1975, p9)

Personal experience, and the active use of language, particularly through talk and writing, became central elements of the English classroom in this model.

Dialect/Register/Language Learning

The importance of personal experience meant a necessary respect for the language which students brought to the classroom and a recognition that identity was bound up with that language. As language learning up to school-age had been based on an active use of language in varying contexts, the school ought to attempt to replicate that situation, rather than to engage in "dummy runs" at language. Thus, drama and role-play were to become central to developing language use in a range of contexts. Drama was basic because of the need to try out language in different roles, to develop control of registers. The stress was to be on the roles, and the language would incidentally follow.

The Curriculum

An approach that emphasised contexts and use, rather than isolated skills, required an integrated approach to curriculum structure, rather than the fragmentary approach of treating different skills on different days of the week. Thus the integrated curriculum became a keystone of the growth model. Alongside this, and replacing the single-minded lesson plan, was an approach of the teacher's being prepared for the many possible avenues that a lesson might take. Flexibility of structure was the key.

Talk was central to the growth curriculum. Dixon believed that skills in such things as the manner of speaking would only become meaningful when students were talking to real audiences for a purpose of significance to them.

Dixon also saw Britton's notion of the shaping of experience to be important to approaches taken to writing. Previous approaches had so stressed the social conventions that the shaping experience of writing was neglected. Talk and writing should be closely related and forms of writing should be left to student choice in order to leave the stress on what it is that students have to say.

The material of the classroom on which students brought to bear their organising and learning powers had usually been literature. Dixon wished to see other experiences valued as well, since "one can also look at people and situations direct". The life of city children, if it was to be valued as classroom experience, needed to have aspects of that experience examined. So, a thematic approach to curriculum organisation was envisaged as part of Dixon's model.

As his very definition of literature is Britton's "spectator role" language, such that "literature" falls on a continuum from gossip to high art, then logically the students' own stories and poems were to be regarded as part of the literature of the classroom.

Dixon's approach to traditional literature was a reader-response one ("There is no short cut ... to each pupil learning to read for himself"). He saw much previous literature teaching being in fact the teaching of literary criticism because that provided a defined content, in place of attempting an active engagement of the student with the literature itself.

In dealing with the issue of language in other subject areas, Dixon captured the spirit of the language-across-the-curriculum movement of the times and, interestingly, conceptualised the terms of the later genre debates of the '80s and '90s (See Sawyer and Watson,1991; Sawyer,1993; Sawyer and Watson, 1995). The issue for Dixon (and for Harold Rosen, who is quoted extensively at this point in the book) was that of distinguishing between the "linguistic-conventional" and the "linguistic-intellectual". Subject knowledge is often expressed in a language divorced from students' experiences, and the efforts of teachers are directed at trying to teach the linguistic forms rather than the subject knowledge:

> *Is there only one possible statement of Boyle's Law?...scientists are not made by teaching pupils the passive voice and the avoidance of the second person, but by inculcating awareness and attitudes (towards certain kinds of data) that will draw on the necessary linguistic forms.*
>
> (Dixon, 1975, pp 67-69)

The traditional view of language as a 'vehicle' for knowledge anticipated Barnes' and Shemilt's later characterisation of the Transmission teacher as one who values the language of the textbook and sees language as a tube down which knowledge is passed for later regurgitation (Barnes and Shemilt, 1974). It was a view of language use across the curriculum rejected in the growth model.

What is a program of learning in English under the growth model? The Dartmouth conference began with the "provocative statement that English has no content"(Dixon, 1975, p72). The search for content, argued Dixon, had be-devilled English curriculum, and was responsible for such traditional concerns as the history of literature or grammar as the content of English. The latter study particularly, argued Dixon, is best seen as a sub-set of the study of language generally and best kept for the later years of schooling, because of its abstract nature.

Assessment under the growth model was to eschew the debilitating effects of the examination system on the curriculum and the Dartmouth Seminar called for a complete review of examinations in the light of its curriculum principles.

Sequencing a Program

Dixon's famous statement that English curriculum design needed "something less specific than a curriculum and something more ordered than chaos" (Dixon, 1975, p91) characterises this section of his book – a recognition of the need for a sense of order, but less certainty about direction than is the case in the rest of *Growth Through English*. Dixon rejected a list of skills, proficiencies and knowledge as the basis of a curriculum and canvassed "not a single level of abstraction, but a hierarchy of levels" (Dixon, 1975, p85), which revolved around teachers setting up frameworks within which pupils could make choices suited to their developmental levels and interests. Dixon's example was that of reading interests and the role of the teacher in both opening possibilities and allowing choice.

He also detailed Moffett's series of hierarchies of language development from what was very soon to become *Teaching the Universe of Discourse:*
+ from immediate and present experience to what is coming next, to the past and finally to potential experience;
+ from myth to naturalistic fiction;
+ growth in explicitness about language and in tentativeness;
+ from immediate and familiar audiences to unknown and distant ones;
+ from language about experience to language about things.

Dixon's ultimate answer to the issue of sequence and continuity was "to know the individual and work from there" (Dixon, 1975, p91).

In-School Organisation
Recognising that changes in the central activities of the classroom implied changes in the classroom itself, in the English department and in the school as a whole, Dixon advocated 'workshop' classrooms, team teaching and mixed ability classes.

Teacher Education
Importantly, Dixon also drew out of the growth model a vision of what appropriate training for teaching under this model might look like. This included:
+ experience in wide language use, such as drama, writing, response to literature;
+ a disciplined study of language in society, including practical investigations;
+ developmental studies;
+ continuing in-service education;
+ close attachment of school staff and teacher education staff.

Critiques of *Growth through English*

Despite its huge importance in the history of English curriculum, Dixon's work has not been without its critics.

Literature-Centred English
From the 70s on, criticism came especially from a literature-centred school of English curriculum yoked to the cultural heritage which Dixon was in part questioning and who vigorously rejected the widened definition of literature at Dartmouth that would include all writing in Britton's spectator role as

'literature'. Especially rejected was the notion of defining the pupil's own work as suitable 'literature' for classroom consideration (Whitehead, 1976, 1977; Allen, 1980). 'Substitution' of the pupil's experience for the elevating effects of literature was seen as a denigration of the curriculum, particularly when the experience being privileged was now that of the urban poor. Such thematic teaching was often parodied in defence of the heritage:

> relevance in English classrooms meant the presentation of local material to stimulate talk. 'What's it like in your house when the truant officer comes?' ... The urban poor were marked for salvation ... English teachers began to cut back on the freight of literature or jettison it altogether. If all pupils cannot cope with literature, then none need have it.
>
> (Hansen, 1979)

Thus shifting the curriculum towards the concerns and lives of the majority of students was seen in this view as a downgrading of the curriculum and a lowering of standards. 'Experience-centredness' and 'literature-centredness' soon began to look like opposing notions as the basis of curriculum choice.

What Does "Growth" Stand For?

David Homer's critique of Growth Through English covered more basic issues. Homer argued that Dixon substituted 'aims' for 'activities' and hence there was nothing that made his curriculum 'English'. The only thing that made Dixon's program recognisable as 'English' was that much of the material for discussion and drama was 'literature' (organised thematically). Moreover, argued Homer, Dixon seemed to want to stay where the child 'was' and there seemed to be no encouragement to look outside the self, so that growth looked like "growth ... towards egocentricity" (Homer, 1979, pp 192ff). Growth, methodologically, had 'nowhere to go'; it was loosely defined; the suggestions for practice were vague and while the content was being defined as "the whole of living experience", the teacher's job was being made impossible.

Critical literacy/genre schools

More recently, criticism of the growth model in general and of Growth Through English in particular has come from the critical literacy and genre schools, both of whom oppose Dixon's work on the grounds of its emphasis on the individual over the social. In this view, Dixon is seen as characterising all that is represented by the Progressive and the Romantic:

+ stressing personal, individual experience and individual needs
+ emphasising the relevance of each child's culture and seeing working class culture in particular as a valid alternative to the middle class culture usually represented in schooling
+ advocating mixed-ability classrooms
+ calling for a pedagogy that is 'relevant', 'pupil-centred', 'creative'.

Critical Literacy

Opposing this progressive view is a pedagogy labelled 'radical', which moves beyond a celebration of working class culture into an explication of the political and economic conditions that produce social inequality. This stance emphasises the social and economic reproduction of injustice. Linking knowledge with power, it aims to produce a 'critical literacy'. In such a literacy, the unit of analysis is not individual, but social, and the key concern is not with individual interests but with individual and collective empowerment. It is oppositional and subversive. Critical literacy celebrates the social and argues that growth model curricula place too much emphasis on the notion of the individual, without recognising that language users are socially constructed. Growth pedagogy is seen as 'individualist', 'liberal', 'progressive', 'naturalising' and 'expressive'; critical literacy, on the other hand, is 'social', 'radical', 'problematising', 'cultural' and, of course, 'critical' (McCormick, 1994; Peim, 1993; Griffith, 1992; Patterson, 1992; Ball, Kenny and Gardiner, 1990; Boomer, 1989). One aspect of Dixon's growth theory that particularly draws criticism is the emphasis on a reader-response approach to literature, which is rejected because of the focus on the individual as the centre of response (Patterson, 1992; Patterson 1993). Based on this model, it is argued, growth-oriented teaching practices also encourage students to envisage literature as if it represented a slice of real-life and hence fail to take the opportunity of teaching students that literature and its characters are social constructs. The problem with this, it is argued, is a lost opportunity to critique the ideology of the text (Mares, 1988).

Genre

From the genre school, what particularly draws criticism is the emphasis on personal writing, which is said to favour those most literate, hence disenfranchising those not from the dominant culture. Genrists reject the assumption that writing is primarily an individual act originating in the individual mind to express the ideas of the individual and to communicate them in a social context. They, and social constructionists in general, see writing as a social act in which the writer's language originates with the community and is used to join communities he/she does not yet belong to. Allowing pupils freedom to write of their own experiences only reinforces the success of those already dominant and does nothing to aid the disenfranchised to improve their position (see, for example, Christie, 1987).

Growth Through English Today

Growth Through English is of course the product of a particular historical moment, yet in many ways it remains a remarkably modern document.

The Historical Moment

The argument over the place of literature in many ways identifies the historical moment. It had been unfolding since the '50s as the London Association for the Teaching of English (LATE) reacted against the influence of Leavis and the Cambridge School. LATE, the National Association for the Teaching of English (NATE) and the University of London under the influence of James Britton, had made the 'London School' by the '70s a dominant voice of English curriculum. This school saw English as being about the pupil's language, while Cambridge saw the heritage as the basis of curriculum. In one view of history the Dartmouth conference is itself seen as the victory of London over Cambridge (Ball, 1987), though other commentators emphasise the lack of unity at the conference (Allen, 1980; Homer, 1973, pp 199-202.). The point is that the two schools represented two essentially different constituencies and views of the world. Leavis-Cambridge 'literature-centredness' represented an elite's missionary endeavour against the evils of industrial society and mass popular culture. Dixon and the London school turned their experiences in inner-city schools into a belief that their pupils' culture had as much right to be represented in their education as those other cultures represented in their reading materials. In any case, Dixon's view seems to me to be one of counter-balancing, rather than rejecting. He argued that "the Seminar was united in the essential value of the literary experience" (Dixon, 1975, p58). What *Growth Through English* tries to do is simply to widen the definition of literature to include not only pupils' writing and other "spectator role" language, but also "participant role" language so that biographies, essays, journals etc, can also be included. Championing Orwell, Hazlitt and Defoe is hardly a rejection of the heritage.

In some ways Homer's critique of Dixon also identifies the historical moment. Dixon's conceptualisation of the skills/heritage/experience triad is obviously a reaction against certain kinds of knowledge being privileged in the curriculum over others. But it is also a reaction against objectively-testable content at all being the basis of a curriculum to the exclusion of processes. The growth model certainly emphasised the personal growth of the individual as being an important aim of language development. Even more important, though, was putting the user of language at the centre of the curriculum at a time when curricula were characterised by lists of concepts about language or by notions of inculcation into 'high culture'. Dixon recognises that the Dartmouth Seminar moved from "an attempt to define 'What English is'...to a definition by process, a description of the activities we engage in through language" and that this definition was a shift from describing English in terms of a set of nouns like skills, proficiencies, set books etc to describing English in terms of a set of verbs (Dixon, 1975, p7). That was a genuine paradigm shift and the notion of the student as a user of the language being at the centre of the curriculum is not a notion to be given up easily. The shift from English as content to English as activity is a profound one and part of Homer's objection to Dixon's lack of clear aims that could objectively be called 'English' can be located in the fact that this paradigm shift had yet to work out its boundaries. What exactly would 'growth' look like? The notion that 'growth' referred to a kind of '60s New Age notion of 'personal growth' aligned with a Romantic obsession with the individual has usually underlined criticisms of the growth model; but this ignores a much more hard-nosed notion of 'growth' as referring not just to the user of language but to growth in the use of language itself (that is, being about language development).

What has gone down in history almost to the exclusion of all else about *Growth Through English* is the skills/cultural heritage/growth triad. This ignores, it seems to me, one of the book's central themes – the search for what constitutes 'growth' in reading, writing, listening and speaking. In later editions, it was this idea to which Dixon returned and on which he expanded. In his 1975 *Growth Through English in the Perspective of the Seventies*, Dixon's extra chapter, entitled "In the perspective of the Seventies" is almost entirely about the issue of what constitutes such growth and how we would recognise it. In a later review of Moffett's work, Dixon characterised Moffett's schematic formulation of discourse development in *Teaching the Universe of Discourse* as exemplifying mid-sixties Structuralism and representing the spirit of Jakobson and Levi-Strauss and Chomsky and the New Curriculum projects (Dixon, 1988). While not himself so schematic, in returning in 1975 to the issue of what constitutes growth and how we would recognise it, it is Moffett's structures that he attempts to refine. He does this by discussing them in relation to particular implications of the London Writing Unit's division of language into the transactional-expressive-poetic schema. Much of Dixon's later work – such as his work in analysing staging points in writing at 16+ – continued to be concerned with this attempt to characterise growth (Dixon and Stratta, nd).

It is remarkable, given the '70s criticism of his neglect of literature which is discussed above, that some modern criticism has also linked Dixon to a Leavisite tradition (Christie, 1993; Christie et al, 1991; Patterson, 1992). It seems a particular case of special pleading to emphasise the commonalities between 'cultural heritage' and 'personal growth' on the tenuous grounds that they both value individual voices when so much of the work of Dixon and other 'growth model' advocates has obviously been to distance themselves from, and provide a balance to, the view of curriculum represented by the Leavis/Cambridge School. Indeed, the notion of 'personal response', which Christie and others see as almost equivalent to 'personal growth' has a quite different origin and meaning in both response theory and in *Growth Through English* from what it had for Leavis.

The Modernity of *Growth Through English*

Two other critical literacy arguments are basic to the continuing relevance of *Growth Through English* today. One of these sees personal response pedagogy as the product of an historical moment that needed to find alternative ways for engaging the attention and supervising the moral development of an increasingly diversified secondary school population, especially an increasing group of reluctant readers. The practices that resulted from this need, it is argued, looked to individual psychology for its pedagogical response (Patterson, 1993). The other argument simply sees Dixon as progressive Romantic.

How much one accepts either of these depends on how one views the notion of 'oppositional' and whether Dixon's can claim to be a 'radical' stand. Like the critical literacy school itself twenty-five years later, Dixon is effectively stating that a cultural heritage curriculum gives one kind of student whose culture is represented in that curriculum a voice and hence a competitive edge in the social power that education helps distribute. But his answer, unlike that of the genre school, is not to help his working-class students into the corridors of power by inculcating them with the socially powerful curriculum. The critical literacy school accuses growth pedagogy of not critiquing, or aiding students to critique, the conditions of working-class life. But it could be argued that in celebrating the immediate life, culture and language of the working-class student, Dixon is taking the far more radical stand of presenting a new social basis to the curriculum. Undoubtedly, there is a genuine radical element in early growth pedagogy, an element that concentrated on the causes of social inequality, helping pupils to understand these and emphasising solidarity rather than upward mobility (Rosen, 1973; Hodgson, 1974, pp443ff).

The universe of English teaching has moved on since Dixon wrote his ground-breaking report on the Dartmouth conference. Some of the report's values have been left behind; some of its important recommendations have never been implemented in widespread practice. Nevertheless, the bulk of what it has to say has underpinned leading-edge English practice for thirty years. It is worth re-visiting for these historical reasons, as well as investigating what it still has to say for the future.

---

* Page references are to the 3rd edition, 1975.

References

Allen, David (1980) *English Teaching Since 1965: How Much Growth?* London: Heinemann.

Ball, Stephen J (1987) "English Teaching, the State and Forms of Literacy", in Kroon, Sjaak and Sturm, Jan (eds) *Research on Mother Tongue Education in an International Perspective: Papers of the Second International Symposium of the International Mother Tongue Education Network, Antwerp, December, 1986*, Enschede: International Mother Tongue Education Network.

Ball, Stephen, Kenny, Alex and Gardiner, David "Literacy, Politics and the Teaching of English", in Goodson, Ivor and Medway, Peter (1990) *Bringing English to Order: The History and Politics of a School Subject*, London, New York and Philadelphia: The Falmer Press.

Barnes, Douglas (1976) *From Communication to Curriculum*, Harmondsworth: Penguin.

Barnes, D and Shemilt, D (1974) "Transmission and Interpretation", *Educational Review*, 26:3, June.

Boomer, Garth (1989) "Literacy: the Epic Challenge Beyond Progressivism", *English in Australia*, 89: September, pp 6-17.

Britton, James (1970) *Language and Learning*, Harmondsworth: Penguin.

Christie, Frances (1987) "Genres as Choice" in Reid, Ian (ed) *The Place of Genre in Learning: Current Debates*, Deakin University: Centre for Studies in Literary Education.

Christie, F. (1993) "The 'Received Tradition' of English Teaching: the Decline of Rhetoric and the Corruption of Grammar", in Green, Bill (ed) *The Insistence of the Letter: Literacy Studies and Curriculum Theorising*, Pittsburgh: University of Pittsburgh Press.

Christie, F, Devlin, B, Freebody, P, Luke, A, Martin, J R, Threadgold, T, Walton, C (1991) *Teaching English Literacy: a Project of National Significance on the Preservice Preparation of Teachers for Teaching English Literacy*, Canberra: DEET

Dixon, John (1975, 3rd edn) *Growth Through English*, London: Oxford.

Dixon, John (1988) "Exploring Models of Discourse" in Dixon, John and Freedman, Aviva, *Levels of Abstracting: Invitation to a Dialogue*, Carleton Papers in Applied Language Studies, Occasional Paper 1, July.

Dixon, John and Stratta, Leslie (nd) *Achievements in Writing At 16+*, University of Birmingham.

Griffith, Peter (1992) *English at the Core: Dialogue and Power in English Teaching*, Milton Keynes/Philadelphia: Open University Press.

Hansen, I V (1979) "The Case for Literature Study in Secondary Schools: Some Difficulties", *The Teaching of English*, 36, May.

Hodgson, J T (1974) *Changes in English Teaching: Institutionalisation, Transmission and Ideology*, Unpublished PhD thesis, London University.

Homer, David B (1973) *Fifty Years of Purpose and Precept in English Teaching (1921-71): An Overview With Special Reference to the Teaching of Poetry in the Early Secondary Years*, Unpublished MEd Thesis, Melbourne University.

Mares, Peggy (1988) " 'Personal Growth' as a Frame for Teaching Literature" in Hart, Kevin (ed) *Shifting Frames: English/Literature/Writing*, Deakin University: Centre for Studies in Literary Education.

McCormick, Kathleen (1994) *The Culture of Reading and the Teaching of English*, Manchester/ New York: Manchester University Press.

Moffett, James (1968) *Teaching the Universe of Discourse*, Boston: Houghton Mifflin.

Patterson, Annette (1992) "Individualism in English: from Personal Growth to Discursive Construction", *English Education*, 24: 3, October.

Patterson, Annette (1993) " 'Personal Response' and English Teaching", in Meredyth, Denise and Tyler, Deborah (eds) *Child and Citizen: Genealogies of Schooling and Subjectivity*, Griffith University: Institute for Cultural Policy Studies.

Peim, Nick (1993) *Critical Theory and the English Teacher: Transforming the Subject*, London/New York: Routledge.

Rosen, Harold (1973) *Teaching London Kids*, London: LATE, Autumn.

Sawyer, Wayne (1993) "Writing Genres, Writing for Learning and Writing Teachers", *The Advanced Skills Teacher*, 3: Autumn.

Sawyer, Wayne and Watson, Ken (1991) "Writing to Learn: Standing Against the Genre Position", *Teaching and Learning*, 11:2, January.

Sawyer, Wayne and Watson, Ken (1995) "Writing in Science", in Sawyer, Wayne (ed) *Teaching Writing: Is Genre the Answer?* Sydney: Australian Education Network.

Whitehead, Frank (1976) "Stunting the Growth", *The Use of English*, Autumn.

Whitehead, Frank (1977) "The Present State of English Teaching", *The Use of English*, Winter.

A Note on *Teaching the Universe of Discourse*

Wayne Sawyer

James Moffett's 1968 classic, *Teaching the Universe of Discourse*, was a seminal work in curriculum theorising about language development. In brief, Moffett argued that development as a user of language occurred along two key lines:

1. Increasing distance between audience and speaker (the 'I-You' continuum). The key stages here he called:

Reflection –	intrapersonal communication;
Conversation –	interpersonal communication between two people in vocal range;
Correspondence –	interpersonal communication between remote individuals or small groups with some personal knowledge of each other;
Publication –	interpersonal communication to a large anonymous group extended over space/time.

Each stage was more selective, composed and public than the one preceding and at each stage feedback was slower, until it disappeared altogether.

2. Increasing distance between speaker/writer and subject, that is, increasing abstraction of subject matter (the 'I-It' continuum). The key stages here were represented in the following table.

What is happening	Drama	Recording
What happened	Narrative	Reporting
What happens	Exposition	Generalising
What may happen	Logical argument	Theorising

The first column represents what Moffett saw as paradigmatic verbal forms in which particular abstractions (the third column) take place. The second column is the traditional discourse categories of schooling represented by those levels of abstraction.

According to Moffett one of these stages cannot take place until the ones before it have, and outer events are increasingly substituted for by inner events. One of his most influential statements in this section is that "Whereas adults differentiate their thought into specialised kinds of discourse such as narrative, generalisation and theory, children must for a long time make narrative do for all", echoing Barbara Hardy's famous statement of the same year about narrative as "a primary act of mind".

In the 'fictive mode', however, growth occurs in the reverse order, with the child beginning in the far fetched (fantasy, folk heroes etc) and moving, with psychological growth, increasingly towards the self, studying inner experience. In a fascinatingly suggestive statement, Moffett argues that this latter progression "recapitulates the history of the species" in the sense that (Western) literature has moved from epic and myth towards inner and underground fiction.

Moffett, of course, is a creature of his time and John Dixon has given a very useful account of the mid '60s influences behind Moffett's book: the popularity of structuralism, particularly of the Levi-Strauss/Jakobson kind; the fascination with the mind and symbolism; the post-Sputnik obsession with science; the growth of the new curriculum projects and the general revolutionary spirit of the age. Dixon also reveals many of the tensions in Moffett's thinking: the possibility that more than one "order of discourse" may be operating at any one time; the notion that what accompanies increasing generalising is increasing particularising; the notion that narrative is itself a generalisation (Dixon, 1988).

Moffett's key contribution is in the twin areas of:

✦ stressing *activity* rather than *forms* (verbs rather than nouns) as the basis of curriculum continuity: the student should learn to *do* recording, reporting, generalising, theorising, with their requisite mental processes;

✦ stressing psychological development as the basis of curriculum sequencing, rather than the sequencing of particular categories of content ("The structure of the content must be meshed with the structure of the student").

It is in these areas that Moffett had influence on documents such as the revolutionary 1972 NSW English 7-10 English Syllabus and, thirty years on, his book continues to have more than historical importance.

References

Dixon, John (1988) "Exploring Models of Discourse" in Dixon, John and Freadman, Aviva, *Levels of Abstracting: Invitations to a Dialogue*, Carleton Papers in Applied Language Studies, Occasional Paper No 1 (July).

Hardy, Barbara (1977) "Narrative as a Primary Act of Mind", in Meek, Margaret, Warlow, Aidan and Barton, Griselda, *The Cool Web: The Pattern of Children's Reading*, London: Bodley Head.

Moffett, James (1968) *Teaching the Universe of Discourse*, Boston: Houghton Mifflin.

The Contribution of Barnes, Britton and Rosen: Language Across the Curriculum

Michael Kindler

The late 1970s witnessed the development of the still-innovative notion that all secondary teachers (irrespective of subject discipline) needed to develop language practices which nurture learning. The underlying concept of 'language across the curriculum' (LAC) was that every secondary teacher was a teacher of language, and therefore each had a responsibility to foster reading, writing, talking and listening as tools for effective learning. This notion of language for learning encouraged pupil engagement with, rather than passive reception of, knowledge. It tried to do this by not forcing students to operate too early in the jargon of the subject.

Jargons of Disciplines or Language for Learning?

Hence, LAC was a paradigm shift in that it altered the previous relationship between teacher and learner, in which the teacher's language as subject jargon had been privileged. Students had been the passive receivers of this language and only those who mastered it had gained access to the subject-knowledge. This process disempowered the learner in that the teacher had acted as gatekeeper.

Now if a learning community is truly such, then language is shared to learn; it ought not to privilege the teacher so that he/she teaches only within his/her frame of reference. The pupils will always learn in their frame of reference in any case. Thus, 'taking in the teacher's words', which 'mean' something different to them can become a struggle to incorporate this meaning into their frame of reference. So, the language which is an essential instrument to the teacher can become a barrier to the pupil.

This recognition that an individual's language is a significant factor in the learning process was central in shaping thinking about learning through the 1970s. "We learn by using language, and we learn language by using it." (Britton) In the 1990s, we need to retain this valuable insight, which in the present outcomes-oriented context is at risk.

The Work of Barnes, Britton and Rosen

Three influential British writers who set out to examine the role of language in the secondary classroom were Douglas Barnes (Leeds University), James Britton (University of London Institute of Education) and Harold Rosen (University of London Institute of Education). Together they co-authored *Language, the Learner and the School* (1969, revised 1971). Written for the London Association for the Teaching of English, the three chapters of this work examine language in the secondary classroom (Barnes), explore the role of talk in learning (Britton), and take steps towards articulating a language policy across the curriculum (Rosen).

Barnes: Lower Order Versus Heuristic/Higher Order Questions

In analysing a number of observed classroom lessons, Barnes' categories include the following (simplified) question types:

✦ Factual ('What'? questions)

✦ Reasoning ('How?' and 'why?') – both 'closed' (ie questions to which there is only one possible answer) and 'open' (ie questions to which there are a range of possible answers)

✦ Open questions not calling for reasoning

He also described one kind of questioning that emerged as 'pseudo-questioning' – that is, a question which appeared open but was treated by the teacher as closed. These questions were also 'pseudo' in the sense that they led the respondent, as with 'closed' questions, to 'guess what is in the questioner's mind'. These questions were not designed to promote learning, but became part of an information exchange ritual whereby the learner was initiated into the culture of the teacher, but did not use language to grapple with his/her own learning.

Barnes analysed the degree of pupil participation in lessons and described the following findings:

✦ teachers talk far more than pupils can reply;

✦ pupils are normally expected to reproduce information rather than to think for themselves;

✦ heuristic questions which ask the student to think aloud in order to discover for themselves are the least frequently asked questions;

✦ lower order questioning abounds.

Further, Barnes described the language of secondary education as being potentially of two kinds : 'socio-cultural' and 'conceptual'. Now the way language is used in the former kind is 'linguistic- conventional', while in the latter it is 'linguistic-intellectual'. The language across the curriculum in the secondary context that is best suited to promoting learning is that which asks open questions, triggers heuristic inquiry and calls for respondents to grapple with their understanding in the process of responding:

> Here lies the importance of pupil interaction. It is when the pupil is required to use language to grapple with new experience or to order old experience in a new way that he is most likely to find it necessary to use language differently. And this will be very different from taking over someone else's language in external imitation of its forms: on the contrary, it is the first step to new patterns of thinking and feeling, new ways of representing reality to himself.
>
> (Barnes in Barnes, Britton and Rosen,1971, p61)

It is only when students try out language in reciprocal exchanges that they come to modify their language in order to organise reality and that they are then able to find new functions for language in thinking and feeling. By encouraging students to speak freely within their everyday speech, they can bring from their own lives what is relevant to what is being talked about.

The Centrality of Talk Within Learning

Thus, Britton's contribution to *Language, the Learner and the School* on the role that talk plays in the classroom seemed at the time also a reasonably new concept. Previously, language generally was largely considered a means to an end, and, in particular, the spoken language used by teacher or learner was considered secondary to that more tangible educational product, writing. Indeed, speaking, prior to the 1970s, had not enjoyed parity of esteem with writing, just as reading had held a higher value than listening. One of the most important outcomes of this volume was to argue for increased recognition of what were hitherto considered to be these less relevant uses of language, and to do so across all curricula, rather than solely in subject English. The significance of this shift is not to be understated. Britton draws attention to the living organ of language as being the instrument for learning, and this (for its time) was revolutionary. Nevertheless, in addressing the previous imbalance, it is the importance of talk that Britton especially advocates. He argues that talk is the essential tool for effective learning because it is in talk that we engage and wrestle with ideas, feelings and concepts.

Principal architect of the Bullock Report (DES, 1975), Britton argues that in the act of articulation, learning happens, concepts take shape, relationships are established, and recognitions become possible. LAC seriously suggests that quiet classrooms are, in learning terms, deadly. Britton supports his perception of the central role of talk in a chapter which examines adolescents talking amongst themselves in a range of contexts (Barnes, Britton ard Rosen, 1969, pp 82-115). His observations on the centrality of talk in learning include the notions that:

- some talk is for the record, to establish common currency;
- some talk is problem solving, clarifying, talking to learning jointly;
- talking is collaborative in the sense that there is a listening and participating, responding, evaluating audience in a group;
- speakers speak their own minds;
- spoken language is relaxed, self-presenting and self-revealing;
- spoken language approximates and does not aim at polished performance (as written work usually does);
- talk is a group effort at understanding and thus promotes learning from others;
- a talking classroom provides an opportunity and an atmosphere of confidence and encouragement;
- talk offers opportunity for 'sympathetic circularity' (Bernstein);
- talk is an area of agreement where students can discuss their differences;
- expressive speech is a means to learn – such things as scientific hypotheses come later.

A Whole-School Policy

Rosen's chapter draws attention to the jargons of content areas. He challenges the self-importance which is often attached to subject specific linguistic registers (jargon), and describes such language as 'impersonal' – a problem because, again, it locks out the pupil's frame of reference.

Rosen, in this third and last part of *Language, the Learner and the School*, explores reasons why it is necessary to move towards a Language Policy Across the Curriculum.

Rosen recognises that some kind of spoken contribution by pupils helps them to learn. So in moving towards such a policy, focus emerges on the pattern of interchange in classrooms. He conservatively estimated that two-thirds of classroom talk is teacher talk. Such practice does not encourage learning – it encourages conformity and a narrowing of possible responses which in turn restrict imaginative possibilities:

We are saying that it is as talkers, questioners, arguers, gossips, chatterboxes, that our pupils do much of their most important learning. Their everyday talking voices are the most subtle and versatile means they possess for making sense of what they do and for making sense of others, including their teachers. School should be a place in which we can hear the full sound of the 'conversation of mankind' (Oakshotte)... When pupils are free to talk, teachers are free to observe and to understand what kind of learning is going on. For in the end, the teacher can only make sense of pupils making sense. He can only work with their meanings. (Rosen in Barnes, Britton, and Rosen, 1971:127).

A Language for Teaching,
or a Language for Learning?

Two other texts were seminal to the LAC movement in the 1970s. One was Barnes' *From Communication to Curriculum*, and the other Britton's *Language and Learning*. The former contains Barnes' and Shemilt's hypothesis, concerning the distinction between Transmission and Interpretation teachers, which in turn illustrates well the distinction between a language of teaching and a language for learning:

The Transmission Teacher	The Interpretation Teacher
1. Believes knowledge to exist in the form of public disciplines which include content and criteria of performance.	1. Believes knowledge to exist in the knower's ability to organise thought and action.
2. Values the learner's performances insofar as they conform to the criteria of the discipline.	2. Values the learner's commitment to interpreting reality, so that criteria arise as much from the learner as from the teacher.
3. Perceives the teacher's task to be the evaluation and correction of the learner's performance, according to criteria of which he is the guardian.	3. Perceives the teacher's task to be the setting up of a dialogue in which the learner can reshape knowledge through interaction with others.
4. Perceives the learner as an uninformed acolyte for whom access to knowledge will be difficult since he (sic) must qualify himself through tests of appropriate performance.	4. Perceives the learner as already possessing systematic and relevant knowledge, and the means of reshaping that knowledge.

Barnes (1976: 144-145)

Britton in *Language and Learning* (1970) stresses that we cannot afford to underestimate the value of language as a means of organising and consolidating our accumulated experience, or its value as a means of interacting with people and objects to create experience. Language is the basis of all the predictions by which we set the course of our lives. In particular, Britton postulates that as participants we use language to interact with people and things and make the world, for good or ill, go round. As spectators, we use language to contemplate what has happened to us or to other people, or what might conceivably happen; in other words, we improvise upon our world representation – and we may do so either to enrich it, to embroider it, to fill its gaps and extend its frontiers, or to iron out its inconsistencies.

Britton's principal argument is about the centrality in learning of oral language – 'that reading and writing float on a sea of talk'. He expresses the view that:

> . . . it is the child's intention that above all releases the tacit powers that lead to mastery; freedom on the part of teachers to provide suitable activities adapted to particular children's needs, and allowing for individual choice, therefore, becomes crucial. We believe that the considerable degree of freedom that teachers in the United Kingdom have hitherto enjoyed has enabled language programs in our schools to play a leading role as models in the international community.

(Britton, 2nd edition, 1993, p8)

In the preface to this later edition of *Language and Learning*, Britton recognises an altered learning climate in the UK of the early 90s that had come about as a consequence of the tight specification of teaching objectives and attendant methods of assessment. He expresses the view that teachers in schools no longer possessed the freedom to suit educational provision to particular needs. Clearly, part of his concern is the contemporary obsession with outcome over process, in which he perceives the value of talk as threatened.

The Absence of Quiet in Classrooms

Arguably the most powerful argument for a language across the curriculum is the notion that the language in the textbook, on the blackboard and in the mouth of the teacher can be aped relatively easily, but this does not make it available for considered, appropriate, individual use. So talk lifts above the conservatism of the written word. Talk is live.

Since the 1970s, theories about educating young people have continued to move from teacher-focused delivery to pupil-focused learning. In the history of education, this is hardly a new idea, but paralleling this development, and reinforcing its direction, LAC recognised that learning is powerfully influenced by the way questions and answers, dialogical exchanges, are shaped in the classroom. It was possible for writers to postulate from this the centrality of oral exchange (between pupil and pupil, as well as between pupils and teacher) as being in the middle of effective, active, positive learning environments.

In fact, it was this emergent understanding of LAC which brought about the realisation that a quiet classroom is not necessarily a learning classroom. It might just be busy or occupied in some industrial-age rote task.

Education into the next millennium is working in a post-industrial context, and therefore to treat classrooms as industrial manufacturing plants of robotic knowledge is to profoundly miss the opportunity of getting onto the information superhighway, because the way information in a post-industrial context is treated differs fundamentally from an unrevised industrial context. One of the learning businesses that had to rethink this paradigm in recent years was *Encyclopaedia Britannica*. Until very recently EB insisted, to their own economic disadvantage, that what the consumer wanted was hard copy. Even though Microsoft adapted a 'less scholarly' encyclopaedia (*Funk and Wagnalls*), because Microsoft packaged it electronically, they came significantly closer to how the learner wanted to access information. LAC is about using language in a more learner-friendly way, just as the example of encyclopaedia information has shown. In both cases, format matters.

On that highway we as teachers have (frequently) moved beyond the task of information provider, because students have ample and speedier access to it than we can give them. Instead, LAC concentrates on how students process, internalise, transform knowledge into meaningful and applied forms. Learning how to learn, encouraging mastery processes rather than force-feeding geese for their *foie gras*, is the essential benefit of a Language Across the Curriculum approach. As secondary teachers we too often take refuge in the sanctity of our discipline. If we are honest, school reports across subject areas are in fact looking for similar competencies, understandings, skills and attributes, and perhaps we are all guilty of being just a little too precious about our subject area's accessibility.

Implications

LAC helped establish that a successful classroom environment included noise; that oral exchanges are, ipse facto, a good thing, and that such language-based interaction promotes purposeful, individually-driven learning. The recognition that comes from that change is nothing less than a transformation from a Dickensian understanding that classrooms must resemble industrial models of silently producing writing to a post-industrial notion that values talk for learning's sake. This increases the quality of understanding that accompanies the processing of information. The primary locus of value is in talk, not in silent listening. Listening has its place, but listening to a teacher descanting in his/her *Discourse (Gee et al, 1996) is disempowering. LAC is about equality of access to the learning discourse.

*   'Discourse' is the language of a closed community, such as Education, while 'discourse' is language accessible more widely.

Bibliography

Department of Education and Science (1975) *A Language for Life*, London: HMSO.

Barnes, D, Britton, J, Rosen, H (1971) *Language, the Learner and the School*, Harmondsworth: Penguin.

Barnes, D, (1976) *From Communication to Curriculum*, Harmondsworth: Penguin.

Britton, J (1993, second edition) *Language and Learning*, Portsmouth: Heinemann.

NSW Department of School Education (1997) *Focus on Literacy: Discussion Paper, Strategy and Position Statement*, Sydney, April.

Gee, J P, Hull, G and Lankshear, C (1996) *The New Work Order: Behind the Language of the New Capitalism*, London: Allen and Unwin

Marland, M (ed.) (1977) *Language Across the Curriculum: the Implementation of the Bullock Report in the Secondary School*, London: Heinemann.

Sawyer, W, Watson, K, Adams, A (eds) (1989) *English Teaching from A-Z*, Milton Keynes: Open University Press.

Torbe, M (1980) *Language Policies in Action: Language Across the Curriculum in Some Secondary Schools*, London: Ward Lock.

Working Party on Literacy Teacher Education. (1994) *Review of Teacher Education in English Literacy and English as a Second Language in the School and Adult Education Contexts*, Canberra: NBEET, September.

A Note on *Language in Use*

Ken Watson

As part of the UK Schools Council Program in English and Linguistics, a team led by Peter Doughty produced *Language in Use*, which consists of 110 units, each providing an outline for a sequence of lessons. The units are grouped into three divisions: the internal organisation of language; the use of language by the individual to order and interpret his/her experience of the world; the individual's use of language to initiate, maintain and control relationships with others.

Two typical units from the book are entitled "National Characteristics" and "How Adults See Teenagers". The first "considers the extent to which our most firmly held assumptions about the world are often bound up with our use of common words, because the assumptions become attached to the words, and we acquire the words unreflectingly through their presence in our language." Here the class, working in groups, would compile lists of common characteristics assigned to particular nationalities and discuss how belief in these characteristics comes about. In later sessions students could examine some stereotypes in fiction (eg, in the novels of Ian Fleming), comics and television, and could prepare and perform short dramatic sketches based on stereotypes.

"How Adults See Teenagers" explores the distinctive features of the language of teenage magazines, with discussion of the degree to which the language used gives support to the idea of 'teenager' as a distinctive identity.

Language in Use is a particularly valuable resource for teachers, but it does require time and effort to turn a unit outline into a sequence of lessons for classroom use. The book is now out of print, but since several thousand copies were sold in Australia it is probably gathering dust in your school or in a secondhand bookshop.

References

Doughty, P, Pearce, J and Thornton, G (1971) *Language in Use*, London: Arnold.
Doughty, Peter and Anne (1974) *Using Language in Use*, London: Arnold.

Reading: SSR and DEAR

SSR (Sustained Silent Reading) and DEAR (Drop Everything and Read) are similar programs designed to reinforce the importance of reading in the eyes of students and to improve reading skills. At a set time each day every student in the school (and every teacher) reads silently an individual selection for a substantial period of time without interruption. It is imperative that each teacher be seen to be reading in front of the class in order to provide a good model of interested, sustained silent reading. The students also must be reading, not simply browsing through magazines, but there is no requirement that they report on their reading at the end of each session.

There is research evidence that, provided the conditions outlined above are adhered to, reading levels are raised and reading as an activity gains prestige.

References
Kefford, R E (1982) "Sustained Silent Reading – Does it Work?" in *Developments in English Teaching* Vol 1 No 2, August.

Trelease, Jim (1984) *The Read-aloud Handbook,* Harmondsworth: Penguin.

Students Reading Their Own Writing

Students simply *do not* learn to link paragraphs better, write stronger conclusions or eradicate run-on sentences by our telling them that they need to do those things. The perception of a need to change must be part of their experience, not just ours. This means that if students are to develop their writing, they must be able to read their work and see the need for the change themselves. Our principal role is to show them how we and others read their work, and to teach them different ways of reading it themselves, so that they can develop as writers.

Here is an approach which I have used. . . . it provides a practical and effective way of thinking about and responding to writing in the often noisy atmosphere of the classroom. There are three questions which I ask of a piece of writing:

1. What do I find as the key idea or centre of gravity of the piece?
2. Can I see a pattern in the writing which indicates how the elements in the piece relate to each other?
3. Did the writer lead me to appreciate the centre and how the elements in the piece relate to each other?

Brian Johnston (1987) *Assessing English: Helping Students to Reflect on Their Work,* Milton Keynes: Open University Press, 2nd edition.

Section II: Taking Stock

3 Reconceptualising Experience: Growth Pedagogy and Youth Culture

Brenton Doecke and Douglas McClenaghan

Growth pedagogy affirms the value of a student-centred curriculum, of the meanings that students construct in classroom settings as they draw on their existing understandings and experiences to create new knowledges.

That much we have learnt from John Dixon and other leading language educators in the post-war period (see Dixon, p74). And yet it is not as though the idea of a student-centred curriculum has remained fixed or constant. We adhere to the principle of a student-centred curriculum – we have subscribed to this value throughout our teaching lives – but this has meant continually reflecting on our practice and scrutinising what it means to place students' experiences at the centre of the curriculum, along with all the attendant notions (of interaction, or interpretation, as opposed to transmission; of dialogue and negotiation, as opposed to merely handing 'official' knowledge down from above). In this essay we propose to look at one significant way in which we have been prompted to reconceptualise the nature of a student-centred curriculum, namely through our continuing efforts to acknowledge the validity of youth culture (ie the cluster of cultural activities in which our students engage outside school) and to make it a legitimate frame of reference in our classrooms.

Negotiating Meaning and Value

The experiences which students bring with them to school are all mediated in textually complex ways. There is, indeed, much to be gained from treating their experiences as 'text' – so we might usefully conceive of the rich linguistic resources which students bring to school. And yet much of the wide array of languages and discourses that our students speak (or which 'speak' them) remains part of the school's underground – discussed, debated and enjoyed during lunch breaks or outside school hours, but ignored during class time, when students are obliged to focus on the 'official' school genres. That such a division continues to figure in many students' lives can only be a matter of concern. It is, in fact, arguable that much recent curriculum development (eg the unsmiling neo- Hallidayan view that it is the business of literacy educators to teach the 'powerful' school 'genres') threatens to marginalise youth culture and its genres and it is partly our intention here to address this problem.

Developing a teaching program which draws on the linguistic resources which students bring with them to class involves more than simply adding another element to the existing curriculum. It is not enough to acknowledge the books and magazines which our students read, the TV shows, films and videos they enjoy, the music they listen to, the computer games they play – important though such an acknowledgment is. We also need to focus on the ways our students use these texts to negotiate issues of meaning and value. This means eschewing the stereotypical image of teenagers as being manipulated by popular culture, as though they are all mindless dupes who will consume anything which is served up to them.

Against this view, we would argue that the texts and cultural activities in which our students engage outside school are neither homogeneous nor commonly shared. Popular music is a good example. Rather than supposing that it is one thing (the list of songs that currently get airplay on the most popular FM stations), it is crucial to recognise that it is divided into many genres and subgenres (rap, hip-hop, gangsta rap, hardcore), each with its devotees. The body of work of many artists is also complex; dedicated fans are very knowledgeable about significant aspects of their favourite artist's output, and they have worked very hard to become expert (cf Buckingham and Sefton-Green, pp60-83). Although there is likely to be a degree of commonality in the music enjoyed by kids of the same age, there is also diversity, depth and specialisation, and it is worth focusing on the discriminations that students exercise in their efforts to differentiate amongst artists and genres.

When kids debate the merits of the latest episode of *The Simpsons*, or pass around issues of their favourite magazines or comics, much is at stake. Through such textual exchanges students test their beliefs and values and speculate about their identities. They explore a range of significant issues, from their sexuality and gender to their ethnicity, social status and politics. Such exchanges presuppose quite sophisticated understandings of meaning and interpretation – far more sophisticated than those reflected in many classroom reading practices, which are often limited to reading the set text and writing the mandatory book report. When placed alongside the lively exchanges in which students engage outside the classroom, such sterile textbook activities are (at best) ludicrous and irrelevant and (at worst) very dubious learning.

Through swapping notes about their favourite books or videos, students implicitly acknowledge the social character of reading, recognising (as Buckingham and Sefton-Green have put it) that meaning is not something "which is produced in the isolated encounter between the reader and the text", but that it is a process through which readers are able to define and negotiate their "individual and collective identities" (Buckingham and Sefton-Green, p38). By expressing their tastes and values, students attempt to affirm their individual identities and their membership of specific groups or communities. They recognise the importance of belonging to a reading community – a community reflecting similar tastes and values, similar views about being in the world. They don't simply watch films or listen to songs – they discuss them, constructing shared meanings on the basis of their readings of these texts. Young people don't go to movies on their own, or even in pairs – they descend on cinema complexes in groups, and they leave the movies loudly proclaiming their opinions of what they've seen. But they do not only engage in such public constructions of meaning when discussing films; this is also an aspect of their encounters with other texts, as any teacher who has tuned into their conversations knows. Some students are into Manga comics, and they parade this allegiance in a variety of ways (by drawing on folders, reading the comics in class, watching Manga videos), thereby distinguishing themselves from other students with different interests and tastes.

Critical Discourses

Acknowledging the importance of youth culture does not mean that teachers should feel obliged to share in young people's tastes and interests – the idea of forty- and fifty-year-old teachers enthusing over *silverchair* would be ridiculous (Molly Meldrum notwithstanding). Paradoxical though this statement might appear, we are not advocating that particular texts or artists should be brought into the classroom. To use any of *silverchair*'s songs as a prompt (say) for thematic work would be to reduce it to the status of a set text, and kids would be entitled to feel resentful about their teachers using such material in this way. The primary focus of classroom exchanges should be less on popular texts themselves than on the processes of interpretation and discrimination in which students engage whenever they talk about their interests and enthusiasms. Our aim should be to affirm the vitality and salience of such processes of valuing without pretending to be up with the latest.

Of course, students themselves will invoke examples from popular culture when exploring texts within classroom settings, provided that the legitimacy of such a frame of reference is accepted by teachers and pupils alike. This can range from drawing parallels between Arnold Schwarzenegger's *Total Recall* and John Fowles' fiction (cf Faulkner) to consciously exploring the imaginative possibilities of teenage romance (cf Moss). Teachers do not always react enthusiastically when students choose to write in certain popular narrative forms, such as sci-fi, horror, action adventure or romance – judging such writing as cliched or derivative. Somehow it is frightfully witty for a student to write a narrative poem about school in the form of (say) Edgar Allen Poe's "The Raven", but it is uncritical and tacky for students to emulate the forms and conventions of popular culture. Gemma Moss has usefully demonstrated how young writers are able to explore questions of identity, including gender and social class, by experimenting with popular genres. She shows that by adopting the conventions of teenage romance, young people are often doing more than slavishly imitating the genre. They are, instead, testing its boundaries, exploring its possibilities and limitations, its contradictions and complexities.

We have already observed the complexity of the rich world of texts that our students inhabit – a complexity which is matched (we would argue) by the critical discourses in which they engage. In comparison with their vigorous debates about books, videos and other texts which interest them, more conventional discourses of value can seem wooden and untheorised. We are thinking, for example, of recent attempts by Kevin Donnelly to argue the importance of an Australian cultural literacy as against an "increasingly diverse, global environment." "The icons and images that young people in particular are overwhelmed with", writes Donnelly, "are international in flavour. Whether it be American baseball caps, Walt Disney films, *The Simpsons* or rap music, the reality is that many students know more about America than Australia" (Donnelly, p7). What is striking about Donnelly's 'cultural literacy' is the complete absence from his thinking of any notion of value as a function of social relationships, as a quality which must be constantly negotiated in the process of negotiating our relationships with each other and the society around us. It is as though the traditional icons of Australian culture – Donnelly waxes sentimental about "The Drover's Wife", Simpson and his Donkey, Mulga Bill and his Bicycle – are simply there, and their value is self-evident. Lawson, Furphy, Paterson – these are the 'great' writers of our culture, and it is our job as teachers to instil in our students a proper respect for their canonical status (cf. Doecke).

Needless to say, students themselves often hold different views about the centrality of such writers and texts to their lives, views which manifest themselves in a variety of ways, from yawns and groans of boredom to sustained critical analysis of the gaps and silences in such Great Texts. Once again we would argue that the issue is less to do with the merits of the texts themselves (if it is ever really possible to speak of 'the texts themselves') than with the ways in which those texts get appropriated by certain types of readers for certain purposes. We have ourselves used "The Drover's Wife" with students to promote critical reflection on its iconic status and the gendered character of Lawson's picture of the bush, encouraging them to write their own late-twentieth century versions of "The Drover's Wife" (a la Murray Bail and other contemporary writers). Where we part company with Lawson-groupies like Donnelly is in our sense that the distinction between 'high' culture and 'popular' culture cannot usefully be imposed on texts, without doing considerable violence to their complexity. Donnelly writes from a position outside classrooms; his judgements about cultural value have all been reached without regard to classroom contexts. We would argue that classrooms should be sites where such judgements are negotiated, where students themselves should be placed in a position where they can articulate their tastes and argue the validity of their perspectives on culture and society.

The distinction between 'high' and 'popular' culture merely signals different social and cultural contexts for making judgements about texts. 'High' culture is not the province of a more refined sensibility as opposed to the vulgarities of popular taste. 'High' and 'popular' culture signify different contexts in which people make distinctions in their continuing efforts to interpret their cultural landscape. By clinging to a wooden notion of the Great Texts that are supposedly central to Australian culture, Donnelly effectively precludes any possibility of exploring the contrasting regimes of value (Frow, pp144-145) or "reading formations" (Bennett) that construct some texts as being of value, while treating others as of less worth. His is a very uncritical – indeed, anti-intellectual – stance, which would prevent students from developing a critical awareness relating to their tastes and discriminations. Our students, on the other hand, are well placed to reflect on the operation of different regimes of value, drawing on their sense of the discriminations they exercise in respect of 'popular' cultural activities. And it is our responsibility as teachers to enhance their critical awareness, making much that is implicit in their judgements explicit.

Conservative commentators like Kevin Donnelly, however, pose less of an obstacle to the textual practices which we have been celebrating than the accumulated weight of traditional curricula and pedagogy. The place which *To Kill a Mockingbird* continues to occupy in the secondary English curriculum cannot really be explained as resulting from traditional discriminations and aesthetic judgements, as though syllabus writers depend on arbiters of taste like Donnelly to hand down their verdicts, which they then dutifully translate into secondary curricula. We suspect that certain texts have remained at the core of the secondary English curriculum, despite significant changes in taste and fashion, because they are all 'safe' books that lend themselves to conventional treatment (reading assignments, comprehension tests, vocabulary lists). Leavisism, Reader Response theories, feminism and poststructuralism – they have all come and gone, and the old hands amongst us have simply continued to inflict *To Kill a Mockingbird* on their Year 10 classes or *Macbeth* on their Year 11s.

Charles Sarland, in *Young People Reading: Culture and Response*, has explored the ways in which students react to set texts, drawing on the critical acumen they have developed through their cultural activities outside school. Students are very conscious of the ritualised practices associated with reading set texts, and they dutifully regurgitate what their teachers want, without ever seriously engaging in issues which are of any moment to them. When interviewing a group of girls about their experience of reading Steinbeck's *The Pearl* (the set text which they had all been obliged to study), Sarland observes how they were unable to "find themselves in the text" and simply passively resigned themselves to working through the book. It is not that these students did not have interesting perspectives on the text, but the routinised practices of the classroom prevented them from articulating their views (Sarland, pp79-101). Sarland also interviewed a Year 7 girl, who gave the following advice about how to get through the set text: "I just get the book and start going through the pages til I get to the end, then I go back to the front, just keep doing it" (Sarland, p100).

Against such practices, it is vital to assert the value of a student-centred curriculum that embraces the tastes and enthusiasms of the young people in our classrooms.

Case Studies

Here are two case studies that illustrate the kind of dialogue that is possible in classrooms when students and teachers engage in critical discussion about popular culture. We would like to underline the word 'critical' because these case studies show how classrooms can be used to prompt students into reflecting on their experiences of popular cultural forms and the discriminations they make.

To exclude popular culture from the classroom is to close off the possibility of this kind of reflection and evaluation. This does not mean making negative judgements about the supposedly 'manipulative' character of popular culture, as though as teachers we should see our role as one of saving students from such harmful influences. Throughout this essay we have affirmed the ways in which our students' experiences are mediated by popular culture – they inhabit a rich semiotic environment – but we do not assume that they are always fully conscious of the processes of valuing in which they engage, or that they always make considered judgements about the images and texts which they encounter. By making popular culture an object of attention in the classroom, we enable our students to reflect on their experiences, on their tastes and discriminations, their values and identities.

We're all 'Doomed'!: Case Study 1

The Year 8 class were doing work on issues and argument. They had begun by drawing on their own experiences to examine different meanings of 'argument' and had discussed some issues that were important to them. Their main task was to examine an issue and to present a point of view on that topic to an audience (this meant members of their class). They were encouraged to use other means of persuasion than traditional forms such as the formal argumentative essay. (For a detailed account of this approach to teaching argument see McClenaghan, et al, 1995/96)

The class had shown themselves to be enthusiastic participants in all kinds of oral work, and so it was no surprise that many students chose to give oral presentations. One group of boys decided to do something on computer games. It so happened that at that time the media were whipping up a moral panic about graphically violent computer games. *Doom* had just been released and was state of the art: fast, realistic graphics with lashings of mayhem, gore and death. According to the media, our children were in imminent danger of growing addicted to *Doom*, becoming desensitised to violence, and thereby developing anti-social and violent behaviours. One of the boys in the group had played *Doom* and, unsurprisingly, his ideas about the game were quite different. So the group decided to do some research on computer games; they surveyed other students in different levels about playing computer games, then gave a talk to the class about the issue, their findings, and their opinions on the topic. They'd originally intended to demonstrate the game in class, but the school lacked the necessary hardware, and so they had to make do with describing the game and how it was played.

For their survey they focussed on the main issues related to their topic. They found that the issue broke up into a cluster of issues: the violence and realism of games and the possible effects these might have on players, the possible addictive qualities of computer games, the (at that time) mooted ratings classification for computer games, the gendered nature of computer gaming, and the media treatment of the issue. The boys concentrated on the first three topics as being the most interesting and relevant. The question of media treatment they dismissed with scorn. Their opinion of the newspaper articles on the issue was that the writers didn't know what they were talking about.

The group's presentation was thought-provoking and entertaining. As Year 8 boys, they believed that they should be allowed to play whatever games they wanted. From their own experience and the evidence of the survey, they concluded that playing the games did not, for kids of their age and older, have any adverse effects because of the violent content. However, they did support a simple classification system, arguing that younger kids could be influenced or disturbed by the graphic violence. They appeared to want to distance themselves from younger kids and position themselves with older students. Their findings regarding the addictive qualities of computer games were interesting, as a number of other students they'd surveyed confessed to spending too much time playing computer games, although – significantly – not only violent ones. The boys argued for parental intervention to stop kids becoming computer addicts.

These students had built bridges between their culture and their schooling. It was a two-way affair, where their schooling informed their cultural lives and their culture had provided a significant focus for their language and learning.

Fascists in Space: Case Study 2

The Wave is an unpromising novel for study as a set text. It raises some political and social issues, but the story is dated and thoroughly anaemic: teaching it requires the use of life-support systems. A Year 10 class studying *The Wave* had suddenly come alive when they began to relate the novel to the story of Hitler's Third Reich. There were plenty of analogies between the two and the novel quickly became subsumed by intense and powerful depictions of fascist Germany, gleaned from television documentaries. When students came to present a piece of work on the novel, they were allowed considerable leeway, as most of them wanted to explore the ideas rather than the set text.

One boy had noticed some similarities between fascist Germany and events and circumstances in *Star Wars*, and he decided to write about them. His idea caught hold and soon there were two small groups of students writing about the parallels between *Star Wars* and fascist Germany. They also decided that they wanted to approach the topic in a relatively scholarly fashion. Teacherly suggestions that they show bits of the trilogy to the class and talk about the parallels fell on deaf ears. They each chose to develop their ideas in formal, analytical essays, with an introduction, paragraphs of substance, and a conclusion.

As the students nutted out what they wanted to say in small-group discussions, they demonstrated considerable knowledge of the *Star Wars* trilogy, relating their new ideas about fascism to their existing knowledge. Their understanding of fascist Germany was, of course, much less comprehensive than their knowledge of *Star Wars*, and yet they were able to make some vital connections between the two. One example was the concept of totalitarianism: they noted how the Empire in *Star Wars*, like the Third Reich, functioned as a totalitarian regime. They then explored ideas about totalitarianism and related concepts, such as extreme authoritarianism, the cult of personality, militarism, violence, suppression of individuality and dissent.

On the basis of this large body of material the students planned a formal essay. They were familiar with writing formal essays, but they had so much to say that they needed help to organise and structure their essays. As with the computer games example, there was interaction between the students' understandings and the knowledge and skills traditionally exercised in the classroom. It wasn't enough just to let them be the experts, and to sit back and applaud their expertise; the students needed help to re-frame their cultural knowledge and experience in the context of the demands of their schooling.

Conclusion: Maintaining Dialogue

Within the last decade, writers have increasingly noted the distinctively postmodern character of the culture which young people enjoy, arguing that teachers are now faced with unprecedented challenges in their efforts to engage students in dialogue and negotiation in their classrooms. Instead of students, teachers must now contend with "aliens in the classroom" (to borrow Green and Bigum's resonant phrase).

We have major reservations about this claim. Although it is made from a stance that is sympathetic to youth culture, in a paradoxical way it reflects many of the assumptions shared by conservative critics. Green and Bigum refer to "the convergence of contemporary discourses on youth, media culture and postmodernism" (Green and Bigum, p120) and the inevitable result is to make youth culture seem more homogeneous or monolithic than it really is. Such a view diminishes the sense in which young people use the cultural forms available to them to make new meanings and values.

We are sceptical as to whether notions of the postmodern subject can ever be very useful in our attempts to understand the complexities of classroom exchanges. Our view of the student-centred curriculum – of the interactive nature of classrooms – presupposes that students are engaged in a wide range of discursive and non-discursive practices. 'Postmodern' may indeed be an apt way to describe some of these practices, but it does not comprehend them. Young people live in multiple contexts that are often contradictory and confusing. Rather than passively assuming the status of subjects that have been pre-determined for them (postmodern or otherwise), they continually struggle to define their identities, attempting to negotiate the subject positions available to them. We would argue that vis-a-vis postmodern society and culture, students are often resistant readers, although this is not to suggest that they are necessarily engaged in rational reflection or choice. Often their resistance is more forcefully expressed by their behaviour, by the things that they do. And often they do not understand the reasons for their resistance, or why they do what they do.

As teachers, we can hardly feel comfortable about their views; very often their words and actions express a cynical contempt for schooling and society, and it is almost impossible for us, as representatives of authority, to know how to engage in a dialogue with them. In significant respects, we are inevitably positioned as authority figures, embodying a complex set of rules and regulatory practices, and it is almost impossible to escape a notion of 'us' against 'them' (as is shown by the very language we are using here). For a lot of young people school sucks and they have a cynical contempt for government and media rhetoric about education. Kids in disadvantaged schools in particular know how the cards are stacked against them, and much of the language they speak is directed against schooling and society (cf Kent, McDonald, Tsiolkas, Wheat).

The kind of dialogue that we are envisaging with kids can be a very uncomfortable one. This has nothing to do with the comical spectacle of middle-aged teachers aping young people's enthusiasms and interests. The scenario we are imagining is more threatening, in which teachers are confronted by young people's anger at a society increasingly characterised by obscene inequalities. Such adolescents (we are thinking of the young people described by Kent, McDonald, Tsiolkas and Wheat) know that beneath the smooth and shiny look of things there is suffering, dislocation, social anomie – thus they experience the paradoxes of postmodern society.

We must provide space in our classrooms for students to articulate these experiences. It is simply not acceptable to exclude such experiences from our classrooms, marginalising them as part of the unofficial school culture that we glimpse in snippets of lunchtime conversations or graffiti scrawled on toilet walls. Much of the rhetoric currently being peddled by governments and the media constructs an ideal image of education and schooling which is completely at odds with our students' experiences. The languages and discourses which our students share – ranging from expressions of cynicism and contempt to good-humoured irreverence and stoicism – are perhaps the only justification we have for thinking that it is possible to imagine worlds other than the one we currently inhabit.

Cultural studies in the classroom means affirming the intelligence and imagination of young people. It is for that reason that governments and the media will do their best to keep youth culture out of classrooms, filling the school day with irrelevancies such as standardised testing , cultural literacy and formal learning outcomes. English teachers, however, should be doing all they can to affirm the centrality of student-centred teaching, and accepting the challenges that this entails.

References

Bennett, T (1984) "Texts in History: The Determinations of Readings and Their Texts", *Australian Journal Of Communication*, 5 and 6, 3-11.

Buckingham, D and Sefton-Green, J (1994) *Cultural Studies Goes to School: Reading and Teaching Popular Media*, London: Taylor and Francis.

Dixon, J (1967, rpt 1972) *Growth Through English*, Huddersfield, Yorkshire: NATE/Oxford.

Doecke, B (1997) "Disjunctions: Australian Literature and the Secondary English Curriculum" *Southerly*, Vol 57, No 3.

Donnelly, K (1996) "Understanding Australia Project". *Victorian School News.*

Faulkner, J (1996) "Popular Culture and Text Response or: How I Put Shakespeare on Hold and Learned to Love Arnold Schwarzenegger", *Idiom*, Vol xxxi No 2, October.

Frow, J (1995) *Cultural Studies and Cultural Value*, Oxford: Clarendon Press.

Green, B and Bigum, C (1993) "Aliens in the Classroom", *Australian Journal of Education*, Vol 37 No 2, August.

Kent, V (1996) "I Want You to Write Me a Poem . . . and I Don't Want it to Rhyme", *Responding to Students' Writing, Idiom* Special, Carlton: VATE.

McDonald, T (1995) "Why VCE Fails the Disadvantaged", *Idiom*, Vol xxix No 2, August.

McClenaghan, D, Doecke, B and Parr, H, (1995 and 1996) *Englishworks 2*, (Student Resource Book and Teacher's Book), Oakleigh: Cambridge University Press.

Moss, Gemma (1989) *Un/Popular Fictions*, London: Virago.

Sarland, C (1991) *Young People Reading: Culture and Response*, Buckingham: Open University Press.

Tsiolkas, Christos (1997) "Hyphenation: Reflections on Language and Identity in Australia", *English in Australia*, 118, May.

Wheat, Chris (1997) "Bad Luck Loser! Sunshine and the VCE", *Idiom* Vol xxxii, No 1, April.

Headlines

The ABC program *Media Watch* delights in picking up ambiguous headlines from Australian newspapers. Here are a few, which as well as providing amusement can be usefully explored in class to see where the ambiguity lies:

CARDINALS OPPOSE DOCTOR KILLING
POLICE SHOOT MAN WITH KNIFE
KILLER·DOGS TERRIFIED DEAD WOMAN
FISHTAIL PALM BREAKS WIND
STUDENTS TAKE FIRM STAND ON LANDMINES
DEAD MAN RUN OUT OF TOWN
CURTIN A FORGOTTEN MEMORY

Often ambiguity arises because one tends to read a headline as though it should conform to the normal English sentence pattern of Subject – Verb – Object/Complement, as these famous examples, from British newspapers, show:

GIANT WAVES DOWN LINER'S FUNNEL
and (from World War II)
BRITISH PUSH BOTTLES UP GERMAN REAR

Students can be invited to search out their own examples from newspapers.

4 Imaginative Re-creation of Literature: a Critical Examination from the Perspective of the '90s

Peter Adams

Few ideas can have had greater success in the world of English teaching than "imaginative re-creation". It has become so much a taken-for-granted part of what English teachers 'do' in relation to the teaching of literature that it requires a certain effort to recall the terms in which it was originally presented by Leslie Stratta, John Dixon and Andrew Wilkinson in their 1973 book *Patterns of Language: Explorations in the Teaching of English.*

It is a surprise, for instance, given the carpet-bag capaciousness of the term as it is currently used, to realise that Stratta, Dixon and Wilkinson discuss "imaginative re-creation" only in relation to the shared novel and recommend it as a way of helping students to read and interpret novels which they "would find it impossible to read on their own but which, nevertheless, with help from the teacher, they can appreciate to a quite considerable extent."[1]

The activities or 'devices' which the authors group together under the collective heading of "imaginative re-creation" represent one form such teacherly assistance might take. Furthermore, these activities are intended as a kind of half-way house between, on the one hand, the unreflective enjoyment and absorption afforded by "wide and discursive silent reading" and, on the other, critical analysis, "that exact consideration [of] word values which is the traditional discipline of literary criticism." (I suspect it was this seductive combination of rigour and pleasure, of reflective distance and emotional engagement, which made imaginative re-creation so potently appealing to a generation of English teachers who were looking for an alternative to the dry-as-dust analytical approaches to literature upon which they themselves had often been brought up).

As defined by Stratta, Dixon and Wilkinson, imaginative re-creation involved students in adopting "a creative role in relation to the work of fiction" in order to "imaginatively re-create for [themselves] the experience of the novel. . . ." These creative roles included:

+ *changing the narrative viewpoint* of part of a novel: "one effective means of getting inside a novel is to require the pupil as writer to take up a part and a role other than the one chosen in the original";
+ *making a radio adaptation* of part of a novel;
+ *re-writing* part of a novel *in another context* (for example, modernising or up-dating a section of a classic text like *Silas Marner*);
+ *making a television or film version* of part of a novel;
+ *dramatising* part of a novel.

What these activities had in common, the authors pointed out, was the way in which they required students to focus on both *form* and *meaning*:

> *Each one of these roles will require the reconsideration of the original text in a different way. But in all cases they require interpretation by re-creation, and re-creation by interpretation. The pupils must ask themselves questions of interpretation before they can bring their new creation into being. These questions are of two kinds. The first is: what is the meaning of the original? In the transition of a novel from a traditional to a modern form, for instance, two different frames of reference are brought into juxtaposition, so that comparison can be made [...] In ways such as this the pupil begins to gain insights into the quality and texture of life represented in a particular novel, whether historical or contemporary. In writing a radio play, pupils find [...] that interpretation of the emotions involved is particularly urgent as they have to be represented in the voice. In writing a play or a film, not only these matters but also problems of how does this character look and move, how does this scene appear, may have to be answered from what evidence the text supplies, or by the pupils themselves.*
>
> *The second kind of question such work raises is that of form. The pupils are required to make distinctions between classical and modern writing, between how a novelist presents in commentary, description and dialogue, and how a radio dramatist has scarcely anything but dialogue; or how a film or TV maker conveys a good deal of his message by visual symbols, more than the stage dramatist who seems verbose if translated straight into another medium.*

(Stratta et al, 1973, p87)

However Leslie Stratta, John Dixon and Andrew Wilkinson may have originally conceived of "imaginative re-creation", both in relation to the purposes it could serve and the forms it could take, the term was enthusiastically taken up over the succeeding years and its meanings rapidly extended.

Ten years after *Patterns of Language* was published, "imaginative re-creation" had come to mean any activity which . . .

encouraged students to 'get inside' the text, consider it from different angles [or] extend their understanding of it without resorting to parcels of organised adult information about the text[2].

(Sawyer, Watson and Adams, 1989, p82)

The following list, from the same source, indicates the ways in which the original concept was expanded:

Oral

✦ Role play a scene from the novel/play/poem.
✦ Improvise a scene with a similar setting or similar characters or similar themes.
✦ Interview a character from the work.
✦ Improvise being the author and explain the title or significant scenes.
✦ Put a character on trial.
✦ Make the work into a radio play and tape it (or a movie and film it).

Written

✦ Write a diary for a character in the work.
✦ Change the point of view of particular incidents.
✦ Write newspaper reports of incidents from the work.
✦ Change the ending or add another chapter.
✦ Letters: from one character to another, to the author, to a friend discussing the work.
✦ Make a film script for incidents from the work.

Other

✦ Cast the film of the work and justify your choices.
✦ Make a map/draw the setting of the work.
✦ Design a cover for a new edition of the work.
✦ Draw a poster advertising the work.
✦ Do a comic strip of incidents from the work.
✦ Make a game of the plot.

Clearly, there have been losses and gains. The very proliferation of activities suggests just how eagerly English teachers had embraced the possibility of developing forms of response to literature texts which did *not* involve writing literary-critical essays or the dreary grind of close textual analysis[3]. On the other hand, it is hard not to feel that some of the original clarity of focus has been lost or, at the very least, blurred.

For instance, it is difficult to see how some of these activities – pleasurable and worthwhile as they may be, in certain contexts – require the kind of "interpretation by re-creation, and re-creation by interpretation" which Stratta, Dixon and Wilkinson had in mind and which is so well illustrated in the examples they provided. Designing a cover for a new edition

---

of the work being studied may certainly be said to involve **interpretation** but the **kind of interpretation** involved is of a different order to that which is at work in the following extract from a discussion between a group of eleven- to twelve-year-olds who are dramatising for tape part of Chapter 3 of Ian Serraillier's *The Silver Sword*, in which Joseph Balicki, a Polish refugee who has escaped from the concentration camp at Zakyna, is hidden by an old woman when the Nazis search her cottage:

The old woman was moved by his story.	C: *Think of something for the old woman; she was moved by his story.*
	A: *I feel very sorry for you.*
	C: *But you've got to get the right sort of voice for that.*
	A: *I feel very sorry, I wish I could do something for you.*
	B: *I know, she could have said: It must have been horrible. Have a bit of food – would you like some food to cheer you up?*

In their commentary, the author's point out the significance of this tiny exchange:

> *The group is seeking out language for the old woman's sympathy. They are not satisfied with the first suggestion, but perhaps if it is said with appropriate feeling that will help. Even so the words aren't strong enough – but if she expresses a desire to help that will be better. ("I feel very sorry, I wish I could do something.") The last speaker both strengthens the expression of sympathy, and gives embodiment to the help ("It must have been horrible. Have a bit of food/would you like some food to cheer you up?")*
>
> (Stratta et al, 1973, pp76-7)

The "exact consideration of word values" that is displayed here is, in fact, a defining characteristic of imaginative re-creation, as Stratta, Dixon and Wilkinson originally presented it. Elsewhere, for example, they examine a number of extracts from a discussion between a group of thirteen-year-olds, who had been asked to modernise a short passage from *Silas Marner*, re-writing it as though it were from a modern English novel describing contemporary events[4]. At one stage, the group turned to the problem of finding a modern equivalent for Silas Marner's profession. A farrier, their teacher had informed them, was "a blacksmith, his job's restricted to shoeing horses":

> Say he's in the shoe business *(half-jocular reference to "shoeing horses")*.
> A steelworker now.

The boot business *(serious)*: there's a lot of
people in the boot business.
There used to be only **one** *blacksmith*.

*The group is attempting to get an equivalent profession in terms of
manual labour and is succeeding. But the final speaker makes a
comment which throws into contrast the nineteenth-century village
community compared with modern industrial society: the fact that the
blacksmith's place and status depended partly on the fact that there was
only one of him.* (Stratta et al, 1973, pp81-2)

The other thing that seems to me to be crucially absent from the
extended list of possible forms of imaginative re-creation from Sawyer,
Watson and Adams which is quoted above, is *a controlling sense of purpose.*
In the absence of any statement to the contrary, it would seem as if *any* of
these activities could be applied, equally usefully and with equal justification,
to *any* text: I might just as well ask the students to role play a scene from
the novel, play or poem as invite them to change its ending or make a game
of its plot.

However, Stratta, Dixon and Wilkinson were perfectly clear about the
fact that they were not recommending a set of all-purpose activities. Each of
the activities or 'devices' (a revealing choice of word in the context of the
present discussion) they propose is designed to achieve a particular end. For
instance, in their discussion of the 'device' of changing the narrative
viewpoint of a text, they chose to focus on Chapter 39 of *Great Expectations*,
in which Magwitch visits Pip after many years in order to claim what he
considers to be his rights of affection and gratitude:

*This is told in the first person and from Pip's point of view: "Again he
took both my hands and put them to his lips, while my blood ran cold
within me", and "Nothing was needed but this; the wretched man, after
loading me with his wretched gold and silver chains for years, had risked
his life to come to me, and I held it there in my keeping! If I had loved
him instead of abhorring him; if I had been attracted to him by the
strongest admiration and affection, instead of shrinking from him with
the strongest repugnance; it could have been no worse. On the contrary,
it would have been better, for his preservation would then have
naturally and tenderly addressed my heart."* (Stratta et al, 1973, p71)

As the authors point out:

*Two other viewpoints are possible: the section may be written from the
viewpoint of Magwitch – how sensitive would he be to Pip's coldness?
How far would he feel the repulsion? How far would he be surprised
by the response? Or the passage could be re-written from the viewpoint
of a detached observer who would comment as he [sic] saw it on the
reactions of both characters, and the nature of the emotions going on
between them.* (Stratta et al, 1973, pp71-2)

It is clear from the way in which these possibilities are presented that changing the narrative viewpoint is seen as a *technique* for investigating the inter-relationship of form – in this case, the point of view from which a set of events is related – and meaning. Change the point of view and different possibilities – and different challenges – emerge. For instance, adopting the viewpoint of the convict not only involves a radical shift in the emotional *locus* of the narrative, but it also raises a new set of technical challenges – how to incorporate into Magwitch's account of this meeting evidence of Pip's horrified shrinking from him *without Magwitch realising its significance?*

I want to draw this examination of the possible uses – and misuses – of imaginative re-creation to a conclusion by briefly considering two examples of students using forms of imaginative re-creation which are not to be found among the original list of activities described by Leslie Stratta, John Dixon and Andrew Wilkinson:

TEXT 1 (extract)

Dear Diary,
As I sit here thinking, I cannot help but wonder why my father would be so angry with me, as Edmund informed me earlier. Some villain must have altered his opinion of me, but why, I do not know. I am thankful for Edmund's assistance. If not for him, I should never have known, for father and I parted on good terms last night and I found no displeasure in his countenance. Edmund has warned me to go armed if I am approached, and I do not know why, but my brother obviously knows best and he has no reason for deceiving me. I shall wait and see what is to happen.

Edgar

Dear Diary,
I am utterly confused as to what I am supposed to have done. Edmund questioned me whether I had said anything upon the party of the Duke of Albany, but I informed him I had not. Edmund then drew his sword upon me, as a pretence of course, when he heard father approaching. I also drew, to seem to defend myself, though not knowing why. He then warned me to fly, and so I did, and here I am, out in the cold night, alone, and confused. If only Edmund could tell me what is going on and why I had to flee so suddenly.

Edgar

Dear Diary,
I heard myself proclaimed, and now am disguised as the basest and most poorest of men, to avoid the hunt for myself. I have grimed my face with filth and knotted my hair, and clothed myself scantily. I plan to take on the personality of a mad-man, so as to ensure my noble

features are not recognisable to others. It seems the only way for me to survive, for to be known for Edgar would be my end.

Edgar

The teacher's intention, in asking his Year 12 students to write Edgar's diary, was presumably to help them to more fully realise ('get inside') Edgar's feelings about and responses to the events in which he is involved. By expanding upon – and rephrasing – what the play provides in relation to these things, the students would (it seems) be both **consolidating** and **displaying** their understanding of the text. However, as this extract from one girl's work demonstrates, there are a number of difficulties associated with this activity and the way in which it has been conceived.

First, the task itself seems to work against its ostensible purpose, which is to encourage the students to enter more fully into 'the reality' of Edgar's situation. The inherent absurdity of Edgar maintaining a diary once he has adopted the persona of Poor Tom – "the basest and most poorest shape / That ever penury, in contempt of man, / Brought near to beast" – makes it very difficult to think of this as more than merely an exercise. (If we set aside for a moment the question of **when** exactly Edgar/Poor Tom would find the opportunity and leisure to write in a diary, a far more serious objection to the task is the difficulty of conceiving of a genuine purpose which such an activity would serve **for the character**.)

Moreover, even if it is just an exercise, the student betrays considerable uncertainty about what exactly is being required of her. Should the diary be written in modern English – in which case she will need to translate Edgar's language, when she uses it, into a more modern idiom – or in some equivalent of Shakespearian English? What is the relationship between the diary and the text? What sorts of things should be recorded in it? How far beyond the limits of the text is it permissible to venture?

In the end, the student has adopted the strategy of writing an entry after every scene in which Edgar makes an appearance. Each entry consists essentially of a brief paraphrase of the text – with the occasional embellishment ("I am utterly confused as to what I am supposed to have done") as a gesture towards 'inwardness' – and is written in a judicious mixture of idioms, intended (presumably) to demonstrate both her understanding of the literal meaning of the text – was this not part of the purpose of the task? – and her ability to 'convincingly' adopt the Edgar persona.

The result is, of course, lamentable, but it could hardly have been otherwise. So fatally misconceived a task is a long way from the sharply focused "approach to the study of texts" which Stratta, Dixon and Wilkinson were advocating twenty-five years ago:

> *If pupils are to re-create imaginatively the experience expressed in the abstractions on the page, **they must have the motivation and a sense of point which is so often lacking in much teaching of [literature]**. One way of re-creating experience for oneself is that used by a translator*

from a foreign language. He [sic] has not only to translate the words, but he has to attempt to express the experience in his own language and in his own terms. He also has an audience in mind, an audience who understands the language into which he is translating. Now in first language teaching the equivalent exercise is paraphrase. But the paraphrase notably lacks the context and point of the translator's work. Whereas he takes an original and writes a version of it in other words in another language, paraphrase is done primarily as an exercise in paraphrase. The work described [in this chapter] avoids such problems: **it is motivated, it has a context, it has an end in view.**

(Stratta et al, 1973, pp70-1. Emphases added.)

At first glance, it may seem that there is little to choose between "Edgar's Diary" and the following example, in which a Year 10 girl is retelling Charles Causley's well-known poem, "What has happened to Lulu?". The differences, however, serve to bring home the crucial significance of such factors as 'motivation', 'context' and purpose ('a sense of point') in successful uses of imaginative re-creation:

TEXT 2

Lulu was furious. For once, couldn't her mother take her seriously? She was sixteen now, a woman. Yes, a woman ... soon to be a wife. Couldn't her mother even try to understand? No! All she'd done was yell when they'd told her. Yell and scream. Well, Lulu had no choice. She had a child to think of now, the child growing inside of her. She would leave anyway, run away! Elope! Andrew would take care of her, look after her and the baby. He wanted to be with her and she loved him. Why couldn't her mother understand? Yelling had just made it worse, made Lulu realise she could never bring her baby up here. She had a part-time job. Well, she would make it full-time, and who needed school anyway? She would raise her child and when it fell in love she would be very supportive. Yes, she would call Andrew now and tell him. They would leave tomorrow.

> *She picked up the phone and dialled the number she knew so well.*
> *"Hello," she said. "Is Andrew there?"*
> *What a relief! He was there after all.*
> *"Yes, hi, Andrew ... Yes, I know, very unreasonable."*
> *Lulu's mother walked into the room and stared at her.*
> *"Yes, Jane," Lulu spoke loudly, "very sure."*
> *When Lulu's mother was certain it was Jane, she left the room and Lulu continued.*
> *"Andrew, I can't talk. Come tonight, late. I'll be ready."*

Later that night, as Lulu was packing up her things, she heard her mother walk past her door to bed. She crept out of her room and gathered her things from the bathroom.

Looking around her, she paused and silently said goodbye to the house she had lived in for fifteen years. Then she dropped the note on the table.

Returning to her room, she saw Andrew waiting outside her window. She walked towards him and opened the window wide. Forgetting it was a slippery window, she let it go and it crashed down onto the sill. She waited in silence. Not a sound. How lucky she was!

Just then her door burst open and her mother ran in. Lulu grabbed her bag and, forgetting her favourite doll, lunged for the window. He mother grabbed her.

"No, Lulu, don't go!"

Her shoe fell to the floor with a bang.

"Let me go!" she screamed.

With one leg through the window and with Andrew's help, she shook her mother off, leaving a red scratch the length of her leg. She ran to the car and they sped away.

Falling to the floor, her mother clutched the doll and cradled it to her, crying loudly.

When morning came, she placed the doll and the shoe on Lulu's bed and left the room, forgetting the daughter she had once had.

Natasha

This piece of writing was produced in the course of a unit of work exploring traditional and literary ballads. (In addition to "What has happened to Lulu?", the students had read "Angel Hill", also by Charles Causley, and a number of the Border Ballads, including "The Twa Corbies", "Lord Randal" and "Edward".) The focus of the classroom investigation of these texts was upon the way in which ballads tell stories. For instance, in discussing both "The Twa Corbies" and "Lord Randal" the teacher had asked the class to compile a list of "Things the poem leaves unexplained" and "Things the poem spotlights". These lists served to highlight the way in which the poems focused on the elemental starkness of the human tragedy without bothering to record such circumstantial details as the **when,** the **where** and – most significantly – the **why** of the events with which they were dealing.

As the next step in their investigation of the ways in which these texts went about the business of telling a story, the teacher asked the students to choose one of the ballads they had studied and to retell it as 'a proper story', supplying all the information that a reader would expect to be provided with in a conventional narrative.

Essentially, this activity – changing the way in which the story is told – involved the students in grappling with an important distinction made by the French narratologist, Gérard Genette. He points out that narrative fictions have three basic aspects: the events ('histoire'), their verbal representation ('récit') and the act of telling or writing ('narration'):

'Histoire' (what we might call 'the story') designates the narrated events, abstracted from their disposition in the text and reconstructed in their chronological order, together with the participants in these events.

Whereas 'histoire' is a succession of events, 'récit' is the spoken or written discourse in which they are related. Put more simply, 'récit' is what we read or listen to. In it, the events do not necessarily appear in chronological order, the characteristics of the participants are dispersed throughout the text, and all the items of narrative content are filtered through some perspective or point of view.

Since the text is a spoken or written discourse, it implies someone who speaks or writes it. The act or process of production is the third aspect – 'narration' [...] Within the text, communication involves a fictional narrator transmitting a narrative to a fictional naratee.

(Rimmon-Kenan, 1983, pp3-4)

In writing 'proper' versions of the stories told in the ballads, the students were involved in trying to work out the 'histoire' implied by this particular 'récit', then, having made decisions about the most appropriate form of 'narration' to adopt, recasting that 'histoire' into another 'récit'.

What Natasha's re-writing of Causley's poem demonstrates is just how crucially a writer's decisions about such matters will affect the meanings that a particular 'histoire' can assume. Natasha's decision to begin her narrative *after* a show-down between Lulu and her mother ('récit') has a significant effect upon its emotional 'centre of gravity' – what is now emphasised are Lulu's feelings of frustration, anger and disbelief (things whose existence is only very indirectly implied in the poem, if at all) and the way in which she feels herself *driven* to take this particular course of action. Natasha's choice of an appropriate form of narration – in this case, *free indirect narration,* which, though employing the third person, is able to move fluidly into and out of the character's private thoughts and feelings – reflects the same orientation towards the story events: this way of telling the story ('narration') privileges *Lulu's* feelings. The cumulative effect of these choices is to shift the focus of the story onto Lulu's need for recognition as something more than a mere child. Natasha's story is essentially about a young woman's need to be recognised as someone who is capable of making and exercising her own choices.

Causley, on the other hand, chose to begin his narrative *after* the events had taken place. The dramatic moment – of conflict and escape – is not related as it unfolds – as is the case with "Lord Randal" and "Edward" – but in retrospect. This has the effect of distancing us from a direct emotional involvement in the drama of the night and foregrounding its aftermath. Furthermore, Causley has chosen to have the story unfold through the questions of a child who does not fully understand the significance of the events to which she (?) has been a witness. This creates the possibility of developing a subtly ironic perspective upon events, in which the reader is invited to see more in the story than the child herself is able to see. Causley's poem is less about a young woman's need for self-assertion than it is about the pain her abrupt departure has caused and it leaves us contemplating the poignant possibility that Lulu may not quite as grown up as she thinks – she leaves her rag doll behind (because it represents the childhood she is so emphatically renouncing?) yet all the money she has to start her new life with is in ... her money-box!

The most important difference between the activity which produced 'Edgar's Diary' and the one in which Natasha was engaged is the way in which the latter involved investigating the *inter-relationship* of form and meaning: what narrative choices (about both 'récit' and 'narration') are involved in re-telling the different stories that we can discern behind the poem's enigmatic surface, and how does any act of re-telling serve to foreground different meanings? Furthermore, the relationship between the original text and the student's re-creation is a *reciprocal* one: each serves to illuminate the other, both in terms of form and meaning.

❋　　❋　　❋　.　❋　　❋　　❋　　❋

Imaginative re-creation activities are perhaps best thought of as exercises in *translation*. Students may, for instance, be involved in translating part or all of a text from:

◆ one *medium* to another –
  ❖ adapting a printed text for radio, television, film, the stage, etc;
  ❖ role-playing a scene from a novel, short story or poem;
  ❖ turning a poem or short story – or a chapter of a novel or a significant incident from it – into a play, a storyboard, a comic strip, etc.;
  ❖ making a visual representation – a map or other form of illustration – of some part or aspect of a printed text;
◆ one *form* to another –
  ❖ changing a mystery story into a fable, then into a newspaper report, and so on, as a way of investigating how it is possible for the same story to take on very different meanings when it is realised in different narrative forms;
◆ one *narrative viewpoint* to another –
  ❖ re-writing an incident from another character's point of view or through a different 'focaliser';
  ❖ creating a first-person account of events – in the form of a character's diary, for example – from a third-person narrative;

- ✧ writing about the same incident from a number of different possible viewpoints;
- ✧ writing an account of an episode from the point of view of an imaginary 'eyewitness reporter';
- ✦ one *context* to another –
  - ✧ up-dating a section of a classic text;
  - ✧ re-writing a classic text – such as a myth, legend, fairy tale, fable, parable, etc. – as a contemporary story;
  - ✧ locating a classic text – *Romeo and Juliet, Julius Caesar* and *Hamlet* have all been attempted, for example – in another time or place[5].

A simple taxonomy like this is useful if it helps us to think more clearly about the range of *purposes* which imaginative re-creation can legitimately serve. Originally, Stratta, Dixon and Wilkinson conceived of the purpose of imaginative re-creation rather narrowly, in terms of helping students to "imaginatively re-create for [themselves] the experience of the novel . . .", which they saw as being "a far more difficult task for the pupil ... than watching a film or television play". However, it quickly became evident that imaginative re-creation was too valuable an addition to the English teacher's toolkit to be restricted to just helping students to 'get inside' a novel. Not only could it be used with texts other than novels, but its purposes could obviously be extended beyond the "reception-centred" paradigm within which it was first proposed. For instance, it rapidly became apparent that imaginative re-creation need not be confined to assisting students, in the initial stages of their acquaintance with a text, to more fully possess the experience it had to offer; it could also be used to help students to explore, express and represent their responses to a text (or an aspect of a text) – and the issues, themes and ideas with which it was concerned – in ways which involved *the sustained and focused exercise of their imaginative and creative capacities*[6].

While locating imaginative re-creation within a more "production-centred" paradigm[7] turned out to be an enormously important and liberating development – it meant that the texts students produced in the course of engaging in re-creation activities could be valued as more than merely stepping-stones towards an appreciation of someone else's text – it also created the possibility of "imaginative re-creation" simply becoming a catch-all term for *any* kind of imaginative or creative response to literature. However, if the term is to have any meaning at all, it seems to me, the activities which it includes should all involve the *re-creation* of part or all of the text under consideration. Going beyond the bounds of the text – for example, by writing a new ending or a new beginning, a sequel or a prequel, or by supplying missing episodes in the characters' lives – may be a valuable and interesting activity for a student to undertake, in certain contexts, but it gains nothing from being called "imaginative re-creation". At the heart of all imaginative re-creation activities, as Stratta, Dixon and Wilkinson observed twenty-five years ago, are the complementary and inter-dependent processes of "interpretation *by re-creation*" and "re-creation *by interpretation*".

If the shift from an exclusively "reception-centred" to a more "production-centred" paradigm represents one way in which the uses of imaginative re-creation have been legitimately extended, a number of post-structuralist and critical literacy theorists have demonstrated how imaginative re-creation activities can be used to help students develop "critical perspectives on texts"[8]. For instance, amongst the range of suggestions Jack Thomson offers teachers for using post-structuralist literary theory in the classroom are some which clearly involve imaginative re-creation:

❖ *[C]hange the setting of the text in place or time*

❖ *Re-write fairy tales for modern times, and review what changes and what remains the same, and draw the implications from this*

❖ *Change one element in a novel (or part of it) and keep the other elements as in the original. For example, retain the same characters, events and setting, but change the time and, therefore, the social conventions and values*

❖ *Re-write sections of novels from the viewpoints of minority, marginalised and suppressed characters, as a way of resisting the dominant, privileged reading*

❖ *Re-write texts in another genre, form or medium. For example, rewrite a short story as a radio play, a poem as a diary, etc. and explore the purposes and formal characteristics of different genres and media*

❖ *Re-write a character's viewpoint in a different narrative mode. For example, rewrite a third person perspective in interior monologue, or as first person, present tense, etc.*

(Thomson, 1996, pp204-5)

However, some of the other ways of re-writing texts that Thomson suggests do not seem to me to be usefully considered as examples of imaginative re-creation:

Transpose the constituent elements of texts as a way of revealing the embedded ideology. For example: change the age, sex, nationality and race of characters; change characters to their opposites (strong to weak, old to young, male to female, poor to wealthy, etc. and reverse)

(Thomson, 1994, p204)

Such 'transpositions' are mechanical rather than 'imaginative'. They are things you simply 'do' to a text in order to reveal features of it that are not immediately apparent – in Jack Thomson's words, its "concealed ideologies, marginalisations, silences and contradictions". They do not involve the tentative, exploratory process of searching out equivalents that was illustrated in the discussion between the students who had been set the task of re-writing a section of *Silas Marner* in a modern context.

I want to conclude, therefore, by looking at an example of imaginative re-creation being used in relation to another classic text ... but for very different ends from those envisaged by Stratta, Dixon and Wilkinson.

David Whitley puts his finger neatly on one of the major problems facing anyone who wants to introduce fables to children. It is, he says, "the issue of power":

> [T]he earliest recorded instance of the fable in Western literature [...] occurs in the epic **Works and Days** of the Greek poet Hesiod, who may have lived as early as the eighth century BC. The story which Hesiod interpolates into his epic narrative begins: "And now I will tell a fable for kings even though they are wise." He proceeds to tell the story of a hawk's relentless demonstration of its power over a helpless nightingale:
>
>> Thus spoke the hawk to the speckled necked nightingale as he seized her in his claws and carried her up among the clouds – and pitifully did she whimper as the crooked claws pierced her through. The hawk then spoke to her masterfully: "Simple creature, why do you cry aloud? One far mightier than yourself now holds you in his grip, and you will go wherever I take you for all your singing, and I will make a meal of you if I choose, or I will let you go. Foolish is he who would match himself against those who are stronger; he is robbed of victory and suffers pain as well as shame."
>
> The moral wisdom wrung out of this earliest of written fables would seem to be that the vulnerable should accept that their fate is controlled by forces far more powerful than themselves. This attitude of resignation to the terms of an implacable and often cruel fate (which is ideologically aligned to an extreme form of quietism) is common in the very early literature of the ancient world. It derives in part from economies in which substantial proportions of the population have slave status and consists in a compelling recognition of powerlessness. But it also connects with a substantial number of stories within the traditional Aesopic corpus – "The Wolf and the Lamb", "The Eagle and the Tortoise", "The Town and Country Mouse", for instance – which can be read as instances of the foolishness of claims for equality and justice, or of the painful consequences awaiting those who attempt to move beyond the horizons within which they are currently circumscribed. It connects also with what is perhaps the central problematic of the fable tradition, **where the perspective on power is generally from the bottom end of the hierarchy looking upwards, but where the moral wisdom advocated often meshes with the ideological interests of those at the top.**
>
> (Whitley, 1996. Emphasis added)

The ideology of a text like "The Hawk and the Nightingale" is no doubt transparent enough but it is not always the case with texts of this kind. Not only do many fables work in the way Whitley describes – that is, to conceal the issue of whose interests they really serve – but the animal characters in fables often act as "ideological decoys" (Stibbs 1990, p128). Portraying animals as humans 'naturalises' the social interactions and power relations depicted: "Masked as part of a natural and animal domain, societal configurations and ethical issues become "invisible and self-evident" (Luke, 1993, p37).

How can imaginative re-creation help students to explore issues such as these?

One of the briefest fables in the Penguin edition of Aesop's fables is the following:

The Lioness and the Vixen

A vixen sneered at a lioness because she never bore more than one cub."Only one", she replied, "but a lion".　　　(Handford, 1954, p120)

In this edition of the fables, the moral of the story is the proverb, "It's quality, not quantity that counts". Certainly "The Lioness and the Vixen" *can* be read as a neatly pointed and economical illustration of a commonly held belief, and from one point of view, it is. But since fables invite us to read their animal characters as standing for human characters or types, it is worth asking what this fable implies about the way things are in the human world.

The first thing to note is that 'quality' is not something that everyone in the world of this fable enjoys. It is the possession of certain animals and not of others. Not only do some characters not possess it, they never can: the vixen, for instance, can never be a lioness, and the lioness's single cub will be born a lion, whether it likes it or not.

As the fable presents it, this state of affairs is simply 'natural', 'the way things are'. And since 'quality', as far as this fable is concerned, is a matter of being stronger and more powerful than others, this text can be read as supporting a view of the world in which it is regarded as right and inevitable that some people are born to positions of power and influence – as members of an hereditary ruling class, for example – and some are not.

Students can begin to investigate these issues by re-writing the fable, in two different ways. In the first instance, they can be asked to work in groups *to substitute appropriate human characters for the animals in the fables.*

This produces very interesting results: students frequently produce fables which involve a king and a commoner comparing their offspring (it's worth asking the students why they felt they had to replace the lioness with a male equivalent) but sometimes they produce fables in which the names of powerful families or dynasties appear ("Only one," he replied, "but a Packer"). Such re-writing serves to foreground the ideology of the text, making it more readily available for discussion and critique.

In the second instance, students can be asked to work in groups to write a fable which illustrates the moral of "The Lioness and the Vixen" but which *does not employ characters who are polarised in terms of their relative power.*

This tends to shift the domain of the fable ("Only one," he replied, "but a Lamborghini") and so further highlights the way in which "The Lioness and the Vixen" is doing something more than simply providing a neat illustration of the moral.

✳   ✳   ✳   ✳   ✳   ✳   ✳

Imaginative re-creation has proved itself, over the twenty-five years of its existence, to be a remarkably Protean set of practices. Originally conceived as a limited set of 'devices' for helping students to 'get inside a novel', imaginative re-creation has not only come to include a very wide group of activities – all of which, however, should involve the mutually inter-dependent processes of "interpretation *by re-creation*" and "re-creation *by interpretation*" – but it has proved itself to have a much wider range of applications than its progenitors could ever have envisaged. It therefore seems reasonable to assume that, in another twenty-five years time, imaginative re-creation will still have a significant role to play in both the theory and practice of English teaching.

References

Australian Education Council (1994) *A Statement on English for Australian Schools*, Carlton, Victoria: Curriculum Corporation.

Handford, S A (1954) *Fables of Aesop*, Harmondsworth: Penguin.

Luke, Alan (1993) "The Social Construction of Literacy in the Primary School", in Len Unsworth (ed) *Literacy Learning and Teaching: Language as Social Practice in the Primary School*, South Melbourne Victoria: Macmillan Education.

Rimmon-Kenan, Shlomith (1983) *Narrative Fiction: Contemporary Poetics*, London and New York: Methuen.

Sawyer, Wayne and Watson, Ken (1995) "Misleading Metaphors and New Models: Personal Growth for the 21st Century", paper delivered at the Sixth International Conference of the International Federation for the Teaching of English, New York.

Sawyer, Wayne, Watson, Ken and Adams, Anthony (1989) *English Teaching from A to Z*, Milton Keynes: Open University Press.

Stibbs, Andrew (1990) *Reading Narrative as Literature: Signs of Life*, Milton Keynes: Open University Press.

Stratta, Leslie, Dixon, John and Wilkinson, Andrew (1973) *Patterns of Language: Explorations of the Teaching of English*, London: Heinemann Educational Books.

Thomson, Jack (1996) "Literary Theory: why, what and how ..." in Ken Watson, Calvin Durrant, Sandra Hargreaves and Wayne Sawyer, *English Teaching in Perspective in the Context of the 1990s*, Sydney NSW: St Clair Press.

Watson, K D and Eagleson, R D (eds) (1977) *English in Secondary Schools: Today and Tomorrow*, Ashfield NSW: ETA of NSW.

Witkin, Robert M (1974) *The Intelligence of Feeling*, London: Heinemann Educational Books.

Whitley, David (1996) "Aesop for Children: Power and Morality" in Morag Styles, Eve Bearne and Victor Watson (eds) *Voices Off: Texts, Contexts and Readers*, London: Cassell.

Further Reading

Greenwell, Bill (1981) "English and Art: a Joint Venture" in Adams, Anthony and Hopkin, Ted (eds) *Sixth Sense: Alternatives in Education at 16-19*, Glasgow and London: Blackie. (On pp121-137, Bill Greenwell describes the Canterbury Tales Project, in which a group of A-level students studying Chaucer worked together to find ways of representing "the essence of each pilgrim" and "the social, moral or ideological relationships between the pilgrims" in an elaborate, three-dimensional art work.)

Lorac, C and Weiss, M (1981) *Communication and Social Skills*, Exeter: Wheaton. (Pages 67-72 contain an example of low ability students successfully adapting a short story for television, using a mixture of story telling by a narrator, vocal dramatisation and still pictures drawn by the students.)

Watson, Ken, Sawyer, Wayne, et al (eds) *Reading is Response* series, Sydney, NSW: St Clair Press. (These books contain, *inter alia*, many suggestions for imaginative re-creation activities.)

Watson, K, Wilson, R, Foster, J and Adams, R (1972) *Explore and Express Book 2*, London: Macmillan. (Pages 111-135 contain a comparison of treatments of the same episode from the novel, play, musical and film versions of *Oliver Twist* and suggestions for further re-creative work.)

Footnotes

1. However, it should be noted that the examples given by Stratta, Dixon and Wilkinson testify to a wider conception of the uses of imaginative re-creation than this would suggest. No one would imagine for a moment that *The Silver Sword* (one of the novels the authors discuss) is the kind of text that students would find "impossible to read on their own". In this case, it's clear that the purpose of the activity – making a section of the novel into a play for radio – is to help the students:
   a. 'read between the lines' of the prose text; and
   b. extend their understanding of the limitations and possibilities of narration in the two media, written and aural.

2. See also "Imaginative Re-creation of Literature" by Ernie Tucker (in Watson and Eagleson, 1977, pp398-9) which recommends such activities as:

   ▪ adopting the role of one character in a novel or play and writing a personal letter to another character;

   ▪ writing a character's diary;

   ▪ writing about the main characters from the perspective of a minor character;

   ▪ going beyond the bounds of the text in various ways (new endings, new beginnings, sequels, supplying missing episodes in the character's lives);

   ▪ writing newspaper reports of particular incidents in novels.

3. The need for such alternative forms of response is put in the following terms by Wayne Sawyer in *English Teaching from A to Z*: "the central problem for teachers of literature is how to extend students' responses beyond their initial unsophisticated reactions without losing touch with these felt responses. How do we extend students' understanding without killing simple pleasure or turning literature teaching into a catalogue of detailed minutiae on plot, character, setting and something called 'theme'?" (Sawyer, Watson and Adams, 1989, p82)

4. Although this 'device' may appear to have a rather restricted application, it can be put to very powerful uses. After all, this is exactly what Alan Garner did with the Welsh myth upon which *The Owl Service* is based – translate it into a modern story involving contemporary characters and events.

5. These examples are, of course, intended to be suggestive rather than exhaustive.

6. Robert Witkin spoke of such an approach to the study of literature as "creative appreciation". In an important passage in *The Intelligence of Feeling*, he contrasted "creative appreciation" with "analysis and criticism" which, he remarked, while having "an important part to play in English studies ... is in no way a substitute for, nor is it synonymous with creative appreciation. The latter requires that realised form [works of literature] be closely related to the pupil's creative expression and that he [sic] express his feeling response in a direct and personal way. *It requires that he make an 'artistic' response using the 'artistic' work of others.*" (Witkin, 1974, p68. Emphasis added.)

7. I have taken the idea of conceptualising imaginative re-creation within these two paradigms from a recent paper by Wayne Sawyer and Ken Watson: "We would argue that 'imaginative re-creation' has been an apt label for a set of sound teaching practices looking for a good theory and, while there is no doubt that theorists make strong connections between reader-response theory and re-creation activities, imaginative re-creation could equally well be argued as underpinned by theories which issue from rhetorical studies. We would want to emphasise these practices (that is, imaginative re-creation) as reflecting as much a 'production-centred' paradigm as a 'reception-centred' one. We would want to stress the notion of 'creation' in 'imaginative re-creation' and to conceptualise these activities as *creating the possibility of authorship as much as the possibility of response to other people's texts.*" (Sawyer and Watson, 1995. Emphasis added.)

8. This phrase is taken from *A Statement on English for Australian Schools*, 1994, p16.

5 Towards Critical Literacy: The 'Cultural Studies' Model of English

Robin Peel

I f life is full of contradictions and paradoxes, then so is the idea of a 'Cultural Studies' model of English. The emergence of the set of practices known as 'Cultural Studies' arose from a feeling of dissatisfaction with the perceived limitations of more established subject disciplines such as English. There is consequently more than a little *chutzpah* in seeming to want to cram Cultural Studies back into the English bottle. At the same time, failure to address Cultural Studies in a book for English teachers would leave an unacceptable gap. After all, the approaches known as 'Cultural Materialism' in England and 'Critical Literacy' in Australia, owe much to earlier – and continuing – work in a field that was originally an offshoot of English.

'Cultural Studies' emerged in a recognisable form in Birmingham, England, when the Centre for Contemporary Cultural Studies was founded in 1964. From the beginning, its approach showed the influence of the founder, Richard Hoggart, and two Marxist critics from the British New Left: Raymond Williams and E P Thompson. As early as 1950, eight years before the appearance of the seminal *Culture and Society*, Raymond Williams had given an indication of what a post-Leavisite model of English/Cultural Studies in schools might look like (Williams, 1950). Such a model would be interdisciplinary, drawing as much on History and Sociology as English, thus placing literary ideas in the wider cultural context. When, in the years following the foundation of the CCCS, Cultural Studies ideas eventually found their way into schools, it was English, passing through a particularly vigorous expansionist and evangelical phase, that gave them a home. In secondary education, English Departments as a whole did not change, for this was the historical moment when literature and creative writing were seen as the badge of English. Some *schools* may have established 'Humanities' courses during this period, but in England, as in Australia, virtually no English departments shed their old identities and renamed themselves 'Cultural Studies'. The vigour of the debate may have made things look radical, but they were not *that* radical. In the newer universities and polytechnics the position was different, and Cultural Studies mushroomed.

During the seventies and eighties, Cultural Studies in higher education grew and evolved as it absorbed, adopted and adapted the theories of, among others, Levi Strauss, Althusser, Feminism, Structuralism, Foucault, Bakhtin and Saussurian linguistics. The political critique was given edge by Gramsci and Jameson, the psycho-analytical by Lacan and the philosophical/linguistic by Derrida. Cultural Studies in the nineties continued to draw an even wider net, absorbing such theorists as Giroux for a critique of pedagogy and Judith Butler and Eve Kosofsky Sedgwick for its critique of gender. Collectively, this amounts to formidable intellectual baggage. Teachers and students at whatever level find the sheer quantity and density of this theory intimidating, and there is no space here to concentrate it into a summary, even if such a thing were possible. Instead, I shall try to identify the global changes that have been conducive to the development of Cultural Studies and those features of a Cultural Studies approach which inform so many of the critical literacy practices that have appeared in Australian secondary school classrooms. For reasons that will later be made clear, it is worth pointing out that with the notable exception of media studies, this process has not been paralleled in secondary schools in England.

The aims of Cultural Studies are broad and political. In their 'General Introduction' to *A Cultural Studies Reader* (Munns and Rajan, 1995), the editors speak of cultural critique as a "mode of challenging and refining the foundational assumptions of any field of enquiry" that is "more than an interdisciplinary solution (in that) it provides a spectrum of approaches to questions that are raised in today's global, multiclassed, multiracial, and multicultural societies". These questions include the "relationship of cultural productions such as art, literature, music and theatre and the social value of these forms in a democratised and computerised *multimedia* society" and "questions of cultural identity *vis-a-vis* the roles played by citizens in these societies, (which) are raised where *gender, class and race* factor into their value as citizens" (Munns and Rajan, 1995, p2). Finally there are "questions as to the meaning of migrant, diasporic, and transnational identities (that) have been raised by post-colonials, where the politics of *representation and nationhood* come into play" (Munns and Rajan, 1995, p2). Such considerations inevitably raise questions about the place of subject English itself, and serve as a reminder that it was only in the late nineteenth century in England, the United States and Australia that departments were created to teach specific national literatures.

But what, in practical terms, are we talking about when we refer to Cultural Studies? In trying to pin it down, I would tentatively draw attention to five broad attributes of a Cultural Studies model of pedagogy:

1. As a term, 'culture' is used in its broadest sense to include anything produced by a society, from novels to supermarket architecture.
2. The approach is interdisciplinary, drawing on ideas from such fields as sociology, politics and semiotics.
3. The influence of Marxist and Gramscian criticism is apparent in much of the discussion associated with Cultural Studies, which is assumed to have a social purpose.
4. Cultural products are seen as artefacts that now transcend national boundaries, and are located in the context of a global, technocultural economy.
5. At the same time, the importance of specifics such as the historical moment, gender, class and race must be attended to in any discussion of the way cultural products are conceptualised and represented.

For the teacher of English, this has one immediate and obvious consequence. The pedagogical practices of Cultural Studies involve a shift in emphasis from 'Literature' and 'Language' to 'literatures' and 'languages', and from the idea of 'literary heritage' to the idea of 'text'. There has often been – and there continues to be in some quarters – a resistance to such a shift.

Now for the series of paradoxes. First the personal, then the professional, and finally the theoretical.

Research (Peel and Curtis, 1996) shows that when students in school, college and university are asked what they like about English many tend to identify the way in which English provides a space in which they can talk about human issues and problems, and is a subject in which their own experience, perceptions and imaginations are given expression and value. They do not feel that they start from a deficit, as they do in, say, Chemistry. Such a reaction is testimony to the enduring legacy of personal response English, which so successfully replaced rhetorical models of English in schools in the nineteen sixties and seventies, particularly in England and in Australia. The paradox here is that many English teachers who themselves were excited by personal response and creative writing approaches at school are now equally excited by the possibilities of critical literacy approaches precisely because they offer a more rigorous and interesting awareness of the social construction of the self, the personal, and of subjectivity. This enthusiasm may collide with what students sometimes perceive to be the less complicated pleasures of English in primary and lower secondary education. Historically, Cultural Studies may have been an offshoot from English, yet its practices of analysis and interpretation and its rejection of a romantic 'self' which can find expression in a voice unique and intrinsic to the individual can appear to give it the coolness of science rather than the 'warmth' of creativity. This is a false binary which underestimates the creative element in both science and criticism but it leads directly to the professional paradox.

The professional paradox haunts many English teachers and heads of English. We can all see what students read for pleasure, know what they do in their spare time, be aware of the films they like and so on. We realise that it is important pedagogically that we draw on what students know already, and where necessary help them to 'read' it more critically. More than this, we want them to produce as well as consume, and so make space for filmmaking and radio program making in English, because that is part of the domain. But we also like the fact that English enjoys a certain status in schools because literacy is seen as such a fundamental skill. We like the fact that people care about English, even if the English that they care about is a very narrow version of what we see English as being about. So I think that on pragmatic grounds there has been a reluctance for English Departments to dissolve themselves and assume the mantle of Cultural Studies Departments. Even in universities, where Cultural Studies is strong, the position is complex. In some universities, Cultural Studies has its home in Political and Social Science faculties; in others it sits happily alongside English and Film Studies, while in a number of universities it is a separate department. It is interesting that the first department, the Centre for Contemporary Cultural Studies, was originally a research group within the English Department, and that one of the key figures in establishing the centre, Richard Hoggart, also had his roots in literary studies. The same is true of Raymond Williams, whose *Culture and Society* (1958) was influential in the early development of Cultural Studies.

The theoretical contradiction comes from the fact that the interdisciplinary nature of Cultural Studies creates a paradox: here is a *subject* that is trying to break down the barriers between subjects. As Jeremy Hawthorn says, "Right from its inception .... Cultural Studies was academically expansionist, if not downright colonialist" (Hawthorn, 1992). Encouraged by the anthropological approach of Levi-Strauss, Hoggart, Martin Green and Stuart Hall published papers which drew on a variety of disciplines, represented in the following:

A CULTURAL STUDIES MODEL

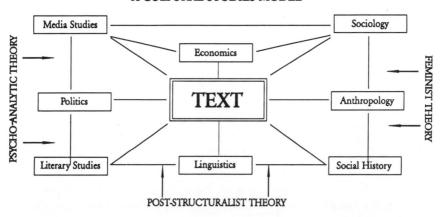

What a Cultural Studies Model Brings to a Text

As I have already implied, certain concepts are absent from this model. Where are personal response, pleasure and enjoyment? Largely because they are seen as social constructs determined by the dominant ideology of the time, notions of value, spirituality, the self, beauty and aesthetics cannot have a fixed, uncomplicated place in this model and are thus missing. In post-post-structuralist literary theory this absence itself is now regarded as problematic. The place of aesthetics in a critical literacy pedagogy is currently the subject of research by Wendy Morgan and Ray Misson and has been the subject of recent Cultural Studies conferences in England. Some English teachers have always been a little uneasy about the perceived relativism of Cultural Studies, and have been reluctant to abandon a literature-centred approach which they themselves found stimulating. The reluctance to let go of what is often seen as a hard-won imaginative writing/literature-based curriculum is not surprising, and may perhaps explain why Protherough and Atkinson (1991) can write so confidently that in Britain ...

> As different models (or paradigms) have come under attack, it has become plain both that there is no return to some 'innocent' English and also that there is little prospect of replacing English with some agreed alternative, whatever it might be called (Cultural Studies or Textual Studies according to some).

This is much less true in Australia, where a critical literacy approach is a key strand in nearly all of the state English profiles – an approach supported by publications for both students and teachers and publicised through many workshops, seminars and keynote addresses at national and regional conferences throughout the country. Even so, 'English' remains the name of the compulsory core subject in the state and national curriculum profiles, and will continue to do so in the foreseeable future.

Cultural Studies and the English Teacher: Classroom Implications

Cultural Studies has a voracious appetite, and has shown itself willing to consume a vast range of topics. Any products of culture, from Ned Kelly (most readers will have encountered Wendy Morgan's *The Example of Ned Kelly*, 1993) to shopping malls can appear on the menu as texts for study. Recent subjects of books appearing in Britain include *High Streets, Shopping Malls: Shopping in Britain Since 1945; Lifebuoy Men, Lux Women: Commodification, Consumption and Cleanliness in Modern Zimbabwe* and *Sport, Culture and Identities in South Africa*. Subjected to discussion and analysis, whether it is of the representation, the subtext or the historical and gendered contexts, these topics, which can and have been readily adapted for secondary classroom use, invite questions such as "*Why and with whom* is (or was) this phenomenon popular?" "*What* implicit messages is it sending out?" and "*How* is it read?". In the English classroom, where different kinds of text, including poetry, fiction and advertising copy can be placed alongside science and medical writing, photography and painting, such explorations can often be the starting point for imaginative, interesting and meticulously researched work from individual students or small groups. One of my students produced as a piece of coursework for her Year 11 folder a study of representations of Marilyn Monroe. Quite unprompted by me, she discussed the half-lidded, down looking gaze of the majority of posed photographs in a way that would have delighted John Berger (Berger, 1972).

But there is more to Cultural Studies than an analysis of consumerism. Representations of war, ethnic groups and religion in literature, film, art, television and press have been explored in studies of the Vietnam War, Aboriginal people, and Islam. Recent studies have looked at the stereotypes in colonial photography and the way that we display the past in museums. Then there are opportunities to investigate other aspects of culture – songs, games, superstitions and folk tales from the rich variety of communities that are now a feature of most countries in the world. In pairing with a school in Britain or America, a class can explore what images one community has of the other, and then try to explore the source of those images. In a recent European example, a German teacher asked a class to look at the way Germany was represented in English foreign language coursebooks, while in England a class looked at the way England was represented in books for German students learning English. The two then compared their findings.

But traditional literature need not be abandoned, for not only does it remain influential culturally, its analysis demands more of students than, say, does the analysis of an advertisement. Romanticism, representations of madness in 19th century novels, young adult fiction – all of these can be accommodated by the Cultural Studies model. Two simple examples, by way of illustration: they come from my undergraduate classes but serve to illustrate a point. In a module called *The American South* I ask my students to look at three representations of the Confederate flag. One is in a scene from *Gone With The Wind*, where the camera pans back from Scarlett O'Hara crossing the square of the ravaged Atlanta, to the flagpole from which the battle scarred flag still flutters proudly, a symbol of southern heroism. The next is a paragraph from *South of Haunted Dreams: a ride through slavery's old backyard*, a travel book by an African-American writer, Eddy L Harris, who describes the effect of seeing a rebel flag, symbol of racism and hate, painted on the front of a truck, thundering down the road towards him at great speed. Finally we look at a description from *Dixie Debates* of the way that the flag, particularly in Japan, represents Lynryd Skynryd and southern rock music and not the southern states at all. With these examples of changing representation students may or may not choose to talk about shifting signifiers, but I hope a point about history, context and point of view has been made. Similarly, in a module on Edwardian writing, we look at the way suffragist women in England appropriated the image of Joan of Arc to further their campaign, and the way that this image had been used before, and has been used afterwards, by sometimes opposing groups. In both cases the aim is to focus on the importance of the historical moment, and the way that certain ideas and tropes were read at a particular time, and where that reading came from. Print text is not neglected: students read carefully *The Times* report of the Derby incident in which Emily Wilding Davison was killed by the King's horse, and for the erasure of women and Edwardian models of masculinity in *The Wind in the Willows*.

Problems

Those not wholly ready to embrace a Cultural Studies approach will raise a number of objections, and three in particular. One concerns time: where is there space on the timetable to do all these things, and do all the things with which English has very rightly been concerned: improve literacy, talking, a range of reading? The positive answer is that a Cultural Studies approach permits all of these, and is likely to improve standards because it is building on those things which students like and already know something about. It validates student experience, rather than trying to impose one culture on top of another. But if reassurance is needed, we do read demanding, canonical novels, short stories and poems in the *American South*, just as we do in *Edwardian Writing*.

This covers another objection: surely students should be introduced to more than just contemporary or near past, more than soap operas, shopping malls and Ned Kelly? Is there no space for Shakespeare or Greek tragedy? The answer is yes: it is quite possible to adopt a Cultural Studies approach which includes a reading of *Hamlet, Romeo and Juliet* or *Oedipus Rex*.

A third objection is that any approach drawing as heavily as it does on an enormous body of theory is inaccessible and elitist, and not democratic at all! Wendy Morgan and Andrew Stibbs have argued that the important thing about the influence of theory is the way that it impinges on and modifies classroom practice, and that students do not need to grapple with dense theoretical discussion not written with school students in mind. The theory is embedded in the practice.

A related objection is that sometimes the phrase 'Cultural Studies' is used very unproblematically by people who have not really had the time to get to grips with what are quite difficult theories. This means that students are given over-simplified versions of what the theories say. This seems to me a serious criticism, particularly in higher education because the teacher is put in the powerful position of *transmitter* of versions of these theories – versions that may themselves require some deconstruction. The best way of resolving this is to be frank about the problem, as Wendy Morgan is at the end of *Ned Kelly*.

There are many more questions (such as 'Does Cultural Studies encourage debate or is it doctrinaire and inflexible? Is it an intellectual straitjacket?') that are likely to worry English teachers, particularly those worried about the space left for imagination, personal response and creativity. Some of these are addressed in David Harris's book on the effect of Gramscianism on Cultural Studies (1992). The simple answer is that if done well it can be empowering, whilst if done badly it can be superficial and unchallenging.

What's in a Name?

Does English include Cultural Studies or does Cultural Studies include English? Those who deride contemporary theory and regard its influence as wholly baneful will not have reached this point in the argument, but I think it is fair to say that the majority of English teachers are at least interested in, and sometimes excited by, the possibilities opened up by these approaches. In England the restraints caused by the restriction on the amount of coursework for Year 11 and Year 13 examinations has forced some teachers to move from 'English' syllabuses to Media Studies. In Australia that kind of divisiveness may be avoidable. What is more, much of the impetus for curriculum development in schools along Cultural Studies lines is now coming from Australia rather than from Britain, with a different set of concerns from those addressed in England thirty years ago. These shifts and changes are well described in Relocating Cultural Studies (Blundell et al, 1993).

Many would regard Cultural Studies as a curriculum development suitable for the world our students will inhabit in the twenty-first century. Far from being an argument that we want an education system defined purely by the philosophy of market economics, and the demands, systems and paradigms of the internet, these practices provide an opportunity to interrogate that world, which is our reality, just as the industrial world was the reality for the mass of people in England in the nineteenth century.

I started this inevitably partial and limited reading of Cultural Studies by referring to the contradictions and paradoxes that any discussion must confront. The future of Cultural Studies will be decided by the eventual dominance – or hegemony, to use Gramsci's term – of one of two apparently contesting forces. On the one hand, we hear from politicians and some employers' organisations an insistent call for 'basic' literacy. In England where the school curriculum is controlled centrally and monitored through a system of testing this is setting an agenda which teachers cannot ignore. Simultaneously – and this is a continuation of a move that has been underway for a number of years in Australia – there is a willingness and a pressure to reconfigure or go beyond English, and to embrace interdisciplinary approaches with pluralistic models of language and literacy.

Yet English has refused to play the role of Titanic to the iceberg of Cultural Studies. Anxieties about the perceived self-referentiality of critical theory and the failure of Cultural Studies to engage with questions about aesthetics and quality – all of these are forcing the subject to ask fresh questions of itself. But it is not going to melt away.

The argument for a Cultural Studies approach is heard in England most persuasively from those who teach it in higher education:

> *Students from culturally-based courses emerge with a critical orientation and broad-based media literacy. They are likely to initiate, and respond to, cultural transformations, throughout their lives – as active citizens, paid workers or entrepreneurs. The rate of technological and cultural change is so fast that it is impossible to predict what will be taken for granted in five or ten years time . . . Curiosity about the culture we live in, research skills to work collaboratively, the ability to innovate and use new technologies creatively – these are the general dispositions (which a three year degree course should develop.)*
>
> J Arthurs, 1997

The same argument can be made for more practice of a Cultural Studies approach in schools. I do not think that many would demur if the phrase of Jane Arthur's I have placed in brackets were exchanged for something like "which students leaving school should have had the opportunity to develop". The question that remains unresolved is whether English can – and should – be the place on the timetable where such opportunities are provided.

References

Arthurs, J (1997) "Opinion" in *The Guardian*, Higher Education 26/8/97, London: Guardian Newspapers.

Bennison, S and Spicer, A (1991) "Cultural Studies at A Level", *Magazine of Cultural Studies*, No 3 Spring, Bristol: Bristol Polytechnic.

Berger, J (1972) *Ways of Seeing*, London: Penguin.

Blundell, V, Shepherd, J and Taylor, I (eds) (1993) *Relocating Cultural Studies*, London: Routledge.

Fiske, J (1989) *Understanding Popular Culture*, London: Allen and Unwin.

Frow, J and Morris, M (eds) (1993) *Australian Cultural Studies – a Reader*, Allen and Unwin.

Green, M (ed) (1987) *Broadening the Context: English and Cultural Studies*, John Murray for The English Association.

Green, M (1976) "Cultural Studies at Birmingham University" in Craig, D and Heinemann, M (eds) *Experiments in English Teaching: New Work in Further and Higher Education*, London: Arnold.

Harris, D (1992) *From Class Struggle to the Politics of Pleasure*, London: Routledge.

Hawthorn, Jeremy (1992) *Contemporary Literary Theory*, London: Edward Arnold.

Mascord, G (1990) "Is Vietnam Non-fiction?" in *A Level English: Pressures for Change*, Sheffield: NATE.

Munns, J and Rajan, G (1995) *A Cultural Studies Reader: History, Theory, Practice*, London: Longman.

Peel, R and Curtis, F (1996) "Becoming and Being a Specialist: Anticipating and Experiencing Higher Education English" in *Teaching in Higher Education*, vol 1 no 2, Oxford: Blackwell.

Protherough, Robert and Atkinson, Judith (1991) *The Making of English Teachers*, Buckingham: Open University Press.

Sarland, C (1988) "Reading Pulp: Seeing the Response Through the Fog", *English in Education*, Summer 1988; vol 22, no 2.

Scott, P (1989) *Reconstructing A Level English*, Milton Keynes: Open University Press.

Williams, R (1950) "Stocktaking I – Books for Teaching Culture and Environment", *The Use of English*, 1.3.

Satire: *The Devil's Dictionary*

Senior students should become acquainted with Ambrose Bierce's *The Devil's Dictionary* (first published in 1908). Bierce, a friend of Mark Twain, satirised the follies and delusions of American society in a series of brilliantly epigrammatic definitions, for example:

Aborigines, *n.* Persons of little worth found cumbering the soil of a newly discovered country. They soon cease to cumber; they fertilise.

Alone, *adj.* In bad company.

Bigot, *n.* One who is obstinately and zealously attached to an opinion that you do not entertain.

Bore, *n.* A person who talks when you wish him to listen.

Dejeuner, *n.* The breakfast of an American who has been to Paris.

Dictionary, *n.* A malevolent literary device for cramping the growth of a language and making it hard and inelastic. This dictionary, however, is a most useful work.

Education, *n.* That which discloses to the wise and disguises from the foolish their lack of understanding.

Man *n.* An animal so lost in rapturous contemplation of what he thinks he is as to overlook what he indubitably ought to be. His chief occupation is extermination of other animals and his own species, which, however, multiplies with such insistent rapidity as to infest the whole habitable earth and Canada.

Self-evident *adj.* Evident to one's self and to nobody else.

6 Questioning Popular Culture

Ray Misson

One of the perennials of the popular press is the article about whether popular culture should be taught in schools. The headline almost invariably sets some popular text *(Neighbours, The Simpsons, Melrose Place)* up against Shakespeare, and there is a certain ritual quality as the various protagonists in the debate (in Victoria I seem invariably to be one of them) go through their usual paces.

Actually, it seems to me that popular texts have now firmly established their place in the English curriculum: they are after all enshrined, even mandated, in various curriculum documents. The arguments about why this is a good thing have been widely canvassed, the two main ones being:

✦ that English should be concerned to engage with the textual world of the students and prepare them to read intelligently the central texts of their culture; and

✦ that these texts have the potential to exert great power, and so it is important to see how they are operating.

Such arguments, I think, have generally won the day, so they don't need to be developed in detail again here. What is interesting however is that the media 'debate' about popular texts in the curriculum refuses to go away.

Predictably the contest is always set up in binary terms ("Bart v the Bard" etc), and no amount of reiteration that it is not a matter of mutually exclusive options but of inclusiveness and complementarity seems able to shift the basic binary belief. Binaries always exert a great attraction, but there does seem to be an unusually strong desire to cling to this one, long after its validity or usefulness has been discredited.

The impulse largely comes from the cultural heritage lobby (some of whom are English teachers), who believe in the unique value of working on classic texts, a belief that doesn't want the supremacy of these texts questioned in any way. They see the decline of the teaching of such texts as a sign of moral and intellectual decay amongst (other) English teachers. (The word 'trendy' usually gets used somewhere around this point.) Popular texts are the last straw, because they believe it is precisely popular texts that the study of the classics is meant to protect one against. English teachers are ideally seen as the champions of a conservative, exclusive culture, i.e. one which has to conserve itself by excluding the kinds of texts most people are most interested in.

What such people are unwilling to contemplate is a broadly inclusive English classroom in which all kinds of texts are seen as manifestations of textuality and looked at with comparable attention in terms of how they are working, what they are saying, and what their value might be.

For the interest in popular culture is not simply an interest in bringing different kinds of text into the classroom, but is more fundamentally concerned with the question of what is to be the attitude to those texts, and by extension to all texts. The work on popular culture is an adjunct to two other areas of intellectual work, themselves closely related: Cultural Studies and Critical Literacy. Both Cultural Studies and Critical Literacy are predicated on the sociocultural nature of textuality. They use conceptual tools largely derived from structuralist and poststructuralist theory, including poststructuralist inflections of feminism and Marxism, as well as post-colonial studies, queer theory, etc. which provide a powerful set of questions to ask of texts, whether they be popular, classical or anything in between.

Thus, while the inclusion of popular culture in the curriculum is certainly important in that it extends the students' knowledge of textuality by opening up the possibility of working on a much greater range of texts, it is even more important in that it brings with it a different way of looking at texts. This is in one sense a historical accident. One could look at *The X-Files* in exactly the same way *Wuthering Heights* was looked at thirty years ago, and dismissively judge it on those terms. However, in another sense, the conjunction of particular newer ways of working on texts with the interest in popular culture is no accident, since the new frameworks show us interesting things about popular texts, things that would not have been seen if the old questions were still being asked. The newer modes of analysis help us understand better both the attractions of a text like *The X-Files* and also how it embodies our current social and cultural priorities and beliefs. One of the payoffs, too, is that it may teach us and our students new questions to ask of *Wuthering Heights*.

Since both Cultural Studies and Critical Literacy are being treated elsewhere in this volume, I will not go further down his path, but turn to look at some of the specific issues involved with teaching popular culture.

The first question is, of course, one of definition. There are a number of axes on which the popular might be defined, many of them to do with audience. In historical terms, popular works are considered to be those produced either by 'the people' – ballads, folk-songs – or with a lower-class audience in mind – penny-dreadfuls, music hall – as opposed to the high art work produced for the upper and aristocratic classes. The class assumptions here are ones that obviously need contesting and that, I suspect, have largely broken down. One is as likely to hear a *silverchair* CD being played in wealthy as in industrial suburbs, at least among a certain age group.

Then it might be argued that it is not the class of the audience but its size that makes a text part of popular culture, and, indeed, there is a certain validity in the notion that popular texts are those that command a mass audience. But here again the category doesn't quite fit easily. There are many texts that one would put under the heading of popular culture that are in fact very much a minority taste - one only has to think of the various youth sub-cultures to realise this. In terms of number of people who have seen them, the films *Trainspotting* and even *Pulp Fiction* may well be less popular than the BBC *Pride and Prejudice* or even the Ang Lee/Emma Thompson *Sense and Sensibility*, whereas for most people the first two are definitely popular culture, while the latter two might not be thought of as such.

Or they might be, since for some people, the medium can be a determining factor. Film and TV are popular media, whereas a book is at least inherently less likely to be popular culture, although this can of course be overridden by the nature of the book, and even the format and point of sale (thick books in newsagents). It is true that, because of their wide dissemination and mass reproduction, TV programs and films are inherently more likely to be considered popular culture than a hardback novel published by a specialist publishing house, but this is, of course, only the grossest of generalisations. Neither *The Singing Detective* nor Peter Greenaway's *The Pillow Book*, for example, are exactly broadly popular texts.

Popular culture might be considered to be entertainment, but one would not want to suggest that Shakespeare's plays were not entertaining. It might be considered to be escapist, but most people would see newspapers and television journalism as a facet of popular culture, and although there is no doubt that these things have a function beyond the simply informative, they could not be labelled purely escapist.

Thus it is almost impossible to define popular texts easily, which is a good thing. The idea should be resisted strongly that there is a defined corpus of works that are popular that can be set up against another defined corpus that isn't, and so the difficulty of definition is in fact strategically useful. One can break down the easy categories and develop a textually rich and varied English classroom.

One of the features of many popular texts (like most texts) is that they are very much targeted to particular audiences (albeit sometimes very general ones) and work with particular audiences in mind. They address the target audience very specifically, and play strongly on that audience's beliefs and fantasies. This means that there are different problems when working with different kinds of text, depending on how the student audience relates to them.

If one is looking at teenage texts, the advantage is that students are likely to be interested because the texts do speak to them so directly, but the very fact that the students are the target audience makes the texts harder to analyse in the classroom. As an initial analytical move, one needs to objectify the text being worked on, make its construction apparent, but because in this case it is so directly shaped to implicate teenage readers in its vision of the world, the work of distancing can be very difficult, and there may be some considerable resistance to doing it. Thus the argument that one looks at popular texts because they are relevant to and interest students needs to be seriously qualified. Their closeness to students may in fact make them less readily available for analysis, not only because of the difficulty that they are so naturalised, but because of the students' intense investment in them. Analysis can easily become an invasion of private space, unless it is very delicately managed.

On the other hand, texts that are targeted at other audiences – either older or younger, historically or ethnically distanced – will in obvious ways denaturalise themselves. The ways in which they are playing to a particular perception of the world and set of values will often be glaringly apparent. This means that it is very easy to do analytical work that shows up the text's limitations, and that highlights its constructedness.

The problem here is not to stereotype, and not to let the analysis feed an easy sense of superiority: "Aren't women/children/people from earlier generations/ etc stupid for being taken in by such texts!" The focus needs to be on developing a sense of how all texts work, that all texts are implicated in ideology, rather than simply showing that Mills and Boons are inherently patriarchal, or that advertisements are exploitative. It is too easy to play hunt the stereotype, and not recognise that we are all implicated in stereotypes, and that we could not operate in the world without the easy categorisations they provide.

It is also very easy to criticise a text for its limited inclusiveness in terms of class, ethnicity or gender ("what is not being included, what is not being given a voice"), but lessons in which this is done can soon become repetitive and rather pointless as text after text is found to be wanting. Acknowledgement needs to be made that no text is totally inclusive, since it is impossible for any of us to rise totally above a particular positioning in terms of class, ethnicity, gender, etc. (This is not a vindication of sexism, ethnocentrism, heterosexism or any other such thing because one must be vigilant against insidious and distorting exclusions, but there are often other things that need to be said about texts, and the limited concentration on what is not in the text can not only distract one from this, but is too easy a point to make and can quickly strike students as mechanical and irrelevant.)

There are two crucial issues that immediately confront the teacher of popular culture:

✦ pleasure;
✦ value.

Scandalously to those who dislike the teaching of popular texts, these texts are not generally geared to producing deep intellectual engagement, but rather more often they rely on calling forth more direct and accessible pleasures. It is difficult, but important, not to moralise on this. Pleasure in itself is not a suspect phenomenon, and it is a worthy aim of texts to create it. The teacher of popular culture must at some level feel the attractiveness of the text being worked on, otherwise the analysis is drastically limited, since the text is often so specifically constructed to create pleasure. One needs to allow the pleasure and not be simply critical of it, while still realising that it is performing an ideological function by positioning the reader in a particular way.

Similarly one must keep the value of the texts in proportion. One does not want to fail to do justice to a text by treating it as rubbish compared with more complex, classic texts, but equally one does not want to inflate its value and make extravagant claims for it. There are some who wish to move outside the value game altogether, and who imply that all texts are of equal value, or see value as purely subjective. However, this is not how we operate on texts, indeed on anything, in the real world. We are constantly valuing. The trick is to be flexible in the criteria for our valuations and do justice to the positive aspects of a text while being fully aware of both its negative aspects and its limitations.

The interest in popular culture has been productive in loosening up the canon of texts that can be looked at in the English classroom. It has been important in breaking down conventional exclusive categories and validating the everyday textual experience of the large majority of people. The work on popular texts is at its most successful when they are seen as part of the continuum of texts naturally up for investigation, not as something to be looked at for the sole purpose of castigating them, nor as a sop to keep the more troublesome troops in the classroom happy. The negativity of both those attitudes inevitably produces bad work, not to mention bad feeling amongst those who enjoy the texts. One wants the students to be able to recognise the value (or lack of it) in any text, and not fall into the easy binary categorisations that the cultural heritage believers promote. If one wants to criticise popular texts – and much of popular culture is open to a great deal of criticism – one must earn the right by first acknowledging the experience the texts have to offer and understanding why they are popular.

Popular texts may generally be accessible, but the analysis of them is not easy, and indeed, as I have said, there can be particular dangers for teachers in working with texts that are immediate and particularly valued parts of the students' own culture. But the intellectual demands combined with the immediacy of involvement make the teaching of these texts both particularly valuable and particularly significant in the English classroom.

7 Peeking Out From Between the Covers: An Historical Overview of Teaching the Media in English

Calvin Durrant

I n the early 1980s, ATOM (Australian Teachers of Media) sponsored Len Masterman, the British media educator, to come to Australia where, amongst a number of other engagements, he delivered a keynote address to the 1982 National Media Education Conference in Adelaide. In this address, he spoke about the origins of media education being essentially middle-class and deeply paternalistic, and that of all the notions about teaching the media in schools, discrimination has proved to be the most deeply ingrained, resilient and chameleon-like in the way it has adapted itself to new theories and practices.

For Masterman, this represents the most potent reason why "... media education, in spite of reports, recommendations and conferences urging its implementation over the past twenty-five years has made somewhat halting progress in the classroom" (Masterman, 1983, p5).

His concluding challenge to the conference delegates has a number of familiar echoes in more recent work on the new media technologies and their potential impact on the school curriculum:

> At the beginning of the 1980s we are standing on the threshold of the most enormous and unprecedented expansion of television and video. Those teachers who continue to ignore or deplore these developments, will be opting for the role of educational dinosaurs . . . . I hope that, within the next decade, Media Education will move significantly from the peripheries of the curriculum towards its centre.
>
> (Masterman, 1983, p10)

Despite a number of such predictions and the undoubted changes that have subsequently taken place, there still remains a widely held suspicion about the nature of the role that the media should play in school education and in subject English in particular.

In a recent keynote address to Queensland English teachers, Bill Green posed the generative question: "Why have we embraced so enthusiastically the so-called new technologies, when by and large we have shied away from systematic engagements with the media?" (Green, 1997).

It seems to me that there are at least two reasons why English teachers in Australia were slow to take up the media education debate: firstly, because they weren't encouraged to, and secondly, because it was not a subject of examination in English for school leavers, and therefore media education didn't rate as being worthy of classroom consideration.

The study of media in schools is said to have begun in response to the ever widening impact that popular culture enjoyed in pre-World War II Britain (Masterman, 1983). Significantly, this initiative was not the result of an enthusiastic embrace of popular culture by the establishment, but a "call to arms" to stem the rushing tide of "exploitation of the cheapest emotional responses" (Leavis and Thompson, 1948, p3). In looking at the way the study of the media has progressed in school education there appear to be at least two levels or strands of influence under which English teachers have operated, though I am not suggesting here that teachers necessarily adhere to any one theoretical foundation to their teaching methodology. Indeed, the research suggests that English teachers have quite an eclectic view of their subject (Peel and Hargreaves, 1994, p45).

The first concerns the underlying tension of whether or not the serious English teacher should in fact be dealing with the media, and the history of this debate is well documented by Andrew Goodwyn (1992) and David Buckingham (1991), amongst others. The second relates to the various media theories that have dominated academic circles since the 1930s (Wilson, 1987).

The serious treatment of media in schools arose from fears surrounding the potential influence of the mass media on young and impressionable minds. This form of media study had as its general aim the development of students' discriminatory powers. Supporters of this view, which early on included F R Leavis and Denys Thompson and later on, the arguably more strident versions of David Holbrook, Fred Inglis and Frank Whitehead, argued that the development of discrimination, fine judgment and taste ". . . depended upon pupils grasping the basic differences between the timeless values of authentic culture as embodied in the traditional arts (in which teachers were themselves initiated) and the essentially anti-cultural values of a largely commercial mass media" (Masterman, 1989, p13).

Of course, as Andrew Goodwyn (1992) so rightly points out, discrimination of itself is not the problem; there are few contemporary English teachers who would not want their students to discriminate when making personal choices, whether they be in the selection of texts or in the realm of personal values. The difference perhaps lies in what might be explored in the contemporary classroom that would help students to know and understand why they exercise particular choices or discriminate among a range of texts, behaviours, beliefs or values. In the Leavis and Thompson classrooms, and perhaps even more so in the neo-Leavisian English teaching arenas inhabited by Holbrook, Inglis and others up until the late 1960s, all elements of the mass media were to be discriminated against, as exemplified in the following extract from Frank Whitehead:

> Yet the disturbing fact is that in the Western world of the mid-twentieth century this power of discrimination has become more difficult of attainment than ever. Never before has there been such a strident multitude of siren voices beckoning us away from the pursuit of true judgment, by playing ruthlessly and insistently on our complacency, cupidity, social timidity, frustrations, prejudices, irrational fears, prurience and mental laziness.... From the moment they acquire language, our children are assailed day in and day out by advertising slogans – from the television set, on cereal packets, on hoardings, in comics.... Moreover, underlying the ethos of the entertainment industry is an assumption even more pregnant with consequences for the educator: the assumption that what we all need in our leisure hours is distraction, an effortless, painless (and pleasure-less) time-killing which demands of us no more than glancing at illustrations, scanning headlines, or gazing in mild stupefaction at a flickering screen for thirteen minutes which separates one commercial from the next.   (Whitehead, 1966, pp 85, 86).

However, such missionary zeal has its downside. Teachers can to a limited degree control what students do in their classrooms, but they cannot hope to put lasting fences around their recreational reading and viewing. Consequently, teachers who genuinely wished to do both the right thing by their students but also adhere to the prevailing literary attitudes of their professional colleagues, were faced with an awkward dilemma: ignore the reading and viewing preferences of their students and thereby risk their scorn and derision, or teach against the grain for popularity's sake and risk being disenfranchised by the local version of the literary establishment. I suspect many elected to pick and choose depending on which classes they were teaching at the time, but it does highlight the difficult situation many English teachers find themselves in even now where they have come through university English departments still largely informed by New Criticism and yet are thrown into teaching environments saturated by popular culture texts.

The shift in attitudes towards the media that took place at the end of the '60s came about not as a response to such thinking, but rather as an indirect consequence of the changing definitions of English itself. John Dixon's *Growth Through English* did not so much legitimate the inclusion of media study in English as broaden the overall outlook on what it was that needed to be the subject's focus – the individual student's personal path to growth rather than a discrete and Establishment-approved set of contents. That this might involve exploring that student's life outside of the classroom became more apparent as the decade progressed and English teachers around the world picked up on the need to alter the curriculum in order to cater for such growth. A new emphasis on the needs and aspirations of working class students and the consequent shift in view of what it is to think culturally became the basis of the establishment at the University of Birmingham of the Centre for Contemporary Cultural Studies in 1964 (Fleming, 1993, p54). While there may have been no formal connections between the Birmingham school and the expanding personal growth movement, there are certain resonances apparent in the ensuing work of "the London school" of Britton, Barnes and Rosen and their concentration on the role of language in learning (Green, 1995).

But formal connection or not, classroom treatment of media texts began to switch from the negative coverage spawned during the post-war years to a new recognition of the potential such texts had for sparking creative debates in English. As a plethora of theme books flooded the school market, increased attention was given to the types of media texts with which school age children were familiar. [See, for example, the popular *Themes and Responses* series by Delves and Tickell, claimed in the advertising to be "(T)he most successful Creative English Course of our time...." (*English in Australia*, No. 9, March, 1969, p36) and also the widely used four-volume *English Part One* series by Hannan, Hannan and Allinson.] But what of the teachers?

While English teachers continued to have a sense of confusion over what their responsibility was, that is, handing on the literary tradition or becoming broad specialists in social communications, they were at least prominent in their awareness about students' fascination with the media compared with teachers of other subjects. In the Murdock and Phelps UK study, seventy percent of English teachers recognised the extent of the influence of the media on their students compared with less than fifty percent for the remainder of the teaching service (1973, p21). Teachers were broadly categorised as adopting one of the following approaches in their classrooms:
1. Mainly favourable towards but rarely dealing with the media.
2. Deeply troubled by the media and thus excluding it.
3. Hostile towards media influence, thereby introducing it for the express purpose of developing discrimination and resistance.
4. Identifying the media as a natural extensions of students' experiences and hence dealing with it regularly as a means of enriching student understanding of it.

English teachers in the main fell into approaches two, three or four, further reinforcing the contention that the profession continued to have mixed feelings about media education (Goodwyn, 1992, p23).

In 1975, the Bullock Report was released, and while it did not attempt to push any new methods of pursuing the study of media in English, it provided express confirmation that media texts were both legitimate and desirable subjects of examination in the English classroom. Further, acknowledgment is made of a perceived move away from the old Leavisite discrimination focus to a new emphasis on appreciation:

> *Although there is unquestioned value in developing a critical approach to television, as to listening and reading, we would place the emphasis on extending and deepening the pupil's appreciation.* (DES, 1975, 22.14)

Whether or not such a message took a long time to reach the teaching force Down Under is not absolutely clear. However, an examination of the treatment of media in subject English as found in the Australian Association for the Teaching of English (AATE) journal, *English in Australia*, provides us with some idea of just how little public attention was being given to the study of media in English even late into the 1960s.

By the early seventies, writers still felt compelled to justify any reference to the inclusion of media studies in English when writing in the national journal. Here is Bill Menary attempting to answer his own question of 'Why screen?':

> *It is simply that our students spend a great deal of time in viewing images on screens of different size, and that whether we like it or not a great deal of their impressions of the world are transmitted through these screens. The starting point is that we surely cannot ignore the twin visual media, film and television.* (Menary, 1971, p11)

In his conclusion, he refers to the small but growing number of teachers moving into screen work in schools:

> *If this article has any value, it may be just this, that it tries to tempt colleagues waiting on the fringes of media study, and I am sure there are hundreds out there, to make a beginning.* (Menary, 1971, p17)

Of equal interest is Menary's series of suggestions for teachers who might find themselves teaching film studies to a number of parallel classes. He outlines four different approaches that might be broadly categorised as:

✦ class appreciation based on students' TV or movie-going habits;

✦ aesthetic treatment of films screened in class;

✦ technical analysis of content and meaning in those class screenings;

✦ critical analysis leading to students' own productions (p13).

Menary's claim that "... one of the most dynamic educational situations is precisely when teacher and pupil are learning together" strikes me as being decidedly progressive for an English teacher at this time (p14).

The last of Menary's suggested approaches rapidly gained in popularity during the seventies and early eighties.

While it appears that from the beginning of the '70s, public debate – at least in the national journal – had shifted towards the growth model view of English, this is not to say that the notion of discrimination had entirely disappeared. In 1973, David Mallick, reporting on some active research he had conducted with a group of his teacher education students, claimed that students were being set up to become passive victims of the ubiquitous forces of the media and declared that:

> *... our teaching is grounded in consciousness, in learning to discriminate and, often to resist. It is no longer possible to release a child amid a bewildering crowd either of diverse writings or of television images, clamorous, undifferentiated, and expect him (sic) to make his own path through the tumult. Criticism is indispensable to sustained and ordered growth, and it is conscious.*
> (Mallick, 1973, p52)

Herein lies a key to the second strand that I referred to earlier that appears to run approximately parallel to the way education moved in the late '70s and early '80s to adopt the media as useful subjects of examination if not exactly as welcome allies in the sphere of public education. From the early '30s, the sociologists of the Frankfurt School had viewed the mass media as being both powerful and relentless in their manipulation of the masses. In the late '40s and through the '60s, research in the United States particularly began to draw attention to the fact that audiences appeared not to be as heavily influenced by the media as was originally thought. As with the endless educational debate over violence on television and its effects on the behaviour of child viewers, research findings were ambiguous and at times downright contradictory (Duhs and Gunton, 1988; Cullingford, 1988). It seemed that there was more to the debate than slavishly assimilating whatever one viewed or read.

With the arrival of the '70s, critical theory came to the fore, though arguably its influence on teaching media education did not take full effect in Australian English teaching circles until the mid 1980s after Len Masterman had delivered a number of conference papers here and his books, particularly *Teaching the Media*, began to have a significant influence on the teaching methodologies of a large number of teachers worldwide (Goodwyn, 1992, p46). Critical theory looks at society as a whole and examines the place of media in it. It views society as being dominated by a small number of elite groups who, because of their economic power, are able to use the media to promote their views, attitudes and values as being natural or self evidently right. The media, then, serve to perpetuate the status quo by legitimising the dominant ideologies and undermining or dismissing opposing views. Critical theorists examine media industries ownership, and they look at "... the media messages themselves, analysing the visual and aural signs being broadcast or projected or printed. They look at the professional practices of media workers and the political economy of the media" (Wilson, 1987, p21). In some ways, this view can be seen to be returning full circle to the early observations of the mass society theorists.

As Andrew Goodwyn observes, an examination of such a critical theory as Masterman proposes in *Teaching the Media* provides us with a very useful insight into the struggle between the nature of media theory and the nature of teaching and learning:

> *First, he is close to the Leavis and Marxist views in positing a media establishment whose effect is to support and generally promote the*

capitalist status quo. Second, one of his principal aims is to help pupils become more critical and resistant viewers. Third, his pedagogical approach to achieve this aim is to attempt to abolish the teacher as an authority figure and to create a non-hierarchical classroom.

(Goodwyn, 1992, p45)

The latter point highlights the progressive nature of Masterman's pedagogy, but it also raises the inherent problem of the teacher knowing more about the media (at least its structures if not its programs or products) than the student, yet having to 'pretend not to' in order for the learning process to proceed. If this is the only teaching strategy used, then it does not seem to me to be an entirely economical use of available English classroom time. Ironically, as I have commented elsewhere, Masterman is a staunch opponent of English being the principal subject domain where media education takes place because of the Leavis heritage that many secondary English teachers still carry (Durrant, 1996, p144).

An examination of the issues of *English in Australia* from the 1980s on, reveals a growing number of teachers both concerned about the place of the study of media in English and, relatedly, how it might be taught. David Homer referred to English teachers at the beginning of this period as being ". . . ostriches where the electronic media are concerned. By and large they are either waiting for them to go away as an issue with which they should be concerned, or pushing responsibility for education in and about the media off to other areas of schooling" (Homer, 1982, p35). He drew attention to the fact that the Third International Conference on the Teaching of English held at the University of Sydney in 1980 ". . . largely ignored the existence of the electronic and other mass media". In a warning that now has an all too familiar ring to it, he suggested that "(U)nless we actively involve ourselves in coming to terms with these issues, by 1990 it will probably be too late" (p46).

In the October 1982 issue of *English in Australia*, Barry Dwyer presented an integrated unit on the mass media for the Resources Section. It is instructive to note some of the emphases here. Firstly, it was presented very much as an across the curriculum exercise, particularly linking English with Social Studies, Science, Maths and Art/Craft. It should be noted that this was an angle that Masterman and others were pushing in Britain at the time. Secondly, it was framed specifically as a ". . . comprehensive approach to a critical study of the mass media" (Dwyer, 1982, pi). Thirdly, a major emphasis is placed on the active roles viewers play rather than on their passive receptivity. The latter point is again stressed in the section on evaluation:

Be guided by this thought: **Media competence** *in a pupil is more than an understanding of the structural-technical features of the media; rather it is an ability to* **respond critically** *to the content-message of the media, both verbal and non-verbal. That is, an ability to select, talk and write* *critically in relation to the media – in short to **act** instead of being passive! (px).*

In 1988, *English in Australia* devoted an entire issue to the "Non-Print Media". Marnie O'Neill elected not to preface it with an explanatory editorial, which is probably a sound (and encouraging) indicator that the editor saw no need to justify her thematic selection to her readership. One of the writers, Cedric Cullingford, outlined the way in which television was shifting in public perception from being seen as the omnipotent Plug-in-Drug (See Winn, 1985) to the recognition that in fact it was not powerful enough to transform society after all.

> *It has taken many years for people to realise the power of the audience over the medium, and the resistance or indifference to much which is offered.* (Cullingford, 1988, p27)

Cullingford explains this view in his outline of a series of ways in which the freeze, rewind and fast forward capacities of the video recorder can serve to open up classroom discussion about program structure, narrative style, balance between action and dialogue, characterisation, genre styles, prediction, the nature of media messages, the establishment or conveyance of mood, the role of music and soundtrack, and the nature of the editing process (p31). His view that classroom talk – or response of some description – is critical to school students paying any heed to what they watch – and hence learn – is a timely reminder of the essential role of the teacher in both the use of and study of media technology.

Brien Hallett's article in the same issue highlighted some of the problems that are still frequently raised by English teachers about using the "film of the book" as an adjunct to the study of the literary text, particularly with senior classes where factual differences between the film version and the written text can cause students some confusion in their external exam responses. He traced the different teacher motivations for using film versions: as an illustration of the literary text, as a reward for wading through the assignments relating to the set text, or as yet another interpretation of the literary text. Hallett stressed the differences between the two media forms rather than their respective artistic merits, and suggested a number of classroom activities that might help students both identify and articulate those differences (Hallett, 1988).

In his article "Recalling & Remodelling Textual Interpretation – English Teachers Approach the Commercial Mass Media", Peter Lumb prefaces his introduction with one of the last of what I would classify as the long chain of 'media apologies' appearing in *English in Australia*:

> *To suggest that English teachers should then broaden their teaching activities and move beyond working with print texts seems more then a little churlish.* (Lumb, 1989, p63)

Perhaps so, but one would have thought that developments in English curriculum and syllabus support documents from around the country would have rendered such a statement unnecessary by 1989. Be that as it may, by quoting the well known statistic that by age fifteen, Australian children were spending more hours in front of television than they were in classrooms, Lumb had a strong argument in targeting the national journal for its slim treatment of the study of media in English over the years, a claim that I would argue continues to be a valid one:

> When one considers the few papers published by **English in Australia** on media or the little time allocated to media issues in national English teaching conferences, or the few chapters in 'how to' books, it would seem clear that we continue to work in print with students as they negotiate our culture, while they prefer to, and do involve themselves with our culture, elsewhere. Interest in our teaching may well be low.
>
> (Lumb, 1989, p65)

Here is one of the early recognitions of what has become a common theme in the 1990s, that school education continues to be a bastion of the print dominated past, while the students it purports to focus on are subjects of a new non-print-based age. Bill Green and Chris Bigum identified it as being part of a much wider cultural shift, ". . . not simply from *literary* culture to *popular* culture, but also, more specifically, from *print* culture to *visual* culture (Green and Bigum, 1993, p127). More recently, Bill Green (1997) has suggested that today's school students constitute a new "Post-Print Generation" – whose "... primary field of reference, their 'cultural capital' if you like, is popular culture and the media" (See also Ulmer, 1989 and Tuman, 1992).

It would seem to me that such a change, far from presenting a dire threat to subject English, has the potential to enable the English classroom – and the English teacher more specifically – to operate at a level of relevance beyond the capacity of most of the other school subject disciplines. The increasingly significant role that media study has assumed in Australian English syllabus documents since 1970 means that English teachers should be broadening their expertise in dealing with an ever widening media domain. Equally, however, there is a danger that having made significant gains – particularly during the '80s – English teachers may settle into a sort of middle-age comfort zone in relation to the media – that having adopted the tools of critical literacy in relation to dealing with the media, the learning curve has now reached a stable plateau.

Speaking to the delegates at the *Mediascape 94* conference held in Adelaide, Robin Quin identified some of the challenges facing the study of media in education:

> Here in Australia ... we have successfully waged a twenty year battle to fix a place for media education in the curriculum. Certainly the situation is not perfect, but nevertheless media education is assured of a place within English and media studies within the Arts and Technology area. This is not to argue for complacency because although we are not coming

of age we might be facing a mid-life crisis. ... I think there are three aspects to our mid-life crisis. ... First, the media have changed. Second, thinking about the media has changed, and third, the education systems are changing. (Quin, 1995, pp 48, 49)

Subject English is inextricably caught up in these dramatic changes. In the 1990s we have seen the emphasis shift from concern about the traditional mass media forms of television, radio, newspapers and popular magazines to the domain of the new media forms dominated by computer technology. This is leading to new ways of thinking about what constitutes the media, how it might best be addressed and accommodated in the classroom and whether education should continue to rush headlong into becoming part of the new information age in a way that it never did with what could now be referred to as the 'old media'. As Bill Green comments, this is in all likelihood going to mean "... increasing attention given to television, film and video in English classrooms, as well as computing and other information technologies, and hence in broad terms a shift from print-based forms of culture and literacy to electronic – and image – based forms and orientations" (Green, 1995). Just what this shift will replace in the English curriculum is something that is likely to be highly contested. With governments and educational agencies looking to greater accountability of public money and increased evidence of improvement in students' level of skills, the battle over media education in subject English is likely to be stepped up a notch into the new millenium.

References:

Buckingham, D (1991) "Teaching About the Media" in Lusted, D (Ed) *The Media Studies Book*, London: Routledge.

Cullingford, C (1988) "Children, Television and Classrooms" in *English in Australia*, 83, March.

Delves, A and Tickell, G (1968) *Themes and Responses*, North Melbourne: Cassell.

DES (1975) *A Language for Life*, London: HMSO (The Bullock Report).

Dixon, J (1967) *Growth Through English*, Oxford: Oxford University Press.

Duhs, L and Gunton, R (1988) "TV Violence and Childhood Aggression: A Curmudgeon's Guide", *Australian Psychologist* Vol 23 No 2, July.

Durrant, C (1996) "Media Education in English" in Watson, K, Durrant, C, Hargreaves, S and Sawyer, W, eds, *English Teaching in Perspective: In the context of the 1990s* Sydney: St Clair Press.

Dwyer, B (1982) "The Mass Media: An Integrated Unit", *English in Australia*, 62, October.

Fleming, D (1993) *Media Teaching*, Oxford: Blackwell.

Goodwyn, A (1992) *English Teaching and Media Education*, Buckingham: Open University Press.

Green, B and Bigum, C (1993) "Aliens in the Clasroom", *The Australian Journal of Education*, Vol 37 No 2, August.

Green, B (1995) "After the New English? Change and (Dis)continuity in English Teaching", paper presented at the combined International Conference of the National Council for Teachers of English and the International Federation for the Teaching of English, New York, USA, July 7-14.

Green, B (1997) "Interfaces: English and Technology", Keynote Address at the State Annual Conference of the English Teachers Association of Queensland, Brisbane, August 23.

Hallett, B (1988) "The Novel and the Film: Teaching the Differences to Senior Secondary Students", *English in Australia*, 83, March.

Hannan, L, Hannan, W and Allinson, A (1967) *English Part One*, Melbourne: F. W. Cheshire.

Homer, D (1982) "English and the Electronic Media", *English in Australia*, 60, June.
Leavis, F and Thompson, D (1948) *Culture and Environment*, London: Chatto and Windus.
Lumb, P (1989) "Recalling & Remodelling Textual Interpretation – English Teachers Approach the Commercial Mass Media", *English in Australia*, 87, March.
Mallick, D (1973) "A Small But Disturbing Experiment",*English in Australia*, 25, November.
Masterman, L (1983) "Media Education: Theoretical Issue and Practical Possibilities", *Metro*, 60, Summer.
Masterman, L (1985) *Teaching the Media*, London: Routledge.
Masterman, L (1989) "The Development of Media Education in Europe in the 1980s", *Metro*, 79, Autumn.
Menary, W (1971) "Why Screen?", *English in Australia*, 16, May.
Murdock, G and Phelps, G (1973) *Mass Media and the Secondary School*, London: Macmillan.
Peel, R and Hargreaves, S (1995) "Beliefs About English: Trends in Australia, England and the United States", *English in Education* Vol 29 No 3, Autumn.
Quin, R (1995) "Our Very Own Mid-Life Crisis", *Metro*, 102.
Tuman, M (1992) *Word Perfect: Literacy in the Computer Age*, London: Falmer.
Ulmer, G (1989) *"Teletheory: Grammatology in the Age of Video*, New York: Routledge.
Whitehead, F (1966) *The Disappearing Dais: A study of the principles and practice of English teaching*, London: Chatto and Windus.
Wilson, B (1987) "Theories of the Mass Media", *Metro* 72, Summer/Autumn.
Winn, M (1985) *The Plug-in-Drug*, New York: Penguin.

Grammar Poems

Even the strongest opponents of the teaching of Latinate grammar feel that the names of the main parts of speech ought to be known by pupils. One way to keep such terminology in front of pupils is to ask them to write 'grammar poems' to prescribed patterns. For example:

One noun	Tree
Two adjectives	white, tragic
A phrase	with uplifted arms
Verb and adverb	asks mutely
Interrogative	why?

8 English and the Mixed-Ability Classroom

Wayne Sawyer

'Mixed-ability' is not a concept suited to the closing years of the twentieth century in Australia. An approach to educational arrangements that uses terms like 'co-operation' and 'egalitarianism'does not sit easily in a world where 'individualism', 'competitiveness', 'efficiency' and 'enterprise' (for each, read 'exploitation' and/or 'greed') are the espoused values. What saturates educational debate in the '90s is the language of the market. 'Productivity' is what governments expect of teachers; students have become 'clients' and schools must 'add value' to them. 'Accountability' will deliver productivity and 'measurement' of 'outcomes' will be the instrument of accountability. In a world where taxation reform is a great adventure, the accountant is hero and the production line provides the ideal model of education, egalitarianism and co-operation seem very '60s' ideas (but then, even discussing values seems very "60s' today).

Indeed, the really major research into mixed-ability teaching was largely done in the '60s and '70s. While it would be untrue to say that mixed-ability research was always unequivocally against streaming, the general tendency, especially in those comparative studies that became selected for 'best-evidence' syntheses, was to show rather hard-nosed '90s' results in favour of mixed-ability classrooms.

Early Research

In 1962, Goldberg et al studied 3,000 pupils in New York over forty-three schools in which the pupils were in bands of varying ability ranges. After two years, ten of the eleven statistically significant comparisons on academic performance favoured students in classes with the broadest ability ranges.

In Sweden, Swennson investigated 11,000 pupils in 1962, and found initial academic advantages for streamed groups, but these disappeared by age 14 -15.

Borg's 1966 study of of 4,000 pupils in Utah from Grades 4 to 9 also found initial gains for the brighter students in streamed classes , but these gains, again, disappeared by 9th grade, while lower ability pupils in mixed-ability situations developed better study habits and better self-concepts.

In the UK, Barker Lunn studied 5,500 children in the late '60s in seventy-two schools and found no differences that could be attributed to streaming, in formal academic attainment in primary schools. On measures of social and emotional attainment, however, children of average and below-average ability showed improved attitudes to school work in a non-streamed situation.

McPhee's study of one Scottish secondary school in 1978 found no differences in the first year between graded and non-graded classes, and a shift in favour of the non-graded group in the second year, including among the most able students.

The studies of Banbury School in the mid-'70s (a school divided into parallel 'halls', two streamed and two mixed-ability) found social advantages in the mixed-ability situation, with clear academic gains for the least able students and slight academic gains for the most able (Newbold, 1977; Postlethwaite and Denton, 1978).

The evidence from this kind of research was convincing enough to have Elley draw the following conclusions by 1984:

✦ Streaming had not been shown to be superior to non-streaming as a method of promoting pupil achievement. What achievement differences did appear tended to favour pupils in non-streamed classes.

✦ Non-streamed classes enhanced the social and personality development of pupils.

✦ The attitudes and practices of teachers were shown to be more important than school organisation. Non-streaming lost its positive effects where teachers opposed it.

✦ Streaming exerted a polarising effect on achievement levels – the bright becoming brighter and the slow becoming slower.

Recent Syntheses of Research

In 1990, Slavin published an influential 'best-evidence synthesis' of research to date in which he concluded that "ability grouping plans have little or no effect on the achievement of secondary students . . . decisions about whether or not to group by ability must be made on bases other than likely impacts on achievement. Given the anti-democratic, anti-egalitarian nature of ability grouping, the burden of proof should be on those who would group rather than those who favour heterogeneous grouping, and in the absence of evidence that grouping is beneficial, it is hard to justify continuation of the practice."

Harlen and Malcolm's 1997 'best-evidence synthesis' concluded that in primary schools "it is of benefit for pupils to learn in mixed-ability groups, even if at times they are separated into ability groups", while in secondary schools, the research showed that streaming offered "no advantages for pupils'achievement, for any levels of ability. At the same time the research shows clearly that there were disadvantages: reinforced social class divisions, increased likelihood of delinquent behaviour in the later school years, lowered teacher expectations of the less able, bias and inconsistency in allocating pupils to ability groups, anxiety for pupils in the top streams struggling to keep up with the pace of the class." Like Elley, Harlen and Malcolm found that teacher behaviour had far more effect on pupil achievement than grouping, but that streaming as an answer to catering for individuals produced mostly negative efects on pupil motivation and the quality of their education.

Empirical research, then, seems to favour mixed-ability over streaming in a number of areas, including academic achievement, student motivation and student atttudes towards school. The moral arguments are even more clear:

✦ streaming is based on an assumption about the 'fixedness' of intellectual capacity;
✦ streaming is rarely accurate, whether based on IQ or examination results, and initial placement is usually irrevocable, especially as a self-fulfilling prophecy undoubtedly sets in;
✦ streaming strongly reinforces social stratification;
✦ the homogeneity of a streamed class is largely an illusion and yet it can lead to teachers not considering the individual needs of pupils.

General Mixed-ability Principles and English

Research has also shown what seem to be the characteristics of successful mixed-ability teaching. In summary, these seem to be:

✦ student-centred rather than teacher-dominated approaches – engaging students in active *doing* and working largely through small-group activities with whole class work as focus sessions, reporting sessions or for sharing;
✦ flexible class groupings;
✦ allowing student choice of activities;
✦ the availability of 'extension' activities for *all* students, but especially the most able.

Such characteristics are tailor-made for English. That list could easily appear in a how-to manual specific to English teaching. It has certainly been my experience that English teachers operating in the spirit of post-Dartmouth English, from the 'Growth model' through to 'Critical literacy' do not need to do anything very different in mixed-ability classes.

Flexible Grouping

This appears to be the key to successful mixed-ability teaching in English. While there are times when the class will operate as a single unit, particularly for 'focus' sessions, the bulk of mixed-ability teaching will be in small groups- sometimes pairs, sometimes larger groups and with groups varying according to the task. Tasks are simply typical English 'project' tasks – imaginative re-creation of literature, production of a class newspaper, improvised drama etc. Individual work will also occur, particularly for writing, silent reading and working on specific individual weaknesses.

Mostly (but not always) within-class streaming should be avoided.

Worksheets

One of the 'traps' which mixed-ability teachers seem occasionally to fall into is a stage in which they try to cater for individual abilities and needs through individual worksheets. In a well-meaning attempt to 'individualise', teachers create for themselves the problem of planning, in effect, up to thirty lessons/sets of activities per class lesson. To survive this, they are soon forced to produce worksheets demanding very low-levels of thinking as 'busy work' which is easily marked. Across the curriculum, this can be avoided by adapting the flexible grouping principle, rather than trying to individualise, AND by planning together across-the-year (eg across Year 9) as a faculty, rather than trying to plan only for one's own class in isolation.

Individualising

One of the advantages of mixed-ability teaching is the opportunity it provides for 'freeing up' teachers to work with individuals. I'm always amazed when teachers say that low achievers get lost in mixed-ability classes. I wonder if they've ever taught the bottom level Year 9 in a large comprehensive. Those students who formerly were in remedial classes obviously do need careful thought when planning, but working individually with three kids in your class who have real problems is a lot easier than trying to work with twenty-eight who do. This is also one case where having work-cards, used sparingly, but based on addressing specific weaknesses, can be an advantage. Also, use should be made of the support teacher on a rotating basis.

One answer to the issue of catering for the top students in these classes has been to provide 'extension' activities. Compulsory 'extension' activities may be perceived by capable students as punishment for 'finishing early' , but if a range of challenging elective activities were available for *all* students, the completion of which was attended by some recognition, this problem would be largely overcome. It is worth stressing again that in English classes, different levels of ability do not require different tasks. Avoiding the savage increase in planning and marking is built-in for English teachers, since *all* students can respond to an imaginative re-creation task such as re-telling a scene in a novel from a particular character's point of view. As Peter Jones argues, to such a task "we can expect a very wide range of responses, from the complex, subtle and exciting to the mundane ... Through various student interactions we can reasonably expect to increase the number of interesting responses and decrease the number of mundane ones" (Jones, 1991).

Assessment

An appropriate assessment policy is absolutely crucial to successful mixed-ability teaching. Placing weaker students in a mixed class and hanging onto competitive assessment is a recipe for disaster. Ranking is made to destroy any workshop/group/co-operative atmosphere in these classes. Brian Johnston's system of work-required contracts is an extremely useful one in mixed-ability. Work-required assessment is essentially goal-based, with students judged not against each other or against some ideal teacher norm, but purely on whether they achieve the goals set for particular tasks.

Students contract to complete certain tasks, with 'successful completion' being awarded a grade 'S' . Tasks 'not completed' are awarded the grade 'NC' and tasks for which students still need to master the skills are awarded a grade 'NS' ('not yet successfully completed'). In the latter case, the students and teacher work together to help the student gain the necessary skills and knowledge to successfully complete the task. There are no ranked grades and no ranked students. The assumption behind work-required assessment is that what the teacher offers is designed to help the student learn and that if the task is successfully completed, then nothing else needs to be said in terms of assessment – successful completion means learning and progress.

Standards for 'successful completion' are negotiated between teacher and student and students must be clear as to what 'success' in this task means before they begin. In a unit on *Bridge to Terabithia*, the teacher might set the task of writing as Jesse to an out-of-town friend reporting the death of Leslie. Successful completion of this task might well mean conveying a previously discussed set of emotional reactions which Jesse would have and which he woud be likely to convey to another friend. His plans for his sister May Belle with respect to Terabithia might also be discussed. Length might also be a criterion in successful completion.

I believe teachers ought to be rigorous in applying the standards for successful completion, so that this form of non-competitive assessment is not perceived as 'soft' and so that students do gain the sense that successful completion is genuinely associated with more learning. The problem then becomes, "What about the weaker student who tries and tries and just won't get there on 'X' task?" Teachers will have their own answers to this. My own is to say that I'll work almost endlessly with the student to get him/her there and, in the end, if they don't make the standard, I'll sometimes drop it to meet them, but reluctantly – because I'd rather walk the tightrope of deciding between absolute standards and weaker students so as to be able to reject the complaint that work-required assessment is about lower standards.

One Teacher's Story

From the mid-'80s to the mid-'90s, I worked in two English departments in the outer western suburbs of Sydney at a time when those departments were going over to entirely mixed-ability teaching in Years 7-10. In one of these – Blacktown Girls High School – I was Head Teacher of English. Both departments contained highly experienced, committed and innovative teachers, though the degree of commitment to mixed-ability differed in each at the beginning of the move away from streaming.

One of the issues in mixed-ability teaching is of course the defining one of catering for differing levels of ability in the class. There are of course many ways to address this issue, but one of the ways both faculties explored was through faculty programming.

Programming Writing:

One of the things to which we felt a faculty needed to be particularly committed was a strong writing program. We adopted an approach of basing the faculty program around, among other things, a sequenced series of writing assignments, so that, whatever else students 'did' in writing in their individual classes over the four year period from Years 7-10, they would have had a sequence of common experiences. The program used was James Moffett's *Active Voice*, in which Moffett sets out a series of writing assignments that, in sequence, take students through increasing degrees of abstraction and increasingly remote audiences. It is, of course, these two sets of sequences on which Moffett's influential theory of language development in *Teaching the Universe of Discourse* is based. Over four years, students in these schools would complete the full *Active Voice* program to run alongside their teacher's chosen activities.

We were aware of the problems of this kind of approach to programming. A sequence like Moffett's is meant to be adapted to individual abilities, rather than imposed regardless of where individual students are 'at'. Some students may never reach the most abstract, remote-audience activities in Moffett's sequence. It could justifiably be argued that we were imposing a sequence on our student population rather than developing programs from what we knew of the students. Teachers were, however, free to develop their own units for classes other than a requirement to include a form of the appropriate *Active Voice* activity. It was rarely difficult to find ways of integrating the particular *Active Voice* assignment into the current class unit and, at the same time, we were able to say that built into each class' every unit was some kind of measure of development simply from successfully completing a task that was theoretically more difficult than an equivalent task in the previous unit. No-one could claim that mixed-ability was 'diluting' the 'rigour' of our work. Paradoxically, then, the common tasks which were increasingly challenging were seen as providing a strong underpinning for writing in our mixed-ability classes.

We also decided that in a group workshop approach to writing, which was virtually universal across these two departments, we were happy for students to be working on common tasks for some, even for much, of the time. Students could achieve at their own level on these tasks, but at the same time, there was a sense of moving forward as students also moved along Moffett's two sequences of development through successful completion of these assignments.

Programming Reading:

I was fortunate to be at this time in two departments that were relatively 'resource rich' . In one this was because the school was still relatively young and still resourcing off its 'establishment grant'. In the other, I was very lucky to be a Head Teacher under a Principal who believed in the rather quaint notion that government money to education ought to be spent on the kids. When NSW introduced global budgeting in the late '80s, he devolved money to faculties and developed an allocation formula that saw the greatest amount of money going to where the numbers of kids were greatest – that is, to English! At the same time, in both departments, there were a core of people very up-to-date on adolescent literature.

Thus mixed boxes of books became the staple diet of these classrooms. Every Year from 7-10 had a large collection of such mixed sets of books – usually 4-5 copies of 6-7 titles in a box, occasionally 30-35 individual titles. Whole-class novels were, of course, still taught, but 'class sets' in the bookroom(s) became the minority category. It is often difficult to find a novel to appeal to all members of a class at any time. Mixed-ability classes show up this problem clearly, so providing a range of novels with a range of interests and a range of reading 'levels' is important.

Both departments sought to create and continue a 'culture of reading' in the schools and boxes of new, appealing, high quality adolescent literature with a good variety of titles went a long way to achieving this end. Part of this thrust was a faculty policy of every student reading a minimum of two novels in every five-week unit, regardless of whether the class was studying a common novel. The boxes of books again meant that this was genuinely not difficult to achieve.

If 'resource richness' is not the reality in a faculty, there are still a number of ways in which the aims of mixed boxes can be achieved:

✦ class libraries where teachers have 'home rooms'. Municipal libraries' book sales, second hand book stores and 'op shops' are a good source for cheap and often surprisingly recent titles for this purpose;

✦ a temporary/ frequently 'turned over' class library can be made from the teacher's borrowing a box of forty titles from the school library for a number of weeks to be loaned out within the class;

✦ if the librarian won't allow even this option, then *frequent* and *regular* borrowing visits to the school library become necessary.

Conclusion

If English is about developing as a user of the language, then being exposed to a variety of language uses ought to be the norm in English classes. The mixed-ability classroom is the classroom in which this is most likely to occur. As long as teachers are committed to a model of teaching which allows for flexibility in class arrangements and are prepared to use the 'freed up' class time to work with individuals, then a view of education that emphasises egalitarianism and co-operation can be made to work even in the '90s. Both experience and research say that results for all students should even improve – something even the economic rationalists would have to applaud.

References

Carey, Mark (1991) "Mixed-Ability English Resources", *Priorities 1*, Sydney: Australian Education Network.

Barker Lunn, J C (1970) *Streaming in the Primary School*, Slough: NFER.

Borg, W R (1966) *Ability Grouping in the Public Schools: a Field Study*, Madison: Dembar Educational Research Services.

Elley, W (1984) "To Stream or Not to Stream?: A Review of Research on Streaming". *Set, 2*.

Goldberg, M L et al (1962) *The Effect of Ability Grouping: A Comparative Study of Broad, Medium and Narrow Range Classes in the Elementary School, New York*, Columbia University: Teachers College Press.

Harlen, W and Malcolm, H (1997) *Setting and Streaming: A Review of Research*, Edinburgh: Scottish Council for Research in Education.

Johnston, Brian (1987) *Assessing English*, Milton Keynes: Open University Press.

Jones, Peter (1991) "Mixed-Ability Teaching and English", CASE Conference, Wahroonga, NSW, May.

Jones, P and Tucker, E (eds) (1990) *Mixed-Ability Teaching: Classroom Experiences in English, ESL, Mathematics and Science*, Sydney: St Clair Press.

McPhee, A (1978) *Mixed Ability and Streamed Grouping in Third Year Secondary English*, Edinburgh: Scottish Curriculum Service.

Moffett, James (1981) *Active Voice*, Montclair, NJ: Boynton/Cook.

Moffett, James (1968) *Teaching the Universe of Discourse*, Boston: Houghton Mifflin.

Newbold, D (1977) *Ability Grouping: the Banbury Enquiry*, London: NFER.

Postlethwaite, K and Denton, C (1978) *Streams for the Future*, Brackley: Pubansco.

Slavin, Robert E (1990) *Achievement Effects of Ability Grouping in Secondary Schools: A Best-evidence Synthesis*, University of Wisconsin-Madison: National Center on Effective Secondary Schools.

Swennson, N-E (1962) "Ability Grouping and Scholastic Achievement", *Educational Research*, 5:1, November.

Reading: *RIB-IT* (Read-In-Bed)

At Swinburne Technical School in the early 1980s, Andrew Taylor, Gary Shaw and Jo Goodman launched RIB-IT, a program to promote reading. The program began with Years 7and 8, constantly stressed reading for enjoyment, made sure that all materials were attactively presented, carefully selected the recommended books and offered a variety of post-reading activities designed to promote books to other students. The program was quickly adopted by other schools (at least one as far away as Canada!).

Jo Goodman (nd) *RIB-IT* Melbourne: VATE

9 Small-Group Work

David Baxter

Background and Theoretical Underpinnings

"How do I know what I think until I see what I say?"
(Attributed to E M Forster)

When I began teaching in 1975, this quotation seemed to provide for me a fundamental rationale. I had studied at Sydney University, where the English courses were dominated by the Great Works and the sort of literary analysis which prohibited the word "I" from any essay while the English Education courses were full of the "New English", in which the word "I" was a privileged participant in student writing and speaking. I left the university naively persuaded that English teaching should concern itself with providing a forum for students to articulate their thoughts, ideas and feelings, as well as their analyses, concerning literature, media and life itself. In my innocence, I believed that English had to provide stimulation from an ever-expanding repertoire of material, including that of the students' own lives; it had to entail the freedom of individuals to express passionately held views and it had to develop and refine the language skills needed to create imaginative, personal responses. One of the most obvious classroom implications of such a rationale was a firm belief in the efficacy of small-group work, the scenario within which it would be possible for every student to find out what they thought by seeing what they and others said.

Many of the seminal writers about English teaching in this period, notably Douglas Barnes, Harold Rosen and James Britton in *Language, the Learner and the School* (1969), based their rationalisations of the personal growth model of English on transcripts of students talking in small groups about a variety of topics. Barnes, in analysing patterns of language and teacher-student interaction in a number of classrooms, found that teachers dominated classroom talk and that students were primarily called upon to guess what was in the teacher's mind when asked to participate. He maintained that the ability to merely imitate teacher language was not enough to indicate student learning – "it is only when they (students) 'try it out' in reciprocal exchanges so that they modify the way they use language to organise reality that they are able to find new functions for language in thinking and feeling" (Barnes, Britton and Rosen, 1969, pp61-62). James Britton took this a step further in his analysis of a number of group discussions in which he presented "group effort at understanding" as the key to both learning and growth. All three writers emphasised the primacy of talk in developing both language and thinking skills. Rosen claimed that unless the student encountered other voices, ideas and language patterns than the teacher's, then the "disadvantage of tightly circumscribing the responses and consequently the extent to which a pupil can formulate and represent in words what he is thinking" (Barnes et al, 1969, p125) arises inevitably. Small-group discussion therefore was seen as providing a forum in which the students could feel freer to experiment, theorise and discover by articulating their own versions of learning.

Douglas Barnes, in particular, was concerned to create group situations in which students were given minimal guidelines from the teacher in their dealings with a poem and asked to discuss it in any way that was relevant to them. I remember reading the transcripts of these "conversations" with considerable admiration for the informal depth and freshness of student responses. In this period the overwhelming preoccupation of the post-Dartmouth writers seemed to be to free the classroom from the domination of teacher-talk and teacher-thought and to replace it with structures enabling student response to occur in as unfettered a condition as possible. This is not to suggest, however, that these writers lacked any awareness of the practical problems involved in bringing such conditions to fruition in the classroom – Leslie Stratta, John Dixon and Andrew Wilkinson in *Patterns of Language* (1973), another influential text in my beginning years, included a number of cautionary tales about the nature of group dynamics (especially the destructive potential of participants who see group discussion as a competition and who attempt to dominate it quite ruthlessly) in their chapter entitled "Classroom Interaction", which asserted a definite role for the teacher in managing small-group work.

Since 1975, the theoretical ground has shifted, but the use of small-group work has continued and been adapted to serve newer emphases like co-operative learning, problem-solving and whole language. One of the fundamentals of the last view is that learning should be natural, active and collaborative and therefore that small groups provide an excellent opportunity to use language in a way that allows students to learn new things as well as to express themselves.

The Syllabuses in New South Wales

The use of small-group work has actually been enshrined in NSW English syllabuses for K-6 and 7-10. Both documents present "Talking and Listening" as a discrete strand of equal value with "Reading and Writing", and within that strand emphasise the need to balance whole class discussion with small-group interaction. Thus, in the Years 7-10 Syllabus, Assumption 1 in the "Talking and Listening" Section emphasises the primary role of talking and listening in shaping and revealing students' identities as they strive to make meaning, express their feelings and order their experiences of the world, and gives small-group work equal status with whole-class discussion as a natural way of fulfilling that role in the classroom (*English Syllabus, Years 7-10*, 1987, p22). According to the Syllabus, small groups provide ideal opportunities for students to:

✧ *express and reflect upon experiences and feelings;*
✧ *explore ideas in a consequence-free environment;*
✧ *speculate and hypothesise;*
✧ *talk their way into understanding;*
✧ *argue a case, develop an idea, and solve problems;*
✧ *interact with others to see how they cope with problems;*
✧ *share possible solutions, ideas, and experiences with literature and other texts;*
✧ *develop an understanding of different points of view;*
✧ *extend their experience and repertoire of registers.*
(*English Syllabus, Years 7-10*, 1987, pp 22- 26)

In short, the Years 7-10 Syllabus explicitly acknowledges the efficacy of small-group work in planning for and achieving student language growth and mandates its use in classrooms.

Using Small-Group Work in the Classroom – the Practical Issues

Group work requires planning, preparation and organisation, just like any other lesson or series of lessons. Students cannot be assumed to be able to work effectively in small groups – they need practice and training. Indeed, they need to be convinced of the worth and relevance of group work. Teachers need both to be explicit about why they are asking students to work in small groups and also to ensure that the guidelines and conventions of such work are clear and specific. Students who lack self-discipline in whole-class situations are unlikely to suddenly develop it merely by being asked to form small groups. However, students who appear to lack control and purpose in small groups can be trained (as well as constrained) to contribute meaningfully if certain basic conditions are established:

✦ the size of the group is not too large, but suited to the demands of the task (about four is good for discussion, whereas a smaller number is better for writing, enabling each student to contribute meaningfully);

- the composition of the group enables co-operation and task achievement;
- the activity is interesting and enjoyable as well as challenging and educational;
- the purpose of the activity is clear and precise;
- students are sure of their roles and what they are supposed to achieve or produce;
- a suitable space for working unimpeded by other groups can be created or found;
- the necessary resources for the activity are available;
- the amount of time given for the task is appropriate;
- the rationale for assessing the activity is clear and fair.

Forming groups can be fun. For instance, if an activity requires seven groups, a teacher can create a learning experience by distributing a card to each student with a name or picture on it and then telling the class that the cards fall into seven groups, each with four members who have something in common. Students then need to negotiate with others, use some problem-solving skills, and exhibit some knowledge in order to form themselves into the designated groups. The result is a talking, listening, thinking and co-operating activity which is enjoyable and avoids any problems which may occur if a teacher allows free group choice or tries to be too dictatorial. On other occasions, where discussion about feelings, ideas or responses to literature is concerned, it may be advisable to allow students to choose their own groups as this may facilitate open and sincere exchange of views. Similarly, in a research project, groups of students with similar interests can be formed. Ultimately, the teacher's role is to ensure that groups work well and this means knowing the students well enough to ensure that no disastrous combinations occur no matter what the task. It also means that students should be taught the required skills to be able to function effectively in groups. The rules for behaviour and co-operation need to be explicitly established before embarking on sophisticated tasks in groups. Such rules can themselves be the subject of small-group discussion. Short, specific activities, like pairs of students arranging the events of a story in chronological order, can provide an ideal lead-up to longer, more demanding tasks like drama performances, research projects and written imaginative recreations of literature involving larger numbers in each group.

It is therefore a mistake to think that group work requires minimal contribution from the teacher. The teacher's role does not end with the planning and setting of tasks, but continues as the groups meet and function. The teacher needs to prompt, focus and stimulate discussion without dominating, answer questions, solve practical difficulties, monitor the progress and behaviour of groups, ensure that adequate resources are available and assess both the process and the product efficiently and fairly. In many "whole language" classrooms, while some students are involved in group activities, others are working individually, which gives the teacher the opportunity to interact with individuals at the point of need and to monitor their progress. Reid, Forrestal and Cook in their seminal book, *Small Group Learning in the Classroom*, (1989), recommend that teachers send disruptive students to a desk which is isolated from the rest of the class. They argue that such students need to be closely monitored, but are likely to succumb eventually to the attractions of working with peers rather than on their own.

Some students will claim that they don't like working in groups, but prefer to work independently. This may be because they are not convinced of the fairness of group work – especially if they have had previous experiences where they have done the bulk of the work and other less enthusiastic and responsible students have benefited as a result. Reid, Forrestal and Cook recommend allowing students to work alone when they feel a strong desire to do so, which may be appropriate when the focus is on research, or each group member has a specific role or area of expertise to develop, but can be problematic if a whole-group presentation or performance is the essence of the activity. Perhaps this comes back to the central place of talking and listening in the English curriculum – development of the ability to function orally is as important in the Years 7-10 syllabus as the ability to read and write proficiently and a substantial body of research dating back to Dixon, Barnes and Britton has established the efficacy of prior talking and listening in promoting good writing. Consequently it is the responsibility of the English teacher to ensure that each student be given the opportunities to develop both oral and co-operative skills and experiences.

Teachers need to establish the significance of group work (the extent to which employers value their employees being able to work in teams may provide some incentive here) and to provide a range of tasks that seem fair and achievable for everyone, including the socially isolated. While there may be occasions when students need to be allowed to work independently, separately from the groups, this should not diminish the teacher's expectation that the benefits of small-group work should be shared by all students. Drawing unwilling students into a group is often a matter of finding a topic in which they are interested and ensuring that the role assigned to each student in the group entails equality of effort and/or caters for the perceived strengths and comfort of the student concerned. Thus it's often a matter of tactics, manipulation and judgement rather than of enforcing hard and fast rules. If group work is fun, then students are generally keen to participate in it, if for no other reason than that they are afraid of missing out on something.

The plenary follow-up to group work also requires teacher management – it is all too easy for reporting back sessions to bog down and bore both students and teacher if they go on too long or are too detailed. Presentations can be visual (a poster, a mind map, a poem) or a performance (a short drama scene, a poetry recital replete with actions, a mime) or a summary involving group choice of the major priorities of a task (the ten commandments of writing poetry, or the top seven reasons why Baz Luhrmann's *Romeo and Juliet* is better than *The Simpsons*).

Group work also requires (and encourages) responsible contributions from students. For those new to group work, it may be helpful for specific roles within each group either to be assigned to or chosen by its members. Some commonly used roles are the Leader/Organiser who keeps the group on task (without resorting to fascism), the Reporter who is responsible for presenting the group's deliberations to the class, the Scribe who takes down the group's ideas and consensus and the Timekeeper who watches the clock. However, Reid, Forrestal and Cook maintain that fixed roles can be counter-productive, with the position of Leader being particularly problematic if it inhibits the other students from contributing to or experiencing ownership of the group's work (Reid et al, 1989, p. 38). They also encourage all students to take their own notes rather than rely on a single designated Recorder – again in the name of responsibility, ownership and the clear establishment of the idea that group work is a meaningful part of the learning process and should be taken seriously by every learner (p39).

Group work lends itself quite naturally to peer assessment and evaluation. Peer assessment can enable a teacher to monitor each group closely and to get a feel for the quality of interaction within groups. It is important that the criteria for any assessment of group work be clearly established at the very beginning of the activity, that it be perceived by students to be fair and, above all, equitable, in terms of the effort required of each student.

Where groups produce an assessable product, for which all group members are to receive the same mark, grade or comment, it is important that it be a genuine team effort and not the result of the major contribution of any individual within the group. Activities need to be designed in such a way that all members have ownership and responsibility for the product of their labours.

Of course, not all group work results in the production of something assessable. Where students are discussing their reactions to a poem, TV program or story, for instance, and report or display their ideas, this may be simply part of a process which will be assessed later in individual writing. Some of the most powerful achievements of small groups comprise the informal sharing and exploration of ideas and experiences and are blessedly free of assessment overtones.

Suggestions for Further Reading

In 1982, the NSW Department of School Education produced a booklet, *Planning for small-group Work in English*, the major purposes of which were to demystify group work for teachers, to provide them with "Seventy-Seven Great Ideas" for integrating it into mainstream English teaching and to address the practical issues in managing it effectively. It is still a useful document, particularly for the beginning teacher.

Since then, small-group learning has increasingly been seen as more than just a teaching strategy but as the fundamental unit of organisation in classrooms based on the principles of co-operative learning. This perspective is particularly applicable in the primary school, where the opportunities for sustained and intense interaction and the development of long-term patterns and rituals of classroom process and management are unrestricted by forty-minute periods or a succession of different teachers.

Reid, Forrestal and Cook, in one of the most influential recent books on the subject, use group work as part of an overall view of optimal, collaborative learning in which students are divided into Home Groups, Sharing Groups and the Whole-Class Group depending upon the needs of the particular task they are performing. Their model of learning is a process involving the stages of Engagement (in which students encounter new information), Exploration (in which students grapple with this new information), Transformation (in which students in Home Groups use or work with this information), Presentation (in which students present the products of their work to an audience) and Reflection (where students evaluate their learning). Group work here is more than an occasional classroom strategy but becomes instead an integral part of each learning experience within the class. It seems true to say that the relatively unstructured approach to group work of the pioneers like Barnes and Britton has been replaced by a highly organised classroom regime in the name of the same student-centred principles which so drove the Dartmouth generation.

Co-operative learning theory and methodology can be seen as representing an attempt to fashion and develop a rigorous practice from the insights of those who saw English as a vehicle for the personal growth of students. This philosophy moves beyond the early emphasis on liberating and legitimising student attitudes, experiences and beliefs, to locating small-group work within the context of learning about the external world and using it as an organisational principle for engaging with that world. There is a sense, then, in which this sort of co-operative learning ethos is a direct legacy of the "New English" of the Sixties and Seventies.

References

Some useful books dealing with the principles and mechanics of group work from the collaborative and co-operative learning standpoint are:

Reid, Jo-Anne, Forrestal, Peter and Cook, Jonathan (1989) *Small Group Learning in the Classroom*, Rozelle and Scarborough, PETA: Chalkface Press.

Dalton, Joan (1985) *Adventures in Thinking*, Melbourne: Nelson.

Hill, Susan and Hill, Tim, (1990) *The Collaborative Classroom*, South Yarra: Eleanor Curtain.

Bennett, Barrie, Rolheiser-Bennett, Carol and Stevahn, Laurie (1991) *Co-operative Learning – Where Heart Meets Mind*, Toronto: Educational Connections.

McGregor, Robert (1989), *Working Together – The Co-operative English Classroom*, Melbourne: Nelson.

Another useful book containing international perspectives is:

Brubacher, Mark, Payne, Ryder and Rickett, Kemp (eds) (1990) *Perspectives on small-group Learning – Theory and Practice*, Ontario: Rubicon Publishing.

Other References

Barnes, Douglas, Rosen, Harold and Britton, James (1969), *Language, the Learner and the School*, Harmondsworth: Penguin.

NSW Board of Secondary Education (1987), *English Syllabus, Years 7-10*, Sydney.

Stratta, Leslie, Dixon, John and Wilkinson, Andrew (1973) *Patterns of Language*, London: Heinemann Education.

Fun With Words: 'Misprinted' Titles

The Folio Society, which produces deluxe editions of books for its members, in 1997 ran a competition which invited competitors to produce misprinted titles (with accompanying blurbs) for famous books. Some entries were inspired by food: Golding's *Lord of the Fries*, Hugo's *The Lunchpack of Notre Dame*, Theroux's *The Mosquito Roast*, Haggard's *King Solomon's Mints*. Others thought of animal stories: Dickens' *Bleak Mouse*, Graham Greene's *A Gnu for Sale*, Melville's *Moby Duck*. Other titles included *The Thirty-Nine Stops* ("an exciting tale of life on a London bus"), *The Honda of the Baskervilles*, *Gullible's Travels* ("he believed in travel brochures"). Then there was *Scent and Sensibility*, in which the Dashwood sisters show that aromatherapy makes everything come up smelling of roses: "Every single man in possession of a good fortune must be in want of a whiff."

Your seniors could be invited to produce their own misprinted titles, accompanied by appropriate dustcover blurbs.

10 Second Language Learners in the English Classroom

Barbara McLean

Introduction

"How can I teach these kids – their writing is incomprehensible, and it's so hard to get them to participate."

Words similar to the above might be heard on many an occasion in a range of staffrooms, and the students being referred to are most likely to be learners of English as a second language. In all English classrooms there will be a range of ability. For native speakers of the language this range in performance can be attributed to things such as interest, previous experience and whether there is some develop- mental disability. For second language learners, even though these same attributions may apply, the source of any weakness in English is likely to be different and is complicated by the reduced exposure to English. Thus, even though a native speaker and an ESL student may score similarly on assessments, it is highly likely that the underlying factors which contributed to this score were different and therefore the approaches to teaching and the content of the teaching will not necessarily be the same for the two groups. One implication of this is that teachers should think carefully about grouping ESL learners with native speakers who are themselves having problems with their English classes. This is not to suggest that ESL students should not be in classes with native speakers. Indeed, the social integration and potential for role models in language in such a situation is much higher. Rather the issue becomes one of *which* native speakers it is more appropriate for ESL students to be grouped with. One of the worst situations would be a group of low-achieving native speakers who are also disruptive in class.

In the following pages several aspects of English will be touched on in relation to ESL students in the English classroom with the aim of providing teachers with some insight into their needs and some suggestions as to how their language development may be furthered.

Oracy

"They won't speak up. It's so hard to understand them"

Speaking and listening are increasingly being recognised as substantial parts of the English program and this is an area with which ESL students often need specific help. It is of course not easy to generalise, as some students will appear very fluent when engaging in normal, everyday conversation, while others are so painfully shy it is hard to get a word out of them. For others, accent may exacerbate difficulties in communication. In such a situation, the emphasis in teaching needs to be on developing student confidence and a positive attitude, on using prosodic features well, and on knowledge of appropriate registers. Each of these will be explored further in the following paragraphs.

Reticence in Speaking

Confidence is a major issue for many students. Tsui (1996), reporting on some action research in relation to student participation in class, noted that over 70% of a group of 38 English teachers in Hong Kong secondary schools identified getting more oral response as one of their major problems. While level of English proficiency was a factor in this result, also significant were lack of confidence and fear of making mistakes, together with teacher behaviours such as inadequate wait time, vague questioning, and uneven allocation of turns. One teacher found that most of her students thought there was no incentive to speak in English, with 82% of them giving lack of confidence as a reason for not trying. In the same class, students often responded almost inaudibly, resisting teacher efforts to get them to speak up. In a Year 9 class, students commented that they were afraid their answers would not satisfy the teacher.

One of the strategies which seemed to improve response was to actually give the students time to write down an answer before being called upon. Another was to allow the students to first check their answers with peers, or to engage in discussion which enabled them to rehearse their thoughts in a supportive environment. When confronted with a question, another teacher gave students the option of answering the question, asking for more time, or asking for more help. This approach had the advantage of putting responsibility on the student to respond in a positive way, and avoided the uncertainty of silence. The use of strategies such as these demonstrates the role the teacher can play in facilitating and supporting student response, as distinct from laying the blame for lack of participation on student inadequacies.

Prosody

In relation to prosodic features, it is widely accepted that difficulties in communication arise not so much from accent, but from intonation, stress, and rhythm. These of course are not totally separate entities, but interrelate significantly with each other. They are also things for which teachers can provide input. Prepared *choral reading* is one obvious technique which focuses on rhythm and much poetry lends itself to this. The key to success here is the preparation, involving much discussion and rehearsal of the lines. With a focus on rhythm, *jazz chants* are another useful technique which can be both creative and fun – creative in that they lend themselves to students writing their own, and fun in the performance itself. A variant of choral reading is the more dramatic presentation of *Readers Theatre* (see also p305). In Readers Theatre, two or more participants present a prepared text, reading from handheld scripts. It is different from a play, in that characters do not necessarily read whole parts, and the focus is on the language rather than the action. The story is brought to life through voices and minimal gestures rather than broad scale action. Initially, the teacher would need to demonstrate and then model how a text could be adapted. The different ways of assigning lines help students focus on the interpretation. For example, all the narration can be given to a narrator, and dialogue to the characters. Alternatively, phrases can be highlighted by being spoken by different people, having the effect of emphasising particular thoughts, or narration can be spoken by a chorus, which tends to give an impression of universality. Perhaps a brief extract from a well known poem may illustrate some of the potential of Readers Theatre.

Narrator A:	At last the people in a body
	To the Town Hall came flocking
Group 1:	Tis clear
Narrator B:	Cried they
Group 2	Our Mayor's a noddy
Group 3:	And as for our corporation
All:	Shocking
Man:	To think we buy gowns lined with ermine
Woman:	For dolts that won't determine
All:	What's best to rid us of our vermin.

From *The Pied Piper of Hamelin* as interpreted in Sloyer, S (1982)

For ESL students in the mainstream classroom, working on something like Readers Theatre in small groups provides them with a supportive structure in which they are able to discuss, to practice, and then to participate with more confidence. Excellent texts to work with for Readers Theatre include narrative poetry and picture story books which tend to have been written to be read aloud in any case, with shorter sentences, a good plot and quite often some degree of humour. This can particularly be found in the alternative versions of various fairy tales such as *Prince Cinders* by Babette Cole, *The True Story of the Three Little Pigs by A. Wolf* written by Jon Scieszka or other sources such as *Politically Correct Bedtime Stories* by James Finn Garner. These stories appeal to the more sophisticated teenager who might at first be put off by the notion of reading fairy tales. However, if such materials are used with ESL learners, it will be essential to check they have an understanding of the original story in order to be able to appreciate the humour of the variation.

Register

For ESL students, with their more limited experience of the wide range of uses of English, interpreting different registers is often a challenging task. How many different ways are there to say "Hello"? *Hello* to a friend you haven't seen in a long time. *Hello* to a friend you saw recently. *Hello* to an acquaintance you don't particularly like. *Hello* to a superior. This is just looking at the way it is spoken rather than the different forms that could be used from the more colloquial *Hi!* to the more formal *Good morning.* In what situation would you choose one form rather than another? Interpretation or 'reading between the lines' is also just as important in listening as it is in reading. Focus on activities which give students practice in guessing situations from listening to spoken excerpts can help strengthen their skills in this area.

Knowing that ESL students are likely to have more difficulty in picking out main points from the spoken word, and in remembering large chunks of information, teachers themselves can help by providing a clear context for what is being talked about by engaging in appropriate pre-listening activities, and also by writing key points on the board.

Reading

"You never know if they really understand."

Many ESL students have difficulty with reading. It takes them longer to process material, and they are often hesitant in reading aloud. Even should the student read a passage fluently there is no guarantee of understanding. Indeed, it is much harder to read for meaning when you are concentrating on other factors such as pronunciation and looking at individual words. One way to help students with this is to always give them an opportunity to pre-read the passage or prepare for the reading in some other way. Student responses on a typical comprehension task can also mask underlying difficulties. This is largely because many questions require low level responses which can be found and copied out from the text. Alternatively, with higher order questions, the student may lack the language with which to express the ideas. It can be a useful practice therefore to substitute Three Level Reading Guides for more standard comprehensions. These take more time to prepare, but are well worth the effort. The key feature of these guides is that instead of questions, statements are made with which the student has to agree or disagree. These statements are at three different levels – literal comprehension, interpretive comprehension, and applied comprehension. As well as stating *true* or *false*, the student is required to provide evidence for their response. Some examples of these guides can be found in Morris and Stewart-Dore (1984).

Vocabulary

In the area of reading, one of the most limiting factors for ESL students is gaps in vocabulary. This is perhaps a fairly obvious statement, but it is perhaps the nature of the vocabulary gaps that may need more teasing out. All students need to learn the technical and more unusual words of a language, and teachers generally are alert to this and provide specific help. Also, ESL students tend to refer to the dictionary a great deal. However, it is often to refer to the more common words that are not thought unusual enough to explain or to explore different connotations that can cause problems. The other extreme when explaining vocabulary is to focus on almost every second word, with the result that it is hard to see the forest for the trees, and very little else gets done. It is important to remember that the meaning of the text is the main focus – not isolated words.

Teaching vocabulary is much more than giving a definition or encouraging students to look the meaning up in a dictionary. Research quoted by Nation (1990, p42) suggests that many repetitions of a word are necessary before it enters the repertoire of a student. We also need to know a great deal about the word – what it sounds like, what it looks like, in what patterns the word occurs, what words or types of word are likely to be found before or after the word, how common the word is, where it can be used, and what some synonyms are.

Michael Lewis in his book *The Lexical Approach* argues that the kinds of definitions we often give, or that are to be found in dictionaries, are not necessarily the most helpful. He suggests that we gain meaning most easily by focusing on contrast. For example, explaining how a bush differs from a tree is easier and more useful than trying to define exactly what a bush is. (Lewis, 1993, p79). This notion of taking the general exemplar and then identifying the elements that differ has a long pedigree in the literature on learning concepts, and would seem to have very relevant practical teaching application.

Lewis also refers to the importance of lexical environment which is a representation of our world experience in helping us to decide on which of a variety of synonyms is the more appropriate. We know from our experience in which context we would be more likely to use bowl, glass, cup or beaker with reference to a container of water. We know, that within our culture, we would be more likely to refer to a saucer of milk but not a saucer of water, and we would be able to infer, again from world knowledge, that in the latter instance, reference is probably being made to an animal, and specifically to what animal. It is important to recognise that different cultures may have a different set of references for a word, only some of which may overlap English usage. It is quite often this apparent similarity of a word which can interfere with appropriate usage in the new language.

Importance of Cultural Knowledge

Relevant cultural background knowledge is a significant area of need for ESL students. It is likely that much of the students' own background knowledge does not mesh very well with what is being studied within the Australian curriculum and students have had nowhere near as much time or opportunity to build up the same kind of experiences that the Australian born students have had. Knowledge of people and events is different. The effect of this can be illustrated very well from the newspaper article on page 124. While it is written in English, the events referred to are from another country and another decade. This causes problems even for native speakers.

Some of the meaning in this report is lost if the reader does not know who Canute was – or more to the point, that he was famous for believing he was so powerful he could hold the tide back. Even though there are clues in the text, most native speaking readers I have used the text with don't pay attention to them. And second language learners seem to know even less where to look. Then there is the whole scenario related to the Westminster system of government and party politics, as well as a lot of metaphorical language such as "the rising tide of pacificism", "frantically buttonholing colleagues" etc. It is also interesting to note the choice of "rising tide" to fit in with the Canute theme. It is these nuances that are likely to be missed by L2 readers.

There are two main points that I think this text highlights. Firstly, background knowledge facilitates understanding and the ease with which a passage is read and understood. Secondly, gaps in knowledge alone do not make a passage inaccessible. It is more a question of how many gaps. If there is not enough to hang on to, then comprehension fails, and frustration heightens. Clearly in such circumstances, it is really helpful for the teacher to preview material, looking closely at the assumed knowledge, and then providing relevant background knowledge through a range of activities which might include for example, pictorial input, summaries, explanations, analogies, or some key vocabulary.

Media

While not all newspaper reports are like the one referred to above, newspaper work in classrooms can be extraordinarily difficult for ESL learners. One cannot assume that students have familiarity with the events or people being referred to. English newspapers may not be in the home, nor television or

A soaking on tbe beach . . .
a snub by the Left

CANUTE KINNOCK

By GORDON GREIG, Political Editor

NEIL KINNOCK, just elected Labour's youngest leader at 41, saw an old party tide threaten to swamp his new beginning last night.

Once again, the nightmare question came up: How far are you going to dismantle Britain's nuclear defence shield?

The answer helped Michael Foot lose the last election and from the way the argument was boiling at Brighton, it clearly threatened to help Mr Kinnock lose the next one.

His induction to the mantle of leadership began with a soaking on Brighton beach as he stumbled and fell at the sea's edge while posing for photographers. But the embarrassment of that Canute-like ducking was nothing to the problems of a backroom row between Labour's Left and Right over the rising tide of pacifism and one-sided nuclear disarmament in the party.

Suicide

An angry session of the National Executive provided a curtain-raiser to a debate on Wednesday which may nail young Mr Kinnock more firmly than ever to getting rid of all nuclear weapons.

It saw the novice leader frantically buttonholing colleagues in an attempt to avert what he sees as political suicide. It also saw Denis Healey angrily pounding the table and warnings from Anthony Wedgwood Benn and Ken Livingstone that Mr Kinnock could blow it in the next year if he does not stick to Leftwing policies.

And there was a blunt message to Mr Kinnock from veteran Leftwinger Joan Maynard at a fringe meeting: "If you don't walk your shoes straight we'll have you next year."

But for a few moments the trendy new leader enjoyed the razzamatazz of an election night with an overwhelming victory for the 'dream ticket' – Mr Kinnock plus Roy Hattersley as his deputy.

The result of the leadership ballot with Mr Kinnock streets ahead of his nearest rival, Mr Hattersley, and Peter Shore and E Rick Heffer nowhere, produced an explosion of cheers.

Mr Kinnock clenched his hands about his head boxer-style and gave his wife – and inspiration – Glenys, a hearty kiss.

Mr Hattersley's subsequent election as deputy produced

Turn to page 2, col 1

radio news regularly listened to. Newspaper reports also have a particular style where information is often presented in a rather condensed form. This provides less redundant material to help with getting the gist. The links between paragraphs are also few, which helps to create problems with cohesion. Headlines often involve a play on words that requires a sophisticated grasp of the language. The received wisdom that newspapers are generally written with a reading age of ten in mind does not tell the whole story. As will be readily recognised, there is a wide range of styles of writing in newspapers, from the news report itself through the editorials, the various columns and the feature articles.

Literature

In choosing literature for class study, the issue is not so much the actual text, but how it is dealt with. ESL students are going to need more time to do independent reading, and more support. This may take the form of brief summaries, diagrammatic representations of relationships between characters, or of the plot, or highlighted passages or directed questions to help students know what is important to focus on. Books such as Gillian Lazar's *Literature and Language Teaching: A Guide for Teachers and Trainers* are wonderful sources of ideas for teaching strategies.

Where teachers have the luxury of being able to buy new texts or to choose from a variety of works, it may well be worth considering material written by people from different cultures or which have a cross-cultural theme, as well as those which are quintessentially Australian. One of the particular difficulties with the latter for ESL students is their limited background knowledge, and also the representation of Australian speech or other accents. Not only do many colloquialisms rear their ugly heads, but so do unusual written forms as seen in the following example from *Summer of the Seventeenth Doll:*

Roo: *You was makin' a switch right enough! Your money's runnin' out, you know you can't put the bite on me any more, and so here's the new champion, all loaded and ready. And it wasn't enough to chase after him up north after I walked out on the gang, now you're aimin' to get him in here for the lay-off as well.*   Act II, scene 2, p98

or again from *The Shifting Heart:*

Leila: *What the hell's going on down there. Are you goin' mad, or what? We got a sick girl in here; sicker'n you'll ever be; and she's gotta have quiet, d'y'understand? Now either you shut up or you clear out; if you don't so help me, I'll be down and I'll fix y'up myself.*   Act III, p93

A good source of newer fiction which included cross-cultural themes used to be the Australian Multicultural Children's Literature Award which was sponsored by the Commonwealth Office of Multicultural Affairs. However, this was a victim of Government cuts and ceased in 1995. Nonetheless, for the years in which it operated, information about the winners and the short-listed books is worthwhile following up. In the junior section, the focus was on books which acknowledged cultural and ethnic differences in society and included some practical response to these. In the senior section, it was expected that the books examine more deeply the issues which underlie notions of 'difference', racism and bigotry. Some of the titles in the junior section, for example Errol Broome's *Dear Mr. Sprouts* or Brian Caswell's *Mike* or *Lisdalia* are useful in the early years of high school, while books such as Melina Marchetta's *Waiting for Alibrandi* have become standard fare in the senior high school. Some other titles worth looking at include James Moloney's *Gracey* and *Dougy*. Authors such as John Marsden and Alan Baillie, James Porter, Dorothy Porter and Maureen McCarthy have either received awards or had books shortlisted.

Simply using books with multicultural themes is not sufficient to challenge students' thinking about racism. In one classroom reported by Adams (1995), a teacher decided to use the novel *Roll of Thunder, Hear My Cry* by Mildred Taylor as an impetus for talking about racism. However, the approach taken to the novel was very teacher-centred with weekly quizzes on the book. The students were reticent in talking about the issues – the situation was too close to home, and they did not feel safe in discussing it. Nor was the teacher willing to engage in discussion of contemporary issues. In contrast, the same class had responded with much more verve and insight to *The Diary of Anne Frank*. Adams concludes that:

> . . . having a multicultural English curriculum means that the texts we use, the instructional strategies we employ, the discussions we initiate, the classroom climate we provide, and the student talk we encourage reflect the belief that students have a voice in the classroom and their lived experiences are valued and seen as an important springboard for future learning.
>
> (Adams, 1995, p38)

It is not enough to simply use a novel as a token contribution to a multicultural curriculum.

Reader Strategies

In looking at reading, it is also relevant to consider a student's reading strategies. Mark Clarke (1988) has argued that low proficiency in second language reading leads good L1 readers to 'short circuit' their reading strategies. That is, they tend to revert to more bottom-up processing, focusing on decoding, and individual words – rather than engaging in so much top-down processing characterised by such things as prediction, referring to antecedent information, and using general knowledge to make associations with information contained in the text. Evidence would tend to support this hypothesis, although it may need to be modified to take into account the level of difficulty of the text and the text topic. Davis and Bistodeau (1993), in a study of the reading behaviours of university students in their first language and second language, did find a greater quantity of bottom-up strategies being used when reading in the second language, although this was not to the exclusion of top-down strategies. Indeed the strategy of using general knowledge to make associations with information contained in the text was often used by students to help offset low linguistic proficiency in L2. This sort of evidence highlights the importance of teachers providing appropriate background knowledge and engaging in other pre-reading activities.

Writing

"I'm running out of red pens."

Perhaps of all the areas of English where the weaknesses of ESL students can be observed, writing is the most prominent. Lack of coherent structures, incorrect tense usage, inappropriate article usage, limited vocabulary, poor spelling are some of the common problems. How to improve students' writing is thus a major issue.

One of the current strategies in wide use in NSW primary schools and increasingly in high schools is the explicit study of different genres or text types. While it may seem as if these words are interchangeable, there is a difference in emphasis. The notion of text type is thought by some writers in the field to focus on product – eg, a letter to the editor, a report, an essay, a procedure. Now while it is true that these products are recognisable because they exhibit certain common features both structurally and in terms of language features, there is a potential problem when these text types are presented as recipes. Difficulties particularly ensue when a given response actually invokes several different genres. Rather than teach a description, it may be more useful to teach what is involved in describing, or in explaining, or in arguing – in other words, to think of genres as processes which are applicable to a range of text types. One other thing would seem to follow from thinking of genres as processes, and that is that writers will be more encouraged to focus on the purpose of their writing, and then to make appropriate choices of language based on their knowledge and understanding of the structure and grammar of the different genres.

Grammar

ESL students need even more explicit teaching in relation to language choices than do most native speakers because they have had far less exposure to the written mode. One of the characteristics of early writing by ESL students is that it reflects much more the spoken mode – ie, when read, it seems far more as if the student has simply written in the way they would talk about the topic. Recognising the way students can change the style based on recognition of the purpose of the text, the nature of the topic or field, the tenor or relationship between the writer and the audience, and the degree of distance from the event being referred to and from the reader is important to understand. It is not enough to simply provide examples of different ways of expressing ideas. How this is achieved needs to be highlighted.

Dear George,
Couldn't catch you by phone, so have to resort to writing. We're having a party to celebrate .... It's on Saturday the 15th, starting at 8.00. Hope you can come.
Ginnie
Dear Sir,
In celebration of.................., there will be a dinner on Saturday 15th, commencing at 7.30. Your presence is cordially invited.
Yours sincerely,

The differences between these two 'letters' is captured in choices made in relation to vocabulary, word form and sentence structure.

In writing in a more authoritative or generalised way, students need to be helped to see the power of strategies such as nominalisations. Instead of saying "We will celebrate", the form is changed to "celebration". Instead of saying "The store was robbed on ...", the sentence might begin "The robbery took place ...". Students need to be taught what language structures can be used to change from more personalised to depersonalised writing, for example "I am appalled that ..." to "It is appalling that ...."

From examples such as these, it can readily be seen that a focus on the grammar of writing can be of great help.

Correction

One of the implications which can be drawn from this process approach to writing is that the type of correction placed on students' work needs to be specific and helpful. In many instances it is not enough to simply underline a grammatical error. Students need to know what would have been more appropriate and, most importantly, the reason why. One way of reducing the number of errors in the final product, and at the same time providing opportunities for language development, is to include time for conferencing in lessons. This can be peer conferencing or teacher conferencing. With peer conferencing, it is necessary to provide some training in how to help each other. The idea is to engage the students in supporting and extending each other, rather than simply editing and correcting. If time is short, students might even hand in a draft for teacher comment before the final product is formally graded.

Assessment

ESL Scales

One of the difficulties confronting teachers of ESL students has been the lack of a shared framework or set of benchmarks against which achievement in English can be judged. Several publications have helped fill this gap. In 1991, the ESL Framework of Stages was published by the Curriculum Corporation. This provided descriptions of a series of age-related stages together with objectives and sample activities and assessment indicators. However, as part of the national educational initiative during the early 1990's to produce statements and profiles related to the key learning areas, a decision was made to develop a separate statement for ESL to supplement the key learning area statements. This new project drew upon two other projects which were going on at the same time – one was a project being developed by the Victorian Directorate of School Education and the other was being sponsored by the National Languages and Literacy Institute of Australia (NLLIA). The report of this latter project, *ESL Development: Language and Literacy in Schools*, was published by DEET in 1993 and the *ESL Scales* were published in 1994. One of the major differences between the NLLIA report and the *ESL Scales*, is that in the *ESL Scales* the level statements describing a continuum of skills and knowledge are meant to apply equally to primary and secondary students. In *ESL Development*, the levels and descriptions are related to what would be appropriate for junior primary, middle and upper primary and secondary students. Specific assessment activities are also modelled in relation to the target age group, proficiency level of English, and subject area. In this sense, more detail is provided to guide teachers. Without doubt, the existence of these different publications has provided teachers with a valuable framework for identifying language development and monitoring achievement.

At another level, mention should also be made of the Certificate in Spoken and Written English (CSWE) which was introduced in 1992. This was developed by a team from the NSW Adult Migrant Education Service and was intended to provide a competency based curriculum having clearly identified outcomes which would provide low proficiency adult students with relevant skills and a formal recognition of their attainment. In order to teach the Certificate it is necessary to be specially accredited by attending training sessions. The Certificate is being used in a number of schools to meet the needs of certain groups of students. The existence of such a course is recognition of the need for students to have something which is both useful and achievable. The high level of structure in the curriculum provides much needed support for these students, and the success that they feel is often in direct contrast to their feelings of inadequacy when having to compete with native speaking students in other curriculum areas.

External Examinations

Recognition of the particular disadvantage which ESL students faced in having to compete with native speakers on highly literature-based external examinations in English led ESL teachers in NSW to lobby for a different kind of course. In 1988, a new 2-Unit course called Contemporary English was introduced for Years 11 and 12. It was intended to enable students to "use the English language effectively through developing knowledge of and facility with its cultural, linguistic and textual conventions" (Board of Secondary Education, 1988, p1). There was a much greater emphasis on speaking and listening skills, and the focus for reading and writing as well was to develop effective communication "in a wide range of contexts and in a manner appropriate to audience, purpose and situation."(p2). In the area of oracy, students were to engage in a wide range of activities which allowed them to focus on features which influence effective communication and to recognise why some forms of spoken language are more effective than others in conveying messages. In reading, a wide range of texts including literature, newspapers, and popular media as well as non-literary materials such as graphs and diagrams, were to be accessed. The syllabus document states:

> The approach is not directed so much towards distinguishing the 'literary' qualities of a text as towards understanding the text, pursuing the issues it raises, taking it to illuminate problems of human behaviour or of contemporary society, exploring the cultural context to which it belongs and relating it to other contexts. While the course allows for the study of individual authors, it enables teachers to follow a thematic approach, in which a number of texts are linked, or in which a single text is made the focus of a more wide-ranging study, drawing in ancillary material of various kinds. (Board of Secondary Education, 1988, p11)

Writing was to include personal, imaginative, informative, persuasive and expository texts, and should be viewed as a process directed to achieving a specific purpose.

The unit was first examined in 1989, and over the next few years, the candidature grew to include a large number of native-speaking students. Some of these students were having difficulties with English; others chose the unit because it was perceived to be easier to get a good mark, and others because they simply were not interested in the detailed examination of literature which was a feature of other English courses. This resulted in the course taking on a life of its own which was quite separate from its original intended clientele. As the popularity of the course grew (from 2,000 students in 1989 to 18,300 in 1997), so too did concerns about the move away from the literature-based courses. These concerns were expressed by a number of influential people including some academics, and a perception grew that the 2-Unit Contemporary course lacked rigour, and was a 'cop-out' for many students. Much of this opinion lacked a solid foundation, but nonetheless, in the Government White Paper on reforms to the HSC published in 1997, it was recommended that the Contemporary English course be dropped, and a special ESL course with strict eligibility requirements be introduced in 2000 for first examination in 2001. For other students with a low achievement in English there is to be a Fundamentals of English course only available in Year 11 but which will need to be taken in conjunction with the standard 2-Unit English course. The details of the proposed courses were not spelt out and were to be left for the Board of Studies to start work on. The time frame from conception to implementation is not long, given the number of issues that need to be considered.

With regard to any new course, questions need to be asked about who it is for, and what purpose it will serve. With a special course for ESL students one of the issues is eligibility. What defines an ESL student? Length of time in the country? How would students who move back and forth between countries be categorised? Level of competence in English? There are some native speakers who demonstrate very poor English skills and who may benefit from the approach taken in a course which focuses on language. The reasons for their poorer performance may be quite different, however, and so it may not be appropriate to teach them together with ESL students. Other issues include who would be eligible to teach the course, where it would be taught given the possible small numbers in any one school, pathways for further study, and the status of the course – whether ESL students would be advantaged or whether they would shy away from it. The existence of a separate course however, provides a tremendous opportunity for the cultural assumptions to be made more transparent for the students, as well as for a clearer focus on language appropriate to the level of the students.

Conclusion

In summary, four main points can be derived from this discussion which provide guidance to the teacher with ESL students in the classroom.

✦ Be supportive. Encourage students to take risks without fear of ridicule or failure.

✦ Provide opportunities for students to participate in all aspects of the classroom. This means at the very least giving appropriate turns to ESL students and using a lot of group work which involves students in producing spoken or written responses.

✦ Analyse tasks set in order to identify exactly what is required of the student and what support might be needed for the student to complete the task. Particularly, pay attention to providing appropriate background knowledge.

✦ Beware of equating language proficiency with cognitive level. Because students may have difficulty expressing themselves in English does not mean they have learning difficulties or need to be given simplistic material to work on.

We must aim for a classroom where students achieve success, in which interesting and relevant work is carried out, in which students are challenged to perform at a higher level, in which explicit focus on language occurs, and which is enjoyable.

References

Adams, N (1995) "What Does It Mean? Exploring the Myths of Multicultural Education" in *Urban Education*, 30, 1, 27-39.

Beynon, R (1969) *The Shifting Heart*, Sydney: Angus & Robertson.

Board of Secondary Education (1988) *2 Unit Contemporary English Syllabus and Course Description.*

Clarke, M (1988) "The Short Circuit Hypothesis of ESL Reading – or When Language Competence Interferes With Reading Performance" in Carrell, P, Devine, J and Eskey, D (eds) *Interactive Approaches to Second Language Reading*, Cambridge: CUP.

Davis, J and Bistodeau, L (1993) "How Do L1 and L2 Reading Differ? Evidence From Think Aloud Protocols", *The Modern Language Journal*, 77, iv.

Lawler, R. (1957) *Summer of the Seventeenth Doll*, London: Collins.

Lazar, G (1993) *Literature and Language Teaching: A Guide for Teachers and Trainers*, Cambridge: CUP.

Lewis, M (1993) *The Lexical Approach*, Hove: Language Teaching Publications.

Morris, B and Stewart-Dore, N (1984) *Learning to Learn From Text*, North Ryde: Addison Wesley.

Nation, I (1990) *Teaching and Learning Vocabulary*. New York: Newbury House.

NSW Government (1997) *Securing Their Future. The NSW Government's Reforms for the Higher School Certificate.*

Sloyer, Shirlee (1982) *Readers Theatre: Story Dramatisation in the Classroom*, Urbana, Illinois: National Council of Teachers of English.

Tsui, A (1996) "Reticence and Anxiety in Second Language Learning" in Bailey, K and Nunan, D (eds) *The Language Classroom*, Cambridge: Cambridge University Press.

Section III: Reading Texts

11 Reading – Some Questions and Answers

Ken Watson

Is There a Literacy Crisis?

My favourite shock-horror newspaper headline, at the time of an earlier 'literacy crisis', read

50% of 15-YEAR-OLDS BELOW AVERAGE IN READING

Of course, in the normal meaning of the word 'average' this must always be the case. If a dramatic improvement in literacy levels were to occur next year, the headline would still be true.

The National Literacy Survey released in 1997 was presented by the then Minister for Schools as providing evidence of a major literacy crisis, but a calm appraisal of the evidence suggests that the opposite is true. Amazingly large percentages of Year 3 and Year 5 pupils were able to meet the very high (and quite arbitrary) benchmarks; in writing, for example, 72% of Year 3 students

✦ had mastered punctuation;
✦ could spell not only common words but also words rarely used;
✦ avoided repetitive words and sentence structure;
✦ had no gaps in logic.

In a survey of adult literacy released at the same time, the notion of some previous golden age of literacy was yet again shown to be a fantasy. While 2.3% in the 15-24 years bracket needed help in reading newspapers, 8.3% in the 55-64 bracket needed help.

Nevertheless, it should be borne in mind that today's children are likely to do less and less reading outside school now that the range of leisure activities is much greater (television, video games etc) and the English teacher in particular has an even greater responsibility to encourage reading and writing in his or her classes. Properly run, whole-school programs like SSR (Sustained Silent Reading) and DEAR (Drop Everything And Read) have proved their value (see page 44).

What Do We Know About Reading Processes?

Quite a lot, really. We know that different kinds of reading make different kinds of demands upon the reader, and that one thing young readers need to learn is to adjust their reading to the demands of the text. Few novels or newspaper articles, for example, demand attention to every word, but certain kinds of poetry will make such a demand, as will the wording of a question in an examination.

Theories of how reading takes place are of two basic kinds: 'bottom up' and 'top down'. 'Bottom up' theories see reading as beginning with letter-sound combinations, then the combining of the sounds into words and so on. 'Top down' theories, on the other hand, see the reader's prior knowledge of the language and of the world in general as at least as important as letter recognition, and the extraction of meaning from the text rather than the decoding of words into sound as the essence of reading. While no one would disagree that some phonic knowledge is important, the weight of the evidence is in favour of 'top down' models.

It is important to understand that written language contains three kinds of information (or cuing systems):
1. semantic information (word and sentence meanings);
2. syntactic information (information about word order and sentence structure);
3. grapho-phonic information (information about the relationship between the graphemes [letters] and the sounds [phonemes]).

By the time children are ready to learn to read, they already have a great deal of tacit knowledge about (1) and (2); unfortunately, many early reading schemes fail to recognise this fact and hence do not encourage children to make use of this knowedge when they are confronted with the task of getting meaning from the written word.

A 'top down' model may be rendered diagrammatically (after K Goodman) as:

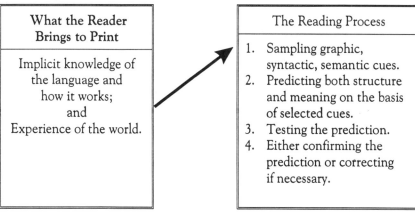

What the Reader Brings to Print	The Reading Process
Implicit knowledge of the language and how it works; and Experience of the world.	1. Sampling graphic, syntactic, semantic cues. 2. Predicting both structure and meaning on the basis of selected cues. 3. Testing the prediction. 4. Either confirming the prediction or correcting if necessary.

All readers, no matter how proficient, make errors when they read ordinary prose. This suggests that reading is not an exact process. But the errors – or, better, *miscues* – of good readers differ from those of weak readers in two significant ways:

1. their miscues do *not* detract from the overall meaning;
2. their miscues maintain the *Englishness* of English. They put verbs into verb slots, nouns or pronouns into noun slots, prepositions in preposition slots, and so on. (Cambourne and Rousch, 1980; Watson, 1985)

Is Phonics the Answer?

While, as already noted, some grapho-phonic knowledge is an important ingredient of successful reading, it is not the only, or even the most important, element – a fact which most people acknowledge when they encounter words which they can understand but do not know how to pronounce. (Few people, for example, know how to pronounce a word like 'victuals', but in reading *Treasure Island* they readily understand its meaning from the context.) It seems that much of the grapho-phonic knowledge that good readers have is acquired *during* the process of learning to read rather than being a prior requirement. This is just as well, since there are hundreds of letter-sound combinations in English! Think, for example, of the many sounds given to the letter 'a': *war, way, card, pat, mountain, care.* One piece of research demonstrated that in a sample of 6000 one- and two-syllable words from the vocabularies of nine-year-old children there were 211 distinct spelling-sound correspondences (Smith, 1973, pp88-89). It follows that a total reliance upon phonic methods of reading would involve a massive overloading of short-term memory.

Studies of weak readers in the secondary school have shown that in the vast majority of cases there is an over-reliance on grapho-phonic cues and a failure to utilise the semantic and syntactic cuing systems. An unpublished study by Watson found that over 90% of a sample of a hundred weak readers in Sydney high schools were in fact quite strong in the processing of grapho-phonic cues. Most of them, however, made almost no use of the other cuing systems, and indeed often failed to see that reading is decoding into meaning, not decoding into sound. Unhappily, most of these students, already strong in phonics, were being given remedial programs which were strongly phonics-based.

A telling example of an over-reliance on phonics to the exclusion of everything else comes from one of Jeffrey Wilhelm's case studies (Wilhelm, 1997):

I was reading a baseball story with Marvin [who often played baseball].
He read aloud that "Jack slid into second and kuh-nocked his kuh-nee,"
pronouncing both silent k's. When asked what a "kuh-nee" could possibly
be, Marvin shrugged. "I just told you what it says. How should I know

what it means?" Marvin often indicated that it was the reader's job to pronounce words, but not to make meaning. (p.96)

At one stage the curious notion was abroad that 'reading' and 'comprehension' were separate entities. Not so; if there is no comprehension, there is no reading. One of the weaknesses of such packaged reading programs as DISTAR is that they present youngsters with largely meaningless passages constructed to drill certain letter-sound combinations, and unwittingly convey the message that reading and comprehension have nothing to do with one another. The following passage, from an American reading scheme, is an extreme example:

ODD OX ROCKS A CLOCK

Tom got Ron's clock off Ron's box. Tom lobs Ron's clock on Dot's Odd Ox. Tom got on top.
Dot's ox jogs off. Odd Ox swats Tom's socks. Tom sobs lots.
Pol hops off Tom's cot. Dot's wand got Odd Ox on Ox's hocks. Odd Ox rocks lots!
Tom hops off Odd Ox. Dot got Ron's clock off Odd Ox.
Don locks Ron's clock on Ron's box top. Ron jogs on Tom's cot.
Tom sobs lots. Pol hops on Ron's clock.

Quiz:

Tom wants Ron's...? (lock, clock)
Dot's...? ox. (off, odd)
Dot got Dot's..? (wand, want)
Odd Ox swats Tom's.....................................? (hocks, socks)
Ron jogs on Tom's ....? (cot, box)

Can Comprehension Be Taught?

Traditional teaching of comprehension, involving regular practice on answering questions on passages of prose and poetry, has been challenged by a number of research studies. For example, the London Association for the Teaching of English, in a major study, found that their subjects, students aged 13 and 14, made little or no gain in reading comprehension from eight months of regular intensive work on selected passages (D'Arcy, 1973)

Most textbooks containing such passages are based on the belief that there are identifiable sub-skills of comprehension, such as 'locating the main idea', 'locating a sequence of ideas', etc, but research by Lunzer and Gardner (1979;1984) and Spearritt (1977) suggests that reading comprehension is a unitary aptitude or skill. To quote Lunzer and Gardner:

. . . individual differences in reading comprehension should not be thought of in terms of a multiplicity of specialised aptitudes. To all intents and purposes such differences reflect only one general aptitude: this

*being the pupil's ability and willingness to reflect on whatever it is he is
reading.*   (1979, p64)

Lunzer and Gardner developed a list of activities that really did seem to
improve reading comprehension, using the acronym DARTS (Directed
Activities Related to Texts). Each of these activities should be undertaken
by small groups (two, three, or four members), using, where possible,
complete poems, short stories etc.

1. Text reconstructions
    a. *Prediction:* stopping a text at particular points to encourage students
        to speculate on what will happen next.
    b. *Cloze:* deleting some key words (not too many – six or seven will
        do) from a poem or prose passage and asking students to discuss
        possible alternatives. First choices are then compared with the
        original – and it may be that the class will find that some of their
        suggestions improve on the original.
    c. *Sequencing:* re-ordering a scrambled text. For example, a poem is
        cut up into stanzas, and the groups asked to determine an
        appropriate order.
    d. *Beginnings and Endings:* students are given the beginning and ending
        of a text and asked what they think the missing section is about.
2. Text Analysis
    a. *Finding boundaries:* students are asked to divide a text which has
        been printed without paragraphing into what they think are its sections.
    b. *Underlining and labelling:* students mark the text in some way to
        indicate its most significant features or pattern.
    c. *Drawings and diagrams:* presenting some of the information in the
        text in a visual way (e.g, drawing, flow-chart, ideas web).
    d. *Role play and improvisation.*
    e. *Responding to statements:* students are presented with a range of
        statements about the text, and asked to discuss which are the most
        important or appropriate.
    f. *Asking questions:* students, in groups, decide on a set of questions
        they want to ask about the text.

A very useful booklet on the subject is Hamlin and Jackson's *Making
Sense of Comprehension* (1984).

How Useful Are Reading Tests?

Reading tests need to be used with some caution. At the beginning of a school
year, a test given to everyone may be a useful means of quick identification
of students who are at risk, who will then need to be assessed individually,
as most mass tests do not diagnose individual weaknesses. A good diagnostic
tool is miscue analysis, a modified form of which is outlined in Barbara

Johnson's *Reading Appraisal Guide* (1979), an excellent handbook for anyone working with a weak reader.

What Else Can I Do to Help the Weak Reader in My Class?

1. Draw on the student's own environment, his (the student is more likely to be a boy) own language. Let him dictate his own stories and experiences into a cassette recorder and transcribe these to use as reading materials.
2. Make use of the printed material that daily assaults the student: car ads, TV programs, pop songs etc.
3. Make a careful analysis of the student's miscues (see above). If the miscues involve confusion of similar words (eg, 'saw', 'was') write a story in which strong syntactic and sematic cues help him overcome the problem. Cloze is useful here.
4. If the miscue analysis shows that he is relying solely on the grapho-phonic cuing system, train him to make use of the syntactic and semantic cues by encouraging him to predict on the basis of the grammar and the meaning. Again, cloze passages which force the student to predict on the basis of his tacit grammatical knowledge or his knowledge of the world are an excellent means of achieving a willingness to predict on the basis of evidence.
5. If the reader is having difficulty with grapheme/phoneme relationships, avoid isolated word drill. Use alliterative poems, jingles with strong rhymes etc.
6. If the student is reading so slowly that he loses the sense, read with him, running your finger under the printed words and reading a little faster that he normally does. Ten minutes of such practice each day often brings astonishing results.
7. Build up a library of taped stories/plays/poems. Students follow the printed words as they listen to the tape. This can be done at home.
8. Writing should go hand in hand with reading.

What About Spelling?

The belief that all children can be taught to spell with 100% accuracy is misplaced: there are some highly literate people who remain poor spellers throughout their lives. Charles Darwin, perhaps the greatest mind of the 19th century, constantly faltered over the spelling of such words as 'school'; to the end of her life Jane Austen remained unsure of how to spell words like ' niece' and 'necessary'. Robert Lowell, one of the greatest poets of the 20th century, was an appalling speller.

The task of learning to spell correctly is much more difficult for speakers of English than for, say , speakers of Italian. In Italian there are only about forty letter-sound combinations, whereas English has hundreds (see above). The position is made more difficult in English because the unstressed vowel sound in words of more than one syllable almost always sounds the same (like 'e' as in 'butter') when people talk. In spoken English, the unstressed vowel in the following words tends to be pronounced in the same way: picture, popular, parent, constant.

Attempts at spelling reform have met with limited success. Even Noah Webster's massive reform project left many inconsistencies, such as 'practice' for both verb and noun, while 'license' is the spelling for verb and noun. Other reform projects have foundered on two great stumbling blocks: the pronunciation of English words differs from country to country and often from region to region, and changes made to match pronunciation often destroy important visual links, particularly where an adjective has a different pronunciation from the noun from which it was formed (eg, 'nation' and 'national'). A further problem is that pronunciation changes over time, though interestingly pronunciation changes are often in the direction of bringing pronunciation closer to the spelling of a word. For example, 'often' used to be pronounced as 'offen', but now a majority of Australians sounds the 't'. Similar changes have occurred with words like 'hotel' (where the 'h' used to be silent).

Sight is the preferred sense for spelling, and weak spellers are most often people with weak visual memory. One technique that should be taught to all students is that of look – say – cover – write – check when learning to spell a new word.

It is important not to undermine students' confidence in themselves as spellers. Marking with red slashes thirty-five spelling errors is likely to cause a bad speller to give up completely; better to draw his/her attention to the three or four misspellings of really common words and set the goal of having the student get those right next time.

A teacher-made difficulty that many students have occurs when an exercise is given asking them to choose between 'there' and 'their', 'thought' and 'through', and the like. Research has shown that such exercises almost inevitably compound the confusion; if a student is having difficulty with such similar words, the important thing is to establish links based on meaning. Thus with a student confusing 'thought' and 'through' an appropriate remedial technique would be to present him/her with a cloze passage where all the blanks would require parts of the verb 'to think'; some weeks later another cloze would require prepositions or adverbs which would link 'through' in the student's mind with 'down', 'under, 'over' etc.

References

Reading

Cambourne, Brian and Rousch, Peter (1980) "There's More to Reading Than Meets the Eye", *Australian Journal of Reading*, vol 3, no 2, pp104-114.

D'Arcy, Pat (1973) *Reading for Meaning Vol 2: The Reader's Response*, London: Heinemann.

Johnson, Barbara (1979) *Reading Appraisal Guide*, Melbourne: ACER.

Hamlin, M and Jackson, D (1984) *Making Sense of Comprehension*, London: Macmillan.

Lowe, Kaye (1994) *Growing Into Readers*, Newtown: PETA.

Lunzer, E and Gardner, K (1979) *The Effective Use of Reading*, London: Heinemann.

Lunzer, E and Gardner, K (1984) *Learning from the Written Word*, Edinburgh: Oliver and Boyd.

Meek, Margaret (1983) *Achieving Literacy*, London: RKP.

Smith, Frank (1973) *Psycholinguistics and Reading*, New York: Holt Rinehart.

Spearritt, D (1977) *Measuring Reading Comprehension in the Upper Primary School*, Canberra: ERDC/AGPS.

Watson, Ken (1985) "Miscuing: Everybody Does It", *English Education*, Vol 17 No 2.

Wilhelm, Jeffrey (1997) *You Gotta BE the Book*, New York: Teachers College Press/NCTE.

Spelling

Bean, Wendy and Bouffler, Christine (1987) *Spell by Writing*, Sydney: PETA.

Jenkins, Rhonda (ed) (1986) *Spelling Is Forever*, Carlton South: Australian Reading Association.

Stratford, Dick (1977) "Spelling" in Watson K and Eagleson R D (eds) *English in Secondary Schools: Today and Tomorrow*, Sydney: ETA of NSW.

12 The Impact of Literary Theory

A NOTE ON READER-RESPONSE THEORY

Ken Watson

The year 1978 was a significant one for teachers of English, since it saw the publication of both Louise Rosenblatt's *The Reader the Text the Poem* and Wolfgang Iser's *The Act of Reading*. Here at last, it seemed, was a literary theory – reader-response or reception theory – that dovetailed neatly with the pedagogical theorising about the nature of reading that had been part of the development of the personal growth model of English.

Actually, reader-response theory had been around for a long time, though few were aware of it. Back in 1938 Louise Rosenblatt had stressed the individuality and creativity of the reader in her *Literature as Exploration*, a book that was, unhappily, ignored by the teaching profession, and teachers (and, it would seem, literary critics as well) remained unaware of what writers had been telling them for centuries. In 1767 Laurence Sterne was emphasising the readers' creativity by exhorting them to fill in the gaps he was deliberately leaving in the text; a century later Walt Whitman was pointing out that

> . . . the process of reading is not a half-sleep, but, in the highest sense,
> an exercise, a gymnast's struggle; that the reader is to do something
> himself, must be on the alert, must himself or herself construct indeed
> the poem, argument, history, metaphysical essay – the text furnishing the
> hints, the clue, the start or framework. Not that the book needs so much
> to be the complete thing, but the reader of the book does.

In this century poets and novelists have continued to emphasise that reading is a creative process. W H Auden had this to say:

> What a poem means is the outcome of a dialogue between the words on
> the page and the person who happens to be reading it; that is to say, its
> meaning varies from person to person.

John Fowles has spoken of the "necessary co-operation between writer and reader, the one to suggest, the other to make concrete", and the Australian poet J S Harry says that she always tries to leave "room . . . for the imagination of the reader".

In contrast to the New Critics, who insisted on the self-contained nature of the literary work, and hence the irrelevance of the reader, reader-response critics emphasise the *active* nature of reading. Louise Rosenblatt has written:

First, the text is a stimulus activating elements of the reader's past experience – his experience both with literature and with life. Second, the text serves as blueprint, a guide for the selecting, rejecting, and ordering of what has been called forth; the text regulates what shall be held in the forefront of the reader's attention...The finding of meanings involves both the author's text and what the reader brings to it.

(Rosenblatt, 1978, pp 11, 14)

This view of reading as a 'transaction' between reader and text can prove immensely liberating for students, and ought, in my view, be made explicit to them. Elsewhere (Watson, 1992) I have described some experiments I conducted with secondary school students in the 1980s, using the picture book *John Brown, Rose and the Midnight Cat* by Jenny Wagner and Ron Brooks. I found that if young readers could be brought to a realisation that a range of responses is not only permissible, but indeed inevitable, they would be encouraged to value their own initial responses, and build upon them, rather than wait for the teacher's definitive interpretation.

This view of reading as a dialogue between the words on the page and person reading them does not mean that all interpretations have equal validity. To quote Rosenblatt again:

The two prime criteria of validity as I understand it are that the reader's interpretation not be contradicted by any element of the text, and that nothing be projected for which there is no verbal basis.

(Rosenblatt, 1978, p115)

The role of the teacher in deepening and refining response involves a valuing of the students' initial responses as a starting point, and giving them the opportunity – through small-group talk, through imaginative re-creation – to test that initial response against the responses of others and against the text.

While believing strongly that teachers need to base their teaching of literature on a reader-response view, I recognise that reader-response theory as defined by people like Rosenblatt fails to recognise that the meanings readers take from a text are to some degree determined by the culture in which they have grown up. This again is something that can be made explicit to young readers, and the booklet I have co-edited with John Stephens (Stephens and Watson, 1994) illustrates one way in which that can be done.

One of the saddest stories about teaching I have ever heard was related to me by an American friend who was teaching in a large high school (about 2,800 pupils!) where English was required to be taken in only one of the two

---

final years of schooling. Encountering in a corridor a final-year student whom he had not taught since her first year in the school, he asked whether she was taking English that year. On learning that she was not, he asked what she was reading for pleasure. She replied: "I'm not reading anything. I don't like reading a book unless there is someone to tell me what it is about." The intervening years had disempowered the student as reader, indoctrinating her with the view that the real meaning of a text is one to which the teacher alone has the key.

References

Iser, Wolfgang (1978) *The Act of Reading: A Theory of Aesthetic Response*, London: RKP.
Rosenblatt, Louise M. (1938/1976) *Literature as Exploration*, New York: Noble.
Rosenblatt, Louise M. (1978) *The Reader the Text the Poem: The Transactional Theory of the Literary Work*, Carbondale: Southern Illinois University Press.
Stephens, John and Watson, Ken (eds) (1994) *From Picture Book to Literary Theory*, Sydney: St Clair Press.
Suleiman, Susan and Crosman, Inge (eds) (1980) *The Reader in the Text*, Princeton, NJ: Princeton University Press.
Tompkins, Jane (ed) (1980) *Reader-Response Criticism*, Baltimore: Johns Hopkins University Press.
Watson, Ken (1992) "Personal Readings, Cultural Readings (*John Brown, Rose and the Midnight Cat*)", in Evans, Emrys (ed) (1992) *Young Readers, New Readings*, Hull: Hull University Press.

POSTSTRUCTURALISM

Ray Misson

I t is usually a feature of anything that is 'post' that it throws the certainties of whatever it is 'post' to into doubt. This is certainly true of poststructuralism, although it is not just structuralism that is questioned, but the whole way of thinking in modern times. For this reason, poststructuralism, particularly in American work, is often subsumed into, and referred to as, postmodernism, but I think we are wise to retain 'postmodernism' as a term for a particular style related to a particular period, and to use 'poststructuralism' to refer to a particular set of intellectual perceptions and preoccupations that have become dominant in the last two decades. The founding ideas of poststructuralism come largely from the work of a number of French writers, but they have been taken up right across the Western academy and beyond.

In the limited space I have, I can do no more than sketch in some of the main contours of poststructuralism, simplifying greatly, and no doubt bringing down on my head the scorn of those with an understanding better than mine of its considerable complexities. It does perhaps need to be said that poststructuralism is no single thing, but rather a loose constellation of ideas and theories out of which multifarious versions of the phenomenon can be constituted. Even those of us who acknowledge our thinking to be so influenced by poststructuralist thought that we might not resist being called 'poststructuralists' exhibit extraordinary variety in the versions of poststructuralism we have built out of this mass of work.

There are two main streams of poststructuralist thought that I want to concentrate on. They have provided a rethinking of two rather different areas and produced rather different outcomes when applied to the English classroom. The first is to do with the reconceptualisation of language that poststructuralism has brought, which has had a powerful effect on the way in which literary texts are read and worked with in classrooms. The second stream is concerned with the theorisation of the relationship between language, ideology and human identity which has been a powerful underpinning of Critical Literacy.

Poststructuralism and Language

The idea that poststructuralism undercuts the certainties of structuralism is perhaps a good place to start our brief exploration of the phenomenon. I don't want to spend time sketching in a summary of structuralist thought: it will be enough to point to a few major features. Structuralism was taken up with such great excitement because it seemed to offer not only a theory of meaning but beyond that a theory of human knowing. Its basic notion, that we have internalised particular structural categories which allow us to sort and interpret the sensory phenomena that the world sends to us, gave a way of analysing all kinds of phenomena in the humanities and social sciences. In particular, its ability to explain how certain things came to carry particular meanings (whether the things be speech sounds, clothes or kinship inter-actions) seemed to offer a theory that would make the whole world knowable and known. Poststructuralism undercuts this vision of glorious certainty.

Take any word, even a simple one like 'dog'. In structuralist terms, this verbal sign 'dog' is a neat and certain package of the *signifier* (the actual marks on the page) and the *signified* (the concept of a certain kind of animal). Poststructuralism questions both the neatness and the certainty. One way in which we can see this happening is if we work with the notion of difference. In structuralist terms, the meaning of 'dog' inheres in its difference from, say, 'dot' or 'log'. We are able to attach the meaning to the symbols because of this difference. But that means that inherently every word depends for its meaning on every other word, depends for its meaning on what it is not. It might be argued that there are traces of all these other words that give the word 'dog' its meaning somehow inherent in the word 'dog', so the differential opposition is not as clear as it seemed. To simplify a very complex argument, the word 'dog' signifies a certain kind of canine animal because it doesn't signify what we call a cat, or a bird, or an elephant, or a rose, or love. And yet, that definition means that our conception of dog is potentially coloured by all these things against which it has been defined.

More than that, we start thinking about the word 'dog' and our mind goes around relays of different aspects of 'dog', and the boundaries of our conception of 'dog' can be seen to be very blurred (even before we get to the things whose difference might be thought to define 'dog'). It's not a neat package at all. We have various cultural connotations of 'dog' (and of course 'dog' means very different things in different cultures, where they might be worshipped, eaten, treated as marauders, treated as pets). We have various personal experiences too that colour our conception. So there is a great deal of instability and indeterminacy even in a seemingly simple word, let alone when the word is a complex notion such as 'pride' or 'friend'. What happens in normal language use is that we arbitrarily close off these relays of meaning and give ourselves the sense of the neat package, but your neat package might be quite different from mine as we have gone round different relays and closed off at different points. Moreover, we need not have imposed this arbitrary closure, but the possibility of meaning could go on and on through the connection of the word with every other word, and so there could be an endless deferral of meaning. Jacques Derrida, the central figure in a great deal of poststructuralist thought, has focussed this view of language in the word *différance*, which does not translate easily into English because it is a pun on the French words for 'difference' and 'deferral'. The nature of language is an endless process of differentiation and deferral, thus undermining any sense of certainty in meaning.

Many poststructuralist writers work by undercutting the stability of meaning by all sorts of techniques. It is why their works are often difficult to read. Puns are everywhere, and various other kinds of wordplay. A favourite trick is to fracture a word to make the reader aware of the elements combined in it, or to bring two meanings together in a kind of pun: e.g. one might get the term 'linguistic in(ter)ference' which would imply that the author is talking about the ways in which inference might interfere with language, or the ways in which inference enables language to interfere with other things, or the ways in which language interferes in the process of drawing inference, or any one of a number of other possibilities.

All this kind of intellectual fun and games may seem a long way away from the classroom, but the implications are enormous. In particular, these ideas provide a theorisation of how people produce different meanings out of words and texts, and warn us of the dangers of closing off the possibility of meaning too quickly. It is not true that poststructuralism claims that words can mean anything and that there is no sanction for saying that a particular meaning is wrong, but it is true that it has given us a great deal of respect for the multiplicity and shiftiness of language.

Just as we can't reach simple and absolute closure on the meaning of any word, there is no possibility of reaching the certainty of absolute truth outside language for any concept. Derrida claims that Western thought is contaminated with what he has called 'logocentrism'. 'Logos' is the Greek word that provides the '-ology' component in words like 'biology' or 'psychology', so it implies 'knowledge', but it is also the word that is translated as 'Word' at the start of the Gospel according to St. John: "In the Beginning was the Word (logos), and the Word was with God, and the Word was God." Thus Jesus is the physical manifestation, the speaking forth into the World of the unknowable God who is the presence behind him. Derrida, through the concept of logocentrism, argues that Western thought relies on a 'metaphysics of presence', a belief that there is a validating reality behind language that gives it its meaning. Language, it is generally believed, is deceptive and inadequate to embody the reality behind it to which it refers. But Derrida, in a famous phrase, asserts "il n'y a pas de hors-texte," there is nothing outside text. Language is all we can know: there is no ideal transcendent presence behind language that fills its emptiness with meaning. All meaning operates within language, and is subject to the vagaries that the indeterminacy and instability of language inevitably imply.

This is particularly significant for writing, for, as Roland Barthes argues in his famous essay, "The Death of the Author" (1977), we have been used to thinking of the author as the validating presence behind the text. The aim of criticism has been to discover the author through the text, and tie down the play of textual meaning through reference to her/him. But, Barthes claims, the author is dead, there is only text, with the free play of meaning of the various discourses out of which it is constructed available for us to disport ourselves amongst. There is nothing behind the text: there is only the ever-shifting surface of the text itself which we move across, making what we will of the multiplicity of meaning available.

Again this has enormous implications for the classroom. It is not that it allows the reader to make any extravagant sense she/he likes out of the text, but it does give tremendous freedom for reinterpreting, following through particular lines on the text, recontextualising it and discovering extraordinarily diverse meaning in it. The text is no longer tied down by authorial intention or even the meaning possible to the author. It has become material to be rewritten over and over again in different constructions in each reading. We can, if we wish, read "against the grain", that is, we can refuse to take the text's implicit or explicit valuations of what it is showing, and follow through other implications of the material that allow us to produce quite different readings. An example of this will be given later.

It was one of the great insights of structuralism that things do not have meaning in themselves but are constructed to convey meaning.

Poststructuralism, in what is probably its most famous manifestation, uses this insight not to explain how things come to mean, but to show up the limits and limitations of meaning. This is done by deconstructing the text. Deconstruction is the analytical process by which the ideology of a text is shown not to be a natural reflection of the world, but a product of certain textual strategies that privilege a particular viewpoint, suppress inconsistent material, or smooth over inherent contradictions. Deconstruction looks for the points at which the strain shows in the text, and works on them, heightening the contradiction, bringing back the suppressed material, exposing the unjustified valuation of one of the terms in an opposition, until the ideology of the text is apparent, and its seeming naturalness has been exposed as constructed.

This has been particularly valuable in showing how discrimination has been perpetuated in texts. We are moving here over into the second strand of English studies stemming from elements of poststructuralism that I want to look at, that which is concerned with questions of the nature of human beings, and particularly how we are positioned in, indeed constructed through, ideology.

The Subject of Ideology

Significantly for English teaching, poststructuralism sees this process of the creation of the individual human being and their positioning within ideology as largely happening through language. When Derrida proclaims that there is nothing outside of texts, the implication certainly is that human beings are not exempt. Human beings do not have an essential being that lies behind the textual practices they engage in – always acknowledging that textual practices are not necessarily linguistic but can be visual, bodily, gestural, etc. – but rather the human self is co-extensive with, and created through, these textual practices.

The idea of 'discourse' as developed by Michel Foucault is crucial here. A discourse in this tradition is a formation of textual practices activated in a particular social/personal arena which brings with it particular ways of being, ways of doing and ways of thinking. There is a discourse that we use with the family; there is a technical discourse we might use in our work; there are discourses of law, religion, and so on. The idea that we talk in different registers in different situations is an old one. However, rather than conceiving us as putting these different ways of talking on as a covering to a stable essential self, rather like putting on clothes to dress ourselves appropriately for particular situations, poststructuralism radically argues that there is no self apart from these ways of talking. The discourses we partake in are what constitute the self. Therefore the self is a social construct (the constructivist position), rather than being a given essence of a person (the essentialist belief).

This provides a strong theory of how we are locked into certain belief systems. We are subjected to various discourses, and these discourses create our subjectivity, ie, our subjective sense of what we are and how we fit into the world. Texts put us into a subject position (the way of seeing the world implied by the text), and we become subjects (ie, experiencing human beings with a particular configuration of attitudes and beliefs) through being positioned in this way. Thus, if I read a fundamentalist Christian tract and fall into the subject position implied, I will be created or confirmed as a particular kind of human subject, a person with fundamentalist Christian beliefs. More subtly, if I see an advertisement for a brand of jeans giving a particularly strong image of the independent, ruthless, macho guy, I might misrecognize myself in the representation, see myself as ideally in my essential self that kind of person, and subscribe to the patriarchal masculinist values implicit in the image.

The examples suggest that the theory needs to be made a lot more subtle and requires a great deal more elaboration than I have given here before it can explain human beings (and there are some who argue very cogently that it will never explain human complexity satisfactorily, particularly because it neglects the disruptive force of the body and desire). At the very least, we need to add a theory of how people come to resist certain discourses, and we certainly need to insist on the extraordinary multiplicity of subject positions possible for any person, and the different prominence any subject position may take within the individual's constitution. We probably also need to assert the fact that the discourses are constantly shifting in relation to each other and in their relative strength within a person's psyche. Nevertheless, given qualifications, it is a powerful theory of how we are made the subject of ideology.

This theory of the discursive construction of subjectivity (ie, the construction of our subjective selves through discourse) does give an urgency to work on examining how texts are positioning us, because these texts may in fact be quite powerfully creating us and our belief systems. We may need to deconstruct the texts in an attempt to defuse their potential power over us. This analysis of textual representations, showing how they are constructing certain ideological messages, has become crucial in many classrooms, and is one of the main thrusts of Critical Literacy, which is discussed elsewhere in this volume.

An Example

It would be impossible to exemplify all the points I have been making about poststructuralism from any one example in a short article such as this, but to finish up, I want to provide some analysis, working within a post-structuralist framework, of one text, showing what might be done with it. The following is a rather beautiful short lyric by the Australian poet, David Campbell:

Night Sowing

O gentle, gentle land
Where the green ear shall grow,
Now you are edged with light:
The moon has crisped the fallow,
The furrows run with night.

This is the season's hour:
While couples are in bed,
I sow the paddocks late,
Scatter like sparks the seed
And see the dark ignite.

O gentle land, I sow
The heart's living grain.
Stars draw their harrows over,
Dews send their melting rain:
I meet you as a lover.   (1968, p42)

I think that there can be little doubt that a conventional reading of this poem would be couched in terms of the aptness of the metaphor of the farmer and the land as lovers, of the sowing of the seed as a gentle act of love in a radiantly beautiful night, nature working with human beings in a productive harmony.

The discourses out of which the poem is built are that of:

(a) agriculture – 'sowing', 'fallow' 'paddocks' 'furrows',

(b) a poetic discourse about nature which allows the anthropomorphization of the land, the stars and the dew, brings in a sense of natural order ("the season's hour") and, of course, draws on a particular range of rather Romantic associations with night – 'moon', 'stars', 'dews', and

(c) a discourse about heterosexual love and procreation which subsumes and metaphorically projects the other two discourses as the overarching frame of the poem.

The notion of 'seed', which of course is a biblical term for semen, provides the major means for linking together the notions of agriculture and sexual love in its romantic inflection ("the heart's living grain").

Thus, the poem is assuming and so calling its readers into a subject position that will acquiesce in a positive view of agriculture, believe in and value the beauty and harmony of Nature and the night, and subscribe to a patriarchal view of male/female relationships with the woman as the passive 'gentle' partner in whose 'furrows' the male plants the seed. Putting it in those terms, of course, makes one aware of how thoroughly the poem is bound up in a particular ideological system. It also makes one aware that the beautiful coherence and sense of completeness that the poem offers is the product of not allowing alternative views in, being silent about the economic purpose of farming, for example, or the negative connotations of night, or alternative, more equal visions of male/female love.

Many a reader many a time will be willing to go into the subject position required and assent to the implicit ideological beliefs, at least for as long as it takes to experience the pleasures the poem has to offer. They will read it as they are being called by the text to read it. But it is also possible to read it "against the grain" (pun with the subject matter of the poem totally unintentional but in itself a demonstration of the power of language to make meaning that the writer isn't in control of). Reading "against the grain", as discussed above, implies refusing to go into the poem's subject position, but highlighting the other possibilities of meaning implicit in the poem's discourses, but suppressed. This has been a particularly powerful strategy for feminist criticism, where one can make explicit the patriarchal assumptions that many texts are built on but remain silent about.

One can imagine with the David Campbell poem, if one were committed to Aboriginal land rights, for example, that one might want to show up the way in which European agriculture has been 'naturalised' within the poem, that is, how what might well be seen as exploitation has been made to appear a natural and benevolent phenomenon by the use of the particular discourses. It would perhaps be easiest to do this by working within the love/sex metaphor and rendering it problematical, as indeed it already at least potentially is, with its traditional images of female passivity and masculine activity, of the male fire 'ignit(ing)' the darkness of the female land. Indeed, it does not take a great deal of reading against the grain to see the image as potentially one of rape, as the land not being acquiescently gentle, but as being helpless before an act of aggression. (This is actually a powerful image underpinning a number of Aboriginal poems.)

When working with the poem in the classroom, one could develop out these ideas in many ways, if one wanted either to make apparent how ideologically slanted the Campbell poem is, or if one perhaps wanted to set up a dialectic between Campbell's views and other possible ones. The removal of any expectation of a single, closed, compliant reading that poststructuralism has brought has freed up the possible ways of working with texts. In particular, the possibility of rewriting the text to expose its absences or its ideological position has become part of the repertoire. Such creative responses are often the best way into developing a sense of alternative views. With the David Campbell poem, since there is such strong anthropomorphization going on, one might ask for the land's response. Or one could ask the students to write a poem that an Aborigine might have written about a European farmer sowing a European grain crop at night on land that once belonged to the Aborigine's people. Something like the following might result. In this case an extra constraint has been set that the poem should follow the same form as Campbell's, and indeed use the same rhyme words:

Night Sowing

O helpless, helpless land
Where green ears are forced to grow,
Now you are drained of light.
The moonshine flees the fallow
Till the furrows run dark with night.

This is the fatal hour
When the ravager nears the bed.
He comes to the paddock late
To fire it with his seed
And make the dark ignite.

O helpless land, he sows
The foreign, depleting grain.
Stars bring the darkness over,
Dews shed lamenting rain,
Violation comes, no lover.

What has happened in this rewriting of the poem, of course, is that negative versions of the positive discourses in the Campbell poem have been activated, producing a kind of inverse version of it. Some may consider that such a process is akin to vandalism, a kind of literary immorality. However, such a view implies a belief in the inviolable integrity of a given text, which ultimately depends on some notion of the author as authenticating presence behind the text. This is not, as we have seen, how poststructuralism views things. In poststructuralist terms, the text has been cut free, the author is 'dead', and we have every right to reread and rewrite the text in ways that suit our purposes. (One may question the purposes, but that's a different issue.) It can also be argued, of course, that it's important to become aware of the implicit ideology of a text, and to have the right to counter it if we wish, so as not to become subject to it.

There is still a great deal of suspicion around about poststructuralism because it does so radically throw into doubt such a lot of the beliefs that people live by, beliefs such as the determinacy of language and the existence of a core self outside society and language. Because so much of it is counter-intuitive, it is, in many ways, easy to lampoon and misrepresent as a kind of highly esoteric, lunatic game that intellectuals play having been deluded into believing it meaningful. However, there can be little doubt that poststructuralism has created a revolution in our way of thinking, and is somewhere behind most of the major innovations and new insights we find occurring in English teaching today.

References

Barthes, R (1977) "The Death of the Author" in *Image – Music – Text*, London: Fontana.
Campbell, D (1968) *Selected Poems 1942-1968*. Sydney: Angus and Robertson.

Writing:
The Bulwer-Lytton Fiction Contest

For many years San Jose State University in the USA has sponsored the Bulwer-Lytton Fiction contest, which challenged entrants to compose the opening sentence to the worst of all possible novels. The contest took its name from the Victorian novelist Edward Bulwer-Lytton, whose *Paul Clifford* (1830) began with the immortal lines: "It was a dark and stormy night...". The actual opening sentence reads:

It was a dark and stormy night; the rain fell in torrents – except at occasional intervals, when it was checked by a violent gust of wind which swept up the streets (for it is in London that our scene lies), rattling along the housetops, and fiercely agitating the scanty flame of the lamps that struggled against the darkness.

Scott Rice has edited several selections from the contest - *It Was a Dark and Stormy Night* , *Son of It Was a Dark and Stormy Night*, *Bride of Dark and Stormy* , *It was a Dark and Stormy Night: the Final Conflict* - all published by Penguin Books.

The 1988 winner, Rachel Sheeley, produced this:

Like an expensive sports car, fine-tuned and well-built, Portia was sleek, shapely and gorgeous, her red jumpsuit moulding her body, which was as warm as the seatcovers in July, her hair as dark as the beads of fresh rain on the hood; she was a woman driven – fuelled by a single accelerant – and she needed a man, a man who wouldn't shift from his views, a man to steer her along the right road, a man like Alf Romeo.

A shorter example (from *Bride of Dark and Stormy*) :

The sun rose slowly, like a fiery fur ball coughed up uneasily onto a sky-blue carpet by a giant unseen cat. (Michael McGarel)

Challenge your senior students to produce equally bad opening sentences!

13 Critical Literacy

Wendy Morgan

Critical teaching presumes nothing more sinister – or trendy – than an active social conscience. But it's also quite uncompromising about the centrality of social conscience in educational practice.

Knoblauch and Brannon (1993), p49

Critical Literacy at Work

A secondary English classroom teacher is introducing his Year 12 students, who are not headed for tertiary education, to the language of workplace relations. In groups, the students are examining a business journal article about new style managers in order to trace its ideology about the management of workers (Morgan, 1997, pp 114-116). In a primary classroom a teacher has set her students to explore the ways mothers are represented in Mother's Day junk mail gift catalogues (Luke, O'Brien and Comber, 1994). In an adult literacy session for students whose language background is other than English, the class are asking questions about where one another's shirts came from: who sewed them, where the fabric came from, who owns the company, and what the conditions of the workers are (in Knoblauch and Brannon, 1993, pp 149-150).

And in another secondary English classroom, one student is sharing with others this poem she has selected for its exploration of language, place and power:

SLOW

I was brought up in a nearly all Aboriginal community.
There were a couple of white bosses and their families.
The first time I ever spoke to a white person,
A kindergarten teacher, I think,
she came up to me,
'Hello', she said.
This really made me think.
Boy, I was thinkin', she can talk our language
(which was English).

Most of the language of my ancestors is nearly dead.
There are only a few words left.
I thought she was talking our language
because I had never talked to a white person before her.
So how was I supposed to know whose language was whose.
Boy was I slow.   Gundy Graham

This prompts questions among the students about who 'owns' the language used in education and other spheres of business, public and government life; and who is 'owned by' (possessed by, framed by) standard English. There is heated debate about whether some forms of English, such as Aboriginal English, are 'sub-standard' or are legitimate versions of the language. They decide they need to understand more about how people feel about their identity and their community when they must use a language which does not conjure up their history, culture and experience (Morgan, "Language, Place and Power" in Morgan et al, 1995).

These are all examples of critical literacy at work. What distinguishes these approaches to teaching from more traditional ways of 'doing English' is not just the expanded range of texts considered worthy of serious scrutiny: critical literacy teachers can also be found engaging with the canonical works of Austen and Shakespeare (and not just in order to catch the wave of popularity of recent film versions). Nor is the distinguishing feature such 'techniques' as group work, role play, or activities such as rewriting a text from the viewpoint of a marginal character: many of the strategies employed by critical literacy teachers are almost the same as those used within the 'progressive' or 'new' English from the 1970s onwards. The difference lies in the beliefs about society and about language which underpin the work of such teachers. This determines the choice of texts and approaches to them; this leads to the asking of certain (different) kinds of questions about those texts; this values different kinds of knowledge from that promoted by the literary and cultural establishment; and this is interested in different kinds of outcomes for individuals and society from the shaping of adults with finely tuned aesthetic sensibilities or competencies in using language in ways that society presently rewards.

Language and Social Difference

What meaning any of us make of that poem "Slow", what significance we give to that situation, will depend largely on our knowledge, beliefs and values that precede and shape them. (When a cluster of ideas and attitudes – for example, that the ways of white Australians are superior to those from other ethnic and cultural backgrounds – is systematic and shared by any group of people in a society we call this an ideology.) For instance, it would be possible to read the poem without irony as the necessary lessons to be learned by those who must assimilate to the dominant ways in order to ensure that there is 'one nation' in this land. Or one could take the poem mainly as an example of the adaptation by indigenous people of the artistic forms of the dominant culture – in this case, the 'free verse' form of written poetry. Indeed, such 'readings' might be discussed in a critical literacy classroom – in order to make their ideologies available for scrutiny.

In that critical literacy lesson around the poem the ideology which frames the teacher's work is broadly one of social justice (which goes beyond the tame and possibly self–interested version promoted by some governments and bureaucracies). It tries to redress the inequalities between groups of people in our society – inequalities which are also inequities (forms of injustice). Those inequalities are not the fault of individuals or groups but derive from the structures and organisation of our society, so that some groups have systematically less opportunity and access to the goods and benefits that others enjoy who are no more deserving. Those who have been positioned as 'different' (not 'the same' as 'us') include groups marked according to race, ethnicity and culture, class, gender and sexuality, physicality, age, geography, and so on. (Of course, any one individual may span several such forms of difference.)

Here is a brief introduction to the base of understanding about language and society on which critical literacy teachers build their curriculum practice:

How could literacy not be social? and not social simply in the sense that any communication is socially addressed, but more fundamentally social in that meanings can only be made with resources: languages, dialects, registers, genres, and discourse forms that are characteristic of communities, and not unique as such to individuals.

Different communities, different experiences of life, different social positions create essential contexts for the unique meanings each of us makes. . . . Difference is as social as community. And where there is difference there is always also inequality, inequity, injustice. Where there is difference there is also power, and power differences pervade our uses of language, and our attitudes toward language used. ... The word critical in critical social literacy reminds us that when we step back from the immediacy of meaning to analyse the forms through which meanings are made, we inevitably also analyse the inequities between our communities.

(Lemke, 1993, pp 9-11)

The following propositions (drawing on Janks, 1993a and 1993b, and Morgan, 1994b) expand on this view.

Language and Power in Society

1. The dominance of any social group is maintained by persuading people to consent to the belief that the status quo and the dominant ideologies

are 'natural' and 'inevitable'. Language is central to such forms of persuasion, for every text is informed by the ideologies and the discourses current at the time; these present a particular – partial and interested – version of reality and invite the reader to accept that interpretation. But language may instead be used to challenge existing forms of power and cultural dominance.

2.   Texts are constructed from a range of possible language options; many of the choices involved are social choices – rules and norms for use, which are a good indication of which group has the power to determine the workings of society. Such rules of use are social conventions, not 'given' or 'natural', for texts are constructed within a culture or subculture and for a society in a particular time and place and with particular relationships of power between people. This context governs what can be said and how.

3.   Such texts not only say certain things in certain ways but do not speak of others: they are partial and incomplete, with silences about certain matters, and incoherences or gaps, which readers are encouraged to make good or fill in with 'commonsense' – that is, unconsciously ideological – assumptions.

4.   Readings produce meanings. There is no single 'author-ised' meaning behind or prior to a text, which determines how it must be read; instead, readers in specific historical, cultural and discursive contexts can produce different, divergent, and perhaps opposed readings. When readers become aware of the choices of language, subject matter and presentation that have been made in constructing texts they are enabled to ask critical questions about those choices, including whose interests have been served by such textual constructions.

Towards a Critical Literacy Curriculum: Reading the Culture for a Critical Consciousness

The three following suggestions for framing a curriculum are only a selection; other approaches can be found in the sources listed at the end of the chapter. All of them build on the understanding of language and society, meaning and power sketched above, and all of them in some way entail these processes:

> Critical literacy teaching begins by problematising the cultures and knowledges of the text – putting them up for grabs, for critical debate, for weighing, judging, critiquing. Learning the linguistic structure of texts can be a crucial part of this process. But a social analysis of texts also requires classroom frames for talking about how and in whose interests social institutions and texts can refract and bend social and natural

*reality, manipulate and position readers and writers. Such analysis can
also provide the groundwork for 'changing the subject' of texts, and for
strategically intervening in social contexts.*
(Luke, O'Brien and Comber, 1994, p141)

1. A Freirean Approach:
Becoming Ethnographers of the Culture

The great literacy educator, Paulo Freire (1970, 1985), who worked with
underprivileged and illiterate peasants in Brazil, used this approach to
consciousness raising, but it can be adapted for a 'first world' context. (See
Lankshear and McLaren, 1993, for discussions which build on his work; and
for its adaptation in first world contexts see Shor, 1980, 1987.)

In brief, this work involves:

✦   identifying key words / concepts / artefacts and 'codifying' these by a
    photo or drawing.
    (Shor used the common hamburger! Note that critical literacy takes as
    its 'texts' whatever in our social institutions and structures can be read
    as text.)
✦   investigating the 'reality' and 'forms of life' they are implicated in.
    (For the hamburger this could include the international economics of
    the beef supply, the environmental impact of the packaging, the working
    conditions of employees, the ideologies promoted in the advertising
    campaigns, the cultural effects of a fast food culture, the nutritional
    effects of such foods on populations and the like.)
✦   engaging in social action as a result of this process of 'conscientisation'.
    (This might take various forms: parodying advertisements; framing and
    distributing   informational   leaflets;   campaigning   to   ensure   that
    nutritionally   sound   food   is   available   in   the   local   canteen   and
    information about its benefits is provided to consumers.)

2. A Focus on the Nature of Reading and Writing

This approach (Wallace, 1992) carries out ethnographic research into
literacy. It means not taking for granted the practices which may be peculiar
to a particular group within a culture. In order to investigate the social, partial
and political nature of the production and circulation of texts, the practices
that surround them and their role in our understanding of our lives, the
following questions are asked:

✦   What reading practices are characteristic of particular social groups?
✦   How are reading materials produced in a particular society, who
    produces them, and how do they come to have the salience they do?
✦   What influences the process of interpreting texts in particular
    contexts?

These could of course be adapted for various forms of text, such as new technologised forms of literacy involving computer games, the World Wide Web and the like.

3. A Focus on Intertextuality: Juxtaposing Texts

This approach can be useful in when a work of literature is set for close study by a whole class (see further Morgan, 1994b for the theory and more detailed suggestions for approaches; for a wide set of such texts and their treatment see Morgan, 1994c). The rationale for such juxtapositions is that when one text is set alongside another it is easier to see where a particular text is 'coming from', what its 'neighbours' are and what is foregrounded or marginalised. In order to create a productive friction, it is most useful to choose texts which:

✦ offer a range of kinds of information, from different fields and disciplines;
✦ are grounded in a range of ideological perspectives;
✦ come from different historical times and cultural locations.

Developing Critical Literacy Reading Skills

Within these or other curriculum frames, the following questions (from Luke, O'Brien and Comber, 1994) may be useful in taking investigations further. Note that these questions guide the teacher's planning; they are not always to be used directly in interrogating students, but may instead be 'translated' into activities which strategically develop understanding of the issues. Such activities may be followed by deliberate reflection to permit the more conscious articulation of these understandings.

1. Situating the Text

✦ What is the topic and why is this topic being written about?
✦ How is the topic being presented?
What themes and discourses are being used?
✦ Who is writing to whom?
Whose voices and positions are being expressed, and whose are not?
✦ How is the text encouraging you to think and respond?
✦ What other ways are there of writing about the topic?
✦ What wasn't said about the topic, and why?

2. Locating the Text in the World

The following set of questions overlaps with the first, but perhaps focuses more explicitly on matters of context:

✦ Where does this text come from? (This deals with the historical and cultural context of the text.)
✦ What kind of text is this? (This asks about intertextuality – how texts resemble other texts in their genre and conventions and draw on them for their meanings.)
✦ What meanings and contexts of meanings are possible from this text? (This focuses on the versions of reality that are constructed in the text.)
✦ What social function does this text serve? (Language may have power to offer us a certain kind of knowledge and belief in its 'truth' – with consequences for our lives and those of others.)
✦ What kind of reader does this text propose and what position is afforded to him/her?

3. The Writer, the Reader, and the World in the Text

The following questions (from Lankshear, 1994) extend that last question and go beyond description and critique to the possibility of reconstruction and textual meanings and social relations:

✦ How does this text construct a version of reality and knowledge? and
✦ What is left out of this story?
✦ How does this text represent the reader and set up a position for reading?
and
✦ What other position might there be for reading?
✦ How does this text set up its authority and encourage your belief?
and
✦ How can you deconstruct its authority?

Developing a Critical Social Imagination

The work alluded to above, of reconstructing texts, reading positions and meanings, hence ultimately participating in the work of building a more equitable democracy, cannot be carried out through analytical work alone. Teachers will need to help foster the imagination of their students – not a capacity for personal, creative fantasy so much as an interpersonal, practical, historical or 'sociological' imagination. This is necessary if students' feelings and attitudes are to be engaged sympathetically with the lives of others and if their speculating is to take the form of a broad social vision. Such a critical social imagination depends on three kinds of understanding (Morgan, 1996):

1. an analytical understanding of how texts and discourses work to represent reality and define what is desirable or possible or necessary for us;
2. a sympathetic understanding of the people who are affected, shaped, by those representations; and

3. a hopeful imagination of how we – teachers and students – can engage with those texts and their debates; how we can help to reconstruct them by constructing our own texts; how through such text-making we can help re-present aspects of reality and re-define what's desirable and possible.

Revolution or Evolution?

After such counsels, it is important to recognise that the work that goes on in actual – messy and mundane – critical literacy classrooms Monday through Friday is inevitably limited and incomplete, always in process towards ends we can never be certain would in all senses be beneficial. For the institutions, discourses and ideologies and systematic practices of schooling and society at large are the contexts which shape our work and us. We can aspire to an ideal of a socially just society, but it will remain just that, an ideal. It will inevitably be a practice shot through with contradictions and tensions, contingencies, self-sabotage and resistances from within us and from beyond. And there are questions, still (always?) unresolved, about such matters as these (discussed in chapter 1 of Morgan, 1997): Are individuals free agents, choosing for themselves, or 'subjects' governed by social forces? (Or both?) Do people give authentic 'voice' to their own thoughts and feelings, or do discourses speak (through) people? If there is no position beyond the reach of ideology, how can people be 'enlightened' about the workings of all ideology, and emancipated from its grasp? If critical literacy teachers are right, are students wrong when they do not see the world in the same way? If critical literacy practises a 'resistant' reading (one that refuses to go along with the meanings the text invites), is there no room for a 'submissive' – aesthetic – reading for pleasure?

Meanwhile, critical literacy education, like any other, is a particular form of contextualised social practice. It may also be marked by shifts of attitude and behaviour in ourselves and our students, and our world. We may not be able to guarantee these, but we can at least practise a practice for language and literacy in the service of a more just world.

The poem by Gundy Graham appears in Mattingly, C and Hampton, K (eds) (1992) *Survival in Our Own Land,* Aboriginal Development Assistance Association: Hodder and Stoughton.

Books about Critical Literacy

Aronowitz, S and Giroux, H (1985) *Education Under Siege,* South Hadley, MA: Bergin and Garvey.
Aronowitz, S and Giroux, H (1991) *Postmodern Education: Politics, Culture, and Social Criticism,* Minneapolis: University of Minnesota Press.
Fairclough, N (1989) *Language and Power,* London: Longman.

Fairclough, N (ed) (1992a) *Critical Language Awareness*, London: Longman.

Fairclough, N (1992b) *Discourse and Social Change*, Oxford: Polity Press.

Freire, P (1970) *Pedagogy of the Oppressed*, New York: Seabury Press.

Freire, P (1985) *The Politics of Education: Culture, Power, and Liberation*, trans. D. Macedo, South Hadley, MA: Bergin and Garvey.

Freire, P and Macedo, D (1987) *Literacy: Reading the Word and the World*, South Hadley, MA: Bergin and Garvey.

Gee, J P (1990) *Social Linguistics and Literacies: Ideology in Discourses*, London: Falmer Press.

Giroux, H (1983) *Schooling and the Struggle for Public Life: Critical Pedagogy in the Modern Age*, Minneapolis: University of Minnesota Press.

Giroux, H (1988) *Teachers as Intellectuals: Towards a Critical Pedagogy of Learning*, New York: Bergin and Garvey.

Giroux, H (1991) "Literacy, Difference, and the Politics of Border Crossing", in C Mitchell and K Weiler (eds) *Rewriting Literacy: Culture and the Discourse of the Other*, New York: Bergin and Garvey.

Giroux, H (1992) *Border Crossings: Cultural Workers and the Politics of Education*, New York and London: Routledge.

Giroux, H and McLaren, P (eds) (1994) *Between Borders: Pedagogy and the Politics of Cultural Studies*, New York and London: Routledge.

Janks, H (1993a) *Language and Position*, Critical Language Awareness Series, Johannesburg: Witwatersrand University Press and Hodder and Stoughton.

Janks, H (1993b) *Language, Identity and Power*, Critical Language Awareness Series, Johannesburg: Witwatersrand University Press and Hodder and Stoughton.

Kecht, M (ed) (1992) *Pedagogy is Politics: Literary Theory and Critical Teaching*, Urbana and Chicago: University of Illinois Press.

Knoblauch, C and Brannon, L (1993) *Critical Teaching and the Idea of Literacy*, Portsmouth, NH: Heinemann/Boynton-Cook.

Lankshear, C (1994) *Critical Literacy*, Occasional Paper No. 3, Belconnen, ACT: Australian Curriculum Studies Association.

Lankshear, C and McLaren, P (eds) (1993) *Critical Literacy: Politics, Praxis, and the Postmodern*, Albany: State University of New York Press.

Lemke, J (1993) "Critical Social Literacy for the New Century" *English in Australia*, 105: 9-15.

Lemke, J (1995) *Textual Politics: Discourse and Social Dynamics*, London: Taylor and Francis.

Luke, A, O'Brien, J, and Comber, B (1994) "Making Community Texts the Objects of Study" *Australian Journal of Language and Literacy*, 17, 2: 139–49.

Morgan, W (1994a) " 'Clothes Wear Out, Learning Doesn't': Realising Past and Future in Today's Critical Literacy Curriculum" Perth, WA: Papers of the Australian Association for the Teaching of English National Conference.

Morgan, W (1994b) "The Play of Texts in Contexts" *Literacy Learning: Secondary Thoughts*, 2,2: 8–24.

Morgan, W (1996) "Critical Literacy: More than Sceptical Distrust or Political Correctness?" Keynote Address published in *Critical Literacy*, ed Morgan, W (with Gilbert, P, Lankshear, C, Werba, S and Williams, L) Norwood, SA: Australian Association for the Teaching of English.

Morgan, W (1997) *Critical Literacy in the Classroom: The Art of the Possible*, London and New York: Routledge.

Shannon, P (ed) *Becoming Political: Readings and Writings in the Politics of Literacy Education*, Portsmouth, NH: Heinemann.

Shor, I (1980) *Critical Teaching and Everyday Life*, Chicago: University of Chicago Press.

Shor, I (ed) (1987) *Freire for the Classroom: A Sourcebook for Liberatory Teaching*, Portsmouth, NH: Heinemann / Boynton–Cook.

Simon, R (1992) *Teaching Against the Grain: Texts for a Pedagogy of Possibility*, New York: Bergin and Garvey.

Slevin, J and Young, A (eds) (1996) *Critical Theory and the Teaching of Literature: Politics, Curriculum, Pedagogy*, Urbana, Ill: National Council of Teachers of English.

Wallace, C (1992) "Critical Literacy Awareness in the EFL Classroom", in Fairclough, N (ed) *Critical Language Awareness*, London: Longman.

Resource and Course Books for Teachers and Students

Gilbert, P (ed) (1995) *Challenging the Text: Critical Literacy Units for Secondary English*, Canberra: National Professional Development Program.

Morgan, W (1994c) *Ned Kelly Reconstructed*, Melbourne: Cambridge University Press.

Morgan, W et al (1995) *A World of Texts: Global Understanding in the English Classroom*, Brisbane: Global Learning Centre.

Martino, W with Mellor, B (1995) *Gendered Fictions*, Scarborough, WA: Chalkface Press.

Mellor, B, Hemming, J and Leggett, J (1984) *Changing Stories*, London: ILEA Centre and Scarborough, WA: Chalkface Press.

Mellor, B, Patterson, A and ONeill, M (1991) *Reading Fictions*, Scarborough, WA: Chalkface Press.

Doublespeak

For many years, the National Council of Teachers of English (USA) has crusaded against 'doublespeak': language that is grossly deceptive, evasive, euphemistic, confusing or self-contradictory. Each year it presents an ironic Doublespeak Award to the American public figure (or organisation) which has been the worst offender. Some examples of doublespeak include:

collateral damage – (referring to civilian deaths in the Allied bombing of Iraq during the Gulf War)

safety-related occurrence – (accident)

advanced downward adjustments – (budget cuts)

period of accelerated negative growth – (recessions)

protective reaction strike – (bombing)

predawn vertical insertion – (airborne invasion)

enhance the efficiency of operations – (sack employees)

dehired – (sacked)

energetic disassembly – (explosion)

> *Quarterly Review of Doublespeak* National Council of Teachers of English, 1111 Kenyon Road, Urbana, Illinois 61801, USA

Any consideration of doublespeak (and euphemism in general) inevitably leads to a consideration of the debate about political correctness. Is there more to political correctness (which has been described as "euphemism with attitude") than a proper sensitivity to the feelings of others? Is it a threat to free speech, as some claim?

Like anything else, political correctness can be parodied. We particularly like one that turned up on the Internet:

It's demeaning and size-ist to refer to Santa's helpers as "Elves". The preferred term is "Subordinate Clauses".

References

Allen, Keith and Burridge, Kate(1991) *Euphemism and Dysphemism: Language Used as Shield and Weapon*, New York: Oxford University Press.

Sawyer, Wayne (1995) *Looking at Our Language*, Sydney: St Clair.

14 Visual Literacy: Enabling and Promoting Critical Viewing

John Stephens

I t is not news to teachers of 'English' that the parameters of their subject have long since expanded beyond its foundations in literacy, literature and drama, so that what English teachers do is much more diverse than might be inferred from the subject name itself. Now, they need to be more multi-skilled than ever before, proficient in working with various visual media as well as print media, and adept in a wide range of cultural formations and the discourses which incorporate them. Moreover, the kinds of knowledge required for these proficiencies go well beyond an understanding of the formal aspects of visual media, or of media with a visual component. A teacher also needs a self-reflexive awareness of the politics and sociology of media production and interpretation – in other words, she or he needs to be aware of how images of society are represented or reflected and of how audiences relate to and interrogate those representations. Visual literacy – the analytical understanding of visual images – addresses a wide range of representational forms, including film, television, paintings, photographs, and so on, and with a wide range of intentions between information and entertainment. For the purposes of this brief discussion, I will draw particular examples from some 'everyday' photographs.

When, from about a century ago, technologies began to evolve which would revolutionise the production and transmission of cultural forms so that visual media took over many of the communicative functions of the printed word, it was assumed that the language of images would be self-evident. Whereas literacy was a developed skill, requiring at least some formal training and not always acquired to a degree which made its proficients even remotely equal in an information-based society, no special skills or training would be needed by consumers of visual images. A photograph, for example, might be viewed as a simple reproduction of empirical reality, and this is probably how people usually think about family snapshots or tourist photographs. Nevertheless, to an outsider the reality so represented may seem quite subjective, a construction of a reality which is not shared and perhaps not particularly interesting. Even with something as apparently straightforward as a snapshot of a street scene, the significance may well lie in the associations brought to it by the viewer. Figure 1 (see page 171) is a photograph of a street in Gamla Stan, the old part of Stockholm. Its function is, let us say, to express an ambience, to remind the photographer of the feeling of being in a part of the world where the streets are narrow and cobble-stoned and there are no high-rise buildings. There are people in the photograph, but they are unimportant, merely part of the ambience; this seems evident from the woman in the foreground, who is unposed and walking away. For a person flicking through a bundle of holiday snaps, the picture would probably not rate a second glance: it is someone else's banal memory. Other viewers, though, may bring memories of their own or even random associations to the picture. Contrast this picture with Figure 2, a fashion photograph taken by Simon Lekias for *Dolly* magazine. The setting is again actual (Campbell Parade, Bondi Beach), but the sense of reality is constructed in a different way, communicating a different interest, and inviting other kinds of association. Now this is evident in the posing of Ali, the model, in the foreground, and the relationship viewers may perceive between that figure and the 'natural' or uninterpreted figures who have apparently strayed into the background – for example, is the function of these background figures to accentuate the element of artifice in the foreground of the scene, or to evoke reality by reflecting the randomness of (irrelevant) figures which appear in a tourist's snapshots, as in Figure 1, or to assert something about fashion photography by the contrast of their winter clothing with Ali's rather skimpy dress? An importance difference between the two photographs also lies in the positioning of the viewing subject, first, as socially located as viewer of a bundle of snapshots or as reader of *Dolly* magazine, and second, as physically situated by the horizontal and vertical angles of scene in relation to viewer.

Reality itself, then, is mediated by visual images. Various visual media – magazines, television, films, and so on – are involved in representing images of society and in presenting information to society, and English teachers have a primary responsibility to incorporate critical media awareness into classroom practice. However, this is not necessarily a matter of enabling students to deconstruct and resist forms of media bias or particular ideological formations discerned in advertising or in television programs, because that may be too simple-minded a view of text-viewer relationships. It is often argued, particularly in relation to television audiences, that viewers are not positioned by a single dominant ideology, but interact with a multiplicity of possible discourses, activated by a viewer's other social, cultural and institutional experiences. If this were not so, and television achieved the kind of cultural hegemony over viewers imagined as a worst case, it would be hard to explain why some programs fail. Nevertheless, inasmuch as "media systems are complex, incomplete, and partially efficient channels for reproducing existing social relations" (Ross, 1989, p106), the extent to which significance is determined by the structures of the viewed text or by the viewer's variously interrogative readings of that text remains a subject of inconclusive debate. What might be developed in classroom practice, then, is an enhanced awareness of how visual images work, how they relate to particular socio-cultural formations, and how viewers go about positioning themselves and relating to the positions implied by a visual text.

The language of visual images is far from self-evident, and in a society as visually oriented as, say, Australian society in the late twentieth century, most people appear surprisingly inept when it comes to visual literacy. This is partly because when we talk about images we tend to do so by narrativising the content, but it is also because we often lack concepts relating to visuality and a language for expressing such concepts. Hence it is important to teach appreciation and analysis of formal properties such as line, shape, space, balance, angle of view, perspective, and colour, though always keeping in mind that students must also develop abilities to go beyond the formal visual elements and gain access to the complexity of meanings, both cognitive and visual, that they offer. This further move will also bring into play such aspects of text-viewer interaction as intertextuality, genre, and culturally-grounded metonymy. By applying such concepts to visual images, viewers are enabled to arrive at both aesthetic and thematic responses and interpretations. The two photographs discussed above will further illustrate this.

By positioning the viewer only slightly left of centre in the street, Figure 1 produces a formal balance between the two sides of the picture which is only to a small extent offset by the figure in the foreground and the uneven height of the roofs. Further, the viewer's gaze is firmly controlled by the one-point perspective: the strong vectors formed by the lines of the buildings both at ground and rooftop levels converge on the centre of the picture where the street happens to end. The gaze is directed towards that point, so that the combined effect of the symmetry and the vectors is to draw the eye past the possible objects of interest in the scene to the light-bleached building in the background. Vectors, lines which are 'a force with a direction and a magnitude' as Zettl defines the term (in Berger, 1989, p47), focus attention on objects of central importance, so if this were a scene inviting interpretation viewers would expect its significance to emerge from this effect. It doesn't, so both aesthetically and thematically the result is dullness and banality. In contrast, Figure 2 cultivates asymmetry to generate a more visually exciting scene. The lines of the building, especially at ground level, again produce a firm vector which could draw the eye towards the background, but this is forestalled in two ways. First, and most obviously, by the human interest of the close-up figure in the foreground, and by the counter vectors established by the curve of her body away from and back towards the door and by the patches of white space (the upper door panels, the model's dress, and the white space behind the background figures), an angular series pivoting on the foregrounded human figure. Second – and this is another point of contrast with Figure 1 – the photographer has used a shallow depth of field to emphasise the sharply focused foreground and de-emphasise the softly focused background. A less artful photograph such as Figure 1, concerned as it is to capture the reality of the scene, will prefer maximum depth of field. In this case, the photographer would be apt to feel quite piqued if a section of the photograph were out of focus, since that would defeat its purpose as a visual recount of a memory.

There are three other aspects to the reading of these photographs which have bearing on their thematic and social meanings. Visual media, including home snapshots, are always a construction drawing on conscious and unconscious decisions about what is socially important – what objects, what knowledge, and what kind of human relations. Second, viewers negotiate meaning by drawing on their knowledge of visual codes, of genres and of intertextual fields. And third, visual messages have the potential to affect social attitudes and behaviour. In *Reading Images* (1996, p119) Kress and van Leeuwen point out that images involve three kinds of relations: that between the people, places and things depicted within the image (the *represented participants*); that of viewer and the represented participants, hinging on the attitude of the viewer; and that of viewer and the producer(s) of the image. Both photographs are what Kress and van Leeuwen describe as an 'offer', that is, represented participants are offered to viewers 'as items of information, objects of contemplation, impersonally, as though they were specimens in a display case' (p124). This is obvious enough in a tourist snapshot. When a travelling companion is included, gazing out at the viewer, the image demands some kind of social response from the viewer, a recognition of some reciprocity.

Figure 2 invites a complex range of possible interactions. An important point to be made at the outset is that the audience for the image is teenage females, and this obviously affects how the picture is looked at, especially since it is an offer, marked by Ali's pensive downward gaze, a configuration further accentuated by the genre. It is a fashion photograph, as the overprinting in the lower right-hand corner, identifying and pricing the clothing worn, reminds the viewer, and appears as one of a sequence of seven such photographs. But it also establishes a playful relationship with the conventions of fashion photography: the sequence is in black and white, whereas the commentary frequently refers to fabric colours, and some garments referred to are scarcely visible at all; many items of clothing are second-hand or the property of the model herself, so viewers are shown a domain of actual possibility rather than exotic, unattainable fashion; and, at the same time, the choice of black and white and various elements of layout and structure suggest an allusion to art photography. The conjuncture of possibilities here is fairly characteristic of the playful, often humorously ironic, interaction amongst producers, images and audiences cultivated in magazines such as *Dolly* or *Girlfriend*. Audiences are encouraged to form different kinds of relationship with the image, though some critics would argue that this only takes place within a particular range of parameters determined on the one hand by what is included in and excluded from represented images, and how those images are controlled, and on the other hand by the ways in which viewers are already positioned towards particular discourses of femininity and fashion (they might be slavish consumers of images; but, oppositionally, they might always consider cowboy boots gross, for example, or short dresses exploitative of female bodies).

Another complex aspect of image-making in Figure 2 lies in the functions of metonymy. Metonymy is an utterly crucial aspect of visual images, in that the extent to which visual media have the potential to manipulate audiences resides largely in metonymic effects. Metonymy is activated when a sign based on culturally determined associations stands as a part to a larger whole by means of an overlap of literal and figurative function. In a simple way, the street in Gamla Stan (Figure 1) is metonymic when reproduced as an image: the street is old, but extremely clean and well-maintained, declaring itself a prime example of cultural heritage and hence cultural capital. In Figure 2, as in fashion photographs generally, the model's clothing has a metonymic function, carrying generalised messages about style, bodily production and 'attitude'. What is signified here is complicated by the relative expensiveness ($155) of a dress a size too small for the wearer, but which appears stylish in contrast with the clothing of the background figures, who are nothing if not daggy (there are hints of anoraks here), and so are appropriately out of focus. What, though, are the metonymic effects of the dilapidated doors, Ali's clutching of the handle, and the pensive, even sad, body language? Is she hesitant about entering? Is she having second thoughts about leaving? Is she locked out? Has she arrived at the wrong time? Has the business (or whatever) closed down? There are multiple possibilities here which enable viewers to narrativise the scene by inserting their own intertextual associations, and these in turn may range from actual-life experiences to myriad 'high' art representations of exclusion and alienation. The image has, in effect, an uncontrolled space here, but its metonymic functions will nevertheless stand in some kind of relationship – contrastive, playful, ironic – to the metonymic functions of the dress. A further uncontrolled element enters this play of discourses from the verbal data: the 'second-hand cowboy boots' are contiguous with the dilapidated doors, so does this affect the associations of *second-hand*, which otherwise tend towards 'resourceful' rather than 'shabby'? It might be better to say that it's part of the picture's self-ironising, blurring the distinctions between the represented and the real and between the romantically dilapidated and the seedy.

The intertextual possibilities of the photo are thus quite open, and the image is a good example of how a particular text exists and is consumed in an intertextual context, a range of generalised textual and cultural knowledges which viewers bring to the viewing (see Fiske, 1987, pp 108-127). Intertextuality poses a particular problem for English teachers now that the dominant notion of textuality has shifted from the 'text in itself' to 'the text in its contexts' and to a sense that meaning lies *between* texts rather than within them. Verbal and visual codes can, and should, be taught, but intertextuality can really only be pointed to, though never comprehensively, and what can be taught is the strategies and functions of intertextuality. Often, too, intertexts turn out to be the domain of sub-cultures (teenage girls from particular socio-economic groups, say) or they pertain to localised discourses. Thus a different intertextual effect seems evident in Figure 3, another street scene, but now of a street in the old part of Tallinn, Estonia, photographed in the spring of 1996. Within cultural experiences, this street might stand in an intertextual relationship with the Gamla Stan street, and does so once I have brought them together in this discussion. The Estonian street is perhaps potentially more aesthetically pleasing (the buildings are varied, individual and architecturally inventive, and the winding layout promises and delivers moments of suspense and surprise). But it is marked by various forms of dilapidation: the focused building in the centre of the picture has crumbling brickwork and peeling paint; paving stones are uneven or missing; the grit spread to enable pedestrians to walk in snow has not yet been cleaned away; and, what in my current discourse constitutes a degradation of cultural capital, the facade of the building in the foreground has been modernised and rendered neutral and characterless. We can interpret this dilapidation literally as the combined effects of the harsh Northern winter and a depressed economy; we can also read it both literally and metonymically as the effect of the fifty year winter of Soviet occupation on an invaded culture. Reading the street in this way in fact constitutes a material example of how metonymies are socially produced, because tourist brochures published in Tallinn in 1996 overtly encouraged such a politically-informed metonymic reading of Tallinn streetscapes. What we have here, then, is one of the more arcane forms of intertextuality, where a particular historical and political awareness enables a more fully informed reading of the scene. This is not to say that the scene will be meaningless for a viewer without access to this knowledge, but the meaning made will be inevitably different. Arguably, it will also be a diminished meaning, but that is another issue.

I have tied this discussion to specific and detailed examples for a reason. In general, I advocate an approach to teaching visual literacy which is grounded in the communication of principles (how various visual media work), the teaching of concepts relevant to the production and interpretation of visual images, and the teaching of an interpretative language which appropriately expresses those concepts. Since the process is always about interpreting cultures, exercises in visual literacy will properly be 'text' centred and involve aesthetic, practical and broad cultural considerations. Visual interpretations of still images begin with literal interpretations based on examination of such elements as the content, the layout, and the relationships between represented participants, and then move to more thematic or metonymic concepts – cultural themes, codes, and messages – that are inferred from that initial analysis. As my discussion of the three photographs has suggested, the kinds of meanings viewers will make will depend on the sophistication of their viewing literacy, the range of intertexts they access as individuals, their individual positioning in relation to the ideological presuppositions of the focused text, and the relative transparency in context of the intended meanings of the producer. In this regard, Simon Lekias' playful photograph for *Dolly* magazine supports a rich variety of interpretations.

What I have said about photographic images generally applies to other kinds of visual media. In watching film and television, for example, viewers need a basic foundation for understanding narrative and for decoding the dramatic and cinematic or televisual elements used to unfold narrative thematically; and they need to understand continuity and closure in order to enable an analysis of whole texts. They also need to be aware of the differences between film and television as media – the different kinds of images they present through their different uses of camera angles and spatiality. It is important to remain alert to the effect of the social, political and economic environment on the production and reception of visual media. And finally, a point commonly made by advocates of critical literacy, and which also lies at the core of teaching media as a form of textual construction: the school curriculum itself represents ideology and values and has social and political implications in its role as a context in which interpretation takes place.

References

Berger, Arthur Asa (1989) *Seeing Is Believing: An Introduction to Visual Communication*, Mountain View, CA: Mayfield Publishing Company.

Buckingham, David (ed) (1993) *Reading Audiences: Young People and the Media*, Manchester and New York: Manchester University Press.

Fiske, John (1980) *Television Culture*, London and New York: Routledge.

Giardetti, J Roland and Oller, John W Jr (1995) "Testing a Theory of Photographic Meaning", *Semiotica*, 106,1-2: 99-152.

Kress, Gunther, and van Leeuwen, Theo (1996) *Reading Images: The Grammar of Visual Design*, London and New York: Routledge.

Morley, David (1980) *The 'Nationwide' Audience*, London: British Film Institute.

Ross, Andrew (1989) *No Respect: Intellectuals & Popular Culture*, London and New York: Routledge, Chapter 4.

Figure 1

Figure 2

Figure 3

15 Wide Reading

Ernie Tucker

Wide reading was one of the most obvious advances and one of the more accessible teaching methods advocated by the post-Dartmouth "new English". To make life even more easy for the reborn English teacher, wide reading was supported by well written, well designed textbooks which came direct from the horse's mouth: Dixon and Stratta (1963) in the UK, Delves, Tickell (1971), the Hannans and Boomer and Hood (1971) in Australia. What happened?

Teachers took up the themes approach to integrate English teaching and release it from the incredible grip of grammar on Monday, comprehension Tuesday, novel Wednesday, Shakespeare Thursday, spelling Friday, composition fitted in once a fortnight at best, and poetry, speech and drama occasionally replacing one of the regulars. Media was the mark of a radical teacher and best avoided. Themes and integration seemed to be the two messages which got through to the majority of teachers. Perhaps because the text books used extracts from novels and plays, wide reading was often ignored. However, with the paperback revolution coming to children's literature in the seventies, wide reading should have flourished. It didn't.

I turn to research to find support for these reflections. From 1981-1985 a federal team created The Children's Choice Project (Bunbury, 1995). They devised a questionnaire followed up by interviews of both teachers, students and parents concerning the reading chosen by children in Years 5, 7, 9 and 11. 3,338 students were chosen from 11,461 students who answered the initial survey and the final results were derived from a selected sample of 936 students and 492 teachers. For comparison, this Australia-wide research also published a valuable review of research into the reading preferences of Australian children since 1929.

From this mass of information, we find that, although children were reading widely for leisure, their English teachers and school librarians were having minimal influence on their choice. Very little reading done at school, or for school purposes, was enjoyed. Wide reading had not taken off in our classrooms. The single text, usually a novel, shared by the whole class was the new orthodoxy. The list of class shared texts makes depressing reading.

A few figures. The "class library" as the source of books read for leisure fell from Year 5, where 12.3% of boys and 15.1% of girls found their books, to 6.6% and 8.8% in Year 7, to 2.0% and 3.0% in Year 9. Contrast that with the students themselves as the source: Year 5, 21.0% of boys and 30.7% of girls, rising to 26.1% and 36.5% in Year 7 before the fall to 23.5% and 30.1% in Year 9. (Bunbury, 1995, p66)

Yet the questionnaires and interviews showed that students do enjoy reading widely and do enjoy discussing their reading with their peers. Students made the distinction between oral discussion of ideas and the accountability concept of the book reports required by teachers. As the project report puts it:

Discussion about books they choose to read was evidently an activity enjoyed by young people, so might it not be possible to provide more time for such discussions (in small groups) in class? Such discussions would be very different in nature and intensity from the oral book reports which occupy a moderate amount of class time for some teachers ... Instead of such small group discussions it is the written book report which occupies an increasing amount of class time ...and while such activities keep the pupils busy and provide a system of accountability, they do not match the lively interchange of oral discussion where one pupil learns most from another. (Bunbury, 1995, p70)

Unfortunately this research, although referred to frequently as "work in progress" during the '80s, was long delayed until it was finally published in 1995. This is one reason for the results being much neglected and I fear that the picture is much the same today: there is a major disparity between students' choice of reading and that selected for them by their teachers and when reading is set, the one novel shared by the whole class is the predominant activity. Death by a thousand worksheets. Trivial pursuit. The only advance that I can detect without research is that booksellers and publishers find that teachers are more mobile in their choice of the class shared text. I almost wrote "adventurous" but I still live in hope.

It seems that once Australian texts by Southall, Wrightson, Marshall and Thiele, English texts by Garner, Dahl and Lewis, and American texts by Byars, Zindel and White were allowed into the classroom, teachers found that this was as much width as they could give. If our selection of class texts has become more wide, I suspect this nine-author band is still about the limit.

Apply this template to your own teaching over the last four years of Years 7 to 11. Around nine authors? Have I stumbled on a new magic number for English teachers? And who would be the authors today? With English writers, Fine replaces Garner but others such as Doherty and Swindells are not perhaps as widespread as Dahl and Lewis still, and great writers such as Howker are neglected. With American writers, Cormier and Paterson; Byars is less there, but otherwise, teachers use single titles such as the amazingly successful and long lasting *To Kill a Mockingbird* and *Z for Zachariah*. Great writers such as Hamilton and Lowry win Newbery medals but are neglected here. But in Australia, and this is beginning to sound just a little like Leporello's catalogue aria, not quite 1003 but it is difficult to guess three who dominate. Marsden, Crew and Caswell? Wheatley, Kelleher and Gleitzman? Klein, Winton and Gleeson? Who have I left out? How often are Southall and Wrightson, our two internationally revered writers, still promoted and used by English teachers? This should start a few staffroom arguments but there's no prize for the dominant single title: *Looking for Alibrandi*.

What has happened has been a wide expansion in the variety of texts used to include feature film, video and written mass media and an increased percentage of Australian texts. One other advance I have seen is some evidence of author study of Crew, Paterson and Voigt. Short stories are beginning to emerge from the 'Henry Lawson only' category with some excellent recent collections, but these appeal to us for the teacher-dominated kind of lessons such as reading aloud. The other use of a short story collection I recommend is that the students be asked to sample the whole book, read it all if they wish but choose just one story for spoken or written response. This makes for different group formations and gives the group responsibility for that story in their response to the rest of the class.

Issues of a more radically wide reading, involving the frightening possibility of twenty-nine students reading twenty-nine different texts at the same time in the same classroom and responding to their reading, lead me to questions about the innate conservatism of schools and schooling.

Any teacher threatened with a choice between new methods and classroom control is likely to choose classroom control. When we are all under continuous media, administrative and politicial attack on our performances in literacy education, we can only be grateful that wide reading survived at all.

A whole generation of teachers was trained in the behaviourist tradition of individualising instruction and most of us found it impossible. We knew it was stupid to try and teach a whole class *Kidnapped* so we found more culturally close texts and graded the classes and the questions to accommodate an approximation of classroom control. To find these texts we did read much more children's literature and we did take more risks and change the texts more frequently as funding improved slightly to allow, but individualised reading remained neglected.

The reorganisation of libraries and librarians into resource-and-information-skills, then technology-skills centres, rather than places for the development of readers, took away another lesson a week, when, typically, Year 7 students would be reading in a classroom situation as individuals.

Various schemes such as RIBIT, USSR and DEAR were introduced to fulfil reading across the curriculum goals for the administration but I suspect that these practices, which were included in the Children's Choice research, gave further comfort to those English teachers who said that they had no time to give to classroom reading when they had already given up x minutes a week to the whole-school scheme.

When schools began to afford quality photocopiers, English teachers rapidly took up word processing and the contemporary worksheet approach to reading was established. If you want proof, simply look in your English department filing cabinets and check the next executive meeting complaint about the budget blowout for paper use and copier maintenance. Worksheets that no longer turn yellow with age are a formidable threat to quality English teaching.

Faced with a static and conservative approach to reading, we now find ourselves further disempowered by simplistic and reactionary methods of assessing literacies. Cheap-fix tests with machine marking, promoted by banks and universities in the name of excellence and required by ignorant administrations and politicians in the name of accountability, reduce reading to the level of sporting contests. However, there may be a hidden and unintended benefit in that they do not use set texts and that the generally well read teachers who get stuck with the job of creating these tests are also media-wise and as a result are able to produce a test which includes a wide range of well presented and interesting reading. Perhaps teachers will decide that the one text class novel is not the best way to prepare students for the test. They may even include the dreaded magazine reading which the Children's Choice project revealed increases in leisure reading from Years 5 to 11 even with boys. (Bunbury, 1995, p50) The danger is that extended texts like novels will be read less often.

The current literacies emphasis in The National Literacy Policy (Lo Bianco and Freebody, 1997) also gives us an opportunity from a conservative government source. Seeing wide reading in the newer context of readings and literacies conveniently concurs with other recent developments in the social nature of literacies and learning. If we can persuade our colleagues to risk being learners while they are teachers in the classroom then a new season of wide reading may begin. It's still a big ask in the context of the architectural and administrative constraints of classrooms and schooling but a minority of teachers have been successfully teaching with multiple texts since Dartmouth.

One key to a successful transformation of these teaching/learning practices is the change of focus from literature to reading; from the passive reception of the canon to the active re-creation of the text. This was inherent in the change from the literary heritage model to the growth model of English teaching but reading became ghettoised in the behaviourist skills area of the curriculum. High school teachers today still think they know little about the teaching of reading. While this humility is commendable, this attitude disempowered the very group who are the elite readers of the educated community. There are now many teaching guidance texts, chiefly from Margaret Meek and Jack Thomson which help us to share the secrets of reading. (Tucker 1988 and 1994)

When reading is seen as a social activity which students enjoy when they select their own texts, the pleasure principle works in our favour. Adult book circles have shown this for more than twenty years. When students use methods such as the reader's journal for private responses and the varieties of classroom talk for more public thinking, teachers can demonstrate how students progress as readers and, by keeping simple records, know where their students have gone and need to go in the future.

And I do mean simple records, such as a class list sent around the class on a clipboard every lesson for students to record titles and/or page numbers for both school sourced and out of school sourced texts. Most commercial homework diaries have a 'books read' space that makes the record personal. A simple rating system also helps to start discussion and promote reading through wall charts. This is the Children's Choice scale: if you use this, it will tie in with the photocopiable questionnaire in their appendix. "I did not like it at all; I did not like it much; I thought it was OK; I liked it very much; I thought it was one of the best." (Bunbury, 1995, p255 ff)

This way, instead of the teacher wrestling with the impossible task of individualising the program, the students are doing it. Think of all the times we tried to emulate the SRA box of cards with questions on an inevitably restricted range of books. The tricky bit is still the creation of the reading environment which encourages trust, experiment, risk taking and sharing , among the myriad of other subtle factors in the classroom learning ecology. However, this is the stuff of good English teaching in all areas of the curriculum. The crucial development in a wide reading classroom is the elimination of fakery, plagiarism and hypocrisy.

For those concerned that I am leaving the students to wallow in their own grey mediocrity (favourite clichés of right-wing critics) I say visit the class, listen to the responses. Making a class video is another useful way of adding to the evidence. Of course I still balance student-selected wide reading with one or two carefully selected whole class texts, book boxes of my own selection and my reading aloud of novellas or short stories. This is obviously important in giving all students access to genres that they are uncertain about or prejudiced against. For example, girls are unlikely to read science fiction and boys are unlikely to read romance and both are unlikely to read books that are poorly packaged.

I use some simple rules to encourage decisions and save time. If you haven't brought your own book, you still have choice but you choose from what I have in the class basket (one of the plastic Coles supermarket variety which I am notorious for carrying to all my classes in a school with stairs. I prefer a library trolley wheeled from the library, bookroom or staffroom.) After time is up for choosing, you have to give the writer a fair go and persevere with the first thirty pages. Then if you still think that you have not made the right choice, you may give your reasons and choose again.

Simple new technology such as Post It Notes assists me. These keep the school's book stock clean from notes and underlining and when removed from the text can be manipulated to help plan writing or talking. They also encourage economy of note making and help to jot down that thought before it disappears. I get the school to buy large commercial quantities of these and I hand them out to the students in reading lessons.

I have written elsewhere about the reading journal. (Tucker 1988 and 1994) Without the development of honest responses from readers, they do not develop the empathy that Jack Thomson's research showed to be essential for the development of readers who can have a conscious understanding of a text as a construct. (Thomson 1987) The most useful addition to my reading journal scaffold since then has been, "If I had difficulties, these are the possible reasons".

"A variety of responses" is a truism for us but allow me to share two methods which I have not seen often. Use the cult of the author and add it to imaginative re-creation techniques to create lively and entertaining interviews between the students acting as 'media persons' and the 'author'. Extend this method to various film production meetings about making the film of the book. (It helps to have seen the films *Barton Fink* or *The Player*.) *For example, your student reader has ten minutes to persuade the producer to love your concept for the film of the book, or your student is the producer at a casting conference. "Brad Pitt! You must be crazy! You think I'm some kind of millionaire? OK I know I am but 'The Lost Day' requires a completely new, fresh face to play Vinny. He's got to look vulnerable like Leonardo di Caprio was when he was a nobody."*

For those of you worried about outcomes-based curriculum, I just turn it around with reverse programming. I take the evidence of what the students have done and compare it with the outcomes required by the curriculum. What I haven't covered well, or not at all, enters my future planning. It's really just the action research cycle of asking a question about an aspect of the curriculum and putting it into a feedback loop. All good teaching is action research whether you have the time to tell anyone else about it or not.

In 1997-1999 I have the wonderful experience of judging the Childrens Book Council of Australia Books of the Year Awards. This is further convincing me that we still have a cornucopia of children's literature written and published by Australians, let alone the New Zealanders, Canadians, Americans and the rest of the English writing world and the increasing number of books in translation. Wide reading, at its simplest, is necessary to give our students access to this intellectual capital. In the more complex social and political questions of schools and schooling, wide reading is essential for students to take on power as learners. In the multiple literacies faced by learners now and during the rest of their lifetimes, we teachers have the responsibility and pleasure of sharing the secrets about reading.

Bibliography

Boomer G and Hood M (1971) *Sandals in One Hand,* Melbourne: Longman Rigby.

Bunbury, Rhonda (1995) (ed) *Children's Choice,* Burwood Vic: Deakin University Press.

Delves, A and Tickell, G (1971) *Taller By Half a Head,* Melbourne: Cassell Australia.

Dixon, John and Stratta, Leslie (1963) *Reflections,* Oxford: Oxford University Press.

Hannan, L M and Hannan, W (1972) *A Reader for English Part Three,* Melbourne: Cheshire.

Lo Bianco, Joseph and Freebody, Peter (1997) *Australian Literacies,* the accompanying document to "The National Literacy Policy for Australia", Canberra: DEETYA.

Meek, Margaret (1989) many references but see especially her 45 page gem, *How Texts Teach What Readers Learn,* Rozelle: PETA/Thimble Press.

Thomson, Jack (1987) *Understanding Teenagers Reading,* North Ryde NSW: Methuen.

Tucker, Ernie (1988) "Teaching in the Private and Public Worlds of Adolescent Literature" in Valerie Hoogstad and Maurice Saxby (eds) *Teaching Literature to Adolescents,* Melbourne: Thomas Nelson.

Tucker, Ernie (1994) "Teaching Reading With Janni Howker" in Agnes Nieuwenhuizen (ed) *The Written World Youth and Literature,* Port Melbourne: D W Thorpe.

Recent Recommended Texts for Wide Reading Classes

Years 7, 8

Baillie, Allan (1997) *The Last Shot,* Norwood: Omnibus Books.

Baillie, Allan and Harris, Wayne (1997) *Star Navigator,* Sydney: ABC Books (picture book).

Barwick, John (1997) *The Warriors of Kaal,* Gosford: Scholastic Australia.

Burgess, Melvin (1995) *The Baby and Fly Pie,* Harmondsworth: Puffin.

Caswell, Brian (1997) *Relax Max,* St Lucia: University of Queensland Press.

Creech, Sharon (1994) *Walk Two Moons,* London*: Macmillan Children's Books.

Creech, Sharon (1997) *Chasing Redbird,* London*: Macmillan Childrens Books.

Cushman, Karen (1996) *The Ballad of Lucy Whipple,* London*: Macmillan Childrens Books.

Doherty, Berlie (forthcoming) *Daughter of the Sea,* Harmondsworth: Puffin.

Doyle, Brian (1982) *Up to Low,* Toronto: Groundwood Books.

Dubosarsky, Ursula (1996) *The First Book of Samuel,* Ringwood: Viking.

Forrestal, Elaine (1996) *Someone Like Me,* Ringwood: Puffin.

French, Jackie (1997) *Soldier on the Hill,* Sydney: Angus & Robertson.

Gee, Maurice (1994) *The Fat Man,* Auckland; Viking.

Gleeson, Libby (1998) *Refuge,* Ringwood: Viking.

Herrick, Steven (1996) *Love, Ghosts and Nose Hair,* St Lucia: UQP.

Heneghan, James (1996) *Torn Away,* New York: Puffin.

Hirsch, Odo (1997) *Antonio S and the Mystery of Theodore Guzman,* St Leonards: Allen & Unwin Little Ark Book.

Hughes, Monica (1993) *The Crystal Drop,* Toronto: Harper Collins.

Jenkins, Wendy (1996) *Killer Boots,* Fremantle: Fremantle Arts Centre Press.

Johnson, Sylvia (1996) *Callie and the Prince,* Sydney: Pan Macmillan.

Lester, Alison (1997) *The Quicksand Pony,* St Leonards: Allen and Unwin Little Ark.

Lowry, Lois (1993) *The Giver,* London*: Harper Collins Lions.

Macdonald, Caroline (1997) *Through the Witch's Window,* Ringwood: Puffin.

Mattingley, Christobel (1997) *Daniel's Secret,* Gosford: Scholastic Australia.

Morgan, Damian (1997) *Pete,* Gosford: Scholastic Australia.

Morimoto, Junko (1997) *The Two Bullies,* Milsons Point: Random House Mark Macleod (picture book).

Naylor, Phyllis Reynolds (1997) *Shiloh Season,* London* Macmillan Childrens Books.

Nieuwenhuizen, Agnes and Duder, Tessa (1995) *Crossing,* Dingley Vic: Mammoth.

Pausacker, Jenny (1997) *The Rings,* Melbourne: Lothian.

Reid, Elspeth (1997) *The Secret Pony,* Milsons Point: Random House Mark Macleod.

Stubbs, Roy (1997) *The Buddha Head,* Gosford: Scholastic Australia.

Wakefield, Kerry (1997) *Young Bloods,* Ringwood: Puffin.

Whatley, Bruce and Smith, Rosie (1997) *Detective Donut and the Wild Goose Chase*, Sydney: Harper Collins (picture book).

Winton, Tim (1997) *Lockie Leonard Legend*, Ringwood: Puffin.

Years 9, 10

Burgess, Melvin (1997) *Junk*, Harmondsworth: Penguin.

Burgess, Melvin (1996) *Loving April*, Harmondsworth: Puffin.

Broderick, Damien and Barnes, Rory (1997) *Zones*, Sydney: Angus & Robertson.

Clarke, Judith (1997) *The Lost Day*, Ringwood: Puffin.

Corbet-Singleton (1997) *The Face*, Gosford: Scholastic Australia.

Caswell, Brian and Phu An Chem, David (1997) *Only the Heart*, Ringwood: Puffin.

Crew, Gary (1997) *Tagged*, Flinders Park SA: Era Publications (graphic novel).

Crew, Gary and Tan, Shaun (1997) *The Viewer*, Melbourne: Lothian (picture book).

De Goldi, Kate (1996) *Sanctuary*, Auckland: Puffin.

Doherty, Berlie (1994) *Street Child*, London: Harper Collins Lions.

Doyle, Brian (1993) *Spud Sweetgrass*, Toronto: Groundwood Books.

Dubosarsky, Ursula (1997) *Black Sails White Sails*, Ringwood: Viking.

Fine, Anne (1997) *The Tulip Touch*, Harmondsworth: Puffin.

Earls, Nick (1996) *After January*, St Lucia: University of Queensland Press.

Garner, Alan (1997) *Strandloper*, London: The Harvill Press Panther Book.

Gwynne, Phillip (1998) *Deadly, Unna?*, Ringwood: Penguin Young Adult.

Harlen, Jonathan (1996) *Fireflies*, Ringwood: Puffin.

Hathorn, Libby (1996) *The Climb*, Ringwood: Viking.

Hilton, Nette (1997) *Hothouse Flowers*, Sydney: Angus & Robertson.

Horniman, Joanne (1997) *Loving Athena*, Norwood: Omnibus Books.

Howker, Janni (1997) *Martin Farrell*, London: Random House Red Fox.

Hyde, Michael (ed) (1997) *"The Girl Who Married a Fly" and Other Stories*, Norwood, SA: AATE.

Jinks, Catherine (1997) *Eye to Eye*, Ringwood: Puffin.

Lowry, Brigid (1997) *Guitar Highway Rose*, St Leonards: Allen & Unwin Ark fiction

McFarlane, Peter (1996) *The Enemy You Killed*, Ringwood: Viking.

Macleod, Mark (ed) (1996) *Ready or Not*, Milsons Point: Random House.

Marsden, John (1997) *Dear Miffy*, Sydney: Pan Macmillan.

Martin, S R (1997) *Swampland*, Gosford: Scholastic Australia.

Metzenthen, David (1997) *Finn and the Big Guy*, Ringwood: Puffin.

Metzenthen, David (1997) *Gilbert's Ghost Train*, Gosford: Scholastic Australia.

Nix, Garth (1997) *Shade's Children*, St Leonards: Allen & Unwin Ark fiction.

Paulsen, Gary (1997) *The Schernoff Discoveries*, London*: Macmillan.

Pausacker, Jenny (1996) *Hide and Seek*, Reed for Kids Mandarin.

Pluss, Nicole (1997) *Beach Baby*, Ringwood: Penguin YA fiction.

Provoost, Anne (1997) *Falling*, St Leonards: Allen & Unwin Ark fiction.

Riddle, Tohby (1997) *The Great Escape from City Zoo*, Sydney: Angus & Robertson (picture book).

Saliba, Sue (1997) *Watching Seagulls*, Melbourne: Addison Wesley Longman.

Southall, Ivan (1997) *Ziggurat*, Ringwood: Viking.

Taylor, Mildred D (1992) *The Road to Memphis*, Ringwood: Viking.

Taylor, William (1994) *The Blue Lawn*, Auckland: Harper Collins New Zealand.

Walters, Celeste (1997) *The Killing of Mud-eye*, St Lucia: UQP.

Wheatley, Nadia, ill Klein, Deborah (1997) *The Greatest Treasure of Charlemagne the King*, Gosford NSW: Scholastic Australia.

Wilson, Budge (1993) *My Cousin Clarette and Other Stories*, St Lucia: UQP.

Winton, Tim (1997) *Blueback a Fable for All Ages*, Sydney: Pan Macmillan.

Zak, Drahos and Holden, Robert (1997) *The Pied Piper of Hamelin*, Sydney: Angus & Robertson (picture book).

Zurbo, Matt (1997) *Idiot Pride*, Ringwood: Penguin YA fiction.

* Originally published in USA but available in Australian shops only in this edition.

16 Picture Books in the Secondary Classroom

Ken Watson

I t has taken twenty years, but the idea of using picture books as teaching aids in classes from Year 7 to Year 12 is now widely accepted. The fear that adolescents would indignantly reject such materials has proved baseless; in the rare cases where there is an initially negative reaction the students are quickly won over, because modern picture books are often very sophisticated. Some, indeed, clearly have an adult audience in mind: one thinks of Raymond Briggs's powerful anti-war books, *When the Wind Blows* and *The Tinpot Foreign General and the Old Iron Woman*. The latter is rumoured to have so enraged Mrs Thatcher that she brought pressure on the publishers not to reprint it. Clearly, if a picture book can provoke such a reaction at an adult level it is not something to be confined to the most junior classes of the primary school.

Apart from the fact that many modern picture books offer challenges (of various sorts!) even to the adult reader, there are at least two good reasons for using picture books in the secondary school. Since the format is large and the text short, a single copy of a picture book is often all that is needed for a stimulating lesson. (Ideally, of course, each group of three or four should have its own copy.) Further, words and pictures in combination are the most common form of communication used today, and hence warrant close attention in the classroom. And because the best modern picture books marry the two most skilfully, they are the ideal vehicle for exploring this medium of communication.

Perhaps the commonest use of picture books in secondary classrooms in the late 1970s and early 1980s was in relation to the exploration of story structure and of the linguistic features of stories for the young. Many teachers at this time discovered how highly motivated their Year 9 and 10 students became when they studied the language and structure of picture books for young children and then put their knowledge to work by creating, in groups, their own picture books and trying them out with audiences of five- and six-year-olds. In the process, they were acquiring knowledge about such things as parallel stories (John Burningham's *Come Away from the Water, Shirley*), circular story structure (Maurice Sendak's *Outside Over There* – and, more recently, the Alhbergs' *It Was a Dark and Stormy Night*), the power of repetition and cumulation (Ruth Brown's *A Dark Dark Tale*; Pat Hutchins' *Don't Forget the Bacon*), the conventions of fairy stories, and the variations that can be played upon them (Tony Ross's *The Boy Who Cried Wolf*).

Since the many awards for picture books (eg, the Australian Picture Book of the Year, the Kate Greenaway Medal, the Caldecott Medal) are judged by adults, some teachers also saw the possibility of sharpening their students' critical judgment (and of having them write in a different register). In groups, students would discuss the merits of shortlisted books, and then write 'judges' reports'. Lively discussion would follow when winners were announced and the actual judges' comments made public.

The appearance of the Ahlbergs' *The Jolly Postman* (1986) gave teachers another valuable teaching aid: a witty set of examples of different linguistic registers. An interesting by-product of this book was the enthusiasm with which young readers from about seven to ten took up the idea, deluging the Ahlbergs with their own 'letters' to and from various nursery-rhyme characters. These letters showed that the formal teaching of such registers is hardly necessary if the natural curiosity and enthusiasm of children can be aroused by some lively examples. Here is one such offering, which neatly captures the register of the official letter:

5 Yoxall Buildings
Derwent
24.11.86

To The Old Woman Who Lived in a Shoe

Dear Madam,

I am writing to you on behalf of the Social Services Department of Housing. I have the pleasurable duty of informing you of our plans to re-house you into larger accommodation. We are all hoping that you are not too hungry, as we are informed by your husband that he has forgotten the code on his "Family Express" card and therefore can send you no maintenance. We are moving you to a large mansion house and hope you will be very happy there.

Yours sincerely,
Ben Palmer
Housing Director

But picture books offer even wider possibilities, as Colleen O'Sullivan (1987) and Wendy Michaels and Maureen Walsh (1990) were to show. Both books tied their suggestions firmly to a reader-response framework (see Chapter 12); both drew attention to the usefulness of picture books in helping students to grasp irony and satire, and of the support given by such books to those learning English as a second or third language.

The explosion of literary theory in the late 1980s forced teachers of senior and middle secondary classes to ponder the question of what literary concepts should be passed on to students and of how such concepts could be explained clearly and economically. After conducting some classroom research (eg, Watson, 1992; Stephens and Taylor, 1992), Stephens and Watson produced, with the aid of a team of experienced teachers, *From Picture Book to Literary Theory* (1994). This book had two purposes: to explain the newer theories to English teachers and to suggest ways of using particular picture books in the classroom so that students could grasp those concepts which the teachers felt were worth passing on.

One of the most important of such concepts is that of ideology. No text is innocent: every text , either overtly or covertly, rests on a set of values that the author accepts and wants his/her readers to accept. It seems vitally important that young readers recognise this fact, and while it is easy enough for them to grasp the ideology of one of the many picture books concerned with the preservation of the environment (eg, Jeannie Baker's *Where the Forest Meets the Sea* ; Jorg Muller and Jorg Steiner's *The Sea People*) or the folly of war (e.g., Junko Morimoto's *My Hiroshima* ; Raymond Briggs' *The Tinpot Foreign General and the Old Iron Woman*), unmasking the ideology of the stories of Enid Blyton or of novels like *The Wind in the Willows* is much more difficult. A careful exploration of picture books like Babette Cole's *Prince Cinders*, comparing it with Perrault's *Cinderella*, or of more ambivalent examples like *Tusk Tusk* by David McKee or *Bear Goes to Town* by Anthony Browne, will help students to pin down this slippery concept.

In the section on reader response theory (Chapter 12) it is argued that this can be a most liberating theory for students from Year 7 upwards, and that the picture book is one way of demonstrating its central tenet. The weakness of reader response, its failure to acknowledge the degree to which we are socially and culturally constructed as readers, can also be demonstrated to students through an appropriate choice of picture books. Through an exploration of picture books like Barrie Wade and David Parkins' *Give a Dog a Name*, students will discover for themselves that factors like gender, race and social class help determine the way we read.

Gerald Graff (1987, p256) has pointed out that "if there is any point of agreement among [the various literary theories] it is on the principle that texts are not, after all, autonomous and self-contained, that the meaning of any text in itself depends for its comprehension on other texts and textualised frames of reference." Hence another concept that ought to be understood by all students, at least from Year 10 upwards, is that of intertextuality. Many picture books, like the Alhberg's *Each Peach Pear Plum*, depend almost entirely upon the reader's ability to make the necessary connections with other texts, and books like Fiona French's *Snow White in New York* and Jon Scieszka and Lane Smith's *The True Story of the Three Little Pigs* simply provide the most obvious examples of intertextuality – something which is a feature of each and every text the students will encounter.

So used are we to 'expressive realism' in fiction that we tend to accept the method of narration as 'natural', and forget that the writer is relying on a range of conventions and codes. In short, we often regard texts as windows on reality, and fail to notice their essential constructedness. A great deal of postmodern fiction is concerned with exposing the constructedness of realist texts, and thus seeks to foreground the devices which in the realist text we accept as natural and normal. The term 'metafiction' is used for such writing, and metafictive picture books are becoming more and more common. A famous example is Anthony Browne's *Bear Hunt* ; another text which engages in metafictive breaking of boundaries is John Agee's *The Incredible Painting of Felix Clousseau*.

The picture book, then, can be a powerful aid in helping students to grasp some unfamiliar literary concepts; it can also be used as a means of promoting visual literacy. Students need to develop skills both in interpreting visual images and in being able to analyse their effect on the reader/viewer. (See also Chapter 14) Almost any picture book will generate questions on aspects of visual literacy:

✦   What is the effect, in Josephine Poole and Angela Barrett's *Snow-White*, of the angle of vision in the double-page spread of Snow-White's flight through the forest?

✦   What ideas about viewing are conveyed in Istvan Banyai's *Zoom* and *Re-Zoom?*

✦   What is the effect of foregrounding the bleeding head of a dead fish in Gary Crew and Peter Gouldthorpe's *First Light?*

✦   What effect do the decorative borders have on our reception of Selina Hastings' retelling of *Sir Gawain and the Loathly Lady?*

Finally, here are some suggestions for using the latest crop of picture books (remembering that O'Sullivan (1987), Michaels and Walsh (1990), Stephens and Watson (1994) and Watson (1997) provide a wealth of suggestions for a large number of picture books published up to 1996).

As an example of oral story-telling, providing opportunities for discussing both the rhythms of the spoken word and the use of non-standard English, look at Bronwyn Bancroft's beautifully illustrated *The Whalers*. *Aphanasy*, by Lilith Norman and Maxim Svetlanov, has illustrations which strikingly convey the Russian flavour of the story, and would make interesting comparison with the earlier picture books of Fiona French, like *Huni*, which adopts the style of ancient Egyptian art , and *Aio the Rainmaker*, where the illustrations complement the tribal African story. Demi's *One Grain of Rice* has illustrations which fit the story by being distinctively Indian, and in addition has a mathematical theme which should challenge and intrigue.

The final illustration of *Billy the Punk*, by Jessica Carroll and Craig Smith, should provoke interesting discussion, as it shows Dad doing his own ironing; older students might pick up the entertaining intertextuality of Bruce Whatley and Rosie Smith's *Detective Donut and the Wild Goose Chase*, which parodies the style of the hard-boiled detective story. The superbly illustrated *Cupid and Psyche*, retold by M C and K Y Craft, can be compared for its visual impact (and for style of retelling) with earlier versions such as that of Walter Pater and Errol Le Cain. Selina Hastings, whose versions of Arthurian tales illustrated by Juan Wijngaard have been highly praised, has teamed up with another artist, Reg Cartwright, to produce a retelling of some of *The Canterbury Tales* with illustrations which echo *The Ellesmere Chaucer*. An unexpurgated 'Pardoner's Tale' is included, together with the tales of the Knight, the Nun's Priest, the Wife of Bath and the Franklin. The teaching possibilities of this version are endless, though, like *Cupid and Psyche*, it is less a picture book (that is, one where pictures and written text complement and are dependent on each other) than an illustrated collection of stories. The same can be said of Rosemary Sutcliff's superb retellings of Homer, *Black Ships before Troy* and *The Wanderings of Odysseus*, excellently illustrated by Alan Lee. These two books would make a wonderful Friday afternoon serial for Years 7 and 8.

Students can investigate the picture book as a means of conveying information, looking at such books as the prize-winning *The Wombat Who Talked to the Stars*, and can also be asked to evaluate the various pop-up books with a similar purpose, like the Nancy Willard/ Bryan Leister 'book-lover's pop-up' *Gutenberg's Gift*.

Could any English teacher who is aware of the riches offered by the modern picture book resist the idea of making use of it in the secondary English classroom? I think not.

References

Benedict, Susan and Carlisle, Lenore (eds) (1992) *Beyond Words: Picture Books for Older Readers and Writers*, Portsmouth, NH: Heinemann.

Doonan, Jane (1993) *Looking at Pictures in Picture Books*, Stroud: Thimble Press.

Graff, Gerald (1987) *Professing Literature*, Chicago: University of Illinois Press.

Graham, Judith (1990) *Pictures on the Page*, Sheffield : NATE.

Hall, Susan (1990) *Using Picture Storybooks to Teach Literary Devices*, Phoenix, Az: Oryx Press.

Johnston, Scott (1992) "Jewels in the Crown: Picture Books in Secondary English" in Jack Thomson (ed.) *Reconstructing Literature Teaching*, Norwood, SA: AATE.

Michaels, Wendy and Walsh, Maureen (1990) *Up and Away*, Melbourne: Oxford University Press.

O'Sullivan, Colleen (1987) *The Challenge of Picture Books*, North Ryde: Methuen Australia.

Stephens, John and Taylor, Susan (1992) " 'No Innocent Texts': The Representation of Marriage in Two Picture-Book Versions of the Seal Wife Legend", in Emrys Evans (ed), *Young Readers, New Readings*, Hull: Hull University Press.

Stephens, John and Watson, Ken (eds) (1994) *From Picture Book to Literary Theory*, Sydney: St Clair Press.

Watson, Ken (1992) "Personal Readings, Cultural Readings" in Emrys Evans (ed), *Young Readers, New Readings*, Hull: Hull University Press.

Watson, Ken (ed) (1997) *Word and Image*, Sydney: St Clair Press.

Picture Books

Agee, Jon (1988) *The Incredible Painting of Felix Clousseau*, New York: Farrar, Strauss and Giroux.
Ahlberg, Janet and Allen (1993) *It Was a Dark and Stormy Night*, London: Viking.
Ahlberg, Janet and Allen (1986) *The Jolly Postman*, London: Heinemann.
Baker, Jeannie (1987) *Where the Forest Meets the Sea*, London: Julia MacRae.
Bancroft, Bronwyn (1996) *The Whalers*, Sydney: Angus and Robertson.
Banyai, Istvan (1995) *Zoom*, New York: Viking.
Banyai, Istvan (1995) *Re-Zoom*, New York: Viking.
Briggs, Raymond (1984) *The Tin-Pot Foreign General and the Old Iron Woman*, London: Hamish Hamilton.
Briggs, Raymond (1982) *When the Wind Blows*, London: Hamish Hamilton.
Browne, Anthony (1982) *Bear Goes to Town*, London: Hamish Hamilton.
Browne, Anthony (1979) *Bear Hunt*, London: Hamish Hamilton.
Brown, Ruth (1981) *A Dark Dark Tale*, London: Andersen.
Burningham, John (1977) *Come Away from the Water, Shirley*, London: Cape.
Carroll, Jessica, ill Smith, Craig (1995) *Billy the Punk*, Sydney: Random House.
Crew, Gary, ill Gouldthorpe, Peter (1993) *First Light*, Melbourne: Lothian.
Cole, Babette (1987) *Prince Cinders*, London : Hamish Hamilton.
Demi (1997) *One Grain of Rice*, New York: Scholastic.
French, Fiona (1975) *Aio the Rainmaker*, London: Oxford University Press.
French, Fiona (1971) *Huni*, London: Oxford University Ress.
French, Fiona (1986) *Snow White in New York*, Oxford: Oxford University Press.
Hastings, Selina, ill Wijngaard, Juan (1981) *Sir Gawain and the Green Knight*, London: Walker Books.
Hastings, Selina, ill Wijngaard, Juan (1981) *Sir Gawain and the Loathly Lady*, London: Walker Books.
Hutchins, Pat (1976) *Don't Forget the Bacon*, London: Bodley Head.
McKee, David (1978) *Tusk Tusk*, London: Andersen.
Morimoto, Junko (1987) *My Hiroshima*, Sydney: Collins.
Morris, Jill, ill Dye, Sharon (1997) *The Wombat Who Talked to the Stars*, Queensland: Great Glider.
Muller, Jorg (1982) *The Sea People*, London: Gollancz.
Norman, Lilith, ill Svetlanov, Maxim (1994) *Aphanasy*, Sydney: Random House.
Poole, Josephine and Barrett, Angela (1991) *Snow-White*, London: Hutchinson.
Ross, Tony (1985) *The Boy Who Cried Wolf*, London: Andersen.
Scieszka, Jon, ill Smith, Lane (1989) *The True Story of the Three Little Pigs*, New York, Penguin.
Sendak, Maurice (1981) *Outside Over There*, London: Bodley Head.
Wade, Barrie, ill Parkins, David (1992) *Give a Dog a Name*, London: Scholastic.
Whatley, Bruce and Smith, Rosie (1997) *Detective Donut and the Wild Goose Chase*, Sydney: Harper Collins.
Willard, Nancy, ill Leister, Bryan (1995) *Gutenberg's Gift*, Baltimore: Wild Honey.

Illustrated Books

Craft, M Charlotte, ill Craft, K Y (1996) *Cupid and Psyche*, New York: Morrow.
Hastings, Selina, ill Cartwright, Reg (1993) *The Canterbury Tales*, London: Walker Books.
Pater, Walter, ill Le Cain, Errol (1997) *Cupid and Psyche*, London: Faber.
Sutcliff, Rosemary, ill Lee, Alan (1993) *Black Ships Before Troy*, Sydney: Angus and Robertson.
Sutcliff, Rosemary, ill Lee, Alan (1995) *The Wanderings of Odysseus*, Sydney:Harper Collins.

Applications: Literature

Developmental Stages of Reading Literature

Jack Thomson

In the developmental model set out below, the kinds of satisfaction students experience in reading literature are ordered in successive stages of increasing complexity. These satisfactions are also cumulative: a good reader who reads at the highest levels also experiences enjoyments at earlier levels. The pleasure that comes from reviewing a whole text as an author's construction (Stage 5) does not supersede, but rather supplements, the pleasures of empathising and analogising (Stages 2 and 3), for example. Similarly, the strategies of reading are also progressive and cumulative. As readers progress from one level to the next they do not, snake-like, shed old strategies like a worn-out skin, but develop those strategies for increasingly complex purposes, as well as adopting new strategies. For example, the reader's predictive and interpretative activity can range from merely anticipating what might happen next, to a continual questioning of the text at each reading moment, re-interpreting the significance of short- and long-term past events and modifying expectations of possible alternative short- and long-term outcomes. Similarly, the mental images readers form range from pictorial stereotypes to complex emotional associations; the literary and cultural repertoires readers draw on vary according to the range and complexity of their reading and cultural experiences; and the reader's active hermeneutic process of filling in textual gaps involves formulating connections (between events, characters and narrative points of view) of increasing subtlety and complexity.

A developmental model that helps teachers to work out fairly easily each student's level of reading, can be very useful in indicating what it is that each student already does competently. At present teachers are often more aware of what young readers don't understand rather than what they do understand. Students are far more likely to progress in situations in which teachers build on the constructive strategies they do possess – and which they are shown they possess – rather than in 'remedial' situations which emphasise their inadequacies and draw their attention to them. In the workshops associated

Reading Literature: A Developmental Model

Process Stages: Kinds of Satisfaction / Process Strategies

(Requirements for satisfaction at all stages: enjoyment and elementary understanding.)

1. Unreflective Interest in Action.	i. rudimentary mental images (stereotypes from film and television);
	ii. predicting what might happen in the short term;
2. Empathising with Characters.	iii. mental images of affect;
	iv. expectations about characters;
3. Analogising: Deriving Insights from Fiction for Understanding Oneself.	v. drawing on the repertoire of personal and cultural experiences; making connections between characters and one's life;
4. Reflecting on the Significance of Events (Theme) and Behaviour (Distanced Evaluation of the Characters)	vi. generating expectations about alternative possible longterm outcomes;
	vii. filling in textual gaps;
	viii. formulating puzzles, enigmas, accepting larger textual hermeneutic challenges;
5. Reviewing the Whole Work as a Construct or Fabrication.	ix. drawing on literary and cultural repertoires;
	x. interrogating the text to match the world view offered by the text with one's own;
	xi. recognition of implied author*;
6. Consciously Considered Relationship with the Text, Recogniton of Textual Ideology, and Understanding Of Self (Identity Theme) and of One's Own Reading Processes	xii. recogniton of implied reader * in the text, and the relationship between implied author and implied reader;
	xiii. reflexiveness, leading to understanding of textual ideology, personal identity and one's own reading processes.

with the research many reluctant readers found how easy it was to enjoy reading and to learn new reading strategies when they started to believe in their own abilities and to concentrate on meaning and their own interests in a story rather than on what they had come to see as teacherly concerns.

As can be seen from the summary above, specific reading strategies were clearly identifiable at each developmental level. Each kind of reading satisfaction or source of interest was found to be associated with particular strategies used by all students reading at that level.

Reference
Thomson, Jack (1987) *Understanding Teenagers' Reading*, North Ryde: Methuen.

Footnotes
* The "implied author" is Wayne Booth's term for the "real author's second self" (Booth, 1961), the kind of person the text implies the author is, and possessing the kinds of values the text implies that the author has. The implied author represents the ideal aspirations of the real author.

* The "implied reader" (Iser 1978) is the kind of reader the real reader is invited by the implied author to become, at least temporarily, so as to participate in the production of the text's meaning.

Approaches to Poetry

Wayne Sawyer

There are a large number of excellent texts on the teaching of poetry in secondary school. A recommended selection of such texts is:

General Professional Reading With Lots of Teaching Ideas
Patrick Dais and Mike Hayhoe, *Developing Response to Poetry*, Open University Press.
Mike Benton and Geoff Fox, *Teaching Literature 9-14*, Oxford.

Anthologies of Poems Especially Compiled for Students with Accompanying Teaching Ideas/Student Activities
Mike Benton and Peter Benton: *Double Vision; Painting With Words; Examining Poetry* and *Poetry Workshop*, all published by Hodder and Stoughton.
Jill Bryant, *Australian Visions: Paintings and Poems*, Hodder.
Mark Carey, Wayne Sawyer, Maurice Saxby and Glenys Smith, *Dimensions, Levels 3 and 4*, Nelson.
Mike Hamlin, *Steps in Understanding* series, Hutchinson.
Mike Hamlin and David Jackson, *Making Sense of Comprehension*, Macmillan.
David Kitchen, *Axed Between the Ears* and *Earshot*, both published by Heinemann, and *Thin Ice*, Oxford.
Paul Richardson and Ken Watson, *Postcards From Planet Earth*, Oxford.

Paul Richardson, Ken Watson and Margaret Gill, *Snapshots of Planet Earth*, Oxford.

Teacher-Resource/Ideas Books with Accompanying Poems to Illustrate these Ideas in Action

Rhonda Brill, *Fire and Ice*, St Clair Press.
Mike Hayhoe and Stephen Parker, *Words Large as Apples*, Cambridge.
Mike Horsley, *Reef, Palm and Star*, St Clair Press.
Ken Watson, *Jigsaw*, St Clair Press.

Anthologies of Poems

Rory Harris and Peter Mcfarlane (eds) *A Book To Perform Poems By; A Book to Write Poems By;* and *Take a Chance*, all published by AATE.
Rory Harris, Peter Mcfarlane and Mark Rashleigh, *Making the Magic*, AATE.
A selection of the approaches to teaching poetry in these texts includes:

✦ DARTS
   A family of activities popularised by Lunzer and Gardner (*Learning from the Written Word*) and later by Moy and Raleigh ("Comprehension: Bringing it Back Alive" in Miller, J, *Eccentric Propositions*), the acronym stands for "Directed Activities Related to Texts" and approaches include such things as:
   ✧ Cloze: deleting key words in order for groups to discuss possible alternatives.
   ✧ Sequencing: re-ordering a poem in which the stanzas have been scrambled.
   ✧ Underlining or Labelling: students mark the text in some way to indicate its most significant features or patterns or against some criteria ("Underline all the phrases with a straight line that you think are negative about 'X' ").
   ✧ Responding to Statements: the teacher puts forward a number of statements about a poem and students are asked to discuss which are relevant, to prioritise, to mark as "True" / "False", etc.
   ✧ Asking Questions: students, in groups, list a set of questions which they need to ask about a text.
   Specific examples of these, and other DARTS, with variations on the approaches can be found in the texts listed above by Benton and Fox, Carey et al, Hamlin, Hamlin and Jackson, Brill, Hayhoe and Parker, Horsley, Watson.

✦ Imaginative Re-creation
   Imaginative re-creation is discussed in greater detail in this book in the chapter by Peter Adams. This family of approaches was first popularised for novel study by Stratta, Dixon and Wilkinson in *Patterns of Language*, but the activities have come to be applied widely to poetry and drama. Typical activities include:

- ❖ Inventing the story behind the poem: What has happened before? What is happening 'off stage'? What might happen later?
- ❖ Rework the poem in a different genre, eg, as a newspaper article.
- ❖ Reply as the poet/narrator/poetic voice to a number of questions asked by class members.
- ❖ Write a poem 'in reply' as another character.

Excellent sources for such approaches are Benton and Fox's *Teaching Literature 9-14* and the anthologies edited by Kitchen. Other very useful texts are those by Benton and Benton and Hamlin.

✦ **'Workshopping' Poetry in Various Media**
Poetry can be used as the basis of filmmaking, dramatic performance, radio programs, art work and a number of other approaches to presenting poems in various media. Hayhoe and Parker's *Words Large As Apples* is an ideal text for many examples of poetry workshops with examples of appropriate poems. Benton and Fox's *Teaching Literature 9-14* is also ideal, while the texts by Benton and Benton, Carey et al, Bryant, Kitchen, Richardson and Watson also take very useful workshop approaches.

✦ **Oral Performance/Readers Theatre** (see page 305)
Verse speaking and choral speaking of poetry is becoming a bit of a lost art, but can be fun in the classroom, especially with younger students. *Fire and Ice* and *Jigsaw* make a feature of such activities with examples of appropriate poems to use.

Readers' theatre has become increasingly popular as a way of presenting poetry in the classroom. In this approach, readers in groups use voices in various combinations to present a poem in ways they perceive as appropriate to highlighting some issue/theme in the poem. Gesture and movement can accompany the reading, but should be reasonably minimal. *Fire and Ice* and *Jigsaw* are again good sources of readers' theatre ideas and examples of appropriate poems. Harris and McFarlane's *A Book to Perform Poems By* contains a large number of poems appropriate for these purposes. Also greatly useful are Benton and Fox, Hayhoe and Parker, Hamlin, Richardson and Watson.

✦ **Writing Poetry**
Writing poetry in the classroom is often regarded as too personal a thing to be approached by formulas or restrictions. Nevertheless, like any other form of writing, teacher demonstration/discussion/modelling which emphasises both craft and the conveying of a message is extremely useful. All the texts by Harris and McFarlane listed above contain examples of various forms and other kinds of models (many by students) that teachers will find useful. Texts by Hayhoe and Parker, Benton and Fox, Hamlin, Hamlin and Jackson, Kitchen, all contain either useful sample ideas on stimulating the writing of poetry by students or specific activities based on particular stimulus poems.

Ways into Novels and Short Stories

Diana Mitchell

While Reading the Literature

1. Questions and Issues

I pass 3 x 5 note cards out and ask students to write down two or three questions or issues that they want to discuss from their reading. I collect the cards as the students finish them, try to skim through them to organise and categorise a bit, then either begin a whole-class discussion on issues brought up or divide the class into groups and give them a few of the cards to respond to. Using this technique usually guarantees student involvement since these are student-created, not teacher-created questions. It is always interesting for me to notice that the questions and issues students want to discuss are often ones that would not have occurred to me.

2. Monologue about and to a Character

When the class gets to an especially upsetting or dismaying part of a book, students can write a monologue meant to be delivered to the character involved. Monologues could be based on student reactions to something the character did, advice to a character, or impressions of the character and where that character seems to be heading. This activity works well at such points as:

+ in *Romeo and Juliet* where Juliet decides to take the poison;
+ in *Of Mice and Men* when George goes after Lennie; and
+ in *The True Confessions of Charlotte Doyle* by Avi when the Captain beats Zachariah.

3. Protest Campaign

If students become upset about something that happens in a novel, let them organise a protest campaign. In *Don't Care High* by Gordon Korman, my students were upset that the principal would not let the student body have a president. In groups, students spent two days writing a speech to rally other students, composing a letter that would be read to the principal, and making posters and buttons in favour of the deposed president. On the third day each group delivered their speech to the rest of the class and tried to rally them to the cause, read their letters addressed to the principal in the novel, and shared any other work they had done on the campaign. This idea works at the point in the book where a person or group is being wronged, such as when the Captain treats the crew cruelly in *The True Confessions of Charlotte Doyle*.

4. Pick an Issue

When a major issue looms up in a novel, such as the lack of personal freedom in *The Giver* by Lois Lowry, I ask students to write about it. I usually give them several suggestions. From *The Giver* I asked them how they felt they would fit in with the typical family in the novel, what they would like or dislike about having their career picked for them, and how they think they would react to the sameness in the society.

5. Editorials

After students understand how to write a persuasive editorial, have them write an editorial about an issue in the book. For instance, while reading Charles Dickens' *A Tale of Two Cities*, students might want to write an editorial beseeching people to stay out of Paris; while reading Cynthia Voigt's *Izzy Willy-Nilly* they might want to write about the hazards of drunk driving.

6. Daily Journal

Students choose one major character and keep a daily journal for that character, reporting what happens to the character as the story progresses. Students can record the feelings and motivations of their chosen character as well as events which affect them from the lives of those near to them. This idea works well with characters who are preoccupied or introspective such as Hester or Arthur Dimmesdale in *The Scarlet Letter*, Myrtle in *The Great Gatsby*, George in *Of Mice and Men* and Jonas in *The Giver*.

7. Letters

While reading the novel, students write letters from one character to another, when the plot seems to merit it. For instance, in *The True Confessions of Charlotte Doyle*, Charlotte could write a letter to the crew explaining to them why they should trust her and give her another chance after she betrayed them.

8. Three Words

Students write down three words which they feel best describe a character. In groups, students share their words and their reasons for selecting these words. Each group decides which three or more words best fit the character. They share their conclusions with the class. This simple activity stimulates valuable discussion as students justify their word choices. I've used this idea with short stories such as Eudora Weldy's "A Worn Path" and am often amazed at all the ways students view the same character. Students have described Phoenix Jackson, the main character in the story as: old, humble, peaceful, stubborn, senile, buffoonish, sly, determined, dignified, angry, dishonest, fearless, selfish, and venerable. The discussions that followed were lively as students disputed or agreed with word choices.

After Reading the Literature

1. Characters' Quotes

Students dig back into the book to find ten quotations or sentences that reveal the character they've been assigned or have chosen, and that show what the character is like. Students explain what these quotes tell or show about their character. Another way I have used this idea is to divide the students into groups of three with certain chapters assigned to each group. They go through the chapters finding what they consider to be important quotes from many characters. I compile all the groups' quotes, duplicate them, and give them out the next day in class. The same groups get back together and try to identify as many of the quotes as they can, using the novel as needed. Of course, they skip the ones they chose the day before. This activity really gets students back into the book as they try to identify who said what and what it shows about the character. Spirited discussions result when students have to deal with the words of Curley's wife in *Of Mice and Men* when she says, "You can talk to people, but I can't talk to nobody but Curley" or when Crooks says, "You guys comin' in and settin' made me forget."

2. Poetry Connections

From collections of poetry, students pick out the poems they believe specific characters would like or poems that speak to issues in the life of a character. Students can also pick out poems that say something about the theme or setting of the book. On the back of the poem they write their reason for choosing the poem. On the day these are due, I collect them, ask students to number a sheet of paper, and begin reading the poems. Students write down how they think the poem relates to the novel or to a character. After I've read three, we stop and discuss student thinking on the three poems before we go on. This can take several days to complete but students are usually enthusiastic about hearing the poems other students pick out and interested in explaining how they think the poem connects to the novel.

3. Awards

After reading a novel or group of short stories, students brainstorm categories for awards that could be given to characters such as 'most caring', 'most dedicated', 'most selfish', 'most troubled', 'most courageous', 'most pitiful', 'most heartless', 'most imaginative', 'hardest role to play', 'person who put up with the most', 'worst parent', and 'most dramatic'. Students then decide which character should receive the award, and briefly write up why that character should get that award.

4. Make a Newspaper

After students have read a novel, they write and design the front page or two of a newspaper that includes stories about the events and characters in the story. They can write news stories based on happenings in the story, interviews with the characters, news briefs about the main events in the story, a weather box, and a "what's inside" box. When my students read Hemingway's *For Whom the Bell Tolls*, one newspaper, "The Republic Weekly", contained a feature about Anselmo called "A Freedom Fighter and His Cause", a news story entitled "Fascist Air Raids Rake Spanish Cities", and another news story, "Peasants Blow Up Train". On the second page there was a letter to the editor about death in the mountains, three obituaries, an opinion piece on why the peasants seemed to have lost their powerful religious faith, and weather reports so both sides could better plan their strategies. Another student paper included an ad for El Bango Munitions which boasted "We specialise in guerrilla services".

5. Pictures

After reading a novel, students bring in a picture that a specific character would like or appreciate or that they feel would have a special meaning to that character. They can share these in groups, with each student explaining what in the picture would appeal to the character. Students can also write up their reasons for choosing the picture.

6. Word Collage

Students cut out thirty to forty words or phrases from magazines that describe the novel or a character in the novel. They write the book title or the name of the character in the centre of a blank sheet of paper and then glue all the words on, filling the entire sheet. Students then write about why they chose the words they did. Although this activity seems easy, and students do enjoy doing it, they often make connections that illustrate deep and sophisticated thinking about the novel.

7. Connecting Poetry to Stories

The teacher brings in poems that relate to the novel or story and asks students to discuss and write about the way the poem speaks to the issues in the novel.

8. Writing a Scene and Acting it Out

Students take a scene that was alluded to but not completely developed in the novel and flesh it out in script form. A scene that lends itself to scripting is the incident in Weed which caused Lennie and George in *Of Mice and Men* to leave town on the run.

9. Gender/Violence Critique

When stories lend themselves to this assignment, I use it as an option. I ask students to imagine that they are members of either the National Organisation of Women or the Coalition to Stop Violence and that they have been asked to write up a critique of this novel in terms of gender stereotypes or in terms of whether or not this story promotes violence. This idea works well with *Of Mice and Men, The Great Gatsby, The True Confessions of Charlotte Doyle* and many, many other novels.

10. Interview a Character

Each student chooses a character to interview. In groups, students first construct a list of questions to ask characters in the novel just read. Then each person writes up the interview by having the character answer the questions. For instance, when we read *The Giver*, students wanted to ask Jonas' parents why they never questioned anything in the society, how Jonas' father could justify killing infants, how Jonas' mother felt knowing that her job in the justice system often meant violators of minor 'crimes' were put to death, and how they felt about being moved to housing for "Adults Without Children" when their children grew up. Students generate the questions together, then individually write up the interviews which show how they think the characters would answer.

Instant Book

Ken Watson

The technique of 'instant book', described in Robert Protherough (1983, pp 64-6), has proved excellent in junior secondary classes in helping weaker readers gain a sense of a novel as a whole, and in senior classes has been found to be a splendid revision activity for the final examination.

With a junior novel, the teacher edits down the novel to thirty passages (or whatever is the number of students in the class). These passages are then photocopied and pasted onto cards, each card being numbered in sequence. On the top of each card (except, of course, the first!) a cue line, the last line from the previous card, is written. The cards are then handed out to the class, and each student told to practise reading his/her passage. If narrative links are needed, these are provided by the teacher as narrator. (Warning: If the students are to practise their passages overnight, have them mark their sections in their books; do NOT let them take the cards home. If you do, someone will lose a card, or a student will be absent and you'll not be able to fill in the gap readily.)

After the students have had the opportunity to practise their reading, the class is arranged in a circle and the 'instant book' presented in readers theatre fashion (see page 305).

With senior classes, 'instant book' has proved an excellent method of revision when two or more groups have made their own selections. Much fruitful discussion is generated when a group is asked to justify inclusion or omission of particular key passages to the rest of the class. Where the novel is being studied for a public examination, classes in different schools have exchanged their 'instant books', and this has aroused great interest where choices of passage have diverged greatly.

Reference

Robert Protherough (1983) *Developing Response to Fiction*, Milton Keynes: Open University Press

Deconstructive Approaches in the Teaching of Texts

Eva Gold

In many texts the presence and authority of the writer are barely discernible because of our acceptance of the textual practices which shape our reading of texts. As readers we are adept at the interpretation of symbols to create a complex and detailed world in our minds. Yet it is not difficult for students to identify these practices and become aware of the ways in which they position us. This gives them the choice of accepting that position to some extent, or of reading "against the grain". Students often find this experience surprising and highly satisfying.

Positioning of the Reading Subject

The Merchant of Venice is a good text to start with because students already find its overt prejudice offensive, recognise the cultural influences that have historically operated on the interpretation of the text and readily reject the subject position created by the text at certain points in the play such as Shylock's forced conversion. Nonetheless there are other occasions where cultural attitudes are more deeply hidden.

✦ Offer students different subject positions from which to read: Watch/listen to/read Shylock's speech to Jessica as he exhorts her to "lock up my house". Groups can create a monologue/dialogue/scene in which they adopt the subject position of

a) one of Lorenzo's friends;
b) a Puritan;
c) a Jew who has been the victim of continued persecution;
d) a young feminist.

A class discussion can then focus on how these different positions influenced our reading of the scene; how the text has positioned us; the kinds of resources a director might use to (re)position the audience of a particular production.

Similarly "My Daughter, My Ducats". Consider who is speaking. (What kind of people are they? What has been their role in recent events?) What attitudes do the speakers bring to the subject? What is the purpose of their duologue? Is there any indication of the author's attitude to the speakers or their subject within the duologue or after it?

✦ Now change the subject position: Rewrite the scene from the point of view of someone who has no fondness for Antonio (because he disapproved of excessive spending and high risk ventures) and who has firm family values and respects the role of the father figure; *or* is a Jew who admires Shylock's success as a financier, despite all the prejudice he has to suffer, and sympathises with his difficulties as the sole parent of a wayward daughter.

How do these different subject positions influence your reading of the duologue? How might a director reposition the audience's perspective on this scene?

✦ Offer students other texts against which to read the original. The Program of Peter Hall's production of *The Merchant of Venice*, Phoenix Theatre, London 1989, (Dewynters PLC) offers some interesting counter texts:

   ❖ While it is accepted that the prosperity of Venetian trade was largely dependent on its banking system, S Schoenbaum (English Department, University of Maryland) describes money lending in England. He writes that despite its illegality, usury was widespread in England and that Shakespeare's father John was prosecuted for this offence twice. He also suggests that William Shakespeare himself may have been prepared to lend money at interest.

   ❖ Half the students could write a character sketch of Antonio from the point of view of someone critical of usury (a representative of the law? the church?) and the other half someone who believes that unless money is available to entrepreneurs the economy stagnates (John Shakespeare? a banker? Alan Bond?).

   ❖ A further commentary on 16th century economic existence in this program calculates the value of 3,000 ducats at 1989 rates (students always ask that one). How informed Shakespeare was about contemporary exchange rates and standards of living is of course up to speculation but a different perspective on the Venetians is gained with the information that 3,000 ducats translated into half a million pounds sterling in 1989.

Students can review Bassanio's speeches about love and debt with this fact in mind.

The Broker of Wall Street

Students can take a scene and adapt its set, costumes, gestures and fixtures to the new context. The key questions are: What changes? What stays the same? What meanings are highlighted by your new reading? Which ones are suppressed?

Conventional Writing/Reading Practices

The accepted conventions of reading and writing texts are particularly concealed in realistic texts. The writer attempts to engage the empathic responses of the reader to the point that the reader can lose him or herself in the text. This is achieved through techniques which create a sense of verisimilitude so that the reader can identify with certain characters and situations.

The following activities help students perceive the ways in which:

✦ the author's voice is muted through the various techniques of focalisation through characters, so creating an apparently realistic world;

✦ the patterning of contrasts and ultimate resolution of oppositions gives the sense of a complex but harmoniously integrated work which gratifies the reader with its sense of order and reassurance;

✦ this popular form of fiction that often purports to present a critique of society and its institutions reinstates society's power structures through its very form.

Authorial Hide and Seek

Is the author apparent? In which parts of the text? Highlight any words that the author says directly: how intrusive are they?

Through whose eyes/mind are we viewing the events of the text? Is it a first person narrator or can the author be perceived standing behind a character through whom we see and interpret the world of the text? How have the perceptions of the narrator or of the focaliser created the meaning of the text (ordering of events, relationships of events/of characters, implied attitudes etc)? How could the meaning change if the events were viewed from the perspective of another character?

Highlight any words that reveal the author's attitude to his/her subject. What happens if you change some of these words to make the connotations more positive/negative?

Simple conversion exercises such as changing the author's (main character's or reader's) culture (class, ethnicity, sexual orientation etc) as in the activities above, assist in foregrounding cultural assumptions. These can form the basis of a range of rewritings which propose other views of reality.

The Illusion of Reality

How has this been created? Consider the ways in which the characters have been made to appear lifelike. (The way into deconstructing this idea often comes from the students themselves as, when confronted by direct speech in a pre-twentieth century text, they question: "Did people really speak like that?" The answer is, of course, "No". Direct speech presents a construct of coherence for a particular purpose. While the use of direct speech is often intended to represent actuality and animate narration, it is too coherent and effective to be completely naturalistic.

Students can be invited to map out the qualities of characters, and then construct a diagram of their actions and their effects. They can then be invited to do the same for their own character or that of a friend – both far more difficult tasks. This is likely to lead them to recognise the imposed coherence of the characters in the realistic novel, the constructedness of logical behaviour, actions and their consequences.

In this way students can demonstrate how characterisation models a certain view of correct social behaviour and so they can understand how the realism is an important element in the confirmation of social values.

Patterning (Frequently Through Binary Oppositions)

The genre of the realistic novel demands resolution of conflict and a pleasing integration of the whole. For this to be achieved, oppositions are set up (good/evil; materialistic/spiritual; generous/miserly; arid/fertile) through patterns of parallels and contrasts.

Structural patterns can be made apparent through a simple chapter summary. Students can prepare a chapter summary each and deliver them orally in order. Notes are taken, one copy on butcher's paper for class use. This can now be used for all kinds of structural analysis.

Possible questions that lead to discovering the patterning of the texts are:
✦ Are there any events/settings that parallel each other?
✦ Do you see any ready divisions for the text?
✦ Is this reflected in the author's divisions into parts or scenes?
✦ At which point does the action seem to turn?

Often students discover patterns that are surprisingly artificial. They can then offer interpretations of the text in terms of its binary oppositions in action, character, setting, imagery etc. These oppositions can then be questioned in such ways as:

✦ Are the contrasts set up truly opposing or is the opposition constructed as such?

✦ What happens if you reverse the order of implied privilege?

✦ How are these oppositions undermined by other texts, for example:
   Jane Eyre/The Wild Sargasso Sea
   The Wind in the Willows/The Wild Wood
   To Kill a Mockingbird/Roll of Thunder, Hear My Cry?

Through the resolution of opposites the realistic text confirms society's traditional power structures by demonstrating its power to accommodate opposition.

Section IV: Writing Texts

17 'Process Writing': Confessions

Brenton Doecke and Douglas McClenaghan

Our aim in this essay is to revisit a significant phase in our professional development, when we both found ourselves teaching at Watsonia High School in 1982, and began exploring the possibilities of 'process writing' in the junior and middle school. Pro-cess Writ-ing. Pouting lips followed by a sibilant 'cess', the death head's grin of 'wriiiiiit', ending with the dull gong of 'ing'. You can always count on a couple of murderers for a fancy prose style. Yet we are not really repentant about embracing 'process writing' pedagogy. We shall try, in fact, to point beyond the empty caricature of process writing that has been bandied about in curriculum debates over recent years, and affirm the promise of that pedagogy – we say 'promise' because we feel that 'process pedagogy' has only ever been partially implemented, and in some schools it has had little or no impact beyond the lip service paid to 'drafting'.

This is despite the claims made during the early eighties that a 'writing revolution' was sweeping through primary and secondary schools. R D Walshe, in the lead essay to *English in Australia 62* (October 1982), announced that there had been a decisive shift away from "the old model of writing teaching (a belief that writing is no more than a skill or set of subskills which can be learnt by repeated drills and exercises and can then be applied mechanically to express 'what you want to say')" to an emphasis on "the process of writing", involving a new focus on pre-writing and first-draft, editing/revision/rewriting – all set out in a neat sequence that we subsequently pasted on to our classroom walls. The whole of *English in Australia 62* communicates the commitment and enthusiasm of many leading exponents of the 'writing revolution', including a seminal essay by Brian Johnston, "How Can I Usefully Respond to Students' First Drafts?" (see McClenaghan, 1996, for a discussion of the continuing relevance of Johnston's work).

The fact that this issue of *English in Australia* was a special AATE/PETA issue edited by Margaret Gill, "in consultation with R D Walshe, Publications Editor of PETA", reflects an attempt by some secondary English teachers at that time to learn from primary educators. The 'process' movement had started in primary schools, and secondary English teachers faced quite remarkable challenges when they tried to implement this pedagogy in a secondary school environment, dominated as it was (and still is) by timetables, bells, room changes, and a curriculum organised according to traditional academic subjects. Those teachers who tried to implement 'process' pedagogy stepped beyond the sense of superiority that secondary teachers have traditionally felt towards their primary colleagues, and they began to listen very earnestly to what primary teachers had to tell them about language and learning. They began to recognise the value of the work done by primary teachers, to acknowledge that their junior school students were already graduates of "a rich learning environment" (to use a phrase coined recently by David Lee), and to try to build bridges between primary and secondary school pedagogies and curricula.

Another feature of *English in Australia 62* is an interview which Barbara Kamler conducted with Donald Murray. Murray was one of the leading exponents of the 'writing process', and we shall lift a couple of quotes from this interview as a way of structuring our essay. By revisiting this issue of *English in Australia*, and using the Murray interview, we hope to evoke the complexities of our professional development at that time. The Murray interview captures two significant tenets of process writing that we applied in our classrooms. We shall first let Murray 'speak' ('process writing' valued the individual 'voice' in writing), affirm what we learnt from him, and then reflect on how our teaching practice took us beyond his understanding of the writing process.

To conclude, we shall make some connections between 'process writing' and 'growth' pedagogy as enunciated in Dixon's *Growth Through English*. We shall consider the extent that we ourselves were working within this paradigm, and reflect on whether this paradigm was as pervasive as some critics have claimed.

1. 'Experience'?

What you don't need is to give them experiences. It's a terrible kind of arrogance that says we have to give kids experience. Try to keep a bunch of eight year olds from having an experience. On the way to school they have nine million experiences but now that they're at school, THE TEACHER WILL GIVE THEM AN EXPERIENCE. It's ridiculous. What you need is to find out what kind of experiences they have had. As they tell you what experiences they've had they will begin to see the

importance of the experience from the response that you are giving them,
which has to be an honest response ....

(Donald Murray in Kamler, 1982, pp26-27)

One of the greatest challenges which 'process writing' posed for teachers was asking students what they wanted to write, instead of continuing with the practice of setting topics for the whole class. What if they didn't have any ideas? What did you do then? But at Watsonia High School we invariably found that they had plenty of ideas. And, having negotiated a topic or focus for their writing with us, they were then prepared to write a first draft, and to 'conference' it in groups. These conferences sometimes included the teacher, sometimes not. Johnston's three step approach to responding to first drafts (outlined in the essay mentioned above) provided a useful framework for both teachers and students to discuss their writing (see p44). We found that after modelling how to apply Johnston's approach, students were able to follow the three-steps independently when discussing each other's writing (cf. McClenaghan, 1996). Not that these things weren't accomplished without any difficulties, or that the students automatically adopted the formulae provided by Graves, Johnston, and others, for writing and conferencing their work. This was a messy, complicated process, full of peaks and troughs, false starts and minor triumphs, anxieties (on the part of both students and teachers) and real pleasures.

After 'conferencing' their writing, students then went through the process of 'revising and editing', 'product and publication', 'reader response', and 'writer's attitude' – the stages of the 'writing process' as set out by R D Walshe in his article in *English in Australia* 62 (9-11). Looking back, we feel that it was perhaps the activity of reflection and evaluation in which students (and teachers) engaged at the end of the process that represented the most significant departure from traditional school practices. Instead of simply handing down a verdict on a student's piece of writing, with a mark out of ten and a summary comment at the bottom of the page, we had opened up the possibility of dialogue with students about what they wanted to do with their writing, where they felt they could improve, what they felt they had learnt – a dialogue that went beyond the moment of 'publication' (in the form of wall stories, bound books, video presentations, etc.) to become a sustained conversation about their language and learning. We can only assume that those critics who have relentlessly panned 'process writing' over the past decade have never had the experience of engaging in such conversations with students.

We must also assume that they have had no experience of the way classrooms were transformed by 'process' pedagogy. Rather than dividing English up into discrete and compartmentalised sections ("If it's Tuesday, it must be spelling....", "If it's Wednesday, we must be doing comprehension ..."), with process writing we were inevitably driven (so it felt) to integrate speaking, listening, writing and reading. The characteristic emphasis on group work illustrates this. Group work could serve as a springboard for a range of activities, including writing and performing plays, making videos, oral presentations, collaborative writing, and book clubs. Again, this change in class routines did not happen overnight. It demanded a lot of energy and patience as we saw our classrooms changed into something radically different from what our colleagues were doing in other classes. Indeed, we often had to battle with the assumptions about 'doing' school work that students brought with them into our classes from their Maths or Science lessons (or from their English teacher of the previous year). We were obliged to struggle with colleagues who saw our classrooms as something weird and aberrant, as 'noisy' or even out of control.

Critics have objected to process writing as a personalist discourse that prevents students gaining any sense of themselves as social actors, or understanding the social character of language and literacy (see Gilbert, 1989; Christie, 1987). Murray's comments above – evoking an image of little children skipping merrily to school, alive to the world around them, ever-eager to record their impressions of the people and things they have encountered – are clearly open to critique in these terms. His vision of 'a bunch of eight-year-olds' is in a long line of other culturally loaded statements by middle class educators, stretching back to John Dixon's *Growth Through English*, that posit individual 'experience' as somehow existing apart from what schooling and society tell us we are, and as prior to language. Critics of 'process' (and 'growth') argue that in attempting to explore this elusive dimension of individual sensibility and values, teachers have deluded both themselves and their students about the nature of schooling and society. They have, in short, been engaged in an ideological game, to the benefit of middle class children (the ones who already speak the language of 'experience') and to the continuing detriment of other social and cultural groups (cf. Boomer, 1989).

We shall limit ourselves to saying two things about 'process' pedagogy in this respect. The first is that for all our knowledge of the way schools 'interpellate' individuals and produce human subjects of a certain type, as teachers we enter into relationships with our students, accepting the rights and obligations that human relationships entail. There is no gainsaying the fact that classrooms are sites for intensely personal encounters, even as teachers and students play out their traditional roles. Our students are flesh and blood people, each a conflicting mass of strengths and weaknesses, possibilities and limitations, hopes and disappointments. They respond when people show interest in listening to them. We may want to dismiss Murray's construction of individual experience, without rejecting his emphasis on the need for teachers to be responsive to the needs of students and to attend to what they think and feel. Through implementing a 'process' pedagogy, we each began to listen more closely to our students, opening up the possibility of a critical perspective on language and schooling, on both their part and our own.

Our second point is that the writing our students produced actually formed a telling critique of Murray's ideal of personal expression. What did our students write about? A list of titles will give you an idea of the wide range of genres they explored: "A Silent Help Saves Two Girls" (a headline for a mock newspaper article describing the plight of two girls who had been abducted), "The News Report" (a script of the *Ten Eye Witness News*, featuring a thoroughly bitchy "Yana Vent" [sic]), "Tennis" (an instructional piece on how to play tennis), "Should I have Tried?" (a fictitious piece about wagging the inter-school cross country, beginning with an excerpt from the Watsonia High School Bulletin announcing the event). Our point is that none of this writing was 'personal' writing to which criteria like 'honesty' or 'authenticity' could be comfortably applied. Nor were we able to respond to the personal 'voice' that we found in any of these texts. The students, in fact, quite explicitly made the move from 'voice' to 'text' (to use Roland Barthes' famous binary), revelling – that would not be too strong a word for it – in the linguistic possibilities of a range of genres. We shall have more to say about the textual character of their writing in the next part of our discussion.

2. 'Spontaneous' and 'primitive' genres?

I don't know why there is an obsessive concern in schools with teaching the forms in advance of writing. I don't think we have to give the kids the form of the story or the form of the poem before they write. The forms start to rise spontaneously from their writing. They can't avoid their form. Once they start to get these primitive forms we can give them names if we want to. That's a narrative. That's a poem. You've got to be writing to see poems. You've got to have the experience of writing before you're introduced to poems. The poems come to you from the writing. You don't get the form and then do the writing.

(Donald Murray in Kamler, 1982:28)

With this quote we are simultaneously confronted by our continuing closeness to and distance from process pedagogy.

The word we trip up on is 'spontaneously' – this does not do justice to the gradual refinement of their writing, to the careful emulation of the conventions of television shows, or their imaginative explorations of detective fiction, horror stories, realistic fiction, court room dramas, weather reports and football commentary in which our students engaged. They were obviously having a lot of fun, but at another level they were taking it all so seriously. Sometimes – despite the example of 'Yana Vent' mentioned above – they weren't even attempting to parody the conventions of TV shows and other popular genres; they were engaged in a serious effort to get those conventions right, to see how language worked in those forms. Their sense of audience and purpose was often subtle, showing that they were capable of judging which forms of writing best suited their purposes; but they approached these judgements gradually – they did not arise 'spontaneously'. Nor does the notion of forms arising 'spontaneously' from their writing do justice to the work we did as teachers in creating situations that allowed them to explore such possibilities. It also ignores those moments when we intervened in our students' writing in order to goad them into a clearer sense of their purpose and audience or to suggest other possible directions for them to pursue.

'Spontaneously' could, however, be unpacked in another way that is more congruent with our current understandings of teaching and learning. To the extent that Murray is arguing that students already have a working knowledge of a range of genres or text types, he has got it right. By encouraging them to choose their own topics and to develop appropriate forms to explore a range of imaginative possibilities, we allowed them to bring such knowledge into the classroom. This is a dimension which is lost when teachers become obsessed with 'scaffolding' a limited range of school genres that are deemed to be the most 'powerful' (ie, limited and conventional) genres in our society. Students invariably have an acute sense of language as play; they know that to explore the linguistic possibilities of any situation or genre is more than to abide by a set of 'rules', but to reformulate, re-invent, usurp and appropriate those linguistic conventions for their own purposes. We have discussed this question elsewhere (see *Englishworks 2, Resource Book* and *Teachers' Book; Writing With a Difference*; Doecke, 1990; Doecke, 1995).

Such classroom practices imply a very sophisticated understanding of the linguistic nature of experience and the lives of our students as 'textual beings' – in many ways a far more sophisticated understanding of the relationship between language and experience than is reflected in the work of critics of 'process pedagogy'. That sophistication is shown by the way 'process pedagogy' encourages students to explore questions about language and experience. The classroom thereby becomes a site for the joint construction of knowledges about language and literacy, rather than 'dummy runs' that reduce students to parroting pre-existing (and officially sanctioned) knowledge. As John Dixon comments in *Growth Through English*, " 'knowledge' may ... arise from pupils learning as well as teachers instructing ..." (Dixon, 1972: 73).

Needless to say, such an approach goes against the grain of much current thinking about curriculum, especially the focus on 'outcomes'. Rather than reducing curriculum to a pre-determined set of outcomes, we hold on to the belief – common to both 'process writing' and 'growth' pedagogy – that teaching should be risk-taking, that it should involve surprises, that it should enable our students to explore possibilities that take us beyond what we may have planned. We want to be surprised by our students' understandings and insights; we want to enable them to achieve 'outcomes' which burst the boundaries defined by the neat grids and tables set out in documents like the *English Profile*.

3. 'Process Writing' and 'Growth'

To gain a sense of the totality of the 'writing revolution', and to appreciate how this emerged out of a 'growth' paradigm, it would be useful to reread the 'big' books: Dixon's *Growth Through English*, Britton et al's *The Development of Writing Abilities*, not to mention the books authored by Donald Graves and Donald Murray. However, such an approach runs the risk of lending the 'writing revolution' a coherence which it did not have. Although advocates of 'process writing' talked of 'revolution' – Walshe even invoked Kuhn's *The Structure of Scientific Revolutions* to suggest that the change was of Copernican dimensions – it is a far more complex process to describe how we personally got to be where we were, why we were open to these ideas, and what we actually did with those ideas when we walked into our classrooms. Or why we are where we are now.

And when it came to implementing the 'new' pedagogy, it wasn't the 'big' books that mattered to us. We have focussed on *English in Australia* 62 because the professional discourse modelled in this journal provided a vital context for our practice. At that time *English in Australia* was a lively and engaging journal at the interface between theory and practice (the subtitle of *English in Australia* 62 was 'Theory into Practice'); it was the ideas about writing formulated in this journal that we took into our classes in our continuing efforts to improve our teaching. Such reading fuelled our endless conversations about English curriculum – conversations which spilled over into English Faculty meetings, where (for a number of reasons) debates became very heated.

'Theory into Practice' is a lumbering phrase which hardly does justice to the complexities of teaching. The phrase will serve, however, to remind us that our 'knowledge' as teachers can never attain the coherence implied by paradigms or models of English teaching. Too often curriculum history is organised around a series of phases or periods, as though ideas march in a neat sequential order, with teachers jumping on to the latest bandwagon. No doubt there are teachers who are prone to messianic fervour, whether it be process writing or other fads (poststructuralism, genre, reading recovery). In their efforts to give their ideas an original stamp, some of the leading exponents of process writing indulged in neat periodisation which divided the old off from the new, as R D Walshe's essay shows. The 'growth' model itself was announced as displacing previous paradigms, most notably 'skills' and 'cultural heritage' – this is probably one of the most problematical aspects of Dixon's *Growth Through English*, although (paradoxically) it has not been an aspect queried by subsequent critics of 'growth', who have invariably appropriated Dixon's periodisation, merely bringing things up to date by adding their own ('latest' and the 'best') model of language and literacy (cf. Christie et al, 1991).

For us, the question of the relationship between 'process writing' pedagogy and 'growth' is therefore in some ways an academic one, at a remove from the complexities of classroom practice. Looking back on our professional development since we started teaching, we can see that the 'writing revolution' crystallised for us many of the issues that Dixon originally posed in *Growth Through English*, although we would not have conceptualised our teaching practice in this way when we were working together at Watsonia. When we attempted to implement process writing pedagogy in the early '80s, we were working within a 'growth' paradigm, but we did not consciously embrace this model of English (we were also unaware of the aura which has subsequently been ascribed to the word 'Dartmouth').

Rather than conceptualising our own practice as an alternative to 'skills' or 'cultural heritage' (the models of English that 'growth' supposedly displaced), we found ourselves struggling with a cluster of assumptions and practices – not simply those of other staff members at Watsonia (although, as we've noted above, English Faculty meetings often became 'heated'), but habits and beliefs that continued to shape our own teaching. The tried and true (and well-worn) reading assignments, each with a million comprehension questions (neatly divided into 'literal' and 'interpretative'), the endless English Faculty meetings when we agonised over the set texts for the following year, the drills and skills embodied in texts like *Word Mastery* or *Mastering Words*, Schoenheimer's 'precis' exercises, the sterility of 'clear thinking' – no doubt these practices could be classified as exemplifying the 'skills' or 'cultural heritage' model of English, but for us they firstly constituted the environment in which we were obliged to operate. This was the context in which we began to reconceptualise our practice, and in comparison with which process writing appeared to offer an alternative. And not only an alternative 'writing' curriculum, but a reconceptualisation of the whole of subject English, with the emphasis now being placed on writing rather than reading, on talk rather than the obedient completion of grammar exercises, on the totality of speaking, listening, reading and writing, rather than on discrete tasks of dubious relevance.

References

Alkemade, K, Lee, D, and Murrell, M (1996) "Not Blank Pages: Literacy, Transition and Changing Practices", *Idiom*, Vol xxxi, No 2, October.

Boomer, G (1989) "Literacy: The Epic Challenge Beyond Progressivism", *English in Australia* No 89, September.

Christie, F (1987) "Genres as Choice" in Ian Reid, ed, *The Place of Genre in Learning: Current Debates*, Typreader Publications, No 1: Centre for Studies in Literary Education, Deakin University.

Christie, F, Devlin, B, Freebody, P, Luke, A, Martin, J R, Threadgold, T, Walton, C (1991) *Teaching English Literacy: A Project of National Significance on the Preservice Preparation of Teachers for Teaching English Literacy*, Canberra: DEET.

Dixon, J (1967, 1972) *Growth Through English*, Huddersfield, Yorkshire: NATE/Oxford.

Doecke, B (1990) "Back to Basics: Exploring Alternatives in English Teaching", review of Pam Gilbert, *Writing, Schooling and Deconstruction*), in *Typereader 5*, Summer, Journal of the Centre for Studies in Literary Education, Deakin University.

Doecke, B (1995) "Language and Silence: English Education and the Problem of Intellectual Elites: Critical Reflections Occasioned by *Teaching English Literacy* (The Christie Report)", *English in Australia* No 114, December.

Gilbert, P (1989) *Writing, Schooling and Deconstruction: From Voice to Text in the Classroom*, London and New York: Routledge.

Johnston, B (1982) "How Can I Usefully Respond to Students, First Drafts?", *English in Australia* No 62, October.

Kamler, B (1982) "An Interview with Donald Murray", *English in Australia* No 62, October.

McClenaghan, D (1996) "A Hardy Perennial: Responding to Students, First Drafts, Responding to Students' Writing", *Idiom* Special, Victorian Association for the Teaching of English.

McClenaghan, D, Doecke, B, Parr, H (1995 and 1996) *Englishworks 2*, (Student Resource Book and Teacher's Book), Oakleigh: Cambridge University Press.

Reid, I, Cardell, K, Doecke, B, Howard, J, Meiers, M, Morgan, W (1988) *Writing With a Difference: Teacher's Edition*, Melbourne: Nelson.

Walshe, R D (1982) "The Writing Revolution", *English in Australia* No 62, October.

In the Middle

From the late 1980s onwards, successive groups of English teacher trainees in two universities have voted Nancie Atwell's *In the Middle* the most helpful book encountered during their course.

Atwell, Nancie (1987) *In the Middle: Writing, Reading and Learning with Adolescents*, Portsmouth, Nh: Heinemann/Boynton Cook.

18 Journal Writing: an Essential Tool of Learning

Jack Thomson

In today's English classes, keeping a journal has become as important for students' learning as working co-operatively in small groups to share ideas and solve problems, and as important as being encouraged to speak informally and to use their own familiar social dialects in the classroom for developing their conceptual understanding. Over the last twenty years most English teachers have come to see these three situations as being related, as they know that the language students use in writing in their journals, in talking co-operatively in small groups and in using their own social dialects is marked by considerable informality of style which, by not being assessed or judged for its 'correctness' – or for its degree of approximation to formal 'standard' English – is so comfortable for the students that in using it they can focus all their attention on what they are saying rather than on their ways of saying it.

I am not saying that English teachers have come to believe that standard English is unimportant for students. We all know that it is essential that all students master it, in both talk and writing, if they are to have choices in their lives and access to power in their society. However, we have all learned from the linguists that standard English is not a universally applicable form of language; that it is but one variety of English among many varieties, and a variety that is not appropriate to use in some (intimate and informal) social situations. Standard English is a final draft kind of language appropriate and necessary for formal situations such as writing for publication or delivering a lecture. The language in which human beings (tentatively) formulate – or grope towards – new understanding is, necessarily, considerably less formal, complete, grammatically assured, coherent and explicit. It is a language which is more comfortable and familiar for users, enabling them to concentrate on the ideas they are grappling with rather than on their forms of expression. Over twenty years ago James Britton called this kind of language, so essential for learning, "expressive", distinguishing it in function from the more formal language of intellectual enquiry (reporting, instructing, informing, persuading and theorising) which he called "transactional" and the more formally structured and shaped language of fiction and poetry, which he called "poetic" (Britton, 1975).

Rationale : What's The Point Of It? Why Do It?

1. 'Expressive' Language and Learning

In the 1970s the work and research of James Britton (Britton, 1970), Douglas Barnes (Barnes, 1976) and many others (including Harold Rosen, John Dixon, Leslie Stratta and Nancy Martin) showed conclusively that the only way that any of us comes to understand new information, concepts and our own experience, is by talking and writing about them in our own comfortable, "expressive" language, either or both to ourselves or/and to interested and trusted others. It is common knowledge among English teachers now that talking and writing are instruments of learning. We have come to see, that is, that language has a purpose beyond communication. However, language isn't an instrument of learning in those schools in which teachers, ignoring the research of the 1970s, continue to see writing as an end in itself and go on setting writing tasks only to give students practice in the skills of writing. In such circumstances, students focus their attention primarily on the language they are using rather than on the subject they are writing about. We not only learn to write by writing but we can learn by writing. However, again, students do not learn by writing when the only response teachers make to what they have written is to correct the errors and to penalise students for making them. In these circumstances students learn to focus primarily on avoiding making mistakes rather than on the information, ideas or experience that is ostensibly the subject of their writing.

2. Language and Thinking

The much earlier research of L S Vygotsky (Vygotsky, 1962) and Jerome Bruner (Bruner et al, 1964) on the relationship between language and thought showed clearly that while neither *telling* children (explanation) nor *showing* children (demonstration) is sufficient for their learning to understand ideas, *getting them to do things themselves* (practice) is not, on its own, sufficient for their learning to understand abstract concepts either. For concept formation, for real understanding of abstract ideas to take place, children need to make explicit their thinking to themselves and verbalise their conclusions in their own comfortable, "expressive" language, in talk and/or writing. In other words, if you don't wrap your own language around your own thinking you don't learn.

3. Language and Social Dialect

Where, then, does the view of language outlined above stand in the late 1990s when English has moved towards an emphasis on a more critical social literacy?

Because of the important relationship between language and identity, it is crucial that students' own dialects are not only accepted but actually valued in the classroom. As Williamson and Woodall (Williamson and Woodall, 1996) have recently shown, all too often the cognitive, affective and social benefits of using one's own social dialect as a tool of learning are ignored in the (vested) interests of dominant social groups who believe that standard English is the appropriate form of language for all people for all occasions regardless of the social context in which they are operating. Williamson and Woodall attack what they call "the materialist, utilitarian and New Right ideologies" that have constructed the new National Curriculum for English in England for aiming to "produce" citizens who will be ciphers for the commercial and industrial machine rather than to educate people who will be thinking, understanding and choice-making human beings. As they so rightly say, rather than being positioned as consumers of knowledge and skills which the teacher transmits, students "should experience the role of producers of knowledge ..." so they can "learn to act in the world and address structures of inequalities" (Williamson and Woodall, 1996, pp 8, 10).

4. Peer Group Pressure and Class Discussion

With peer group pressure being as it is, and operating powerfully in many schools to repress overt displays of knowledge and conscientiousness in class discussion (and with shy students who don't want to make themselves vulnerable to ridicule by exposing their deepest thoughts and feelings in public), the written journal is a particularly good means of helping students to get their own language around their own thinking and, in fact, to get their thinking going and to explore ideas to some depth.

5. Learning Processes Facilitated by Journal Writing

The kind of writing students do in their journals could perhaps best be described as thinking aloud on paper. It is the kind of writing that helps people to assimilate and accommodate to new ideas, to sort out their responses (thoughts and feelings) to something they have read. As the eminent English novelist E M Forster once said, "How do I know what I think until I see what I say?" Keeping a learning log or a reading journal helps students to:

✦ explore and come to terms with new ideas and experience;
✦ organise their ideas before, during and after discussing an issue or topic, with others in a small group, for example;
✦ clarify their ideas and formulate them more coherently for more explicit and public communication.

In the journal, because of its first-draft, instant-response informality, students make discoveries in the act of writing. The personal and exploratory style generates profound interpretive abstractions.

Most importantly of all, I believe, writing a journal helps students to reflect on their learning so they are able to articulate for themselves what they have learnt and how they have learnt it. This metacognitive or self-reflexive understanding of their own learning processes is very powerful knowledge. If you know what you know and if you know how you came to know it, you are in control of your own learning: you have learnt how to learn. The educational power of this metacognition – or self-reflexive understanding of our own learning processes – is supported by the work of Margaret Donaldson on children's language development (Donaldson, 1978) and that of Jack Thomson on secondary students' reading processes (Thomson, 1987). In her book *Children's Minds*, Donaldson emphasises the importance to children's intellectual growth of their being taught in ways that develop their reflective awareness of both the way language works and the processes of their own minds. She says, "If a child is going to control and direct his (sic) own thinking... he must become conscious of it".

Problem Areas

1. The Dangers of Routine and Going Through the Motions

Let me emphasise as strongly as I can that the writing of journals can easily be made educationally debilitating for students if it becomes a new orthodoxy imposed thoughtlessly and practised routinely without the specific purposes for each occasion of use being made explicit to, and negotiated with, students. As Bill Corcoran has so rightly pointed out, the reading journal could easily become "yet another school genre, like a book report for the sake of a book report, or a draft in writing just for the sake of drafting" (Corcoran, 1988). There is a real need for ringing the changes in approach in the reading journal. For example, there seems to me to be no point at all in making students repeat the same activities in the reading journal for every text in a course, or to set exactly the same specifications for a journal in Year 8 as the students had experienced in Year 7.

2. The Need for Common Sense

If you invite students to write anything and everything in the journal and the teacher doesn't read it, then obviously you don't assess it or count it as part of the assessment for the year. You also tell students not to leave it lying around where antagonists might use it to betray them because of what they say about various teachers or other students, or because of the kind of language they use.

Peter Forrestal and Jo-Anne Reid in their book for students, *English Workshop One: Room to Move*, spell out the differences between a journal and a diary, explaining that, for them at least, there is more educational value in keeping a journal in subject English than in keeping a diary, and they include a note from a teacher making some sensible suggestions to students about keeping a journal (Forrestal and Reid, 1983, p17):

> Sometimes you may wish to write about the very personal and private things in your life. Remember that your journal is not the same thing as a diary. In your diary, kept at home, perhaps you write the very personal thoughts you have that no one else is to read.
>
> Because other people might sometimes read your journal, don't write anything in it that could embarrass your group or your teacher. Be sure to avoid writing anything that they shouldn't know.

3. Assessing the Journal

Personally, I believe in assessing the journal, whereas many other teachers obviously do not. Those who don't, generally make sure that students take journal writing seriously by doing something like setting aside 10-15 minutes a day, or every second day, to give students uninterrupted and sustained periods of concentration on it. I also believe in teachers reading students' journals and in replying to them at some length, but not, of course, in 'correcting' or denigrating the language.

An outstanding American English teacher, Gary Lindberg, doesn't read his students' reading journals but assesses their journal work by interviewing each of them individually three times during a course for fifteen minutes and once at the end of the course for half an hour (Lindberg, 1987). This journal conferencing counts for a third of each student's final grade in the course, and students are assessed on what they have learnt from writing the journal. They have to make a presentation to him summarising and interpreting their journal to show him what they have made of the course and what they have learnt about texts and themselves as readers. They can choose parts of their journals to read to Gary in the conferences to illustrate points they make and to particularise for him moments of illumination about their reading processes as they experienced them, for example. Gary says that he doesn't 'grade' the journal itself as that would be, to him, to contradict its nature as informal, expressive writing, but he does grade the students' work in the journal and, more specifically, "what the student makes of that work". This is what he says:

> ... the conferences are reflections on the reflections, and those successive acts of transcendence affect the ways in which the writer returns to the journal for future writing. As in a writing conference the subject is not some ideal interpretation, but the writer's own process of making meaning.
>
> (Lindberg, 1987, pp 123-4)

Whether you take up Gary Lindberg's practice of conferencing with students or not, you will recognise that he does focus primarily on the crucial importance of developing in his students self-reflexive understanding about their reading (and learning) processes. In their journals his students conduct a personal dialectic by interrogating texts and finding answers for themselves and then engage in actual dialogues with him in conferences. In successive stages of "transcendence" (and at successive levels of generality) they reflect on their own reflections of their own reflections on reading and learning. First, they reflect on texts in the actual process of reading them; secondly they reflect on their own observations, interpretations and reading processes; and thirdly, by interpreting their journals in conferences, they get outside their own earlier interpretive frameworks to reach high levels of metacognitive understanding of themselves as readers and learners. I believe that those teachers who don't require their students to reflect on their reflections in their journals so as to progress to these higher levels of metacognitive understanding are leaving out the most important stage of students' learning.

4. The Alleged 'Un-naturalness' of Keeping a Journal

There are some students – and some teachers – who say that keeping a reading journal while reading a book is an 'unnatural' activity. Well, it is in the sense that it disrupts the culturally learned and therefore accepted (and 'naturalised') pace of reading a text. But what law is it that says a literary text has to be read straight through at a constant speed? That is the way machines work. When students complain that the act of having to stop reading a text from time to time in order to write in their reading journals is disruptive of their concentration on the text, when they complain that it 'breaks the flow' of their reading, they show how unconsciously they are compliant to, and victimised by, old theories of reading and the culture in which they live. They have developed the notion that to pause and to reflect on an activity one is engaged in is a bad thing to do. They have learned that to write down one's thoughts, reactions and puzzles as one reads is a violation of the reading experience. Well, there are numerous politicians and business leaders who have a vested interest in preserving these barriers to critical consciousness, because such consciousness makes people less manipulable and more resistant, and as English teachers I think it is our responsibility to help students develop such critical consciousness.

This notion of writing responses during the reading of a text, 'disrupting the flow' of reading, was openly discussed in a Year 12 class in Bathurst, taught by Cliff Smith (Smith,1985). One student said, "I can't stand dissecting a book. It really takes all the enjoyment out of it . . . It takes away the magical quality of the book."

To get students to read at different speeds, to slow down their reading and to become reflective and reflexive about their reading (and thinking) processes means that we have to overcome this mystification and get them to see that there is nothing natural or magical about reading. The magical bit, the mystification, might be fine, but there is pleasure and satisfaction, as well as power, in demystification, in seeing the magician's tricks, the methods of construction. And the reader who might like to be occasionally mystified in reading for 'relaxation' doesn't want to be mystified all the time, surely?

Later on in the year, after keeping a reading journal (to which their teacher responded by keeping up an ongoing dialogue of commentary by writing in their books) the students said things like this:

David: "If you just flow through the book you're not necessarily thinking about it, whereas if you stop and write things you are standing back and thinking about the book and the way you are reading it."

Colin: "With *An Open Swimmer* (Tim Winton) I read the entire book and didn't do a Reading Journal and thought it was just a story. Then I read it again and did a Reading Journal on it and thought it was a bit better than just a good story. Instead of breaking the flow of my thinking it made me think."

Brad: "The Journal helped because I had to read the book more carefully to answer my own questions."

Jason: "In writing the Journal you can see your own vague idea changing and developing in the course of one ten minute entry. First there will be one idea, then a similar one, and so on until a final idea comes that ties the rough ideas together. Sometimes I notice that something is wrong about my thinking when I write it down. Something about writing it out makes me realise that it is not right – like seeing it physically makes me mentally see that it's wrong."

Scott: "Yes, by the time you've finished reading a book and writing about it you've sort of changed your approach so that when you go back and look through what you've written, it's like a revelation of how what you thought when you read it the first time fits with what you've come up with at the end, so that you get a deeper understanding of the book. I find that reading over my journal when I've finished reading the book really helps me see meanings and connections I hadn't seen before and it's great. It's very exciting."

Different Kinds of Journals

Journals can be used in all subjects across the curriculum and for a range of purposes from reflecting on learning processes in general to learning specific skills in specific areas. They are sometimes called 'logs' after a ship's log, being a record of "a journey or expedition into new territory" (Heywood et al, 1995, p17) – in this case, a journey into learning.

1. Learning Logs

In a learning log students are asked to do such things as:

✦ make preparation notes for work in class;
✦ make their first responses to activities in class;
✦ monitor the stages and processes of their own learning of specific activities during a unit of work;
✦ reflect on and evaluate work that they have done in class, what they have learnt and the way(s) they have learnt it.

Peta Heywood, Barry Carozzi and Tricia McCann, in *Englishworks, Teacher's Book 1* (1996, p ix) describe it this way:

> *The Learning Log ... is a place to record the learning that is taking place, the challenges that are faced and overcome, the failures that have been endured, the successes that have been celebrated. We suggest that you encourage students to make entries in their Learning Logs at the end of each lesson, or at least on a weekly basis. The Learning Log focuses the students' attention and assists in developing their capacity to reflect on what they have been doing and learning in English.*

Here are some of the sorts of questions that students might be asked to reflect on as part of the final evaluative stage of a unit of work, in this case one involving performance of literary texts:

✦ What were the problems?
✦ How did you solve them?
✦ Were there any not solved?
✦ Would you go about it any differently if you were starting again now?
✦ What was the effect on your working of knowing that you had to produce a finished product?
✦ How valuable was (what you did) as a way of exploring (literature)?
✦ What did you learn about the text? the context? yourself? your values? their social construction?
✦ What did you learn about your ways of learning?
✦ Consider the kinds of language you used throughout the unit in talking and writing. What would you say about your competence in using (these forms, genres etc.)? What can you do well? What kinds of things do you think you need to do to improve? Can you set these as goals to achieve in your next unit of work?

In their learning logs students can be similarly encouraged to respond to checklists (for speaking, presenting, listening, reading, viewing and writing, for example).

2. Writing Logs

Writing logs can be used:

✦ to record ideas for writing activities;
✦ for word banks and drafts for pieces of writing;

- for reflections on specific aspects of the writing process both during and after the construction of texts.

Writing logs could include, for example:

- ideas culled from newspapers and magazines (speculating or imagining the stories behind many short paragraph page-fillers can be productive);
- bits of interesting dialogue heard in the street;
- first draft narrations of personal experiences that might later be shaped into final draft anecdotes or stories;.
- descriptions of scenes that attract the writer's interest and curiosity in daily life.

In *Englishworks 2* (1995, p36), Douglas McClenaghan, Brenton Doecke and Helen Parr describe the purposes and uses of a writing log as follows:

> Short story writers and novelists often keep logs in which they jot down ideas, quotations, radio jingles or advertisements, scraps of dialogue they've overheard on a bus or train – it could be anything... And when they get around to writing, they often use their log to reflect on what they are doing and to learn about the writing process. They think about different ways their story could develop. They jot down alternative endings. They think about their characters. They also reflect on where their ideas have come from and why they've made the choices they've made.

3. Reading Journals

Entries in the reading journal should include immediate responses to completed texts (as a starting point for small group discussion, for example), as well as responses to texts during the process of reading them, and metacognitive reflections at the completion of a text. In each of these three situations, the writing not only helps the students to inspect and discover their own thinking, reading strategies and problems, but it also helps the teacher to find out what their students' individual strengths and weaknesses as readers are so she can help them. Below, I include an example of detailed specifications for the keeping of a reading journal.

Journal Specifications: An Example (In this Case, a Reading Journal)

It is very important that students understand the point of all that they are asked to do in classrooms by teachers, and the negotiation of activities and the purposes underpinning them is crucial with the writing of journals, whether they be more general learning logs or more specific reading journals, for example. The directions teachers give students can be short and simple or longer and more complex. Here I offer a fairly detailed, more complex example of specifications for a reading journal for students in their first semester of a Primary Teacher Education Course. It is more detailed and specific because of the particular needs of the audience of trainee teachers for whom coming to understand their own productive reading (and writing and learning) processes would seem to be essential as a pre-requisite to coming (in following semesters) to understand the languaging and learning processes of primary school children. I offer it here not as a model for all secondary school students, but as an example of the specific kinds of exploration students at different levels can be asked to engage in at different stages of their school careers. What follows is an edited extract from the outline for the unit "Literature and Learning", first semester Primary Teacher Education Course, Charles Sturt University: Mitchell, 1989:

Reading Journal and Tutorial Preparation Book (30%)

An on-going activity to be submitted at the end of the semester for final assessment and three times during the semester for discussion of progress. The purpose of the Journal is to help you to think about your responses to the texts of the course and to make explicit the significance of these responses to yourself. For this I think you will find an exercise book more satisfactory than any loose-leaf folder system. Your entries should be seen as written conversations with yourself and your tutor in which you explore your own puzzles and meaning-making processes. Through writing the Journal we hope you will learn how thinking on paper is a valuable part of the learning process.

Length

The amount of writing you do is up to you. Our main criterion for assessing the Journal will be the amount you write. The reasons for this are:
✦ we are convinced that writing in this informal way is very productive of learning and language development;
✦ the longer a written response is, the more likely it is that it will become interesting to the writer and reader (and to the writer as reader), as it is difficult to be boring to oneself at length;
✦ the longer a written response is, the more likely it is to be honest, as it is difficult to be dishonest at length (mainly because it becomes unbearably boring).

Suggestions

We suggest that you keep the Journal like a diary, responding to the texts of the unit in turn and writing the date above each entry. You can use the Journal for notes made in preparation for class discussions and to formulate questions you want to ask in class about the texts, as well as for sorting out your approach to the other written assignments.

We want you to use the Journal to make sense for yourself of your reading and learning processes and of the texts and the associated activities of this

Course. That means that your writing in the Journal will be marked by considerable informality of style. As the first and most important audience is yourself, the Journal will reflect your personal needs as well as your ways of making sense of things for yourself. As the writing is all first-draft we don't expect all the sentences to be perfectly formed grammatically. However, do try to write complete sentences. You may include doodling, drawing, even poems. The Journal will present not only your ideas about your reading and writing activities but your feelings about and attitudes towards them. The emphasis should be on what you learn about your own learning (reading, viewing, writing, talking, listening) processes and the significance of this for your future behaviour as a learner and teacher.

For one novel, chosen by you, we require a detailed set of responses written *during* the process of your reading, followed by your final reflections at the end of the reading.

Here are some questions (offered as a guide, not a straitjacket) to help you reflect on this novel and on your own ways of reading it. Answers to these kinds of questions during the progress of the reading could well form the major part of your response.

1. **Predicting, or Generating Expectations**
   At various stages of reading the text:
   ❖ What sorts of things could happen in the short and long term?
   ❖ How might the story develop?
   ❖ Has what has just happened changed your interpretation and/or attitude?

2. **Puzzles**
   What puzzles or problems are you formulating at various reading moments? What specific questions are you asking of the text? Note when and how you get answers.

3. **Filling in the Gaps**
   What gaps are you filling in in the text? What connections between events are you making? What is the point of each event? Why were the different characters included in the novel? What functions do they serve?

4. **Your 'Repertoire' of Personal, Literary and Cultural Experience and Knowledge**
   What connections are you making between events in your own experience and events in the novel? Does the book remind you of any other books you have read? Trace these connections. What cultural and literary knowledge are you drawing on to make sense of the text? If you are having problems in reading, what sorts of knowledge do you think would help you to make more sense of it?

5. **Mental Images**
   What mental images are you forming of characters, places and events in the novel? Consider the nature of these mental images and where they come from. Are they purely pictorial or are they feelings about things?

6. **The Implied Author**

    What impression is the book giving you of the kind of person who wrote it? Do you find it difficult or easy to sympathise with her/his view of the world? Think about the reasons for this.

7. **The Implied Reader**

    What kind of reader do you think the author had in mind as her/his audience for the book? Are you having any difficulty suspending your own beliefs, values, prejudices to take account of those of the author? On the other hand, if you completely share the author's beliefs think about whether you are being manipulated! Explore this. Keep in mind that all texts position their readers to accept certain world-views.

8. **Ideology**

    There is no such thing as an ideologically neutral text or writer or reader. What is the ideology of:
    - this text?
    - the society that values it?

9. **Reflexiveness and Self-Understanding**

    From considering questions like 1-8, what are you learning about:
    - yourself and your beliefs? What has shaped your ideology?
    - your own really productive reading strategies (What are your strengths and weaknesses as a reader? For example, when you come to boring bits, think about what boredom means to you in relation to this text.)

10. If you regard some of these questions as 'non-literary' or 'extra-literary' considerations, as many of those people in charge of the NSW Higher School Certificate English examination do, ask yourself about your criteria for making such judgments and what beliefs or ideology influenced you to develop such criteria. Because you are the only person who can decide what is most relevant to you, no subject or attitude is taboo in the Journal.

    Another way of exploring these issues is to respond to questions like the following after each section or chapter of a novel. (This *doesn't* mean to summarise the content of the text!)

    + What I really liked in this section was ...
    + What I disliked in this section was ...
    + What puzzles me is ...
    + I expect that ...
    + I speculate/hypothesise ...
    + I now understand ...

    At the end of this detailed exploration of a novel in the process of reading it, you are asked to read back over all you have written to draw some conclusions about what you have learned about yourself, your beliefs and your own reading processes. If you are bored by any part or parts, or by the whole text, explore in some depth what boredom means in your particular case.

Retrospective Evaluation

The value to you of this whole course will to a large extent depend on how effectively you can explore your achievements, problems and puzzles to articulate your own reading, writing and learning processes. After tutorial sessions dealing with issues that have particularly interested, annoyed, and/or puzzled you, record your feelings about the judgments made and the points discussed, and specify what you have learned from them.

At *all* stages of the course identify occasions when you feel excited, anxious, annoyed, disappointed, satisfied. Learning is likely to involve all of these feelings. Next, identify actions you might take yourself which might lead to your gaining more satisfaction from the course and from your own work. In class, don't hesitate to make requests of your tutor which might lead to your gaining more satisfaction. These can then be discussed openly.

Finally, in the last week of semester, and most important of all, read over all that you have written in your Journal and make final comments in some detail about what you have learned:

✦ from and about the texts in the course;
✦ about your own reading processes and the strategies you have learned to use consciously and deliberately to make books mean for you;
✦ about texts and the way they work;
✦ about the cultural assumptions that you bring to your reading.

Writing Style

The kind of informal, comfortable writing that I suggest is appropriate for the Journal is a kind of thinking-aloud-on-paper. It reads like written down speech and reflects the ebb and flow of the writer's thoughts and feelings. It is the kind of exploratory language most of us use when we are tentatively grappling with new ideas and feelings and are not yet ready to produce the coherent and logically ordered analysis or narrative that we make at a later stage in writing essays and stories. Try, however, to express your thinking in full sentences rather than jottings. The reason for this is that we believe the more completely you try to formulate your responses, puzzles, hypotheses and ideas, the more you will clarify them for yourself.

So get to it and have a go at wrapping your own language around your own thinking. And keep in mind, that if you are bored while writing your journal entries, I will be bored reading it. I expect to find it interesting.

Jack Thomson

Overleaf are two examples of students' journal responses, one by a sixteen year old, the other by a university student in her first year.

Students' Journal Responses: Two Examples

1. Dialogue with the Teacher

Here is a sixteen-year-old Bathurst boy's comments in his reading journal about his difficulty in becoming the implied reader of Jane Austen's novel *Northanger Abbey*, followed by his teacher's reply:

> *Perhaps I cannot relate to such experiences that Catherine endures because I am not accustomed to going to balls and enduring the pleasure of meeting ODD people and discussing PETTY things such as clothing and hats. I just don't have any sympathy with wealthy people who never work and have unlimited time to gossip.*

His teacher's written question/comment in response shows the way in which knowledgeable teachers can help teenage readers to understand and control both the conventions of literature and their own reactions to texts. This student was an enthusiastic reader of Science Fiction, so what his teacher wrote was this:

> *Would you react in a similar fashion to a Science Fiction novel peopled by weird aliens and set far into the future on another planet? Try to explain your reactions to this question. What are you learning about literature, yourself and your own reactions to texts from this?*

Here the student came to recognise that he objected to nineteenth century literary conventions in a Jane Austen novel but that he was perfectly happy to accept contemporary literary conventions in Science Fiction, and that he did this because he was used to accepting the conventions of Science Fiction. He learnt about his own cultural assumptions. From comments like these, students become more conscious of the constructedness of texts and of the ways they read them, and so develop greater textual power as readers and writers.

2. A First Response to the Opening Section of William Golding's Novel *Free Fall*

> *The disarranged chronology of this book broke my expected frame of reference, making me work harder to piece together the puzzles the book creates. This made me query, predict, judge and over all, read more actively in an attempt to make sense of the events and details. Being structurally baffled actually made me take far more interest in order to work things out for myself. It wasn't totally bewildering to find a structure like this, because it wasn't the first book I've read that plays around with the chronological order of events. This one does it more complexly than others I've read and makes you immediately realise there is real point in trying to work out why Sammy recollected his life's experiences in this apparently random order. You realise that there is a logic in the order,*

a logic controlled by Golding, and the point of that logic will give you
important clues in interpreting the significance of the whole novel. In
The Pyramid *Golding plays around with the time order of events, but*
there aren't so many of the events explored, and also the difference here
is that now Golding has his narrator play around with the events. Here
Sammy is the one consciously examining his past life whereas in **The**
Pyramid, *although Oliver tells the story in the first person he is not*
shown as so consciously sifting his experience and values for their
meaning. Oliver is less conscious than Sammy. In fact Oliver is quite
unconscious of the evil, selfish person he is, where Sammy is very
conscious of this. So, in a way, **The Pyramid** *as well as books with*
disjointed structures such as **Red Shift** *by Alan Garner have prepared*
me for this novel.

This is a very powerful statement about intertextuality. This student has
a clear awareness of textual rhetoric and literary conventions, and the whole
account is very reflexive. It is hard to reconcile the knowledge and confidence
evident here with the claim this student made at the beginning of the session
on *Free Fall* that she didn't understand "any of the first five or six pages". In
the process of writing what she did she discovered how much she knew and
how she could use it to make more sense of the text she was reading. This is
a good example of the way in which writing "expressively" in journals helps
learners.

Suggestions For Further Reading

Forrestal, Peter and Reid, Jo-Anne (1983) *English Workshop One: Room to Move*, Melbourne: Thomas Nelson.

Forrestal, Peter and Reid, Jo-Anne (1985) *English Workshop Three: Time to Tell*, Melbourne: Thomas Nelson.

Fulwiler, Toby (ed) (1987) *The Journal Book*, Upper Montclair, New Jersey: Boynton/Cook.

Heywood, Peta, Carozzi, Barry and McCann, Tricia (1995) *Englishworks 1* (and *Teacher's Book*, 1996) Melbourne: Cambridge University Press.

McClenaghan, Douglas, Doecke, Brenton and Parr, Helen (1995) *Englishworks 2* (and *Teacher's Book*, 1996) Melbourne: Cambridge University Press.

Hyde, Michael, Kesselschmidt, Johnny and Mason, Mary (1996) *Englishworks 3* (and *Teacher's Book*, forthcoming) Melbourne: Cambridge University Press.

McLoughlin, Rosemary, McNamara, Michael and Reidy, Jo (1996) *Englishworks 4*, (and *Teacher's Book*, 1997) Melbourne: Cambridge University Press.

Thomson, Jack (1987) *Understanding Teenagers' Reading*, Sydney: Methuen, and Norwood: Australian Association for the Teaching of English.

References

Barnes, Douglas (1976) *From Communication to Curriculum*, Harmondsworth: Penguin.

Barnes, Douglas, Britton, James and Rosen, Harold (1971) *Language, the Learner and the School*, Harmondsworth: Penguin.

Britton, James (1970) *Language and Learning*, Harmondsworth: Penguin.

Britton, James, et al (1975) *The Development of Writing Abilities*, London: Macmillan and Schools Council.

Bruner, Jerome, Oliver, R R, Greenfield, P N et al (1966) *Studies in Cognitive Growth: A Collaboration at the Center for Cognitive Studies*, New York: John Wiley.

Corcoran, Bill (1988), "Spiders, Surgeons and Anxious Aliens: Three Classroom Allies", *English Journal* Vol 77 No 1, January.

Donaldson, Margaret (1978) *Children's Minds*, London: Fontana.

Forrestal, Peter and Reid, Jo-Anne (1983) *English Workshop One: Room to Move*, Melbourne: Thomas Nelson.

Heywood, Peta, Carozzi, Barry and McCann, Patricia (1995) *Englishworks 1* (and *Teacher's Book,*1996) Melbourne: Cambridge University Press.

Lindberg, Gary (1987) "The Journal Conference: From Dialectic to Dialogue" in Fulwiler, Toby (ed) *The Journal Book*, Upper Montclair, New Jersey: Boynton/Cook.

McClenaghan, Douglas, Doecke, Brenton and Parr, Helen (1995) *Englishworks 2* (and *Teacher's Book*, 1996) Melbourne: Cambridge University Press.

Smith, Cliff (1985) "Expressive Writing in Responding to Literature by Senior High School Students", Unpublished M Ed dissertation, Charles Sturt University: Mitchell.

Thomson, Jack (1987) *Understanding Teenagers' Reading: Reading Processes and the Teaching of Literature*, Sydney: Methuen, and Norwood: Australian Association for the Teaching of English.

Vygotsky, L S (1962) *Thought and Language*, edited and translated by Hanfmann, F and Vakar, G Cambridge, Massachusetts: The MIT Press.

Williamson, John and Woodall, Clare (1996) "A Vision for English: Rethinking the Revised National Curriculum in the Light of Contemporary Critical Theory" in *English in Education* Vol 30 No 3.

Efferent Reading / Aesthetic Reading

Louise Rosenblatt, in her important book *The Reader, the Text, the Poem*, suggests that there are two kinds of reading: that in which the primary concern of the reader is with what she/he will carry away from the reading, and that in which the reader's primary concern is with what happens **during** the actual reading event. The first, more or less instrumental type of reading, she calls **efferent** reading (from the Latin *efferre*, "to carry away"); the second she calls **aesthetic** reading : "In aesthetic reading, the reader's attention is centred directly on what he [sic] is living through during his [sic] relationship with that particular text" (Louise Rosenblatt, *The Reader the Text, the Poem,,* Carbondale, III: Southern Illinois University Press, 1978, p25).

19 Literacy, Genre Studies and Pedagogy

Paul Richardson

L iteracy is a slippery concept which continues to occupy a prominent place in public debate in Australia and other English-speaking countries. Thirty years ago English literacy education in Australia was a silent partner in public policy, where it functioned as an instrument of cultural assimilation of minorities into the majority culture. As a concomitant, little attention was given to the concerns, identities, or languages of minorities (see Smolicz, 1971). Over the last twenty years or so, a succession of Federal, State and Territory governments have disavowed assimilation in favour of more sensitive, less discriminatory policies, embracing diversity and plurality as desirable attributes of Australian social and cultural life. By insisting that one size does **not** fit all, public space has been opened up for a range of discursive practices, identities and minority languages (see Ozolins, 1993).

In Australian multicultural society, the issue of which model of literacy pedagogy is adopted by schools is inevitably the subject of debate and contest. A decade ago Walters, Daniell and Trachsel pointed out that:

> In practice, any use of the term [literacy], especially in educational settings, always carries with it assumptions, again often contradictory, about what counts as a proper text, how these texts may be decoded and interpreted, what variety or varieties of language may be used for interpretation, what kinds of thinking these texts may be said to represent, and finally, what sorts of pedagogy would most likely produce literate behaviours, however defined.
>
> (Walters, Daniell and Trachsel, 1987, p856)

In a multi-ethic society, questions of individual and collective rights are foregrounded when literacy pedagogy and schooling are identified as the equalising instruments in an otherwise complex, heterogeneous and unequal society. Indeed, Federal, State and Territory governments in Australia have pursued educational policies which attempt to ensure that ethnicity, race, gender and poverty are not barriers to access and achievement. Thus education, and particularly literacy education, has been seen as the means by which those at the bottom of the social, economic and employment ladder – Aborigines, white poor, and children from recently arrived immigrant families – are given a leg up to a more secure, financially rewarding occupation and lifestyle.

If over time we have modified our public policies to be more inclusive, less discriminatory and more sensitive, in the area of literacy education, Federal, State and Territory governments have been persistently attracted by programmatic views of teaching and learning literacy which, if not explicitly, implicitly promise cultural transmission, assimilation and reproduction. Despite the rhetoric of 'critique', 'access' and 'empowerment', the curriculum practices of genre-based pedagogy forged into curriculum and syllabus documents in the various States and Territories promise to deliver commonality, if not narrow conformity, of school-based literacy experiences.

This chapter will briefly outline international developments in *literacy studies* and *genre studies* as a backdrop to an account of the development of a genre-based pedagogy in Australia since the early 1980s. In examining genre-based pedagogy and genre theory it will be implicitly argued that while the so called 'genre-process debate' of the 1980s has passed (see Richardson 1991), some of the issues and questions concerning genre-based literacy pedagogy have not been resolved. Recent work in genre studies and substantial critiques of Martin's theory of genre serve as timely reminders of the need for further research.

Traditionally, literacy has been associated with an individual's ability to read and write. In everyday contexts literacy is invoked in these terms – a view which regards literacy as a set of asocial individual cognitive skills dislodged from their sociocultural moorings in human relationships and communities of practice. By neglecting the role and constitutive influence of situation, activities and participants, literacy becomes a set of skills necessary for individuals to undertake reading and writing. Once acquired, these skills are then seamlessly transferable without impediment across contexts and situations. Such a view is not sustainable in the light of findings from new literacy studies.

A growing corpus of international work contributing to the changing conception of literacy has been characterised by methodological eclecticism across a range of disciplines, cognitive dimensions, socio-cultural groups and educational settings. The interdisciplinary roots of the *new literacy studies* can be seen, for example, in the work of researchers who have demonstrated that children progress unequally towards literacy. The nature and extent of that inequality has been revealed through the work of Heath (1982 and 1983), Scribner and Cole (1981), Lankshear and Lawler (1987), Wells (1986), Gumperz (1982), Michaels (1981 and 1985) , Cazden (1979), among others. Similarly, studies by Graff (1979), Cook-Gumperz (1986), Street

(1984), Gee (1996) have brought to our attention two tenets: literacies are 'social practices' and the nature of language is 'dialogic'(Street, 1997). In short, research studies across disciplines have demonstrated the 'situatedness' of literacy and led to the conviction that literacy cannot be defined, understood, learned, studied, or acquired independently of a social context. Moreover, no longer can it be assumed that there are natural or 'naturalistic' conditions for learning literacy, or indeed, that literacy naturally follows on from oral language development. The very constructed nature of all literacy practices and the relationship between literacy, personal identity, cultural identity, and ideology undermine claims that all children, in all social and cultural contexts, learn literacy in the same way. Equally, this same evidence should have rung alarm bells when it was proposed that language and literacy learning could be explained by a single linguistic theory, at least as it has been manifested in Australian genre theory and pedagogy. Those who founded genre theory and genre-based pedagogy in Australia did so by giving little serious attention to the work being undertaken outside of Australia in literacy and genre studies. From the point of view of the sociology of knowledge, such a development in the late twentieth century, even in Australia, is quite unusual and deserving of study in itself.

Coincident with developments in literacy studies over the past fifteen years or so have been studies on several continents, from a number of fields and disciplines, which have resulted in a metamorphosis of the concept of *genre*. Originally a literary concept, genre has now been engaged as a framework for 'analysing the form and function of nonliterary discourse', and as a tool for 'developing educational practices in fields such as rhetoric, composition studies, professional writing, linguistics, and English for specific purposes' (Hyon, 1996, p693). Three publications were seminal in germinating an interest in genre in accounting for the social, functional, and pragmatic dimensions of language use: Michael Halliday's *Language as Social Semiotic* (1978), Carolyn Miller's article 'Genre as Social Action' (1984), and the English translation and publication of Mikhail Bakhtin's *Speech Genres and Other Late Essays* (1986). Differing definitions and analyses of genre with significantly different pedagogical trajectories have resulted in three distinct traditions of genre being delineated: Australian systemic functional linguistics, English for Specific Purposes [ESP] (Swales, 1990), and North American New Rhetoric studies (Freedman and Medway, 1994). ESP and New Rhetoric see genres as dynamic and social texts pragmatically deployed by members of discourse communities. In broad terms, these new theories suggest that genres are typical forms of discourse which evolve in response to recurring rhetorical situations, where they function to address situations and evoke desired responses. In that they place greater emphasis on the explication of the semantic and syntactic features of texts, Australian genre theorists see genres more rigidly and prescriptively.

The project of North American and Canadian researchers has been to explore the 'situatedness' and evolution of genres in response to changing epistemological, ideological, technological and political needs. Unlike Australian genre researchers, who have concentrated their research more on primary and secondary school genres, North American and Canadian researchers have gathered data from professional workplaces and universities. While Australian researchers have found stability and rigidity in curriculum genres, their North American counterparts have detected an essential dynamism and fragility of the genres in their data. From a body of research studies focusing on graduate students learning to participate as professionals in academic cultures, and influenced by Miller's seminal study, Berkenkotter and Huckin (1995, p3) arrived at the thesis that "genres are inherently dynamic rhetorical structures that can be manipulated according to the conditions of use, and that genre knowledge is therefore best conceptualised as a form of situated cognition embedded in disciplinary activities".

Even though there are similarities in the way genre has been conceived and has been studied by scholars in North America and Australia, there are also significant differences. Unlike researchers of other continents, the Sydney School (see Green and Lee, 1994) began their research work with the avowed intention of developing a pedagogical program to destabilise, debase and eventually displace process writing pedagogy, then dominant in primary education, and of increasing interest to secondary English teachers (see Doecke and McClenaghan in this volume). In hindsight, it would seem that the pedagogical program of the Sydney School deeply influenced the pace, direction, extent, and nature of the research program – a program fuelled by urgency and evangelism. Publications emanating from members of the Sydney School created a self-referencing genealogy of scholars who contributed to a stream of working papers, journal articles, manuals, teacher and student workbooks, each of which rarified and valorised the notion of genre developed by Martin.

The Australian systemic-functional model of genre theory privileges language and text as a system, locating meaning in the language as system and in text structure. Thus, while Martin, Rothery and Christie argue that texts are produced in a context of culture and situation, they insist that meaning is carried in the text structure and in the grammar of individual texts, and that it is through these that language users construct reality. Although Martin (1986) has posited ideology as a level beyond genre in a paradigmatic model which frames language, register, genre and ideology, his notion of genre as textual object which exists independently of social meaning-making practices has eclipsed questions of ideology. Little explicit attention has been paid to ideology beyond the belief that through the teaching of the powerful genres the powerless and the marginalised in society will gain access to distributed power.

Martin's model of genre, then, is defined as "a staged, goal-oriented social process", where genres are seen as social processes 'because members of a culture interact with each other to achieve them; as goal-oriented because they have evolved to get things done; and as staged because it usually takes more than one step for participants to achieve their goals' (Martin et al, 1987, p59). This staged, purposeful cultural activity includes oral and written language genres and is characterised by having "a schematic structure – a distinctive beginning, middle, and end" (Christie, 1984, p270).

In 1980, Martin and Rothery (1980, 1981) began an analysis of the writing of primary school students collected by Rothery. According to an account compiled by Lorraine Murphy (Cope et al,1993) their analysis, founded on the theoretical work of Halliday (1973, 1978) and Halliday and Hasan (1976), revealed that most texts were quite short, lacked development, and deployed only a few genres – labelling, observation/comments, reports, recounts, and narratives. Although these findings were not particularly new at the time, Martin and his colleagues were sufficiently alarmed to independently set about the task of devising a "theoretically distinctive pedagogy to address this situation" (Cope et al, 1993, p233).

Initially they devised a classificatory typology of the genres written by children in a classroom context which were represented as two strands branching off from observation/comment: one strand identified as narrative genres, the other factual genres – both of which were further divided into sub-categories. Eventually additional work (see Martin 1985; Christie et al, 1990; Derewianka, 1990) produced a typology which Christie and Rothery (1989, p5) have identified as the "generic structures which appear to be involved in order to learn the various school subjects":

factual genres:	procedure (how something is done) description (what some particular thing is like) report (what an entire class of things is like) explanation (a reason why a judgment is made) argument (arguments why a thesis has been produced)
narrative genres:	recounts narrative based on personal experience narrative based on fantasy the moral tale myths, spoofs, serials thematic narratives

The textbook and teacher professional development materials devised by Christie et al. (1990), Derewianka (1990), Callaghan and Rothery (1988), and Macken et al. (1989) ensured that teachers had access to materials and a model for teaching the identified genres. Text samples provided examples of the process by which the structural elements of text organisation and grammatical features could be analysed.

An interventionist role was advocated for the teacher as an element in a curriculum cycle which required the teacher to model the social purpose of the text, jointly construct with students a model of the text, and to provide opportunities for consultation with students during their independent construction of a text. Systemic functional linguistics provided the analytical tools and frame through which to analyse the grammatical features of the identified text types. Essentially, these pedagogical recommendations sought to promote a more explicit model of writing instruction founded on a prescriptive, "static vision of genre", involving deliberate teacher intervention (Freedman and Medway 1994, p9).

Not unexpectedly, the genre school initiated and developed by Martin, Rothery and Christie spawned zealous disciples, critical friends and ardent opponents. A useful introduction is provided by Reid (1987) in which critical friends and spirited critics register their concerns about the apparent rigidity of genres, the process by which genres are learnt, question whether particular forms of knowledge only embed in particular linguistic forms, and whether content can be separated from linguistic form (Sawyer and Watson, 1989).

Thibault (1989), Threadgold (1988), Threadgold and Kress (1988) and Hasan (1995) have all cogently argued theoretical cases against the model of genre and language articulated by Martin, Rothery and Christie. Their critiques focus on the disjuncture between the claim that meaning is encapsulated in textual objects, genres as autonomous systems, and the avowal of a social constructionist functional model of language. Thibault (p346) observes that this instrumental view of genre "both assumes and implicitly conveys the message that the world is organised in terms of an intrumental logic based on linear, one-way models of cause-and-effect or means-and-end, which may have the effect of socialising teachers and students into a reductionist one-way model of causality."

Similarly, in a long and highly technical study, Hasan (1995) systematically critiques the model of genre proposed by Martin and seeks to rectify misrepresentations of both Halliday's and her own work. Works by Halliday and Hasan were set by Martin as keystones in the development of his theory of genre. With these keystones removed, Martin's theory appears unstable, requiring further intellectual scaffolding. Moreover, in writing her paper Hasan intended to show "that Martin's framework for the study of text is inconsistent with the systemic functional model" (p184) and that the theory of genre he has proposed is adequately accounted for by Halliday's notion of register. In suggesting that the pedagogical programs introduced into schooling by Martin and his colleagues have "a lot to recommend them . . .", Hasan nonetheless has her objections (p283):

> Practice can hardly be better than the theory permits; otherwise, the practice is better despite the explicitly held theory. My own view is that

the stratification of genre and register, the collapsing of the social and
the verbal, at both these planes, which in turn entails a questionable
view of language, has a highly deleterious effect: it moves the whole issue
of text structure and its activation from active, feeling, reacting
participants co-engaged in some interaction to given forms of talk that
represent the way things are done in our culture, as if culture is
unchanging and as if the participants are simply preprogrammed.

It was the pedagogical program initiated and developed by Martin et al. which eventually led Kress (1989, p10) to observe that 'genre theory in education is not, at this stage, a highly unified body of theory', and to distance his work from the pedagogical enterprise of Martin and his colleagues. Knapp (1995) has recently reiterated this theme by outlining the differences between what he sees as two broadly different interpretations of genre in Australia: the systemic-functional model, and the 'genre as social process' model – models drawn from significantly different views of language, epistemology and pedagogy. The latter model is more in tune with the orientation and interests of North American genre studies.

It seems ironic that from Martin and Rothery's original data base of children's writing from a primary school in Sydney, children around Australia are now being explicitly instructed in the reproduction of those text forms. If Martin and Rothery had begun their analysis with a data base similar to their North American counterparts, that is, with graduate university students and workplace professionals, would they have arrived at the same conclusions about the stability and rigidity of textual forms?

The influence and impact of the Sydney genre school in dislodging expressivist process pedagogy in primary and secondary schooling in Australia has been profound. English literacy curriculum documents in all States and Territories unilaterally treat genres as unproblematic. English syllabus materials in the state of Queensland are founded on genre theory and genre-based pedagogy, with the genres identified by Martin et al. being prescribed for children to be taught. Curriculum and syllabus writers in New South Wales were for a time influenced by the pedagogy, co-opting it into a wider political agenda. While the pedagogy remains influential with teachers, it is again contentious at the political level. Less contentious has been *First Steps* (1994) from the Department of Education in Western Australia and published in conjunction with Longman, Australia, which has surreptitiously become a 'de facto' literacy curriculum for hard-pressed primary school teachers across the country. This literacy program is an 'elaborate technology' which has been 'neutralised' (Lee 1996, p13) as it has penetrated deeply into the consciousness of teachers and their classroom practices in all States and Territories. Ironically, many classroom teachers no longer know of the original research or the researchers who first proposed the theory of genre and developed genre pedagogy. *First Steps* has become a transparent instrument of instruction with the text types around which the curriculum is formed being taken as givens without regard to context or need. Further, an unexpected outcome has been that classroom literacy experiences for the various grade levels across the primary school years have taken on a conformity and uniformity that might only have been expected to result from a nationally agreed, prescriptive curriculum.

While Australian genre theory and genre-based pedagogy have made enormous inroads into literacy curriculum and teaching at all levels, genre researchers on other continents continue to grapple with fundamental issues. For instance, "Can genres be taught? How do speakers and writers manage to produce outstanding texts rather than ones that are 'generically correct' and merely adequate? How do speakers and writers negotiate dissonances between their intentions and their developing texts in the absence of an ideal or a correct textual model? How are texts and contexts related to one another? How do genres and communities constitute and reconstitute one another?" (Kamberelis, 1995, p165). More importantly, these researchers are sensitive to the way that becoming a competent 'speaker' or 'writer', acquiring new genres, entails a process of identity reconstruction. *New literacy studies* have made us aware of the ideologically constructive and constitutive processes of literacy learning. Similarly, *new genre studies* highlight the fact that genre learning and disciplinary socialisation foreground issues of power and authority in relation to the formation of new subject positions, norms, values and beliefs. Australian genre-based pedagogy has been driven by what Lee (1996, p3) calls "a largely unreflexive promotion of a neo-liberal agenda of access and participation", to the point where proponents have been untroubled by the technical reductionist model of instruction into which teachers and students have been socialised through teacher workshops, curriculum and syllabus documents, and instructional materials.

Part of the attraction for many teachers and educators of Australian genre-based pedagogy has surely been the promise that the model of instruction would empower students with the linguistic resources for success. In attempting to teach marginalised target populations the 'powerful' school genres of **report** and **exposition**, Australian genre researchers garnered support from teachers who daily worked with students with little stake in their own future. Critiques of process pedagogy by Martin (1985), Painter (1986), Gray (1987), Christie (1988) and Gilbert (1990) were important in broadening the range of writing children were being asked to undertake in classrooms in Australia, and it must be acknowledged that teachers of primary school children no longer place the emphasis on narrative writing they were encouraged to do a decade ago. Teachers now look more carefully at the writing, reading, and assessment tasks they are asking their students to undertake. However, the systematic typology of text types derived from Australian genre theory has built within it a linearity which appears to take care of sequence and continuity in the development of literacy experiences. In framing English literacy curriculum documents, matters of sequence and continuity of literacy experiences remain nagging difficulties. Genre-based pedagogy with its emphasis on genres as objects, in conjunction with competency frameworks and assessment programs, has been susceptible to co-option into instrumentalist government policies which promote simplistic notions of literacy and literacy acquisition.

As impossible as it is to turn the clock back, it is always easy to be wise in hindsight. Nevertheless, given the primacy of place Martin gave to the linguistic work of Halliday and Hasan in developing his own theory of genre, and given that Hasan has written seeking clarification of Martin's theoretical work, it now seems unfortunate that Australian genre theory and genre-based pedagogy developed so rapidly in the hot-house environment of the Australian academic community. Australian academic discourse communities are small and invariably riven by personal histories and rivalries. In these 'hot-house' conditions, critique and advice from critical friends may not always be well received. The debate that emerged during the mid-1980s rapidly polarised into two camps: the Sydney genre school and their opponents. Those who wrote seeking clarification were invariably dismissed as opponents and thinly disguised apologists for process writing and progressivist education. These often acrimonious divisions, publicised in the national press, served to indicate to the wider community that literacy educators could not agree on much at all concerning literacy education. Sadly, considerable harm was done to the reputation and standing of the community of literacy educators during this time. The social and political consequences of the debate are still being felt in the late 1990s. In terms of the sociology of knowledge, there is an important lesson for Australian academics which I will state as a small parable: it is possible to grow too rapidly to become a big fish in a small pond; unfortunately small ponds dry up quickly in the blaze of the summer sun, in which case even big fish don't survive.

References

Bakhtin, M (1986) *Speech Genres and Other Late Essays*, Austin: University of Texas.

Berkenkotter, C and Huckin, T N (1995) *Genre Knowledge in Disciplinary Communication: Cognition/Culture/Power*, Hillsdale, New Jersey: Lawrence Erlbaum and Associates.

Callaghan, M and Rothery, J (1988) "Teaching Factual Writing: A Genre-Based Approach", Report of the DSP Literacy Project, Metropolitan East Region, NSW Department of Education, Sydney.

Cazden, C (1979) "Peekaboo as an Instructional Model: Discourse Development at Home and at School", *Papers and Reports in Child Language Development*, 17: 1-29, Standford, CA, Department of Linguistics, Stanford University.

Christie, Frances (1988) "Learning to write genres", in Murray, J and Smith, F *Language Arts and the Learner*, Melbourne: Macmillan.

Christie, Frances (ed) (1984) *Children Writing: Study Guide and Reader*, Geelong: Deakin University Press.

Christie, Frances, Gray, Brian, Gray, Pam, Macken, Mary, Martin, J R and Rothery, Joan (1990-1992) *Language: A Resource for Meaning*, Teachers' and Student Books, Sydney: Harcourt Brace Jovanovich.

Christie, Frances and Rothery, Joan (1990) "Genres and Writing: A Response to Michael Rosen", *English in Australia*, 90: 3-12.

Cook-Gumperz, J (ed) (1986) *The Social Construction of Literacy*, Cambridge: Cambridge University Press.

Cope, Bill and Kalantzis, Mary (1993) *The Powers of Literacy: A Genre Approach to Teaching Writing*, London: The Falmer Press.

Cope, Bill, Kalantzis, Mary, Kress, Gunther, and Martin Jim; compiled by Lorraine Murphy (1993) "Bibliographic Essay: Developing the Theory and Practice of Genre-based Literacy" in Cope, Bill and Kalantzis, Mary (1993) *The Powers of Literacy: A Genre Approach to Teaching Writing*, London: The Falmer Press.

Derewianka, B (1990) *Exploring How Texts Work*, Sydney: Primary English Teaching Association.

Education Department of Western Australia (1994) *First Steps*, Longman.

Freedman, A and Medway, P (eds) (1994) *Genre and The New Rhetoric*, London: Taylor Francis.

Gee, J P (1996) *Social Linguistics and Literacies: Ideology in Discourses*, (second edition), London: Taylor and Francis.

Gilbert, P (1990) "Authorizing Disadvantage: Authorship and Creativity in the Language Classroom, in Christie, F (ed) *Literacy for a Changing World*, Hawthorn: The Australian Council for Educational Research.

Graff, H (1979) *The Literacy Myth: Literacy and Social Structure in the Nineteenth Century City*, New York: Academic Press.

Gray, B (1987) "How Natural Is 'Natural' Language Teaching – Employing Wholistic Methodology in the Classroom", *Australian Journal of Early Childhood*, 12 (4): 3-19.

Green, B and Lee, A (1994) "Writing Geography: Literacy, Identity and Schooling", in Freedman, A and Medway, P (eds) *Learning and Teaching Genre*, Portsmouth, NH: Heinemann Boynton/Cook.

Gumperz, J J (1982) *Discourse Strategies*, Cambridge: Cambridge University Press.

Halliday, M A K (1973) *Explorations in the Functions of Language*, (Explorations in Language Study), London: Edward Arnold.

Halliday, M A K and Hasan, R (1976) *Cohesion in English*, London: Longman.

Halliday, M A K and Hasan, R (1985) *Language, Context and Text*, Geelong: Deaking University Press.

Halliday, M A K (1978) *Language as Social Semiotic*, London: Edward Arnold.

Hasan, Ruqaiya (1995) "The Conception of Context in Text", in Fries, Peter H and Gregory, Michael (ed) *Discourse in Society: Systemic Functional Perspectives. Meaning and Choice in Language: Studies for Michael Halliday*, New Jersey: Ablex Publishing Corporation.

Heath, S B (1982) "What No Bedtime Story Means: Narrative Skills at Home and at School", *Language in Society*, 11:49-76.

Heath, S B (1983) *Ways with Words: Language, Life, and Works in Communities and Classrooms*, Cambridge: Cambridge University Press.

Hyon, S (1996) "Genre in Three Traditions: Implications for ESL", *TESOL Quarterly*, 30 (4): 693-722.

Kamberelis, G (1995) "Genre as Institutionally Informed Social Practice", *Journal of Contemporary Legal Issues*, Vol 6, 115-171.

Knapp, Peter (1995) "The Trouble with Genre", *Idiom* XXIX (2): 34-41.

Kress, G R and Hodge, R (1979) *Language as Ideology*, London: Routledge and Kegan Paul.

Kress, G R (1982) *Learning to Write*, London: Routledge and Kegan Paul.

Kress, G R (1989) "Texture and Meaning", in Richard Andrews (ed) *Narrative and Argument*, Milton Keynes: Open University Press.

Lankshear, C and Lawler, M (1987) *Literacy, Schooling and Revolution*, London: Falmer Press.

Lee, A (1996) *Gender, Literacy, Curriculum*, London: Taylor and Francis.

Macken, M et al, (1989) *An Approach to Writing K-12: Introduction*, Literacy and Education Research Network, Directorate of Studies, NSW Department of Education, Sydney.

Macken, M et al, (1989) *The Theory and Practice of Genre-Based Writing*, Literacy and Education Research Network, Directorate of Studies, NSW Department of Education, Sydney.

Martin, J and Rothery, J (1980) Writing Project Report No 1, *Working Papers in Linguistics No. 1*, Linguistics Department, University of Sydney.

Martin, J and Rothery, J (1981) Writing Project Report No 2, *Working Papers in Linguistics No. 2*, Linguistics Department, University of Sydney.

Martin, J R (1985) *Factual Writing: Exploring and Challenging Social Reality*, Geelong: Deakin University Press.

Martin, J R (1986) "Grammaticalizing the Ecology", in Threadgold, T et al (eds), *Semiotics-Ideology-Language*, Sydney: Pathfinder Press.

Martin, J R, Christie, Frances and Rothery, Joan (1987) "Social Processes in Education: A Reply to Sawyer and Watson (and others)," in Reid, I (ed) (1987) *The Place of Genre in Learning: Current Debates*, Geelong: Deakin University Press.

Michaels, S (1981) " 'Sharing Time': Children's Narrative Styles and Differential Access to Literacy", *Language in Society*, 10: 423-442.

Michaels, S (1985) "Hearing the Connections in Children's Oral And Written Discourse", *Journal of Education*, 167: 36-56.

Miller, C R (1984) "Genre as Social Action", *Quarterly Journal of Speech*, 70: 151-167.

Olson, Gary M, Duffy, Susan A and Mack, Robert L (1980) "Applying Knowledge of Writing Conventions to Prose Comprehension and Composition", in Wilbert J McKeachie (ed) *Learning, Cognition, and College Teaching*, San Francisco: Jossey-Bass.

Ozolins, U (1993) *The Politics of Language in Australia*, Cambridge: Cambridge University Press.

Painter, C (1986) "The Role of Interaction in Learning to Speak and Write", in Painter, Clare and Martin, J R (ed) (1986) *Writing to Mean: Teaching Genres Across the Curriculum*, Applied Linguistics Association of Australia, Occasional Paper no 9.

Painter, Clare and Martin, J R (ed) (1986) *Writing to Mean: Teaching Genres Across the Curriculum*, Applied Linguistics Association of Australia, Occasional paper No 9.

Reid, I, (ed) (1987) *The Place of Genre in Learning: Current Debates*, Geelong: Deakin University Press.

Richardson, P (1991) "Language as Personal Resource and as Social Construct: Competing Views of Literacy Pedagogy in Australia", *Educational Review*, 43 (2): 171-190.

Sawyer, W and Watson, K (1989) "Further Questions of Genre", *English in Australia*, 90: 27-42.

Scribner, S and Cole, M (1981) *The Psychology of Literacy*, Cambridge, MA: Harvard University Press.

Smolicz, J J (1971) "Is the Australian School an Assimilationist Agency?" *Education News*, Vol 13 No 4.

Street, B (1984) *Literacy in Theory and Practice*, Cambridge: Cambridge University Press.

Street, B (1997) "The Implications of the 'New Literacy Studies' for Literacy Education", *English in Education*, 31 (3): 45-59.

Swales, J (1990) *Genre Analysis: English in Academic and Research Settings*, Cambridge: Cambridge University Press.

Szwed, John F (1981) "The Ethnography of Literacy" in Marcia Farr Whiteman (ed) *Writing: The Nature, Development, and Teaching of Written Communication, Vol. 1. Variation in Writing: Function and Linguistic-Cultural Differences*, New Jersey: Lawrence Erlbaum.

Thibault, Paul (1989) "Genres, Social Action and Pedagogy: Towards a Critical Social Semiotic Account". *Southern Review*, 22 (3): 338-362.

Threadgold, Terry (1988) "The Genre Debate", *Southern Review*, (Australia) 21 (3): 315-330.

Threadgold, Terry and Kress, Gunther (1988) "Towards a Social Theory of Genre" *Southern Review*, 21 (3): 215-243.

Walters, K, Daniell, B and Trachsel, M (1987) "Formal and Functional Approaches to Literacy", *Language Arts*, 64 (8): 855-868.

Wells, G (1986) *The Meaning Makers: Children Learning Language and Using Language to Learn*, Portsmouth, NH: Heinemann.

20 Computer Technology and Textual Practices in the English Classroom

Gillian Barnsley

The Dartmouth Seminar not only proposed a personal growth model for the teaching of English, it drew attention to the need for English teachers to have a thorough grounding in language. Psycholinguistics and sociolinguistics became part of the map of the territory that a beginning teacher needed to take on board. The English teacher's brief to attend to the oracy as well as literacy of students also arose. Workshop methods of teaching were endorsed there, as were processes such as working in small groups. As Dixon (1967) put it regretfully:

A 'workshop' method with individuals working with each other in groups of changing pattern, properly begins quite early on in primary or elementary school. It ought to develop fairly smoothly, though with new situations, into the secondary school. At present this is not happening... Even the best English specialists in secondary schools tend to be cut off by training and practice from what the primary schools have pioneered, and to lose by such a discontinuity.

(Dixon, 1967, p98)

Thirty years on, the personal growth model is criticised for focusing attention on the personal rather than on the social nature of literacy. Workshop approaches to teaching writing are far more common in secondary schools, even if they too are being contested and re-negotiated in a period of rapid technological change.

This chapter examines changes in writing curriculum since Dartmouth by focusing on issues of writing and technology. It takes into account the fact that English classrooms mediated by computer technology give rise to different pedagogical practices from those in the pen-and-paper world. In the electronic text world we can publish ourselves for audiences and purposes in our local communities without having to work through a publisher. We can revise our work without ever having to commit our mistakes to paper. Text composed on computers is 'soft' text: it is infinitely malleable. We can enter our texts at any point to revise, recast and polish before printing. We can even publish on the World Wide Web in electronic form, without committing our publications to paper.

A number of researchers have been interested in investigating the differences between pen-and-paper classrooms and computer-mediated ones. Daiute (1985) noticed that secondary students made fewer within-text revisions of computer drafts, preferring to add substantially to the ends of their narratives than to recast or reorder their texts. Snyder (1992) worked with two groups of Year 8 pupils who were all invited to write letters to the School Representative Council arguing whether they thought their school was the perfect school. Both groups had the same teacher, who emphasised explicit attention to different genres: narrative, report, argument. The main difference was that one group composed with computers, the other with pen and paper. Snyder found that in the computer-mediated writing class students were more willing to revise texts in argumentative genre than narrative genre, more willing to work collaboratively, more willing to conference with each other and more interactive than in the pen-and-paper classroom. She attributed this to the fact that writing on screen is public: everyone in the classroom can see an evolving text. She also noticed a change in the teacher's role. The teacher was less interventionist in the computer-mediated classroom preferring to 'work alongside' her learners.

These findings suggest that the computer-mediated writing workshop is a promising site for teaching genres other than narrative. It is also a promising site for collaborative writing practices, rather than purely individual ones. In workplace or community settings many texts are also constructed collaboratively rather than individually. Our writing pedagogy needs to build on these insights. In this light, Lensmire (1994) has argued that process/ workshop approaches to the teaching of writing often fall into the trap of specifying only individual writing practices, and that revisions of the pedagogy need to include a focus on collaborative text construction. Gilbert (1990) has also argued that the emphasis on the personal, the individual in text production in many process writing workshops has obscured the fact that reading and writing practices are socially constructed:

> By placing emphasis on the personal and idiosyncratic aspects of literacy learning, as often applies in schools today, the social and constructed nature of language tends to be obscured. Concepts like authorship focus on the creation of a text, on emotional qualities of a text - but not on how a text is made. The making of a text demands that attention be paid to the textual construction and to reading practices: to the social and cultural nature of literacy. (Gilbert, 1990, p77)

In the discussion which follows, I want to demonstrate that writing workshops mediated by computer technology can place emphasis on collaborative as well as individual textual construction, can implement a process pedagogy in new and exciting ways, can draw attention to the generic features of text types and can draw student attention to the social/cultural nature of literacy. We are on the brink of taking 'two steps forward' into new and evolving literacies. To illustrate this I offer two case studies of classrooms where interesting changes in teaching practices have been brought about in part by the use of computer technology.

My first case study comes from England, the second from Australia. Both teaching sequences involve the production of a newspaper. English teachers have been using the making of newspapers or newsletters since Dartmouth because they provide a 'real' audience and a purpose for writing. They also help students write in what Britton (1975) called the transactional mode: news stories are written to inform, editorials and letters-to-the-editor to persuade others to agree with our views. As an English coordinator at Wonthaggi High School in the late sixties, I had the job of producing the school newspaper. My students drafted articles with pen and paper in a range of factual genres, such as news story, editorial and feature articles. The girls in Year 10 typing classes copy-typed the drafts. The newspaper club members edited the typed drafts using plenty of white-out fluid, often inserting small changes to spelling and punctuation with the pen. Boys did not do typing in those days! Everyone in the newspaper group helped with the illustrations, which had to be drawn to size to fit the columns on an A4 sheet. The school principal acted as the gatekeeper, perusing our mock-ups carefully before the final print-run on the office photocopier. We were frankly into an enterprise (sub)culture, making sure that the newspapers were in print to sell to students visiting the school on inter-school sports days. This helped the English Faculty pay for all the paper.

The two case studies I report from the 1990s reflect both continuities and discontinuities in English teaching practices since that time, focusing in particular on the role new technology plays in text production. The first occurred when I was at the University of East Anglia on a teaching fellowship. I was working in the undergraduate teacher education program, where beginning English teachers were learning to use computers as both writing tools and as resources for teaching. In the course of this work, I was invited to spend a day at Long Stratten Comprehensive School on the outskirts of Norwich, as an observer-participant of a day at which technology across-the-curriculum was going to happen. The IT co-ordinator for the area had a brief to support teachers in their own classrooms to deliver the outcomes of their National Technology Statement. His view of in-service was that it was more effective if put into practice with real kids and real teachers in their own classroom settings. The following comprises my observations from that day.

Case Study I
Long Stratten Comprehensive School

It is 8.45 am on a blustery English summer day, June 13th 1991. I meet the IT coordinator in the staffroom for briefing. I am to be located in one classroom with a group of Year 9s. I am to act as a facilitator rather than a gatekeeper in text production. I must not intervene with teacherly advice to solve the problems that the groups in this classroom are going to encounter. In a group of twenty-four kids I am to rove about, listening to how they solve the problems they will encounter during the day. The simulation of the work of a newspaper office will finish at 2.30pm, when the student groups will display their newspaper front pages to the rest of Year 9 for comment and evaluation. The day will not finish until a debriefing session is held in the quadrangle at 3.00pm. That is where teachers and learners alike will have their say.

What is happening around me is that all of Year 9 is engaged in the one simulation run by computers. One hundred and twenty-four kids, six teachers, one outside IT consultant and a visitor/teacher from Australia are supposed to remain occupied for a full school day. A nightmare proposition! The middle-school classroom block has been taken over for this purpose. We have six classrooms in a modern block, with interconnecting corridors and open spaces. The subject timetable has also been renegotiated. Year 9 will not attend normal classes on this school day. They will work on IT instead.

Each of the six classrooms has a computer in it. The computer is dedicated to running the software simulation *Hijack*. The software has been written in consultation with British teachers. It simulates the ticker-tape machine which delivers items of news interest to newspaper groups around the world. The idea is that students in groups of about eight will act as the editorial board of a newspaper, and produce the front page of that newspaper in the course of the day. At a variable interval the computer will spew out updates of the news: the flasher in the park, the abduction of a child, the hijacking of a British aircraft with a prince on board. The students in Year 9 do not know what is going to happen. We teachers do, because we have previewed the program. It is not the most startling program. Bits of text, ASCII files, just print out from time to time. There are no graphics files. Print-text messages are brief and several potential stories are on the boil at any one print run. Examples are:

✦ 00:10:13 Press Agency News
   Hijack
   More news – airliner believed to be owned by British airline.
   No further details yet.

✦ 00:26:34 Press Agency News
Hijack
Unconfirmed reports from Heathrow indicate that a British Caledonian flight from Cairo, due into Heathrow via Athens and Rome (flight no: BC756Y) is considerably overdue. The aircraft, a jumbo jet (number of passengers not released) is the only aircraft into Britain overdue since the hijack emergency was reported.

✦ 00:14:17 Press Agency News
Prime Minister Recalled
The Prime Minister flies back unexpectedly to London from Birmingham, where she was to have witnessed local party electoral organisation in action. Reason for return to Downing Street not specified, other than "urgent business of State".

✦ 00:55:18 Press Agency News
Multiple Crash Reported
A serious crash has been reported on the M6. Early reports are unclear as to the exact location. Thought to be some way north of Birmingham. Frenetic activity among the emergency services has been observed by correspondents in the Birmingham area.

The students have had some prior work on the differences between broadsheet and tabloid newspapers. They have been invited to examine the differences between what counts as news across a range of British newspapers. The first hour with Year 9 involves a lot of decision making. Who is going to work with whom? What kind of newspaper is the group of eight going to construct? Their first task is to decide what kind of paper they are going to produce, and what kinds of stories are likely to interest their readership. We make a map of the kinds of articles which usually appear on front pages. In my classroom, two groups decide to produce tabloids and one decides to 'go upmarket' for something like *The Times*. Each group has a piece of A3 paper on which to design their front page. The room is a buzz of activity as students think up names for their newspapers, decide which person in the group is going to be the editor for their page, decide who are going to be the hack reporters and which people are responsible for any art-work.

Outside the classroom, in a foyer, another group of students at a terminal is going to act as the government, deciding what information will be released in press conferences, and making decisions to avert a possible disaster as the hijacked plane flies over Britain. The government group has access to more information than the news groups in the classroom. In role they hold press conferences, through an elected spokesperson, every twenty minutes. The whole government group has to attend. They are emulating the kinds of spoken discourses that appear on sound or video broadcasts when a news story breaks. They have to face a 'press gallery' of delegates from the news groups, who are armed with questions. There is another team of eight students who act as the recording team, equipped with video cameras and overhead microphones, to record the press conferences. Delegates from each newspaper group in the surrounding classrooms have to drop anything they are doing, and attend, armed with their groups' series of questions. They want to know what information being dispensed by the computer is actually true, and what information is a construct designed to beguile a passive public into acquiescence with the decisions made by the 'government'. The groups back in the classroom cannot go on writing their stories until the delegates at the press conference come back to brief them about the implications of the answers they have been given. Students in the government group appear very well versed in the use of nominalised discourse: they know how to evade direct answers to awkward questions by using nominalised forms. To questions like *'Is the Prince on board the plane?'*, *'What about the safety of the passengers?'*, the government representative answers: *'Disclosure of the names of passengers is not in the interests of safety'*; *'Everything possible is being done to land the aircraft safely'*.

The hack reporters in each of the groups in the classroom are having a dreadful time of it. News stories they have drafted keep changing as further information comes to hand. This means they are constantly having to redraft their stories. They also have to check with their editor which stories are going to be worth following up for the readership of their paper. What will become the lead story, and why? As a teacher I cannot make these decisions for them: the editor in each group has the power. Arguments break out, then are resolved. One group decides to hide a couple of print-outs from the other groups to 'scoop' the news. Another group sees what they are doing and races for the bit of paper. Boys in Doc Martens boots and girls with Maybelline eyes contest the fairness of this. I step in as negotiator and the problem is resolved. I am to make sure that each group gets access to the information being printed. I am to stand by the printer and to cut up strips of news items: everyone else is far too busy to spare a group member for that kind of job.

The IT co-ordinator makes periodic checks on the classrooms, either to call people to press conferences, or to check that equipment is not breaking down. By 12.30 he calls for a lunch break. The students do not want to leave! What if important news breaks while they are away? The students decide to stay on through lunch hour, by giving two team members ten minutes off at a time. The simulation ends at 2.00pm and groups have half an hour to finalise their front pages, by cutting and pasting their stories, hand drafted to column size, to the A3 sheet. The IT co-ordinator is apologetic that there just were not enough computers available for people to be word-processing their stories. Students are working at large tables made by putting six smaller ones together. Where did that story about the abduction of the baby get to? Two groups have anticipated this problem, and have their drafts of stories and possible editorials pinned to the display boards for ease of handling. What is interesting is how different the front pages are, given that all students have worked with the same information. Some are beautifully illustrated, and in colour. Some are more writerly, including examples of editorial opinion and feature articles. Each group also built a real sense of community as they worked together under pressure to meet the deadline.

We display our finished pages in two classrooms, separating the broadsheets from the tabloids. Students walk around the rooms reading and viewing each groups' efforts. Students have to list the strengths and weaknesses of each front page. Is the language used appropriate for a tabloid? What about the relationship of pictures to text? Do they meet standards of accuracy in reporting the news? Overheard snippets of conversation, as students mill around the displays, indicate that they are critically evaluating each others work: *'D'you see that! They've put the baby story as the lead article. Look at the size of the picture!' 'They didn't do much writing!' 'Where's the story about the hijacking? Unfair! They've put it in the Stop Press column'.* These kinds of comments indicate that students are questioning the truth of the representations of the news, as well as looking at issues like sensationalism which may distort factual information. They are also looking at formatting conventions and text types. Since all have had exposure to the same information base, they are in a position to see how other groups have been selective in their reporting. Students keep notes for the final debriefing in the quadrangle.

By the debriefing, we are all exhausted. Students have brought out chairs to sit on, and the IT co-ordinator leads a discussion on the processes of working in groups. Students are very frank about their difficulties. They are also very positive about some of the front pages. They know why they are good examples of their genre. They know which groups tried cheap tricks, like filling blank spaces with advertisements, or putting in pictures over three quarters of a page in size. The blustery wind is rising, so it is very hard to hear everyone's contributions. It starts to drizzle, so the debriefing is cut short. Students race for cover with their chairs. Classrooms are put back in order. The day is over for the students. Not so the teaching team. We share our experiences and make recommendations for change. The biggest disadvantage we all agreed on was the need to have word-processors available next time, to make the redrafting tasks easier to accomplish. The laborious copying of the final drafts of news stories, feature articles and editorials in careful print did slow down the final paste-up stage of the production.

I offer this classroom observation as an example of how one school worked with limited computer equipment to implement a mandated technology and English framework for Year 9. The first point to make about the experience of working with students through the simulation was the change in teacher-learner stance. The classroom became a workshop in which media skills, technology skills and language skills were put to use to construct a text collaboratively. As a teacher, my role was to work alongside students, not solve their problems for them. I had to do a lot of listening. At times during the day I was asked to read stories in progress. For most of the time I dispensed material from the printer to the three groups, a facilitator role. Sometimes I was called on to give editorial advice. The stance became one of teacher-as-learner, and learners became teachers too.

The second point is that having a meaningful purpose and audience for their newspapers gave students an understanding about how news is shaped, how it is constructed. What you omit saying becomes as much of an issue as what you report. The analysis at the beginning of the day of differing kinds of newspapers, their readership and the kinds of stories or articles which would be appropriate for the intended audience provided modelling of the kinds of written texts students could construct. Other language modes were practised: in the oral mode students were using language to persuade each other, to inform each other, to explore issues together. Opportunities for more formal talk occurred in the press conferences, from raising questions through to giving prepared answers. The literacy practices in the classrooms that day reflected the social practices in the world of work.

The third point is that multiple literacies (Lemke,1996) in text production were being used by students. Literacy was not 'just writing', but rather involved the intersection of print, pictures and technology. Media literacy skills were put to use by videoing the news conferences during the day, as were 'critical' literacy skills, as students challenged where the print text was coming from and whose interests it served. Technological literacy involved designing, making and evaluating the newspaper pages, even if these could not be fully realised given the equipment limitations. A computer at each group for word-processing would have solved this problem. A computer equipped with a page-processing package would have been even better. With the pen-and-paper technology at hand the students were well aware of the limitations in redrafting – copying by hand to a column size is a laborious undertaking. It is a credit to the students that they persisted with their tasks.

Case Study II: Frankston High School

Linda Emery is a teacher of English at Frankston High School situated in a bayside city on the outskirts of Melbourne. Her school has introduced laptop computers for three groups of children in Year 7 as a pilot project. Linda's Year 7s are one of the laptop groups.

Over terms three and four in 1996, the children in Linda's Year 7 class worked on a newsletter project, one period per week. The aim was to produce a two-page newsletter on A4 format. One page of the newsletter (double sided) was to contain articles (factual genres) about the high school for Grade 6 children in the local feeder primary schools. The other page (double-sided) was to contain factual information about a feeder primary school in the area. Folders of writing from the primary school children were collected by their teachers, and given to Year 7s at the start of the project. These folders included write-ups of excursions and sporting events. The students had a deadline of producing the newsletters by the Year 7 orientation day.

Unlike the Long Stratten case study, there is nothing simulated about the audience and purpose of the Year 7 newsletters. They serve a very real audience. The Year 7s have visited all the primary feeder schools in the area to work closely with their audience. They have interviewed and audiotaped the younger children as a basis for some of the reports they are constructing in the newsletter. The overt agenda from Linda's point of view is to see whether laptops improve students' writing over the long term. Another agenda is a school one – if primary school students see how the children in Year 7 are working with computers, they may be attracted to the school. In a market-driven educational economy it is important for schools to attract a Year 7 intake. It wards off school closures or further amalgamations. In this way, Linda's teaching is framed by the wider social practices of her school and community.

Linda is not only a teacher, but an action-researcher in the classroom. She is completing her Masters in Education at Deakin, and I am her supervisor for her research paper. I have not observed her classroom in person, but have had frequent discussions with her about her teaching and observations of the Year 7 group. This has included watching videos of her classroom, as children draft their articles for the newsletters, and watching live footage of their interactions with children in primary schools. As part of our work together I asked her to write up an overview of the changes to her classroom practices brought about by the laptops as writing tools, using her teaching journal as a source for bringing ideas together. Her classroom started off being set in a circle. The back wall is decorated with a large book case. Mobiles of art work hang from the ceiling. It is a cheerful room. The classroom layout has changed since the start of the project. As Linda says in her write-up:

> While each individual has their own learning style or preferred way of handling a task, there is no doubt that laptops have created a more co-operative atmosphere. I have found students tend to share work more readily and there is a great deal of swapping over and reading of each others' screens. There is of course the frequent need to get expert help to sort out a technical hitch, but increasingly I have found students working together in clusters to share ideas about writing. This, in my opinion, has given them a greater sense of purpose and audience. They really see writing as a form of shared communication, more so than students in my other classes. Consequently, I have found that the traditional set up of a room with tables in rows is not appropriate, and so we now put tables together to form small work stations for groups. A lot of what I have observed has already been noted by those working in this area, but I have noticed these changes are happening at a faster rate and are having a significant influence on the whole classroom environment.

During term four, the children took off with technology. They borrowed a digital camera to photograph other students, the principals and teachers so that their newsletters could include real photographs. Their laptops have *Microsoft Publisher* and *Word* on them, both of which are capable of importing digital pictures and making templates for newspaper style layout. Linda was not confident with the digital camera, but the children certainly were. In preparation for the visits to the primary school, Linda helped students construct an interview sheet. She asked students to generate a list of potential questions before their first visit. Following is a sample interview sheet produced by a group of girls with Linda's suggestions:

ACTIVITY 1. Ask your student(s) the questions
QUESTIONS (STUDENTS)
1. Q: Have you had any special events or excursions? A:
2. Q: Are there any upcoming events or excursions? A:
3. Q: How does your school rate in sports against other schools? A:
4. Q: Who are your sporting champions? A:
5. Q: How does your school compare with other schools overall? A:
6. Q: What special facilities does your school have? A:
Thank you from Year Seven students of Frankston HS

2. Have your student(s) do some graphics on the laptop.
GRAPHICS: - water safety;   - star lab;
                - science works;   - teachers;
                - sports;   - school logo;
                - students in the class

Another strategy for getting information from their potential audience was the **What's Hot, What's Not** interview sheet, reproduced below.

What's Hot	What's Not
Clothes	
Sport	
Bands	
Girls	
Guys	
Actors	
Movies	
TV shows	
Food	

MF
Name_____Form_____

Students moved from interviewing younger students, to interviews with teachers and the principals of feeder schools. Out of these interviews, the groups in the classroom constructed news reports for the primary school page. An excerpt from a teacher interview with Miss Thom gives the flavour of their approach:

MISS THOM

Q: *How do you prepare Year 6 kids for Year 7?*

A: *Well one good way that we do it, every Monday we have
platooning, which is they go into three half hour sessions: one's
English, one's Maths and one's Japanese. So they get used to
having to take books to three subjects with different teachers.
That's one way. Did you want me to mention any more? We've
also prepared them for project work, by teaching them resource
skills and that sort of thing.*

The group of students responsible for producing this interview
transcribed their interviews straight onto the laptop. Thus we see this text
has all the features of a spoken rather than a written text. The grammar and
the pronoun referencing (it, we, they) in the first sentence of the answer are
markers of spoken language. The inclusion of Miss Thom's question to the
interviewers 'Do you want me to mention any more?' is also a signal that they
are simply recording speech. This text is not framed by any context which
explains the purpose of the interview, apart from placing the name of the
primary teacher they interviewed at the top. The group seems to go about
the business of collaborative text construction by staying completely faithful
to what was said on the tape. When the interview is placed in the first
pasted-up draft of the newsletter, however, a number of changes occur as
visual texts are imported into the page-processing template. The completed
template is on the following page.

The font and style of the headline focus the reader's attention on the
'Interviews' as the lead article. The students have added punctuation markers
and formatting conventions to distinguish addressor from addressee and set
a three-column layout for their page. They have manually pasted three digital
pictures to spaces in the draft. At this stage, however, it looks more like a
newsletter than reads like one. The sports report by Shaun, Ryan, Ross and
Andrew, located above the Interviews is, by contrast, more 'writerly'. It has
more markers of a report genre. The lead sentence classifies the event, saying
what usually happens: 'Each year, Frankston Heights participates in
Lightning Premiership'. The tenor is impersonal and the personalities of the
writers do not intrude: 'the sports were played', 'teams were filled up',
'Newcomb and Football were the sports played'. By contrast, Julian and
Matthew's Starlab Report is not as sure-footed with the report genre. They
write about when Grade 6 went on an excursion, and where. But their recount
shifts to a procedural genre midway; they focus on how something is done
and the tenor changes from impersonal to personal: 'You had to go through
a tunnel to get inside'. This suggests that across Grades 6 and Year 7 the
range of understandings of report as a text type is varied. When this version
of the Starlab Report is compared, however, to an earlier draft, the editorial
control exercised by the page editor, Peter, becomes visible:

A number of changes have been made. The framing subheading *Activities Report* has been deleted. Information about where the class went, 'the Multi-Purpose Room for an incursion to Starlab' has been deleted. So has the mention of the Grade 5/6 class - it now reads "Grade 6". The personal

Lightning Premiership *by Shaun Brand, Ryan Fischer, Ross Varcoe & Andrew Wilson.* Each year, Frankston Heights participates in Lightning Premiership. This year the sports were played at Mornington District, and teams were filled up with grade six and five students.

Netball, Softball, Soccer, T-ball, Volleyball, Newcomb and Football were the sports played. The school won Volleyball, but came runners-up in every other event. There were breaks throughout the day and everyone enjoyed the day.

Starlab Report *by Julian Leavold & Matthew Taylor.* On the 24-5 Grade 6 went to see Starlab- a great big dome that almost took up the whole room. You had to go through a tunnel to get inside. Starlab taught us all about the ages of a star and made stars shine up on the walls.

INTERVIEWS

Interviews conducted and published by: Lucy Blackmore, Matthew Kyle, Karina Minns, Travis Osborne, Bodie Warne and Peter Webb.

MR STALLARD
Q: How long have you been principal?
A: Nine years.
Q: What do you think are the best features of your school?
A: The kids are the best features, because they're really nice people to work with, and, hardly any of them want to get into trouble and do things wrong. And the teachers are really, really hard working.
Q: What plans do you have for the future of Frankston Heights?
A: We plan to build a big gymnasium in the next 12 months. It won't be quite as big as the Frankston High one but we've only got a quarter of the students to fit in it. And that's our next really big plan.
Q: And where's that going to be?
A: Down the other end of the car park in that big space. The far end of the car park.
Q: How important is it to you, to prepare grade six students for high school?
A: I think grade sixers should be as well prepared as we can make them. I think they, we, want them to leave here with sound academic

skills, and confident that they're ready for the challenges of high school. They're not going to be intimidated as people by so many kids, when they're little ones again.

MISS THOM
Q: How do you prepare Year: 6 kids for Year: 7?
A: Well one good way that we do it, every Monday and Wednesday morning we have platooning, which is they go into three half hour sessions: one's English, one's Maths and one's Japanese. So they get used to having to take books to three subjects, and, having to organise themselves to go to three different subjects with three different teachers. That's one way. Did you want me to mention anymore? We've also prepared them for project work, by teaching them resource skills and that sort of thing.
Q: Could you please explain the Buddy Program?
A: Yes. In Grade: 6, all the Grade: 6 students have a buddy in prep, and when the preps first arrive in the school, at the beginning of the year, one grade six child looks after one

prep child in the playground, initially.
And then after about Term 1 the preps are all right to be in the playgrond themselves, but we do activities with them, called cross-aged tutoring, and sometimes we, have activities like drama activities where we work with grade sixers and preps, or at Christmas time we meet with our buddies again.
Q: Since you've been teaching what have been the highlights?
A: I think I was trained to be a Phys Ed. teacher, I really enjoyed the year which I taught Phys Ed. Many things, I suppose I really enjoy the grade six camps, or any year camp. Just teaching children all through. I went to teach in Adelaide for one year.

Principal: Mr. Stallard

ACTIVITIES REPORT

Lightning Premiership *by Shaun Brand, Ryan Fischer, Ross Varcoe & Andrew Wilson.* Each year, Frankston Heights participates in Lightning Premiership. This year the sports were played at Mornington District, and teams were filled up with grade sixers and fives. Netball, Softball, Soccer, T-ball, Volleyball, Newcomb and Football were the sports played. The school won Volleyball, but came runners-up in every other event. There were breaks throughout the day and everyone enjoyed the day.

Starlab Report *by Julian Leavold & Matthew Taylor.* On the 24th of May, Grade 5/6T went to the Multi-Purpose Room for an incursion to Starlab - a great big dome that almost took up the whole room. You had to go through a tunnel to get inside. Oh, and mind you, it was really dark but you got used to it. Starlab taught us all about the ages of a star and all the made stars shine up on the walls and an inferred torch to point to the stars.

tenor, "Oh, mind you, it was really dark but you got used to it" has been deleted. So has mention of the infra-red torch. What is driving these changes to the text? We might like to think they are driven by considerations of genre, but if that were the case and Peter's group had decided that the personal tenor of the report was a problem, why did they leave in the previous sentence ("You had to go through a tunnel to get inside")? And why did they leave out the scientific information about how Starlab is lit?

I think the first change was brought about by considerations of audience, taken literally. The newsletter is for Grade 6, not Grades 5/6. So Grade 5 is dropped from the report. I think the other changes are being driven by the technology and have more to do with adjusting text to fit page layout. My reason for saying this is the reduction in font size between the first draft and the second. This group of Year 7s want to make sure that all their interviews will appear on the page! Space is at a premium. They have worked out that they are not going to have enough space for the digital photographs, the insertion of the school logo and both reports at the top of the page. The space limitations are thus encouraging them to see editing as a matter of leaving things out, rather than rewriting or recasting. They are making changes to texts at the 'publication' stage of the process of writing, rather than at the 'drafting' stage. They are exercising their power, too, in making sure that their own texts appear in full. It is easier to make substantial cuts to texts which you have not had a hand in composing. What the Grade 6 children think about this will be confronted when they read the final version of the newsletter.

While this newsletter is not yet complete, a number of observations can be made about the writing pedagogy at work. The children are drafting, but in different ways from those available in the pen-and-paper classroom. They are doing more drafting at the production stage of the writing process. Some are drafting to fix surface feature errors, some are 'editing at the point of utterance', some are adding information for a reader, some are deleting information to make their pages fit into the limited space available to them. Graves (1983) argued that the order in which students learnt to draft was to add, to delete and then to re-order or re-write. All these processes can happen at the same time in a writing workshop mediated by technology. They may not necessarily be developmental, but related to the writing tools available to the learner. If you are limited by space, you are going to want to delete text, rather than add.

Linda's observations of the drafting process are as follows:

There are still some students (in this class all of these are girls) who are drafting on paper first, then putting it on computer. They have said they find it easier to think through things this way and that they are faster at writing than typing. The number of students doing this, however, has decreased since the start of the year and it is interesting how many of them do not even carry pen and paper around with them any more. I have tried to encourage them to keep everything on their computers and we do all our note taking and planning on the laptops because I have found they are less likely to lose material this way. Laptops enable them to look back at old files for reference purposes instantaneously.

Linda has also noticed a change in both her conferencing strategies and her role in the classroom:

I read in one study where a teacher did not enjoy working with her computer class as much because she didn't feel as useful or as needed. I would have to disagree with this as I have found working in a laptop class highly satisfying. The students still need you, but in different ways. They don't need you to tell them how to spell something; instead they need you to advise them about how to expand an idea or structure a specific discourse. There is a more meaningful conferencing process. In some ways it is more like how you would operate in a senior class – as more of a mentor and less of a master.

Conclusions

The two classroom case studies presented here are examples of how English classrooms are being reconstructed in the wake of technological change.

Teachers have to do a lot of listening and reading, less telling. Classroom space has to be organised to facilitate group work and movement around the room. School-based literacy practices begin to look more like workplace literacy practices in these environments. Power relations between students and teachers in the classroom are also changed. Anyone who doesn't pull their weight in the group, or doesn't produce their material in time can be taken to task over it by their peers because it becomes a group problem. The teacher can be called upon to mediate when disputes in groups erupt. As Lensmire (1994, p156) says:

Children's activity can turn to many ends, some of which we want to support, others which we do not. With collective projects, we support certain peer relations, not by intervening at the level of outward behaviour, but at the level of curriculum, by directing their attention to a common problem to be solved.

The teacher can work alongside learners as a kind of editor-in-chief, but children learn more if they do the editing for themselves. Any teacher-intervention in the writing process, whether to draw attention to the generic features of a text type or to raise questions about appropriateness of language to an audience has to be done on the run. Other students' voices join in these dialogues. As in all classrooms which have a collaborative atmosphere, there is a good deal of small group talking and the 'teaching' seems to be almost invisible! As Linda comments:

When I had a student teacher recently, she said she felt she wasn't able to gauge what the students were doing or how much they had done because she couldn't see it. By this stage I had overcome this although I did know what she meant. It is much easier to move around a classroom and scan student's work on paper than to read off small monitors. To work in these ways, the teacher is more of a facilitator, less of an authority or surveillance expert.

The preparation involved in running successful workshops is enormous. You can't run a simulation without previewing software and organising technological equipment in advance, or have children visiting local primary schools for interviews without having booked the transport. The behind-the-scenes preparation is critical. The setting up of group collaborative writing projects takes time, effort and judgement but the gains for students and teachers are well worth the effort. Tweddle (1995), in outlining the impact of new and evolving technologies on textual practices in the community, argues that English teachers need to reconstruct the reading and writing curriculum to make it relevant for the future. Some of her recommendations about writing curriculum are:

✦ that learners read and write a range of texts in a range of media;

✦ that individual learners might differ in the texts they read and write, the purposes for which they do so and the ways in which they work with their teachers on them;

✦ that learners are taught to write as collaborators as well as individuals. (1995, p9)

The newspaper workshop mediated by technology gives English teachers a space where these aims can be met. Such workshops allow us to pay attention to a range of genres, both visual and verbal, to explore the generic features of differing text types with learners in dynamic ways, and to use a revised process pedagogy where emphasis can be placed on the social and collaborative nature of text construction. In a period of rapid technological change we may find ourselves, as Linda does, learning together with our students.

References

Dixon, J (1967) *Growth Through English*, Oxford: Oxford University Press.

Britton, J (1972) "A Schematic Account of Language Functions" in *Language and Education*, London and Boston: Routledge and Kegan Paul and The Open University Press.

Britton, J et al (1975) *The Development of Writing Abilities (11-18)*, Macmillan Education, London.

Daiute, C (1986) "Physical and Cognitive Factors in Revising: Insights From Studies With Computers", *Research in the Teaching of English*, Vol 20 No 2, 141-159.

Gilbert, P (1990) "Authorising Disadvantage: Authorship and Creativity in the Language Classroom" in F Christie (ed) *Literacy for a Changing World*, The Australian Council for Educational Research, Hawthorn.

Graves, D (1983) *Writing: Teachers and Children at Work*, Heinemann Portsmouth, N H.

Lensmire,T (1994) *When Children Write: Critical Re-visions of the Writing Workshop*. Teachers College Press, New York.

Lemke, J (1996) "Metamedia Literacy: Transforming Meanings and Media" in D Reinking et al (eds) *Literacy for the 21st Century: Technological Transformation in a Post-typographic World*, Erlbaum.

Snyder, I (1992) "Writing With Word Processors: An Effective Way To Develop Students' Argumentative Writing Skills", *English in Education*, Vol 26 No 2, 35-45.

Tweddle, S (1995) "A Curriculum for the Future: A Curriculum Built for Change", *English in Education*, Vol 29 No 2, 3-11.

Imaginary Island

A popular unit from Year 7 to Year 10 involves drawing a map of an imaginary island on a blackboard or on butcher's paper (every member of the class adds a feature) and then brainstorming possible follow-up activities (eg, history of the island, tourist brochure for the island, the island's newspaper, election campaign for the island's legislature, reference book on the island's wildlife, etc). Then each group in the class selects an activity to work on. This one never fails!

Applications: Writing

Its Process and its Product

R D Walshe

PROCESS . . .

Writing originates in some *experience* which I turn into a *topic* that I believe will be of interest to an *audience* (precisely who?).
I proceed to
limit the subject to avoid attempting too much,
brainstorm what I already know, then
discuss, read, research as needed, *make notes,*
get an insight as to opening and sequence,
plan, or broadly outline, or simply start
draft (first draft)
revise,
re-draft (as often as necessary),
final writing,
proofreading,
presentation/publication to audience, and in time
get a response from the audience.
It is a *process* of think/write.
Process and Product are not separate: the process makes the product.

PRODUCT . . .

A. *Surface* or 'conventions':
alphabet (caps/lower)
punctuation
spelling
handwriting/typing
vocabulary
usage
grammar
sentences, paragraphs,
larger units.

B. *Content:*
ideas, images
emotions, feelings
attitudes
values

C. *Styling* (some aspects only):
order of explanation
economy/conciseness
use of specifics
rhythm, smoothness
freedom from jargon, cliché
clear, lively, graceful, etc.

These two columns together sum up the **Craft Of Writing.**

A Sample of Writing Ideas

Wayne Sawyer

Mini-Lessons

Nancie Atwell's *In the Middle* remains one of the best books ever written on teaching writing in the secondary classroom. Atwell describes a genuine workshop situation in the classroom in which the bulk of students' time is spent writing; effective editing and conferencing are key features and students display great commitment. In such a classroom, one issue that arises is how teacher input might deal with skills and improving students writing as craft – and do this efficiently without repeating for every student – while at the same time giving the bulk of time to student writing. Atwell's answer to this is the mini-lesson. As part of a tightly packed daily routine, Atwell conducts one short five-to-ten- minute burst of direct teaching input each lesson. These mini-lessons deal with either 'craft' or 'skills'.

✦ *Craft lessons* deal with areas such as writing effective openings; 'showing', not 'telling'; voice; point of view; using imagery; developing characterisation and writing in particular genres (such as monologues, dialogues etc).

✦ *Skill lessons* deal with areas such as spelling punctuation and grammar.

The following are a selection of ideas for mini-lessons, derived from a number of sources.

Guided Plot Development

Michael Hyde has an excellent activity for guiding plot development (and teaching a valuable skill to help students 'kick-start' themselves). It involves providing a simple scenario (*'setting'*) and an instruction to go with it (*'instruction'*). Students are to write a paragraph based on the instruction, thus:

Setting	Instruction	Example (My Attempt)
1. A person (male or female of any age) is walking.	Carefully describe what this person looks like.	Sam walked along the street, his leather jacket zipped up against the cold. His long face was drawn and pale. His big eyes were as black as the jeans he wore. He walked in a fast, striding motion.

(Hyde, 1990, pp 52-55)

After eight such paragraphs, with 'Settings' introducing new characters and events, a complete story has been written.

For other examples of such guided plot development, see David McRobbie's excellent series on *Creative Writing Through . . . Stories* , of which one example is listed in the "Important Books" section below.

Writing Leads

Give students a number of opening sentences/paragraphs to novels and short stories that are particularly attention-grabbing. (Suggestions: Ken Kesey, *One Flew Over the Cuckoo's Nest*; Robert Cormier, *The Chocolate War*; Anne Tyler, *Dinner at the Homesick Restaurant*; Morris Gleitzman, *The Other Facts of Life*; Ray Bradbury, *Fahrenheit 451*). Discuss and list what it is that makes these effective. Follow up by selecting a current piece from the class and composing a lead on the overhead. Alternatively, try out four separate leads to a story of your own on the overhead over four consecutive days, each time discussing its qualities. An example of the latter is in Atwell (1987), p138.

Imagery

Budge Wilson's collection of short stories, *My Cousin Clarette*, contains a wonderful story ("The Metaphor") about a teacher having her students write metaphors to describe people they know. The narrator describes her mother as "a lofty mountain capped by virgin snow. The air around the mountain is clear and clean and very cold." After discussing with students what each element in such a metaphor is suggesting, students could be asked to complete a similar exercise. A useful list of potential characters for such description is in Hyde (1990), p45.

Effective Editing

The application of the Graves/Murray 'process-conference' approach to writing can be a disappointment if the key notion of editing is not approached in a systematic manner. Often, editing becomes little more than a quick spelling check as the line of students waiting for you to 'check' drafts gets longer and longer. But editing should be a useful and valuable part of the classroom routine. Some suggestions:

✦ Teach the students how to do it (and, incidentally, take the pressure off you. This means putting in *a lot* of time at the beginning of the year showing them how (through mini-lessons). The best resource for this is the overhead. Put up *extracts* from: pieces from kids who don't mind volunteering; pieces from your past classes; pieces you've written yourself. Each time, point out the *specific* strengths of the extract, but each time have some very *specific* aspect you want to improve (for example, the lead) – and do it on the overhead as you discuss it with them.

Teach them a class set of editing conventions. Such things as asterisks, carets, arrows, circles, particular-coloured pens can take on very specific meanings in your class.

Teach them a *routine* for how to run a group conference without you. For example, "When looking at a 'craft' edit such as effective leads, consider one piece at a time, which is to be read aloud by the author. Focus the talk on that 'craft'. When checking for mechanics, such as spelling or punctuation, pass every book around the group for all to 'correct'." Group conferences are particularly good for mechanics checks, because usually someone can spell 'X', but they shouldn't be confined to mechanics checks alone.

✦ Atwell has a very strict routine for her own role in editing (Atwell, 1987, chapter 5), which involves speaking to every student in every lesson. If you don't think you can do this effectively, a strategy I find effective is to make a brief note for yourself of students' problems/strengths when marking. At the next writing session, bring to you four or five students with some common issue to deal with while the others are writing. Take about ten minutes. Keep a record of whom you've seen in these sessions, so that over time, each student gets 'equal time'.

At the same time, allow ten minutes or so at the end of writing sessions for kids to voluntarily bring problems/drafts to you. Deal with them one at a time.

But, make it a rule that no one brings drafts to you until *after* they've edited themselves (you've taught them how!) and had at least one other person edit (you've taught that too). So, your writing routine can become:

❖ mini-lesson;
❖ students write;
❖ while students are writing, you are conferring with pre-selected students;
❖ students still writing or editing or peer-conferencing;
❖ volunteers bring work to you.

Important Books on Teaching Writing

Atwell, Nancie (1987) In the Middle: Writing, Reading and Learning with Adolescents, Portsmouth: Boynton/Cook.

Frank, Marjorie (revised edition 1995) If You're Trying to Teach Kids How to Write . . . You've Gotta Have this Book! Nashville: Incentive.

Hyde, Michael (1990) The Diary of My Secret Life: A Guide to the Craft of Writing, Cambridge: Cambridge University Press.

McRobbie, David (1989) Gumshoe: Creative Writing Through Mystery Stories, Melbourne: Longman Cheshire.

Smedley, Don (1983) Teaching the Basic Skills, London: Methuen.

Making and Using a Database in the English Classroom

Eva Gold

Create a database of a class's reading preferences.

Brainstorm:
Have the class brainstorm the sorts of criteria they use to judge whether a book is worth picking up and reading. They can do this in groups by listing the three questions they consider most important to ask about a book. These are then shared with the entire class who then choose the ten most important.

Creating Fields:
Groups could then suggest what data fields will be needed and the class can decide which fields will work best for their interests and form the basis of the grid on which data will be entered. Possible fields are: author; title; genre; setting; number of student recommendations; rating; part of a series, etc.

Setting up the Database:
This will vary according to the technology available in each school and the expertise of the students and/or the teacher. Interdisciplinary enterprises with computing studies subjects can be very helpful for the technophobic.

When the database has been set up, each student should enter three books/he has read and enjoyed over the past year. Students should have access to the database so that new books can be added. It is useful to have a master copy on the class computer for this purpose and so that students can copy the database onto their own disks for out-of-class use and extension work.

Using the Database:
Students can use the database to direct their own reading with such queries as: What other books by the same author have been popular? Who is the class's favourite author? What other books have been popular in this genre? etc.

Written Extensions

Reading the Data:
Any writing exercise is possible. For example, write a letter to your friend in which you recommend books for him/her to read based on your class's interests.

Interpreting the Data:
Students can take on the role of a publisher who receives the database from a market research company which has examined the reading habits of

adolescents and produce any kind of text such as a report to the MD commenting on its significance and making recommendations for future publishing, an article in a teen magazine, a defence of literacy, etc.

Oral Extensions

Reading the Gaps:

Students can take a print out of the database sorted by genre and give it to a student from another school or an adult such as a librarian, bookseller, parent, publisher. Interview that person to find out what s/he thinks of the reading habits of the class. Students can tape the interview and record the results.

Students can then take on the role of expert who examines the data to assess what kinds of books the class is *not* reading and then give the class a two-minute endorsement of any kind of book or author that is not represented in the data base.

CONNOTATION

The importance of connotation was neatly illustrated by Aldous Huxley when he changed one of Tennyson's most famous lines, "And after many a summer dies the swan", to "And after many a summer dies the duck".

Advertising provides a fertile source for the study of connotation, a study which can be introduced quite early in the secondary school. Junior secondary pupils, for example, can discuss the connotations of the brand names given to cars: Jaguar, Commodore, Mustang.

Discussion of pejorative connotations (with older students) can begin with Bertrand Russell's famous "conjugation of an irregular verb": "I am firm. You are obstinate. He is a pig-headed fool." A *New Statesman* competition yielded the following:

I am sparkling. You are unusually talkative. He is drunk.

I day-dream. You are an escapist. He ought to see a psychiatrist.

I am beautiful. You have quite good features. She isn't bad-looking, if you like that type.

Senior pupils can develop their own conjugations, starting with statements such as "I am slender".

Section V: Oracy and Drama

21 Re-viewing Talking and Listening in the Secondary English Curriculum

Jackie Manuel

There is no gift like the gift of speech, and the level at which people have learned to use it determines the level of their companionship and the level at which their life is lived. (Newsom in Wilkinson, 1973, p431)

The Role of Talking and Listening

For most of us, talking and listening remain the principal means by which we shape, define and declare our selves. It is through talking and listening that we establish and maintain relationships and strive to make sense of experience. The fundamental human impulse to express and seek fulfilment of our needs and aspirations manifests itself most often in the oral communicative mode. Indeed, so much of what we know, and the ways in which we come to know it, are dependent upon our command of spoken language and our capacity to receive and respond to the messages of those around us.

In his work on oral communication, Andrew Wilkinson clarified the pivotal role of spoken language in the development "not only of the human ability to speak, not only of the human ability to communicate, but the human ability to develop fully a personality, and to develop cognitively" (Wilkinson, 1973, p431). Yet, with the pervasiveness of the printed word and the constant promotion of literacy as the priority of education in recent times, it is easy to undervalue the crucial place of talking and listening in the acquisition and enhancement of literacy within the English curriculum.

The Oracy-Literacy Continuum

It has been over three decades since Wilkinson (and others) argued that literacy – the writing and reading side of the communication equation – could not be artificially separated from what he termed 'oracy' – the talking and listening component (Wilkinson, 1965). "Learning to communicate is at the heart of education" (Barnes, 1976, p20). To communicate, we produce language by both speaking and writing it: indeed, it has been well established that most of us, including the young people we encounter as teachers, spend more time producing spoken language to organise and verbalise experience than we do written language (Plattor, 1984, p3).

Profiting from this natural tendency would entail conscious planning for tasks in the English classroom which would draw upon and strengthen the continuity of oracy and literacy. Reinvigorating the links between the two is particularly pressing in the context of an increasingly complex age that demands of its citizens increasingly sophisticated oracy as well as literacy skills. To be able to understand, critique and learn from spoken information is as necessary as the ability to read and write with precision and clarity. Importantly, students' proficiency in oral language can contribute significantly to their developing capacity as readers and writers.

The Secondary English Curriculum of Today

Secondary English syllabus documents in Australia now reflect research of the past few decades that has established the importance of talking and listening in the very processes of thinking, learning and language development. Incorporated into English programming is an awareness that students are more likely to learn when they:

✦ encounter a supportive learning environment that offers relevant, purposeful and stimulating language activities that are also a source of pleasure and enjoyment;

✦ are given a degree of choice and agency, and sense of responsibility for the 'what' and 'how' of the curriculum;

✦ recognise connections between the language of home, community, work and school; and

✦ are given the opportunity to use talk in and for itself, as an important prelude to writing or performance, and as a basis for coming to terms with new knowledge and experience (Reid et al, 1989).

Earlier models of English that focused substantially on the teaching of measurable 'skills' tended to treat oracy in limited, usually evaluative, ways. Typically, children would be required to present a formal speech to the class and this was treated as the major indicator of oral language competence.

Often students were required to answer a series of comprehension questions from a 'listening test' administered to the whole class. This kind of 'test' was considered a reliable measure of listening skills.

But developing oracy involves far more than delivering discrete or decontextualised lessons merely on the functional components of spoken language. Consider how many of our students actually go on to speak publicly on any more than a handful of occasions in a lifetime. Yet, every day they will almost certainly be required to use spoken language, for instance, to negotiate with colleagues; interact with peers; nurture youngsters; empathise; decipher, decode and interpret complex audio-visual messages; speculate about the future and reminisce about the past; greet and converse with familiar people and strangers; and grapple with an array of challenges in their public and private worlds.

Of course, there will always be a place in the English curriculum for the prepared, formal speech. But in addition to such prepared talking there is also a need for spontaneous talking (Wilkinson, 1975). In other words, the scope and quality of oral work should aim to reflect the vast range of purposes, audiences and contexts encountered within and outside the school. For it is purpose, audience and context that shape and determine the meaning of every utterance.

Programming for Oracy

To fulfil this aim, English teachers need to provide a profusion of "living language" (Wilkinson, 1973, p436) situations. Such situations would seek to offer students real opportunities to use language as a natural outcome for a wide variety of creative, exploratory, imaginative and critical purposes. Oracy, along with writing, is the "major means by which children in our schools formulate knowledge and relate it to their own purposes and view of the world" (Barnes, 1976, p19) so planning not merely for substance but also for sequence in talking and listening programs is a central curriculum objective.

As part of the program design and implementation process, English teachers also need "to be more sensitive to the short and long term strategies they are adopting, and the social relationships they permit within their classrooms, and how these effect learning." (Stratta et al, 1980, pp144-145) After all, the most impressive program can fail if the pedagogy and attitudes of the teacher inhibit students' productive talk. The widely influential Bullock Report, *Language for Life*, suggests that, as part of their professional knowledge, teachers should have:

✦ an explicit understanding of the processes at work in classroom discourse; and

♦ the ability to appraise their pupils' spoken language and to plan the means of extending it (Bullock, 1975, p527).

Making oracy an integrated part of English also requires a willingness on the part of the teacher to overcome some of those processes in classroom discourse that often undermine the positive status of students' talk.

The Status of Students' Talk

It is through talking that we learn, express, and further develop our capacity for learning. Learning usually involves tentative exploration. Yet even in recent times, some English classrooms continue to privilege the modes of reading and writing at the expense of productive talking and listening. How often as a student do you remember the anti-talk mantras such as "don't talk", "stop talking and get on with your work", "with all this talking you must be finished working", and so on. The message here is plain – talk is perceived purely in behavioural terms as deviance and a threat to the 'real learning mission' in the classroom. Such a school is a place where teachers talk and, for the most part, students listen and write in order to gain approval.

When this kind of negative model prevails, students are treated as the passive recipients in the dialogical teacher-student relationship (Green, 1990). In this model, there is tacit agreement that power, knowledge and prestige reside only in the teacher. The student is required merely to respond to questions rather than also to create them, to defer to the presumed sanctity of information rather than to interrogate it, and to use talk merely for narrowly utilitarian rather than also for expressive and exploratory purposes. Here the students' talk is often 'response talk' that aims to identify the 'right' answer to the teacher's questions. In such a setting the opportunities for 'talking-into-meaning' utterances are heavily circumscribed. As a consequence, students prefer to say nothing rather than risk incurring the opprobrium of the teacher-authority with a 'wrong answer', or the ridicule of peers for exposing one's apparent inadequacy.

Counteracting Conditioned Oral Passivity

This kind of conditioned oral passivity is identified by Barbara S Wood:

> *Children form a host of generalisations that associate negative consequences with oral communication. To bring about effective learning, we must insist upon some degree of classroom order. But when students conclude that grades or evaluations are directly proportionate to the amount of talking they do – regardless of its overall quality – something unfortunate is happening. Children are associating a high*

value with quiet learning, while we as teachers are associating positive teaching with the same behaviour. (Wood, 1984, p104)

She goes on to argue that we should not "reject teaching practices that regulate classroom talk" but rather, "begin to regard the 'talking child' as a desirable student, rather than a troublesome one"(Wood, 1984, p104).

If oracy is to be regarded as core work in the English classroom, the teacher must necessarily promote and indeed celebrate the role of the 'talking child'. This may entail 're-defining' students' perceptions about the nature, value and purpose of their classroom talk.

Valuing Talking and Listening as Core Work in English

The class that values productive talk is sustained by two assumptions:

1. The teacher (and by extension, the student) recognises the language that each student brings to the classroom as a resource upon which to build and extend that individual's talking and listening capacities. "Talking and listening activities should begin with the language the student brings to the classroom."(Board of Secondary Education, NSW, 1987, p24) This basic principle is endorsed in a wide range of Australian syllabus documents and in the national paper, *A Statement on English for Australian Schools*:

   Effective teaching is based on what children already know and can do. The teaching of English will achieve most where the considerable informal language knowledge and competence of the students, whatever their cultural or language background, is acknowledged, used and extended.

   (AEC, 1994, p5)

2. The classroom teacher and students alike must assume that students have something to learn from each other. James Moffett comments on the agenda of so much peer group and whole-class discussion when he concludes that:

   . . . a major reason children do not listen to each other is that they do not value what peers have to say. Their first inclination is, in school at any rate, to assume that they can learn only from adults, who are all-powerful and all-knowing, not from other small critters like themselves. If the teacher attends and values their peer talk, they will also. As in many other matters, real attention establishes value. If you praise and blame, or otherwise make yourself the

*centre of the group, children will talk to and for you, not to
and for their peers, and consequently will listen only to you
and use the time while another child is talking to prepare
their next bright remark for you to praise.*
(Moffett, 1973, p58)

Once a teacher has fully acknowledged students' language as the living
resource of the curriculum it is possible to envision the 'teacher-student
partnerships'(Boomer, 1982) operating in a less teacher-centred way. No
longer need the teacher be the keeper and controller of the 'talking space'
(Reid et al, 1989, p11).

The Role of the Teacher

Clearly, the teacher plays a central role in taking forward the development
of oracy for the class and for the individual. To be successful, the teacher
needs to engender an optimal learning environment of psychological safety
and freedom as well as to:

✦ plan, prepare, structure, orchestrate and mediate meaningful and
  enjoyable language experiences to extend the range of accomplishment
  for each student;

✦ establish and affirm through practice the patterns of expectation about
  acceptable and unacceptable talk;

✦ "encourage a view of discussion as a means of enlarging one's personal
  world view and modifying it to take account of other people's" (Bullock,
  1975, p145);

✦ have a repertoire of appropriate questioning techniques;

✦ act as a facilitator, co-ordinator, receptive audience, negotiator,
  consultant, and supportive mentor as students grow in confidence and
  competence; and

✦ intervene when necessary, challenge, redirect or refocus talk to
  encourage students to move beyond "the mere expression of opinion"
  to use language "in an exploratory way". (Bullock, 1975, p145)

But there sometimes exists a reluctance on the part of secondary English
teachers to allow students to participate in self-directed talk for fear that
they will not be capable of creating anything more than chaos and noisy
banter. Adams and Pearce argue that teachers "have to control (an)
obsessive, professional fear of something we call 'irrelevance' "(Adams and
Pearce in Brock, 1990, p7). They go on to say that "given the right starting
point or setting, unsupervised pupils can actually be expected to sustain
thoroughly useful conversations." (Adams and Pearce in Brock, 1990, p7)
Importantly, it is the responsibility of the teacher to gradually move the
students' talk "in the direction of relevance, of objectivity, of depth, and of
reciprocity" (Wilkinson, 1973, p434).

At an organisational level, this objective can be realised through a workshop approach to learning during which the class can engage in well-planned tasks in small groups.

Small Group Learning

The advantages of small group work for students and teacher alike have been well documented. There are plenty of resources that will guide the teacher in the theoretical underpinnings and practical strategies for successful small group learning. (See Bibliography) Small groups can provide a beneficial setting for students to make the best use of the learning time (Reid et al, 1989, p11) and the 'talking space' of the classroom. A small group approach can enable students to:

✦ use language for a range of planned and incidental purposes;
✦ experience a supportive and shared context for learning;
✦ learn to deal sensitively with others' ideas and perspectives;
✦ experience the benefits of working co-operatively and collaboratively;
✦ develop confidence, particularly if shy or reticent, through significant participation;
✦ adopt a variety of 'roles' within the group;
✦ express hesitancy and uncertainty whilst 'thinking aloud';
✦ move from low-level tasks, such as recording and describing, to high-level thought processes of inquiring, theorising, speculating and problem-solving;
✦ benefit from the input of a teacher who is able to interact with and monitor individual's learning in small groups; and
✦ make the transition from exploratory and expressive talk to 'performance' for a range of audiences for a variety of purposes. (Reid et al, 1989)

To be effective, the class should experience regular small group experiences. It is vital, however, that from the outset, the class is allowed the time to learn how to work in these groups. Successful small group learning will not simply happen by chance:

> The ability to work effectively in a group develops slowly in children. They have difficulties in many of the skills underlying effective group work: staying on the topic, reaching a cooperative goal, managing distractions, and making effective contributions. Until children learn these skills, student groups may seem chaotic and results may sometimes appear haphazard. (Wood, 1984, pp117-118)

It is also important that students in small groups experience a variety of tasks undertaken in a variety of ways. The small group approach needs to be dynamic and fluid enough to ensure that students do not become complacent about its function and value. For example, it would be tiresome for students and eventually counter-productive, if each time they work in their small group they discuss questions and report back to the class. Once they have become accustomed to their 'home group', students can work within and across a number of groups, depending on the demands and the nature of the task. Specialist groups, publishing groups and project groups, presenting performances, publications, research findings, and so on, are just some examples of the many ways in which the structure, process and outcomes of groups can be varied.

Five Principles for Successful Group Work

These principles are an amalgam of ideas from a variety of sources and serve only as an initial guide.

1. Inform students about the purpose and processes of group work and allow them to contribute to establishing the 'protocols' for group work. Talk about expectations, group roles, individuals' roles, leadership, group responsibility, seating plans etc.

2. Given the class protocols, students must feel that what they have to say, and the way in which they say it, are acceptable. Barnes identifies the initial step in encouraging constructive talk as developing a 'feeling of competence' (Barnes, 1976).

3. It is important to plan a 'context' for discussion. This may be based on "apparatus, on pictures, on films or on written materials, or it can be based on shared experience inside or outside the school" (Knowles, 1983, p216).

4. Allow time for students to become accustomed to working together in small groups by planning short, focused activities, perhaps using pairs initially. Such a focus may be instructions or questions that allow group talk to be directed to some purpose. Set a time limit for tasks, but do not assume that students are not engaging if they take longer, or if they 'stray' from the focus. "A teacher needs to give pupils time for ideas to be shaped and language developed" (Knowles, 1983, p216).

5. Small group talk is a means of extending the capacities of students, either through the complexity of the issue, focus or problem being explored or through the actual "process used by the group in arriving at its conclusion." (Brock, 1990, p7) Varying and sequencing the substance of group work, and varying the way in which it is handled are important factors in sustaining students' language growth.

Teachers' Questions – Students' Questions

The effective teacher employs a variety of types of questions that encourage students to think critically and perceptively about experiences, issues, stimulus materials and problems. If the 'talking space' of the classroom is shared by teacher and students alike, then the range of the questions tends to be far broader, designed to stimulate students' creativity and encourage constructive thinking. In contrast, the classroom in which teacher-talk dominates is often marked by a proliferation of closed questions that call for short response 'answers'. Of the question types set out below, it is clear that "some are more appropriate than others when one wants the student to be involved in the learning process" (South Australian Secondary English Curriculum Committee, 1976, p37) The effective teacher is skilled in the use of a range of question types:

✦ Naming questions – ask pupils to give a name to some phenomenon without requiring them to show insight into its use.

✦ Reasoning questions – require students to 'think aloud', to construct, or reconstruct from memory, a logically organised sequence.

✦ Recall questions – are concerned with summoning up required knowledge from memory.

✦ Closed questions – have only one acceptable answer.

✦ Open questions – allow a number of different answers. It is necessary to check apparently open questions by examining the teacher's reception of the pupils' replies, which may show that he (sic) will accept only one reply to a question framed in apparently open terms.

✦ Observation questions – require children to interpret what they perceive.

✦ Control questions – are directed towards imposing the teacher's wishes on the class.

✦ Appeal questions – ask pupils to agree with or share an attitude or remember an experience, or occur where the children can see the teacher pondering over meaning. He (sic) makes no direct appeal or demand for an answer. His (sic) very attitude invites the children to help him (sic) explore meaning.

(South Australian Secondary English Curriculum Committee, 1976, p37)

Ideally, the English class should also be a place where students' questions – about experiences, books, poems, plays, films, issues, media and other language contexts – play a major role in the classroom discourse and are valued as a significant indicator of engagement, understanding and learning.

Encouraging Good Listening

Most of the principles for improving students' talking skills are clearly applicable to listening. One of the basic ways of improving the listening skills of students is for the teacher to model good listening – to take a genuine interest in the ideas, responses and contributions of all students. Listening competence involves not only the ability to discern aural variables such as tone, pitch, dialect, stress, rhythm and so on. Students should be able to listen for information and meaning by following, recalling and interpreting connected discourse, discussion, dialogue and drama (Board of Secondary Education, NSW, 1987); listen critically to identify the values inherent in speech and the devices it employs to elicit response, to persuade, to coerce etc.; detect bias; and understand the relationship between the visual and aural components of film, non-print media and so on.

Models of Talking and Listening

There are a number of very useful 'models' of talking and listening that assist in planning and programming for oracy in English. A comprehensive program should incorporate as broad a range as possible of the language experiences and functions set out below.

This model is constructed from the work of Michael Halliday, G Philips, D Butt and N Metzger, W J Crocker and Barbara S Wood.

Language Category	Function
Controlling and regulatory language	communication seeking to manipulate or influence others; talk used to predict, bargain, and respond to the controlling communication of others.
Descriptive, informative and explanatory language	describing events, feelings, phenomena; providing reasons and causes; asking questions; responding to messages.
Legitimating language	speech to rationalise or legitimate one's actions; seeks to confirm authority and competence.
Instrumental language	language for getting things done; satisfying needs.
Ritualising or personal language	intitiating or maintaining social and community relationships; greetings, small talk.
Imaginative language	language to express the symbolic, conceptual; fantasising and storytelling.

Andrew Wilkinson's model also provides for the English teacher a useful classification of language functions that is organised according to the subjective communicative needs of the speaker (Wilkinson, 1975).

Speaker's communicative need	Language Function
Who am I?	1. Establishing and maintaining self. 2. Language for analysing self. 3. Language for expressing self.
Who are you?	4. Establishing and maintaining relationships. 5. Co-operating. 6. Empathising, understanding the other. 7. Role playing, mimicry. 8. Guiding, directing the other.
Who/what is he/she/it?	9. Giving information. 10. Recalling past events (past). 11. Describing present events (present). 12. Predicting future events – statement of intention, hypothesis or what might happen. 13. Analysing, classifying. 14. Exploring; asking questions, but in other ways also, by sounding people out. 15. Explaining, giving reasons for. 16. Reflecting on own/others' thoughts and feelings.

Practical Teaching and Learning Strategies

There are many resources that will provide detailed practical strategies for the teacher. The following ideas have been drawn from a variety of such sources. Most are suitable for small group learning contexts and many are appropriate for a range of audiences beyond that of the teacher and peers.

✦ Describing and explaining – processes, events, excuses, instructions places, things, people, decisions.

✦ Retelling and recalling – stories, experiences, incidents, jokes, memories, and movies.

✦ Reporting – hypothetical events, results of group discussions, experiences.

✦ Exploring – ideas, texts, evidence, stimulus materials.

✦ Narrating – stories, plays, experiences.

✦ Problem-solving, negotiating resolutions – to actual and hypothetical problems, conflicts in texts, school, society.

- Predicting, speculating, theorising – from a range of stimulus materials.
- Generating questions – about texts, themes, characters, issues.
- Classifying, collating, ordering, sequencing – ideas, questions, issues, actions, characters, events.
- Role-playing – characters, stereotypes, hypothetical situations.
- Interviewing – characters, writers, famous and invented people.
- Panels – characters, authors, issues, themes.
- Hot-seating – characters, writers, famous and invented people.
- Discussions and conversations – focusing, reflecting, analysing, hypothesising, musing, between peers, between student and teacher, about texts, events, experiences, issues.
- Staging a play – chosen or written by students.
- Dramatic presentations – of poems, scenes, dialogues, excerpts.
- Debates – issues, themes, laws, current affairs.
- Banquets and Dinner Parties – based on texts, events, themes.
- Casting famous people or classmates for characters in – plays, novels, poems.
- Mock Trials – text-based, invented.
- Prepared speeches – on topics, themes, issues, events.
- Pre-writing – exploring and articulating ideas, themes, issues, perspectives.
- Conferencing during writing – with peers and teacher.
- Tape recorder – recording stories, conversations, ads, mini-sagas, interviews, speeches.
- Using the phone – protocols, reporting emergencies, getting information.
- Questioning games – "Who am I?", "Yes-No".
- Listening for pleasure, meaning and critical understanding – poetry, stories, music, prose, famous speeches, parliament, mystery sounds, recordings.
- Listening for rhythms and rhymes – poems, rhyming games.
- Rehearsed readings – individual and choral.
- Dialogues – from texts, invented contexts.
- Music-story activities – create a story or poem to suit some music and vice-versa.
- Media – press conferences, radio ads, interviews, news.
- Spontaneous talks – one minute sales talk for common objects; "What if..?" games,
- Evaluating – responses, writing, stimulus materials, projects, presentations.

Select Bibliography

Australian Education Council (1994) *A Statement on English for Australian Schools*, Melbourne: Curriculum Corporation.

Barnes, D et al (1971) *Language, the Learner and the School*, Harmondsworth: Penguin.

Barnes, D (1976) *From Communication to Curriculum*, Harmondsworth: Penguin.

Barnes, D and Todd, F (1977) *Communication and Learning in Small Groups*, London: Routledge and Kegan Paul.

Board of Secondary Education, NSW (1987) *Syllabus in English: Years 7-10*, Sydney: Board of Secondary Education.

Boomer, Garth (1982) *Negotiating the Curriculum: A Teacher-Student Partnership*, Sydney: Ashton Scholastic.

Britton, J (1971) *Language and Learning*, Harmondsworth: Penguin.

Brock, Paul (1990) *English Curriculum Support Materials*, University of New England, Armidale.

Bullock, A (1975) *A Language for Life, Report of the Committee of Inquiry appointed by the Secretary of State for Education and Science*, London: HMSO.

Crocker, W J (1977) "Teaching Oracy in the English Programme", *English in Australia*, No 39, February pp48-59.

DEET (1991) *Australia's Language: The Australian Language and Literacy Policy*, Canberra: AGPS.

Downing, David B (ed) (1994) *Changing Classroom Practices, Resources for Literary and Cultural Studies*, Illinois: NCTE.

Green, Bill (1990) "Imagining the Curriculum: Programming for Meaning in Subject English", *English in Australia*, No 94, December, pp39-58.

Halliday, M (1982) "Relevant Models of Language" in Barrie Wade, *Language Perspectives*, London: Heinemann.

Knowles, Lewis (1983) *Encouraging Talk*, London: Methuen.

Linn, Ray (1996) *A Teacher's Introduction to Post Modernism*, Illinois, NCTE.

McClure, Maggie, et al (1988), *Oracy Matters*, Milton Keynes: Open University Press.

Moffett, James (1968) *Teaching The Universe of Discourse*, Houghton Mifflin.

Moffett, James (1973) *A Student-Centred Language Arts Curriculum, Grades K-13*, Houghton Mifflin.

Peters, William H (1987), *Effective English Teaching: Concept, Research, and Practice*, Iliinios, NCTE.

Phelan, Patricia, et al (1989) *Talking to Learn, Classroom Practices in English Teaching*, Vol 24, Illinois, NCTE.

Philips, G, Butt D and Metzger, N (1974) *Communication in Education*, New York: Holt, Rinehart and Winston.

Plattor, E (1984) "Listening and Speaking: Research Implications for Curriculum Development", *The English Quarterly*, Vol XVII No 1, pp 3-20.

Reid, Jo-Anne, et al (1989) *Small Group Learning in the Classroom*, Scarborough: PETA-Chalkface Press.

Rubin, Donald L, and Dodd, William M (1987) *Talking into Writing*, Illinois: NCTE.

Shanahan, Timothy (ed) (1994) *Teachers Thinking, Teachers Knowing, Reflections on Literacy and Language Education*, Illinois: NCTE.

South Australian Secondary English Committee (1976) *Oral Language*, Adelaide: SA Education Department.

Stratta, Leslie, et al (1980) *Patterns of Language: Explorations of the Teaching of English*, London: Heinemann.

Torbe, Mike, and Medway, Peter (1981) *The Climate of Learning*, New Jersey: Boynton/Cook.

Wade, Barrie, (ed) (1985) *Talking to Some Purpose*, Edgbaston: University of Birmingham.

Wilkinson, Andrew, et al (1965) *Spoken English*, Edgbaston: University of Birmingham.

Wilkinson, Andrew (1971) *The Foundations of Language*, London: OUP.

Wilkinson, Andrew (1975) *Language and Education*, London: OUP.

Wilkinson, Andrew (1973) "The Concept of Oracy" in Hipple, Theodore W *Readings for Teaching English in Secondary Schools*, London: Macmillan.

Wood, Barbara S (1984) "Oral Communication in the Elementary Classroom" in Thaiss, Christopher, J, and Suhor, Charles (eds) *Speaking and Writing, K – 12*, Illinois: NCTE.

22 Re-casting Drama in English Education

Roslyn Arnold

D rama teaching is centrally located in English classrooms, even though drama in education has developed as a significant area of pedagogy in its own right since the nineteen seventies. There is something special about the insights to be gained from both the experiences one has in drama classes and about the quality of the reflections, writing and thinking which can arise from such classes. The fact that students often enjoy drama classes more than usual is because they can be active, engaging and collaborative. In so being, they can activate affective and cognitive memories which may serve to promote literacy and expressive development.

Implicit in this theoretical proposition is a concept of development as essentially spirally in its nature (Arnold, 1991, p20), whereby all significant learning experiences, over time, influence abilities to learn, to express and to communicate. This being so, drama in English can serve significant purposes rarely matched by the usual range of pedagogy in English. It would be regrettable if students were to miss the particular quality of experiences which drama can offer, simply because teachers were unaware of, or unconfident about, its underlying theoretical principles and practices.

Since developing a theory of psychodynamic pedagogy, (Arnold, 1991, 1993, 1994, 1996) I have been able to articulate why engaging learning experiences, such as those offered by good drama and English teachers, are potentially effective in enhancing students' learning. Classes which effectively engage students' tacit abilities for communication and expression are rich in learning potential. There are important reasons for this. The shift in responsibility which occurs when a teacher invites students to participate in engaging learning experiences, such as those which involve self-presentation, group collaboration and problem solving, reactivates some of the memories of deeply internalised learning experiences, particularly those which have influenced a sense of self-as-learner. While for some students this re-activation might not necessarily stir positive memories, particularly if their sense of self-as-learner is somewhat fragile, or if this type of learning experience is too novel for them, for many students the thought of working in engaging and interactive ways, actually stirs a sense of hope. Such hope or optimism, of itself, can provide a positive expectation which is dynamically effective. That is, the positive affect and the cognitive experience will interact in the mind to promote a readiness for meaningful learning.

The root of such a fundamentally important affect as hope may be traced right back to early language learning experiences. Most infants express joy and enthusiasm as they experience positive affirmation of their language learning attempts from attentive and empathic care givers. This affirmation, and its affective quality , or emotional colour, is laid down like an affective template in the infant's psyche, to be re-activated and re-shaped throughout the learning experiences of life. Daniel Stern's work on the interpersonal development of infants is particularly insightful here (Stern, 1985), supporting with research evidence a central tenet of psychodynamic pedagogy, that the effectiveness of pedagogy is enhanced by experiences which engage both affect and cognition, preferably in a way which stimulates a dynamic between both.

This encourages me to argue that students come into our classrooms with hopes, expectations, memories and a mind set of themselves as learners, which can all be modified through the kinds of pedagogy they experience. In that argument, English and drama are particularly well placed to capitalise on the positive and hopeful memories students must have had to become effective learners of speech, and later, writing. In English classes, the primary focus of drama work may well be on developing an embodied understanding of the way empathic engagements between participants can influence human dynamics. A simple example might illustrate this point. In a role-play where students might act out the proposal scene in *Romeo and Juliet*, close attention might well focus on an analysis of the spatial relationships between the characters and the felt differences the characters and the audience might experience when those spatial relationships are manipulated for effect. Such an analysis might be apparently non-threatening. What the empathic teacher would recognise is that such a scene, by virtue of its universality, will very likely stir feelings of both hope and anxiety, touching as it does on themes of acceptance and rejection, love and potential loss. What is discussed publicly in class or written about privately in a personal journal might well vary according to the degree of confidence or readiness students feel about exploring their own attitudes and mind-sets relevant to these themes. In other words good art, literature and cultural experiences, of their very nature have the potential to stimulate powerful affective responses. Educators serious about the significance of their profession accept that. However, such is the aesthetic richness and underlying structure of good literature, like Shakespeare's plays, that the language itself offers both invitations to exploration and safety nets for such risk-taking.

Provided we are confident about the potential for development within students' tacit abilities, and confident about the evocative nature of the literature we offer, the empathic teacher can structure interactive discussions and drama classes around the responses students themselves offer from their observations of role-plays, from readings and from their own reflective writings. Underpinning this assertion is my own confidence that students themselves are the real focus of any effective pedagogy. Fortunately, drama, literacy and arts education are extremely well placed to start from that focus point. Indeed, in a psychodynamic framework, there is no alternative.

Barbara Hardy (1977, p12) has argued that "narrative (is) a primary act of mind transferred to art from life", and her point of view has won many adherents. It could be argued that role playing is a primary act of mind which predates story telling historically. Before a story is told or heard, participants **assume a role** of narrator or listener. In so doing, particular mind sets are actuated. Rosenblatt's argument (1978) for reading as an interaction between reader and text involves the reader in assuming a particular dynamic stance in relationship to the text. Readers who see themselves as good readers are more receptive to the text than readers who see themselves as poor readers. The assigned, assumed, or unconsciously internalised role-as-reader, or role-as-listener or role-as-narrator, and the adoption of a positive or negative stance in that role, exercises a powerful influence on the ways it will be enacted, and upon the ways texts will be accessed and meanings created. The empathic teacher reads intuitively and from experience, the complex sub-text of roles, relationships and memories functioning in the classroom 'stage'.

Early Role Assignment and Acting Out

Let's take this point further back in an individual's personal history. The roles assigned to a baby even before its conception can determine how it will be responded to in utero and in the family circle. Drama, particularly role-playing, predates language development in the life of the child. Parents' assumptions about babies as individuals, as learners, as members of the family, as like or unlike other siblings, as potential inheritors of the family estate or as another mouth to feed in an already over crowded family ensure that the baby is handled, cared for, responded to and educated in ways which, often unconsciously, reflect certain role expectations. Models of family, social and individual life are unconsciously internalised by infants long before functional language development. Babies are frequently assigned roles as good or bad infants according to certain behaviour patterns – projecting moral worth upon them very prematurely. Gestures, facial expressions, body language and vocal expressions are assigned meanings by the infant in the earliest days of life.

The fantasies parents and others have about unborn children and the expectations projected onto them, and existing children, create all kinds of positive, negative and even destructive forces which individuals have to deal with in various ways. Should one's self-chosen life roles conflict with those predestined by family and social forces, internal and external dramas will inevitably result. The moment of birth is the first enactment of a role as the infant is assigned the role of the baby in the family. The rest of life is the creation and acting out of a script partly written for us, but ideally capable of much revision and creative input. Some of that input comes from the dramas of family and social life, and from cultural input including narratives heard or read. The personal drama of life and the role of a unique individual challenge us to write and enact our own scripts – depending upon our self-perceptions as agents of change or captives of a system.

The sad case of infants who fail to thrive for no known physiological reason is evidence of infants' need to experience themselves as wanted. In this particularly cruel human drama the victims are both mother and child. The mother is often quite unaware of her unconscious feelings about the child, but with sensitive intervention, a form of drama in itself, the underlying, destructive drama which created the problem can be replayed and rewritten, often with a happy ending. The underlying theme of that real-life drama is that human beings have a primary need to experience themselves as loved, wanted, accepted, valued and esteemed individuals. It is a theme informing all human dynamics, including social life, personal relationships and learning contexts and is underpinned by the self-perceptions we hold and the roles we assume and enact in relation to these perceptions.

To rephrase Barbara Hardy's comment above, I want to claim that **role-playing is a primary enactment of mind** – and as such, role-playing as a learning medium should be the core of institutional learning contexts, just as it is the core of family life, social life, and personal life. Even in monologues with ourselves we create dialogues between different parts of ourself. One part plays the role of encourager, maybe, while the other part might discourage. The dynamics between several parts can create the energy for resolution and enactment, or the blocking which causes irresolution and apathy. In some cases another individual, like a therapist or sensitive informed person, has to enter the stage to advance the personal drama through enforced or negotiated shifts in perspective and altered dynamics.

Drama on the Centre Stage

The reasons why drama has not claimed a major role in school curricula and English can be surmised, albeit briefly, here. The traditional link between drama, theatre and entertainment has possibly done a disservice to the power of drama to educate people – though clearly theatre and entertainment can educate very effectively. One problem is that education is still seen too narrowly as something which occurs mainly through listening, reading, writing and computing. All too rarely is education recognised as occurring most powerfully, most profoundly and most enduringly, through social enactments. Take early child language development. The educating context there is the family with all its role models, rituals, narratives and personal histories to add texture to the child's social and linguistic learning. Much to the despair of feminists and sensitive educators, sometimes no amount of consciousness-raising about gender and roles can counteract the powerful influences of gender-modelling within the home. But one of the unique characteristics of role-play is its capacity to reveal unconscious influences upon behaviour and thinking through the enactment of universal themes and contexts and through close analyses of interpersonal dynamics.

My argument for the centrality of drama in English has evolved through practice and reflection over a decade. Although I have taught drama continuously since the early seventies, within English curriculum and in drama workshops, the focus of my academic work in the past fifteen years has been linguistics, psycholinguistics and literacy education, particularly writing development. I have become aware that drama has the potential to integrate all the major educational influences, both personal and institutional, upon my own life. As well, it can provide insights into aspects of those influences which are not easily revealed and analysed. I have come full circle and can see that the psychodynamic spiral I postulated for writing development, (Arnold, 1991, p20) can apply just as well to drama as a learning medium. To say I have come full circle is an inadequate metaphor, though an easily recognised one. This perspective is influenced by reflection on personal experience and the wisdom received through Vygotsky (1988), Polanyi (1969), Bruner (1986), Dimarsio(1996) and others to argue that drama in the fullest sense of enactment (both text and simulation), role-play, play building, sub-texting and theatre, either alone, or in conjunction with reading, writing and reflection, is a powerful and a much neglected medium for any significant learning which involves the engagement of thought and feeling. Furthermore, that engagement of thought and feeling can lead to the differentiation of such thought and feeling through the clarification and elaboration possible in good de-briefing practices.

An argument for the centrality of drama in English needs to define what is intrinsically educative about drama – role-play in particular. Vygotsky's theory (1988) of the zone of proximal development, whereby attentive and attuned adults often unconsciously set achievement goals for children appropriately, and achievably, just ahead of their current achievement levels, is relevant to this argument for several reasons. In the preparation for role-plays both the teacher and participating students can establish the focus and roles of the activity with a view to exploring known, but not yet deeply understood, situations. The preparation work, important as it is in its own right for its development of creative problem solving, projective thinking and co-operative social planning, is often a very different learning experience to that of the role-play itself. Like most classroom work the nature of the preparation of role-play is usually verbal, cognitive, rational, organised and physically inactive. Role-plays themselves are verbal, physically active, and, in being enactive, give rise to spontaneous utterances, affective responses, unconscious revelations and symbolic gestures. While the nature of role-plays is distinctly different from that of most school learning with its use of role-relationships, time and space dimensions, focus and tension, one of the most significant aspects of the educative potential of role-plays is in their capacity to realise and reveal the unconscious memories, influences and tensions of the participants. This claim, and the implications which arise from it, signal both the power and danger of role-play work.

The power lies in the capacity for this kind of work to reveal to its participants significant insights into human behaviour, learning and feeling. These insights are not necessarily accessible to conscious, verbal, rational thought but can be signalled and realised through the more fully enacted, symbolically and spontaneously patterned expressions of engaging role-play work. The power of role-plays arises from emotions, tone of voice, movement and gesture. Like Promethean fire, this power must be protected. True insights are not gained by playing safe where roles and outcomes are eminently predictable and forgettable. The best drama work is often unpredictable and unforgettable. This is not to say it has to be unsafe or threatening. On the contrary there are important safeguards like boundary setting and de-briefing which protect the Promethean fire without quenching its flame.

Part of the educative power of drama in English arises from the expression of the unconscious in that what was formerly concealed is revealed, what was unspoken is now spoken and what was unembodied in the unconscious is now embodied in enactment. However, the truly educative power arises from the connections created between the enactment and the analyses and reflections made by the actors and audience upon the unconscious material. These connections may occur spontaneously or they may need to be worked through in post-enactment discussions or replays. Preparation is one learning experience, enactment another and reflection yet another. The intertextuality and interdependence of these three experiences is the dynamic underpinning the educative nature of drama in English.

The Place of Writing in Preparation and De-briefing

While it is intrinsic to drama work to focus on experiences which are active and interactive, the fullest benefits of drama derive from interaction between the enactive part of such work and both the preparatory activities and the de-briefing and reflective work. Both these activities can involve writing as planning and writing reflection. They can allow the individual to make personal choices and observations about characters, events and experiences without the pressure to conform to the expectations of the group. At times comformity might be chosen but it is valuable to enrich group experiences with the option for individuals to create their own meaning (or characters, scenes and outcomes) through personal or journal writing. For example, participants in a role-play might be required to keep a journal account for a week in the role-character whom they might eventually play. Guidance can be given about the kinds of entries students might make, with much encouragement given to the kinds of observations and speculations the chosen character might make in a diary or journal. It is my strong conviction that the credibility of a role-play depends upon the actor's belief in her/his role. Some actors are gifted and have strong empathic and interpersonal skills. For them the preparation and role-identification is easy. But for those students who need careful thought and time to develop a sense of role, the preparatory journal/diary 'in role' is very beneficial. Another way to use writing as a preparation activity is to have students exchange letters 'in role' between characters. Letters have been used frequently as a dramatic device in drama texts (*Macbeth, Othello, Romeo and Juliet*) partly because they allow certain information to be conveyed to the audience without the necessity for enactment. What I am suggesting here is something rather different in purpose, in that the students' exchange of letters 'in role' can encourage them to develop roles mutually and co-operatively.

Say, for example, a role-play is being developed around some family crisis such as a conflict between parents and a student – say a daughter who wishes to leave home. Independently, 'the mother' and ' daughter' might write their week's journal entries. Then the 'mother' and 'daughter' might exchange letters, not about the content of the role-play itself, but about the past experiences or fears which account for the position each might take in the role-play. The principle behind the activity is that the actor has to project into his/her own role and into that of the other actors. I'd favour exchanging as much information and writing as possible about the roles and between the participating actors prior to the enactment. This kind of preparatory writing works just as well with scripted work. It also provides a slow, effective build-up of a role in such a way that there is less likelihood of actors becoming exposed through unexpected surfacing of unconscious material in the acting out. Any role-play which deals with a universal theme or context such as family life has the potential to stimulate strong feelings and unconscious responses – part of the reason why good drama, literature and art is so powerful. If the preparatory writing is engagingly done and builds the actor's commitment to and belief in the role, the unconscious material can enhance, rather than threaten, the acting experience.

In a similar way, reflective writing after the acting-out can deepen participants' insights and allow a catharsis of thoughts and feelings arising from either acting out a role or watching an enactment. It is only part of the educative role of drama work and writing about drama work. It is another safeguard and a support to work which can reveal and challenge students' unrecognised assumptions about themselves, about the nature of human behaviour and about the dynamics which influence it. Learning reveals and challenges deeply-held beliefs and attitudes and will be powerfully affective. Some affectiveness can be dealt with in calm, reflective de-briefing sessions; some of it can be worked through in personal writing.

Effective De-briefing

Drama in English is different to traditional classroom-based, teacher-centred work and the time and energy demands it makes on teachers and students need to be acknowledged.

De-briefing involves encouraging students to articulate the feelings and observations which have arisen from the drama work. The teacher's role is to be an accepting, attuned listener who knows how to ask for appropriate elaboration should a student have difficulties with articulation, but who also knows never to probe intrusively.

Apart from giving students a chance to express their responses to the role-plays, and indeed, giving them a chance to save face with explanations should their enactment not have worked as well as they hoped, the de-briefing time can also be used to replay brief moments in the role-plays where a significant movement or word might have had a very dramatic impact on the audience. It can take time and focused experience to teach students to be observant and insightful as an audience. By noting such moments and highlighting them for comment or a replay, debriefing can be cathartic and instructive.

De-briefing time can also be given over to silence. Odd as it may sound, the experience of being silent and contemplative within a group which has shared certain experiences can be both cathartic and instructive. If there is insufficient time to de-brief adequately or to sooth students' feelings after a drama session, at least have them sit silently in a circle for a minute or two. It can help participants to contain their feelings and alleviate some tension.

I have alluded to some of the reasons why drama in English is worthwhile. It is because the nature of the work so closely mirrors some important aspects of early learning. It repeats the exploratory, preverbal, symbolic nature of play, and the acting out of roles, as well as triggering the articulation and expression through speech, gesture and movement, of previously unformulated thoughts and feelings. In re-experiencing through drama work the feelings associated with the early creation of meanings and discoveries about the world, there is a possibility of reshaping both those early experiences and the contemporaneous ones in ways which enhance or even change our patterns of perceiving and construing the world. Certainly other expressive media like writing, dance, painting and composing can provide opportunities for the development and expression of personal meanings. However, some of the special features of drama in English are its social nature, its potential to reveal unconscious meanings, its affinity with other expressive media in a complementary way, and its suitability as a core learning medium in a multidisciplinary curriculum. Its capacity to underpin and enrich the core literacy and literature experiences of English curricula place it at the heart of that subject.

References

Arnold, R (1991) *Writing Development:Magic in the Brain*, Buckingham: Open University Press.

Arnold, R (1993) "Managing Unconscious and Affective Responses in English Classes and Roleplays", *English in Education*, National Association for the Teaching of English, UK Spring, 21:1.

Arnold, R(1994) "Research Issues, Psychodynamic Pedagogy and Drama in Education", *English in Australia*, July.

Arnold, R(1996) "The Drama in Research and Articulating Dynamics – A Unique Theatre", Keynote Address presented at International Drama-in-Education Research Institute, University of Victoria, Canada, July. To be published in conference proceedings, in press.

Bruner, J (1986) *Actual Minds, Possible Worlds*, Cambridge, Mass: Harvard University Press.

Dimarsio, A (1996) *Descartes' Error- Emotion, Reason and the Human Brain*, London: Macmillan.

Hardy, B (1977) "Towards a Poetics of Fiction: An Approach through Narrative" in Meek, M, Warlow, A, Barton, G (eds) *The Cool Web*, London: The Bodley Head.

Polanyi, M (1969) *Knowing and Being*, London: Routledge and Kegan Paul.

Rosenblatt, L (1978) *The Reader, The Text the Poem*, Carbondale: Southern Illinois University Press.

Stern, D (1985) *The Interpersonal World of the Infant*, New York: Basic Books.

Vygotsky, L (1988) *Thought and Language*, Cambridge: Harvard University Press.

23 Teaching Plays as Theatre

John Hughes

Over the last twenty years English teachers have been increasingly concerned with teaching plays as performance pieces rather than merely words on a page. During this period we have witnessed major developments in drama education in classrooms. We have seen the expansion, refinement and elaboration of drama as a learning medium together with the influences of theatre semiotics and performance studies on the analysis of drama as an art form. This paper will focus on the latter while arguing that the former has increased teachers' abilities to encourage their students into an understanding of the richness of the performing arts.

A critical response to a play must reflect the fact that the script is a blueprint for a live happening, the realisation of which will require the creative input of a range of talents. The performing arts involve enactments which bond audiences and performers in a shared set of experiences to which both make differing contributions, hence each performance of the same written text is unique. The dynamics of actor and actor, actor and director, actor and audience, change with every enactment. It follows that students must study a play both in the theatre and as text, and that our study of text must all the time take account of what could be happening on stage.

Readers of play scripts constantly need to ask: who is talking, who is responding, what has happened, what are the characters thinking, where are they positioned and how do they relate to others? In novels or short stories, this information is usually provided by the prose, which establishes the character's mood and non-verbal interaction, the time-duration, the location and atmosphere in which the action takes place. It is difficult for many readers to imagine these elements in the blueprint, which is the play script, and teachers thus need to address the theatrical elements which surround the words.

English syllabuses increasingly guide students to plays where the interrelationships between text and action is all-important. Harold Pinter's *The Caretaker*, for example, does not begin with the opening lines, it begins with a non-speaking character, Mick, on stage. His presence seems threatening because of the way he is dressed. His black leather jacket makes us wonder, is he an intruder? He mysteriously exits the stage, leaving the audience in a state of tension as they anticipate his return. The audience, throughout all of the opening dialogue in the first act, constantly wonders when he will reappear. Mick, although he doesn't speak, dominates this section of the play.

The study of a play as a performance event is a challenge to both students and teachers. The important element of dramatic performance which gives a play its life, that is, the collaborative nature of the art, is now central to contemporary theatrical analysis. In order that students may visualise what could be happening on stage, drama teachers are encouraging them to liberate their imaginations from the hypnosis of print without losing sight of the play altogether. However there are students who write about a play as if it were prose. It is not uncommon to read papers in which students write, "In the novel *Hamlet*, Shakespeare tells us about...". This confusion is not entirely unjustified, because if one looks at the types of critical concerns teachers and students have traditionally applied to drama the following appear: themes, plot, character, structure, symbols, imagery and tone. These foci are reinforced by examination questions in English and drama, many of which until recently did not invite answers about dramatic elements. Typical of these questions is the following taken from a Year 12 English examination:

Part C – Drama
Answer ONE of the questions 20-23.
EITHER
20. William Shakespeare, *The Winter's Tale*.
    "The recurring miracle is that life always does renew itself, in spite of the assaults of time and evil."
    Discuss *The Winter's Tale* in the light of this comment.
OR
21. George Bernard Shaw, *Saint Joan*.
    "Shaw clearly did not know what to do with Joan. She is no heroine, no villain – she is nothing."
    Do you agree? What is your view of Shaw's presentation of Joan?
OR
22. Terence Rattigan, *The Winslow Boy*.
    "*The Winslow Boy* is a play about the social importance of decency and trust in the law."
    How does *The Winslow Boy* deal with the issues it raises?

It is clear that questions 20 and 22 ask the students to write about the themes and issues associated with these plays and that question 21 is a character study. Traditional English teachers, raised in the canon of literature model, would have little trouble teaching for these concerns. However, the following question (23) in this paper caused much confusion and anguish when it was set because it demanded far more than the conventional literary responses to character, theme, symbol, plot and the like:

23. Harold Pinter, *The Caretaker*.

What dramatic techniques do you think are most important in *The Caretaker*? How do they contribute to the meaning of the play?

An answer to this question demands an analysis of performance factors such as the impact of Mick's presence on stage before any dialogue is uttered, a response to his leaving the stage and the tension of his expected return, coupled with a response to the stage setting. This question calls on students to explore the fact that a play script is a springboard for collaborative action. I referred above to the role of English syllabuses in guiding students to viewing a play script as a performance document, however as all teachers know, the back-wash effect of examination questions can be a more powerful determiner of curriculum content and emphasis than syllabus aims and objectives. One of the features of questions in drama sections of senior examinations, throughout the English speaking world over the last ten years, has been the increasing orientation to dramaturgical issues and the concomitant shift in teaching and learning approaches.

Unlike poetry or prose, there is no intimate relationship implicit between the reader and a play script. A play script is written for a team – directors, designers, actors etc. – to bring to life. It is not possible to read a text for performance without responding to the different genres within the script. For example, at one point the reader will need to interpret as an actor, at another as a designer. Critical sensibilities and comprehension strategies must be developed which allow the reader "to recognise that the play script consists of a set of instructions to actors, directors, designers and technicians" (Michaels, 1991).

Theatre and performance criticism within English education therefore has a multiplicity of factors to take into account . The division between a semiology of text and a semiology of performance is now passé, having been superseded by analyses of multiple texts and an understanding of basic principles of the *mise en scene* (Pavis, 1980), including the setting, the acting choices, the organisation of space and time. Signifiers such as: the location of the production and the scenery; the relationship between the theatre goers and the performance space; the relationship between off-stage and on-stage; the dynamic between the play script, the director and the dramaturge; the actors and their movements; the lighting and music/sound elements of the performance; the costumes and make-up employed; the pace or tempo and tempo changes implicit in the script and interpreted on stage; the audience response and expectations, and the problems associated with notating a performance, are now being addressed by teachers within the drama components of their programs. In addition many are now concerning themselves with the semiotic implications of film, video and web-site performances. (Pavis, 1992)

Approaches to Teaching Performance Semiotics in English

Given the scope of this paper it will not be possible to outline methods and approaches being adopted by teachers to cover *all* the aspects detailed above, nor to cover the complex issues associated with socio-semiotics and theatre analysis. I shall, however, outline some key areas and teaching strategies which are being employed at The University of Sydney for the education of pre-service and post-graduate English teachers.

The Performance Space and the Mise En Scene

The architecture and location of performance spaces have historical and performance significance – one only needs to reflect on the relationship between ancient Greek play scripts, the social role of fifth century BC festivals and the theatres of the time, or on the significance of the reconstruction of sites such as *The Globe* in Britain, to glimpse an understanding of the important semiological practice implied. The location can indicate to the audience the environment, atmosphere and often the type of action that will occur even before the actors have entered the stage. The type of theatre space: proscenium, open stage, thrust etc., is itself a signifier. A very powerful example of location significance was the 1988 Peter Brook epic production of the *Mahabharata* in Adelaide, Australia. The theatre space was an open-air quarry with the back drop of a massive worked sandstone rock face. The physical setting predisposed the audience for an epic experience before the performance began.

School students often do not feel comfortable attending live theatre performances in grand venues, and this can greatly affect their reception of the text. An analysis of the status of the performance space, the range of traditions, techniques and implicit selection processes contained therein can explain the way audience expectations may or may not be met. Research undertaken at The University of Sydney in 1996-97, in collaboration with Opera Australia, has shown us that many students are intimidated by the Sydney Opera House building itself. The aesthetics and architecture of the building, its imposing stairs and high sail-like roof, combined with the multi-venued, multi-purposed nature of the performance spaces within the structure, signal an environment alien to young people's experience and this psycho-dynamically reduces their capacity to relate to any performances within the Opera House. The location of the performing space is an important element which needs to be addressed before we begin to respond to the language of a play script.

Activity

Divide your class into groups of 5-6 students. Hand out a copy of a well known nursery rhyme, for example, *Jack and Jill*. Each group devises a short play based on the rhyme to be performed in a the theatre space which is a corner of the classroom, that is, the stage is triangular and the front of the stage is no more than three metres across. Each group performs its version to the rest of the class, who then analyse the performance semiotics with particular attention to proxemics (the spacial relationships between actor and actor, actors and location), gesture, vocal pace and projection, and the audience's relationship with the performance.

Tell the students to imagine they are a touring company and they need to adjust their play to suit various theatre spaces. The first space is a conventional proscenium stage. Use your school hall or theatre, or mark out a suitable space in the classroom. The next space is theatre-in-the-round. Take your students onto the school oval and adjust the work to fit a large space similar to the orchestra in Greek theatre. After each enactment deconstruct the performance and note the changes demanded by the changed spaces.

The Setting

The non-literary, visual aspects and spacial relationships in performance contribute a seemingly self-evident and significant semiology and yet visualising the environment in which a play is established by the script or the director's interpretation is difficult for many students and teachers to do. When this is outlined by the playwright, students need to read efferently (in Rosenblatt's terms) in order to imagine the author's visual intention; that is, they need to read the text as we read a non-fiction piece such as a set of instructions (Michaels, 1991, p70). Katherine Thomson, whose plays such as *Diving for Pearls* and *Barmaids* have proved popular with Australian theatre companies, provides clear evidence of the importance of reading for visual cues. It is worth noting that apart from being an excellent word-smith, Thomson is also a very good photographer; her plays have very strong visual elements in them and an understanding of her work requires students to read both aesthetically and efferently. (Rosenblatt, 1978.)

We find it useful for students to study the instructions of the playwright and to draw the set which is outlined. One such example is Arthur Miller's opening to *Death of a Salesman*. In order to visualise and then draw the set, as outlined by Miller, the students need to read the text as if it were a piece of non-fiction even though it is evocative and aesthetically pleasing. Likewise they need to be familiar with technical terms such as "stage right", "stage left", "cross", "apron", etc.

By contrast, in Act 1 of Tom Stoppard's *Rozencrantz and Guildenstern are Dead*, the stage direction contains no scenic information although there is some indication of costume: "Two Elizabethans passing the time in a place without any visible character. They are well dressed – hats, cloaks, sticks and all. Each one of them has a large money bag." Here the director must determine the physical setting/scene in which the action is to be played. Even when playwrights such as George Bernard Shaw do give detailed and specific directions, many directors will eschew the author's guidelines and adopt their own creative perspective. As a result, some playwrights do not regard it as part of their responsibility to include any stage directions. Michael Gow in the preface to *Sweet Phoebe* writes "I've never been interested in stage directions. As a writer ... my job (is) to keep the action moving using only the things the actors say ... Everything else is up to the actors and the director to discover for themselves." (Gow, 1995, p v) The students, through a process of discussing, designing and drawing the sets for plays such as *Sweet Phoebe* or *Rozencrantz and Guildenstern are Dead*, become the director/designer and actors who collaboratively explore and discover the *mis en scene* .

Even a bare stage has meaning. Its shape, its entrances and exits, its horizons, define the possibilities of action. An initial critical assessment of any drama needs to address the force of the building or setting in which the performance takes place and the significance of the set and stage space.

The Collaborative Nature of Drama

In order to imagine what could be happening on stage students are now exploring the various roles in the theatre in so that they might read a script and construct meaning from an appropriate base. They do not need to become expert directors, designers or actors but they do need to experience what it is like to be part of the team whose function it is to make the script come alive. There are many theatre art books which offer detailed examinations of theatre practice but practical experience in a school play or musical for performance is the most successful method for exploring theatre roles in schools.

It is not always possible to involve students in full-scale productions; however, it is easy for teachers to organise role plays to develop an awareness of technical and production values in theatre. *Tennis Match* is such a role play used by many of our English and drama teachers at The University of Sydney. The teacher asks two students to role play a tennis match. The class is then invited to comment on the performance and suggest ways in which it might be improved. The class is then divided into groups which represent experts in the theatre: directors, set designers, make-up, actors, lighting designers, sound designers, costume designers, etc. Each group researches its profession and what its duties might be in the theatre. They then discuss within their groups how they might improve *Tennis Match*. For example, the directors may decide to plan movements; the make-up team may provide sun tans. Each group reports to the class and a modified tennis match is played involving suggestions from the 'experts'. The difference between the first role play and the second is discussed to highlight the importance of the professional roles. Students are then taken to a professional theatre performance and each expert group notes features relevant to their profession (such as direction, lighting, scenery, or props), and reports its findings to the class.

Once students have an understanding of the professional roles of the team needed to produce a play, they are better able to comprehend play scripts because the instructions relevant to various theatre professionals will have meaning and thus visualising the script as performance is facilitated.

Words and Action

A play script does not provide a straight narrative and, unlike novels, the words in plays rarely reveal all that one needs to know. There is an action which surrounds the words and this can augment, juxtapose or even override the surface meaning of the text. Often the term 'sub-text' is used to refer to this complex area; however, the term is inadequate because it implies there is a single text and underneath the words is a bit of action or motivation which augments or changes the meaning. In fact there is little meaning without the dramatic content, which manifests itself through an interplay of words and silence, action and non-action, space and proximity.

An effective exercise for the exploration of action is the communicative exchange first outlined by Dell Hymes, (Widdowson, 1978, p29).

"That's the phone"
"I'm in the bath"
"OK"

This discourse has little in the way of cohesive ties, no overt linguistic features which link the utterances and yet it has coherence. We can imagine contexts which allow it to make sense and so this exchange can be used to draw attention to the relationship between words and action. We have found the following exercise useful: divide the class into small groups and ask each group to devise a performance containing only the above utterances and which makes sense. Each group performs its scene for the others and the class analyses the differences which emerge. The meaning, the coherence, will depend on the dramatic context: the characters and the proxemics combined with the paralinguistic features of intonation, stress, pitch and pace. Students can then discuss what they would write, as a playwright, to indicate how their scene ought to be performed. Would they leave it to the theatre professionals: director, set designer, actors, etc. as Michael Gow does?

Or do they wish to add extra directions, like Arthur Miller or George Bernard Shaw? In this way students can see that dialogue does not convey all the meaning in a play, and that a play script is a blueprint. Much of spoken language only has coherence because of context and action. Unlike novels, plays contain examples of such discourse and hence the need for the production team to give life to the script. Drama teachers are now helping students, through role plays and exercises such as the above, to view the play script as a script and to then apply their insights to the wider field of dramatic literature.

Developments for the Future

In conclusion, I wish to draw attention to two stimulating developments in the field of drama pedagogy. The first is the elaboration of student-centred drama classroom activities based on improvisation. A particularly fine example of this is Cecily O'Neill's work on 'process drama' in *Drama Worlds*. O'Neill's work is significant for English teachers and their students because this type of approach enables them to explore the complexity of performance and the collaborative nature of theatre from the inside.

> The term **process drama** usefully distinguishes the particular kind of complex improvised dramatic event... from that designed to generate or culminate in a theatrical performance, but the difficulty is that it may suggest an opposition to product and perpetuate the sterile separation of this improvised approach from its dramatic roots. In fact, both process and product are part of the same domain. Like theatre, the primary purpose of process drama is to establish an imagined world, a dramatic "elsewhere" created by the participants as they discover, articulate, and sustain fictional roles and situations. (O'Neill, 1995, p viii)

An added benefit of O'Neill's work in process drama is her notion of *pre-text* which refers to the source or impulse for the improvisation to follow. O'Neill suggests a rich variety of literary pretexts, in addition to other areas, and drama teachers find this integration of dramatic and non-dramatic text particularly rewarding.

The second development which gives one great hope is the rise of qualitative, classroom-based research in the field of drama and arts pedagogy. A good example of this work is Philip Taylor's 1996 *Researching Drama and Arts Education*. In this collection of articles from all over the world, we see a commitment to, and celebration of, quality work by teachers, artists and students in the exploration of drama teaching. English educators will find this type of reflection an inspiration to further growth.

Drama has, at its core, the experience of an imagined existence which is made manifest through playtext, body, time and space. The multiple subjectivities and metaphors of society's historical, moral and spiritual consciousness are given symbolic engagement in performance. English teachers are to be applauded for their role in the promotion of future audiences and participants in the dramatic arts.

References

Gow, M, (1995) *Sweet Phoebe*, Sydney: Currency Press.

Michaels, W, (1991) "Teaching Texts" in Hughes, J (ed)*Drama in Education: the State of the Art*, Sydney: EDA.

Miller, A, (1949) *Death of a Salesman*, Middlesex: Penguin Books.

O'Neill, C, (1995) *Drama Worlds: a Framework for Process Drama*, Portsmouth: Heinemann.

Pavis, P, (1980) *Dictionnaire du Theatre*, Paris: Editions Sociales.

Pavis, P, (1992) *Theatre at the Crossroads of Culture*, London: Routledge.

Rosenblatt, L, (1978) *The Reader, the Text, the Poem: A Transactional Theory of the Literary Work*, Carbondale: South Illinios University Press.

Stoppard, T, (1967) *Rosencrantz and Guildenstern are Dead*, London: Faber.

Taylor, P, (1996) *Researching Drama and Arts Education: Paradigms and Possibilities*, London: Falmer Press.

Widdowson, H, (1978)*Teaching Language as Communication*, Oxford: OUP.

Worth Searching For:
The Group Approach to Drama

From the 1960s to the 1980s English teachers with no training in drama found David Adland's *The Group Approach to Drama* (Harlow UK: Longman, 2nd ed, 1981-2) and the accompanying books for Years 7, 8 and 9/10 a godsend. The students' books were packed with wonderful ideas for drama lessons: story outlines, skeleton scripts, situations, characters, dialogues. If you lack confidence in the area of junior secondary drama, these books are well worth searching for. If the school bookroom and the local secondhand bookshop fail you, don't forget that those universities that have a longish history of training teachers will probably still hold the books, and the Internet has booksearch facilities.

24 The Revolution in the Teaching of Shakespeare

Wayne Sawyer and Ken Watson

A visitor enquired of me recently, "What do you do with a play of Shakespeare?" "Act it," I replied. "What else can you do with a play?"

The time is 1917 and the writer is Caldwell Cook in *The Play Way*. Cook goes on to describe, however, what was obviously the more typical approach to the teaching of Shakespeare in his time:

> . . . the Master reads aloud himself. . . . When he has read twenty or thirty lines the work begins. The meaning is examined: dug out of the words, torn out of the idioms, enticed out of the allusions. Every bush is beaten, and hares that start up, whether historical, mythological, moral, geographical, political, etymological, architectural, or ecclesiastical, are pursued, and, if possible, caught. All this must be done by the Form, and the Master should play the part of huntsman while they are hounds
> (Cook, 1920, p195).

Between Cook's call to "Act it" and the relentless chasing of allusions and historical content, as well as identifying minute aspects of Shakespeare's use of verse, there is, of course, a huge gulf. Anecdotal accounts of teaching practice would seem to suggest that much of the twentieth-century teaching of Shakespeare has probably been marked by the 'huntsman and hounds' approach. Reading around the class, stumbling over the verse, awkward and frustrating attempts at 'translation', painful explanations of every word, 'projects' on the Globe theatre and Elizabethan life – these are the practices no doubt responsible for the reputation Shakespeare has 'enjoyed' in the public mind.

In the mid-'80s, however, particularly in Australia and the UK, Cook's call to "Act it" was taken up with great energy. In Australia, people like David Mallick (1984) and Wendy Michaels (1986), and in the UK, Dr Rex Gibson's *Shakespeare and Schools* project helped bring about a revolution which has transformed the teaching of Shakespeare. What is being popularised is an approach which investigates the plays as scripts to be acted – and hence sees them as open to a multitude of interpretations in the hands of classroom 'directors'.

Shakespeare in today's classroom

The teacher of Shakespeare today has two main problems with which to deal before taking up the fundamental issues of how the plays are to be taught, viz:

1. Convincing high school students in the 1990s that texts written in the late 16th and early 17th centuries have anything to say to them, and – related to this – setting a context for the plays.
2. Dealing with the unfamiliarity of the language.

Parallel Improvisations

The first problem is easily overcome by means of presenting the students, in groups, with the challenge of developing improvisations which open up the issues of the play in modern settings. When studying *Twelfth Night*, for example, students could develop one of the following parallel improvisations and then present it to the class:

❖ *Toby, Andy and Mal decide to go off together to a popular holiday resort. Tony and Andy are intent upon having a good time, but Mal turns out to be something of a killjoy, who disapproves of almost everything they do, and seems to consider himself superior to them. Toby and Mal decide to take Mal down a peg or two, but cannot decide how to achieve their aim*

❖ *Some of Viola's friends dare her to go to a party disguised as a boy. To her alarm and embarrassment, one of the girls at the party is greatly attracted to the 'boy'.* (Watson, 1991)

Similarly, *Romeo and Juliet* has great potential for such improvisations using almost any contemporary situation of civil conflict:

❖ *In modern Belfast, a theatre company is about to put on* **Romeo and Juliet***. The cast discuss the pros and cons of setting the play in modern Belfast, and making the feud between the Montagues and Capulets one of religion.*

❖ *In Australia, a Serb boy falls in love with a Croatian girl. How do their parents react?* (Shrubb and Watson, 1991)

Simply placing the play in a modern setting and improvising a "missing scene" also helps create such a context. In *Antony and Cleopatra*, for example, the play opens with Antony's captains discussing his wasted life in Egypt ("Nay but this dotage of our general's o'erflows the measure"). Clearly this is an opening in mid-conversation. As yet, we don't know what has led up to this comment. A teacher could ask students to imagine any situation in which some leader has let down his/her followers by being distracted elsewhere (high school football/netball team; major corporation; political party etc.) Have them play the scene that leads up to a statement something like "Nay but this dotage of our general's o'erflows the measure" and give it a specific setting. (One group of university students developed this before-scene, at the time of the power struggle between Hawke and Keating, in the men's urinal in Parliament House after a Labor Party caucus meeting.) In addition to giving the play's issues a contemporary relevance, such an activity opens up such questions as how the tone of the opening lines might be decided upon.

Shakespeare's Language

When teaching Shakespeare to a junior class, is it actually necessary to read the whole play, especially if it is the students' first experience with Shakespeare? Why not take a (very) few selected scenes and concentrate on scripting, producing and playing them ? (The teacher can "fill in the gaps" with a good narrative.) If for some reason it is necessary to read the whole play, it is useful to have the teacher simply reading and paraphrasing between those scenes which are going to be read closely and acted/directed.

Most students see Shakespeare's language as a bigger hurdle than it is. Hence it is usually necessary to spend some time getting them comfortable with the language so that eventually, in Brenda Pinder's phrase, "they can walk around inside it". We have found that Pinder's "kaleidoscope" idea (Pinder,1991) is a good one for familiarising students with the language. She suggests that before a play is introduced, students are each given a card on which a different line from the play is written. (The line chosen should be one that will fit a variety of circumstances.) The students silently practise saying the line in different ways (lovingly, angrily, sarcastically, timidly etc.). Then they are invited to stand up and walk around the room, saying the line to other students in different ways, as directed by the teacher. This activity generates a great deal of laughter, thus helping to break down the fear of the language, and also familiarises students with the rhythm of Shakespeare's iambic pentameters. Pinder then suggests that the students, in large groups, pool their lines and try to create a short scene (set in a courtroom, or a cafe, or a classroom, or . . .) in which those lines, and no others, are used. The results can be quite surprising.

With older students encountering Shakespeare for the first time we have found a variant of this activity, one based on Shakespeare's insults, very effective. Here the students are each given a card containing one of Shakespeare's insults (a convenient source is *Shakespeare's Insults* by Wayne

Hill and Cynthia Ottchen, 1991) and, after they have memorised the line, they walk around the room using the insult differently with each person they meet. The first time the insult should be spoken using a friendly tone; the second time as though the insult were really meant, and so on. Here are a few that are useful (for teachers as well as students!):

The devil damn thee black, thou cream-fac'd loon! (Macbeth, V iii 11)

Thou clay-brain'd guts, thou knotty-pated fool! (HenryIV, Part 1, II iv 221)

Out, you green-sickness carrion! (Romeo and Juliet, III v 157)

You baggage! You tallow-face ! (Romeo and Juliet, III v 158)

How foul and loathsome is thine image! (Taming of the Shrew I i 33)

Where got'st thou that goose look? (Macbeth, V iii 11)

How now, you secret, black, and midnight hag(s)! (Macbeth, IV i 48)

[You] beetle-headed, flap-ear'd knave! (Taming of the Shrew, IV i 44)

Group soliloquy is another good way of helping students become accustomed to the language of Shakespeare. From the play that is going to be studied, select a soliloquy (or any long speech) and divide it into sense units of roughly the same number as there are students in the class. Allocate one sense unit to each. After each has had the opportunity to try out his/her line in a number of different ways, arrange the class in a circle (in the correct order) and have them read the speech through. By the second time through, the feeling in the speech will become evident. (At this point we must stress that students should **never** be asked to read Shakespeare – or anything else for that matter – to an audience without having had the chance to prepare beforehand.)

Cloze passages and sequencing activities can play their part in familiarising students with Shakespeare's language, and another important pre-acting activity is for students, perhaps in pairs, to explore how tone, pause and emphasis can change the meaning of a line. David Mallick's *How Tall Is This Ghost, John?* (1984) provides some challenging work along these lines, as do most of the volumes in the St Clair *Shakespeare Workshop Series*. For example, students could try playing Hamlet's "There are more things in heaven and earth, Horatio, /Than are dreamt of in your philosophy" with a strong emphasis on "your" and then with a strong, dismissive emphasis on "philosophy". What differences come across? Or , in Act 1 ii of *Hamlet*, they could look at the lines:

Gertrude:... *Thou know'st 'tis common; all that live must die*
Passing through nature to eternity.

Hamlet: *Ay, madam, it is common.*

Gertrude: *If it be,*
Why seems it so particular with thee?

They could explore the effect, first, of having Hamlet speak his line in passive agreement, and then, with a pause after "is" and a strong emphasis on "common". They are then likely to decide that the line becomes an insult, with a correspondingly sharp tone in Gertrude's reply.

The Story Beforehand?

Opinions differ on whether the story of the play should be told to the class before the text is explored. Our view is that, whatever may have been the case in Shakespeare's day, the desire of the modern reader to find out "what happens next" is a strongly motivating force that should not be discounted. But for teachers who do feel the need to make students familiar with the story line first, then either the videos or the booklets in the series *Shakespeare: the Animated Tales* (1992) could be used. In these, Leon Garfield has produced a carefully edited text in which Shakespeare's words are used but are printed as though in prose. Alternatively, one might use Garfield's excellent prose retellings (better, in general, for this purpose than those of Charles and Mary Lamb) in the two volumes of his *Shakespeare Stories* (1985, 1994). Again, our view is that film versions should be used *after* students have considered how the plays might be performed.

A Workshop Approach

At the outset, the students need to realise that what they have in front of them is not **the play**, but a **playscript** or blueprint that has to be turned into a play, and that the play that is created by one set of actors from the script may be very different from the play created by another set of actors from the same script. Indeed, one might not think of there being a play *Macbeth* so much as a sense of *Macbeth-ness* from which a number of different plays could be generated. Hence the activities undertaken in class should, in general, be designed to encourage students to think theatrically, think dramatically.

The booklets in the *Shakespeare Workshop Series* (1988-1998) and the accompanying *Shakespeare: A Teacher's Handbook* (1994) offer many suggestions for active exploration of the dramatic possibilities of each play. Students, working in groups of three or four (of if the script demands it, in larger groups), should be encouraged to draw blocking plans of characters' movements on stage (using, we suggest, sheets of butcher's paper on which is drawn an apron stage in proportion to the stage of the Globe, which was about thirty feet deep and forty feet wide). They should be encouraged to design sets and costumes, and to prepare prompt copies for key scenes (making decisions on how lines should be said, what movements are needed, what lighting should be used, etc). They should be invited to fill in gaps in the text with scenes of their own, and to imagine themselves, in major scenes like *Hamlet* I ii , as courtiers or other bystanders who then comment on what they have just heard and seen (an idea taken up by Tom Stoppard in his *Rosencrantz and Guildenstern Are Dead*). A key scene like the courtroom scene in *The Merchant of Venice* should be developed to early rehearsal stage.

A particularly valuable activity is that of storyboarding, which consists of the picture frame account of the action in a particular scene. A storyboard (see overleaf) is used by film directors to plan the filming of a scene; unlike a simple cartoon, it indicates by the size and shape of the picture within each frame how the action could be shot with a camera. It would be possible to divide the play up among the groups so that the result would be an 'instant play' in cartoon form. This activity emphasises the visual elements of the play, and is an excellent precursor to the viewing of the film version, in whole or in part. Here we would reiterate that in our view film versions are best screened *after* the students have actually confronted the problem of transferring a play into a film. After groups have struggled to create a storyboard of particular scenes, they will watch with great interest what the professionals have done with those scenes, and much more perceptive discussion will follow.

Some of the BBC TV versions are, unhappily, not worth viewing in their entirety, but even the dreariest have scenes that can provide productive viewing and discussion. Some, of course, like the BBC *Richard II* , with Derek Jacobi, and *Othello*, with Anthony Hopkins, are excellent, as are many of the cinema versions, like Polanski's *Macbeth*, the two versions of *Henry V* (Olivier's and Branagh's), Branagh's *Othello*, the Zeffirelli and Baz Luhrman versions of *Romeo and Juliet*, and McKellan's *Richard III*. All these have altered the text in various ways, and this again can lead to fruitful discussion. *Shakespeare into Film* (Béchervaise, forthcoming) provides illuminating essays on filmed versions of Shakespeare.

Already there is an impressive array of materials on Shakespeare available on the World Wide Web. Many, of course, are of doubtful value, but some are excellent, like:

Shakespeare and the Globe Theatre – http://www.rdg.ac.uk/globe

Shakespeare Magazine – http://shakespearemag.com

Virtual Globe Tour –

http://www.delphi.co.uk/ delphi/interactive/16.Globe/walk_intro.html

With so many teaching resources – books, illustrated materials, films and videos, and now Web sites – there is now really no excuse to be made for teachers who fail to make their Shakespeare lessons lively and exciting. But the revolution in the teaching of Shakespeare goes much further than that, for its main thrust is to develop in students the capacity to visualise a playscript in theatrical terms, enabling a performance staged, as it were, in "the skull theatre".*

* The phrase comes from J B Priestley.

HAMLET III i

Long shot on Ophelia.
Hamlet to camera.
Polonius in view to side.

Long/medium shot on Ophelia.
Close-up on Hamlet's arm /
accusing / camera *is* Hamlet.

Medium shot on Claudius,
Polonius. They are in foreground.
Hamlet and Ophelia in background.

Close-up on
Hamlet's mouth.

References

Béchervaise, Neil (ed) (forthcoming) *Shakespeare into Film*, Sydney: St Clair.

Cook, Caldwell (3rd edn, 1920) *The Play Way: An Essay in Educational Method*, London: William Heinemann.

Garfield, Leon (1985) *Shakespeare Stories*, London: Gollancz.

Garfield, Leon (1994) *Shakespeare Stories II*, London: Gollancz.

Hill, Wayne and Ottchen, Cynthia (1991) *Shakespeare's Insults*, London: Vermilion.

Leach, Susan (1992) *Shakespeare in the Classroom*, Buckingham: Open University Press.

Mallick, David (1984) *How Tall Is This Ghost, John?* Adelaide: AATE.

Mellor, Bronwyn (1989) *Reading Hamlet*, Scarborough, WA: Chalkface Press.

Michaels, Wendy (1986) *When the Hurly Burly Is Done*, Sydney: St Clair.

Michaels, Wendy (1996) *Playbuilding Shakespeare*, Melbourne: Cambridge University Press.

Michaels, Wendy, Hise, Jesse and Watson, Ken (1994) *Shakespeare: A Teacher's Handbook*, Sydney: St Clair.

Reynolds, Peter (1991) *Practical Approaches to Teaching Shakespeare*, Oxford: Oxford University Press.

Shakespeare: The Animated Tales London: Heinemann
    Garfield, Leon (1992) *Hamlet*,
    Garfield, Leon (1994) *Julius Caesar* (and other titles).

Shakespeare Workshop Series: Sydney: St Clair Press Various titles, including:
    Hayhoe, Michael (1988) *Creative Work Ideas for* **Macbeth**
    Pinder, Brenda (1991) *A Workshop Approach to* **Hamlet**
    Sawyer, Wayne (1995) *Some by Virtue Fall: A Workshop Approach to* **Measure for Measure**
    Shrubb, Gordon and Watson, Ken (1991) *Star-cross'd Lovers: A Workshop Approach to* **Romeo and Juliet**
    Watson, Ken (1991) *The Food of Love: A Workshop Approach to* **Twelfth Night**.

Of the various editions of Shakespeare designed for school use, among the best are:

Cambridge School Shakespeare: Cambridge University Press.

Harcourt Brace Jovanovich series, especially the Teacher's Books.

Macmillan Shakespeare for Study and Performance: MacMillan.

Exploring Shakespeare: Oxford.

Applications:

Drama

Roslyn Arnold

Here is an application of psychodynamic pedagogy which incorporates drama work and the teaching of poetry. Consistent with the theoretical underpinning which encourages teachers to engage the tacit abilities of their students through expressive approaches to literature, students are given a copy of a poem, for example, John Donne's famous poem "A Valediction forbidding Mourning" and asked to work on the following tasks.

Individually

Imagine John Donne writing this poem at a desk, or while looking at mementoes of a loved one, pending a separation. Using your empathic understanding of how he might feel in such circumstances, write down beside each line the word/s which you think describe his emotional state. Is he despondent, melancholy, hopeful, confused, defensive, perplexed, depressed, cheerful? Ask yourself, "What was Donne feeling as he wrote these lines?"

What was his state of heart?

The answers will come partly from your recall of your own feelings about separation, and partly from your responses to the words of the poem.

When the task has been attempted individually, students might then work in pairs or groups to compare answers. The teacher could help by providing synonyms for affect words so that students can find the shade of meaning which best suits their sense of Donne's feeling state. Students don't always have a ready vocabulary of affect or mood words if they are unaccustomed to approaching literature in this way. It can also help if students are invited to use appropriately coloured highlighter pens to highlight those words which they think signal affect or emotion. It takes a bit of concentration to keep to the task of identifying, not what Donne is thinking, but what he seems to be feeling.

Group Work

Now the class might be grouped in fives or sixes. Individuals in the group each give a summary of the affect words they chose to identify Donne's state of heart. Some consensus needs to be reached about the most significant affect words. When three or four have been agreed upon, the drama part of the exercise can start.

Group Drama

The group is now to devise a three to four minute movement/mime to express the meaning of the poem to themselves and to the rest of the class. This performance might be thought of as a dance or embodied expression of the poem. The point of the exercise is not only to convey a meaning to an audience, but to allow students to move individually and as part of a group in ways which will give them a personalised experience of the poem. It is important for the exercise to be pleasurable and it is worth giving students ample time to work though the activity. Needless to say, if students are of a mind set which thinks poetry needs to be understood as a form of mental gymnastics, this experience will be novel. University students and teachers who have written essays on John Donne's poetry, or taught it by conventional methods, found new meanings in this poem from working in this way. The compass image at the end of the poem is a particular challenge for expressive movement.

Whatever the outcome of the work towards performance, the engagement of feeling, thought and movement in the interests of relating to the complexity of a poem ensures that students are likely to access responses not readily accessed in conventional analyses. Such analyses might well be undertaken once these activities are completed, but from my experience of teaching in this way, there is an energy level and familiarity with the text which informs discussions which follow an empathic, or psychodynamic approach to teaching and learning.

A further extension of this approach is to invite students to write reflections upon their own feelings when they first read the poem, and their feelings as they begin to work through the activities. The point of this is to encourage students to monitor their felt responses as learners and readers of literature, as part of developing their empathic attunement to themselves and others. This ability will enhance their literacy development and capacity for both individual and group learning.

Readers Theatre

Ken Watson

Readers Theatre should be part of every English teacher's armoury, providing as it does an excellent way of putting the spoken word back into prose and poetry. It is particularly valuable for middle and upper secondary students who may be resistant to the idea of choral verse speaking.

In readers theatre, a group prepares a short story or poem for presentation to the class. Groups are often bigger than the three or four members recommended for other kinds of small group work; often a group of six or seven is needed for effective presentation of a poem. The group decides how best to use the voices at its disposal: in a poem, for example, some lines might be said by a single voice, whilst others might said by two or three, or by the whole group. After such decisions have been made, the group has three or four practice runs before presenting the poem or story to the class. There is no need for memorisation: the students always read from hand-held scripts.

In its simplest form, a readers theatre presentation has the performers standing or sitting in a semi-circle in front of the class (stools from the science laboratory provide excellent seating, for reasons given below). Most groups, however, like to depart from this simple arrangement in ways that will give added emphasis to the poem or story.

Since a major aim of readers theatre is to encourage the audience to use their imaginations, props and costumes are not essential, but again most groups like to use a few key props and sometimes feel it necessary to distinguish characters from one another by using different coloured sashes and the like. In presenting James Thurber's version of *Little Red Riding Hood*, for example, one group thought that a basket and a toy gun were essential.

Again, readers theatre requires very little in the way of action. In fact, excessive movement can distract the audience's attention from the text. If a short story is being presented, and there are entrances and exits, these can be conveyed by the use of the stools mentioned above. Characters who are off-stage at the beginning sit with their backs to the audience; when they enter they swivel round to face the audience and exit by swivelling back again. If a character is going on a journey, he/she simply walks staying in the same place.

Those who have written on the techniques of readers theatre recommend a technique known as 'off-stage focus', where characters never look at each other when they converse, but at some imagined point above the audience's heads where their vision intersects. This ensures that the readers' voices are projected towards the audience.

The relative absence of stage action and props emphasises the importance of the voices of the performers: tone, pause, emphasis (and facial expression) become vital.

Of course, if the groups have plenty of time at their disposal they may wish to experiment with music and sound effects. But one of the great advantages of readers theatre is that it is possible for a group to give an excellent rendition of a poem with only half an hour's preparation, and a good readers theatre presentation of a short story may not require much more time than that.

References

Robertson, M E (1990) "True Wizardry: Readers Theatre in the Classroom" PEN 79, Sydney: PETA.
Sloyer, Shirlee (1982) *Readers Theatre: Story Dramatisation in the Classroom*, Urbana, Ill: NCTE.

The Play Grid

John Hughes

In order to help students understand what happens in a play, teachers can encourage young people to do what many directors do: that is, notate the action of the play via a play grid. For each section or scene in the play the director writes short notes on the following:

✧ Who enters. ✧ Who exits. ✧ What is the setting. ✧ What happens.

The grid can be filled out either by reading the play or viewing a video. It is not advisable to fill out the grid while watching a live performance as this would destroy the essential connection between audience and performer.

Sample grid

Section	Who Enters	Who Exits	The Setting	The Action
Scene 1				
Scene 2				
Scene 3				
Scene 4				

Section VI:
Aspects of
Language

25 Language in Schools: Some Questions and Answers

What Do We Know About Language Development in the Secondary School Years?

Ken Watson

Language acquisition in the early years is extraordinarily rapid : the native speaker has normally mastered well over 90% of the grammar of English by the age of five and by the age of eight has achieved almost complete mastery of the phonological and morphological features of English. This proficiency has come about by using language for real purposes in real situations.

Semantic development, of course, continues throughout childhood and adolescence. One category of words which seems to be acquired relatively late is connectives: many children do not grasp the full import of words like 'although', 'unless', 'thus', 'however' until adolescence.

As far as the secondary school years are concerned, language growth is largely a matter of:

1. a greater sensitivity to the demands of the social context;
2. a growth in the ability to handle the more abstract modes of discourse;
3. an increasing competence in using the language in a variety of written forms;
4. an increasing awareness of the language itself.

Loban's longitudinal study (1976) revealed that a mark of linguistic maturity is the ability to use language to express tentativeness. This suggests that teachers should encourage small-group discussion in a co-operative atmosphere.

What is 'Whole Language'

Ken Watson

Whole language is clearly a lot of things to a lot of people; it is not a dogma to be narrowly practised. It's a way of bringing together a view of language, a view of learning, and a view of people, in particular two special groups of people: teachers and kids. (Goodman, 1986, p5)

Perhaps one should start by saying what whole language is not. It is *not* another name for the look-and-say method of teaching reading; in fact, one of the key research studies that underpin whole language is Ken Goodman's demonstration that it is more difficult for poor readers to read words in isolation than it is for them to read the same words in a meaningful context.

Secondly, whole language is *not* a methodology, but rather a philosophy, a set of beliefs about language, the central one being that language is best learnt in authentic, meaningful situations, not through fragmenting it into decontextualised 'bite-sized' pieces. But the 'whole' in whole language means more than this: it refers to the expansion of literacy learning from narrow notions like 'decoding' ("Decoding?" asked Margaret Meek. "Are we spies?") to concern with the personal and social functions of language.

Finally, as far as the teaching of reading is concerned, whole language does *not* turn its back on phonics, but insists that the grapho-phonic system is but one, and probably not the most important, of the three cuing systems (see page 136) and that the evidence shows that a totally phonics-based program for teaching reading will be counter-productive. Most of those who see themselves as whole-language teachers would adhere to the following:

1. They hold a constructivist view of learning, that is, the learner's constructive mental activity is placed at the heart of the learning process. They reject totally the behaviourist view of learning.

2. They believe that teachers should "work with children in the natural direction of their growth" (Goodman).

3. They believe that teaching should be dialogic and transactional. Most would subscribe to the notion of negotiating, as far as possible, the curriculum with their students. In terms of Barnes's 'transmission – interpretation' continuum (see page 39), they would see themselves as at the interpretation end of the continuum. As Barnes puts it, a teacher who sees language as a means of interpretation "will see discussion and writing as ways of helping pupils to think more effectively, and will credit them with the ability to make sense of experience for themselves by talking and writing about it. For him (sic), knowledge is something which each person has to make for himself." (Barnes, 1973, p15)

4. They believe that language learning occurs best in an environment that encourages risk-taking; they believe in the concept of 'the virtuous error', ie, that making errors is one of the main ways in which children learn.

5. Whole-language teachers are 'kid-watchers', assessing student progress based on observation and concentrating on what students *can do*.

Like all movements, in education and elsewhere, whole language has been misinterpreted – sometimes by its adherents. It is, after all, possible to be *too* child-centred. And it is true that it is only recently that whole language has begun to take on board insights from critical literacy, recognising that it has in the past failed to account for power relations in its analysis of social constructions of meaning.

What Are the Teacher's Responsibilities With Regard to Standard English?

Wayne Sawyer

Standard English is that variety or dialect of English used by educated people in formal situations, particularly in writing. It is the form most widely understood internationally. It is the dialect of English which carries the most prestige. Hence, while there is nothing intrinsically better about this variety of the language, it is the language of power in our society. For this reason, all students need to be able to have access to it since so many social judgements are made based on its use.

In the past teachers attempted to eradicate non-standard usages but now it is accepted that teachers should value students' home dialect as well as help students use the variety of English appropriate to a particular situation. Hence teaching language should be a question of broadening students' linguistic repertoire in order to handle a variety of language contexts, rather than attempting to replace their own language as 'wrong'. One way in which this can be done is through role-playing situations that require the standard form.

How Valuable are the Language Exercises that Require Students to Fill in the Blanks, Correct Faulty Sentences, Detect Punctuation Errors, etc?

Wayne Sawyer

Young children learn language by using it for real purposes in real contexts and there is no reason to suppose that older children will learn in a different way. The trouble with traditional exercises is that they are divorced from meaning and context. Further, most textbooks containing such exercises are so designed that all the pupils are expected to do the same exercises at the same time, though it is extremely unlikely that all would be experiencing the particular difficulty that the exercise is designed to overcome.

Such exercises all too frequently rehearse what the pupils already know through use, and take up time that would more profitably be devoted to meaningful reading, writing and talking.

There are, however, many excellent course books on the market for junior and middle secondary students. These tend to be characterised by such features as:

✦ Activities in all four areas of reading, writing, talking and listening.
✦ The integration of activities in these four areas.
✦ Opportunities for a range of *extended* discourse.
✦ Talking and writing for a variety of audiences, functions and purposes.
✦ Teaching writing conventions and skills in a particular context.
✦ Allowing a range of responses to texts.
✦ Allowing for student choice.
✦ Encouragement of small group work.
✦ Some degree of self-assessment.

Should a Grammatical System be Taught?

Ken Watson and Wayne Sawyer

Research on Grammar and Writing

Language is rule-governed behaviour, but an explicit knowledge of the rules is not required in order to use the language. The five-year-old child has internalised the grammar of English simply by growing up in an English speaking community. As Martin Joos pointed out over thirty years ago, "normal fluent speech obeys about five or six grammatical rules per second: a critic can seldom detect, in a child's speech, more than one conflict with standard grammar per ten seconds on the average" (Mackay, 1968). Research since the beginning of the 20th century has failed to demonstrate any link between knowledge of a grammatical system and an ability to write. Roland Harris's famous UK study is a prime example of the many experiments designed to explore the relationship between knowledge of traditional grammar and ability to write. Harris's study paired groups of classes, with one class in each pair having a formal grammar lesson per week while the other class had no grammar and an extra writing period. At the end of the two-year study, the non-grammar classes had made such significant gains in their writing and use of grammar that Harris concluded that "the study of grammatical terminology had a negligible or even a relatively harmful effect upon the correctness of children's writing". (Harris, 1965.)

In the 1970s Elley and others carried out a study to determine whether *the type* of grammar study made a difference. In this study traditional grammar groups were compared with transformational grammar groups. Elley concluded that "English grammar, whether traditional or transformational, has virtually no influence on the language growth of typical secondary school students."

The evidence in this area throughout the century has been so conclusive that it led Andrew Wilkinson to write in 1986, after summarising the key research, that "there is no point in (any further research). It is, after all, centuries since anyone took the trouble to demonstrate that the earth moves round the sun." Wilkinson also supplies an answer to why politicians continue to insist on the importance of grammar study when he says that "to these people learning of grammar represents a disciplining of the flesh, a punishing of the rebellious spirit, and the ultimate guarantee of a stable society. In its very uselessness lies much of its value." (Wilkinson, 1986, pp23, 34.)

So – No Grammar At All?

Given the kind of abstract study which the study of grammar is, it is not difficult to see why research has shown so conclusively the lack of connection between this knowledge and writing ability. If one draws an analogy with driving, one could ask what it is that makes a good driver. Is it driving under particular road and traffic conditions or being able to describe how the carburettor works? Does knowing how an anti-lock braking system works actually make one react quicker in an emergency? Are mechanics better drivers than everybody else? They may know *how* the car works and *how* the bits fit together, but do they actually operate in traffic better than other people?

Nevertheless, teachers should not avoid teaching some grammatical terminology as a useful shorthand. This is simply part of the language of the subject. (When we talk to the mechanic it is useful to be able to say, "When I let the clutch out, the car slips back a gear" – far more useful than trying to say, "When I take my foot off that pedal on the left, the stick thing I work with my hand shakes and wobbles, the car makes this whining noise and kind of stops suddenly and jumps forward".) This can be done usefully and efficiently through the kind of ten-minute mini-lesson approach that Nancie Atwell has popularised. Very useful teaching techniques are contained in Don Smedley's *Teaching the Basic Skills*. The advantage of such a shorthand terminology is evident when discussing aspects of their writing with children and also when discussing literature with older students.

Proponents of a functional grammar argue that this grammar does aid children's writing (see next section). We would argue that the fundamental research to support this view – equivalent research to that of Harris and Elley – has yet to be done.

A Minimal School Grammar
Bob Walshe

The word *grammar* has twenty or more dictionary meanings. As description of the whole system/structure underlying the language, grammar is too vast to teach in schools. Yet students use grammar all the time. Even five year-olds have a good grip on it, *unconsciously*. However, there *is* a need to teach a minimal grammar that provides a terminology and just enough principles to ensure conformity with a number of conventions of (mainly) the written language. This minimum is not burdensome and can mostly be taught at the point of individual need in purposeful writing, rather than as mechanical exercises. Decades of research have shown no gain to writing from routine grammar instruction.

Let's never forget that writing is chiefly about getting meaning clear for a reader. A writer's main struggle is with ideas, with content. Every writing topic is a question, demanding inquiry, problem-solving, the most rigorous thinking of which the writer is capable. And mixed up in that complex think-write process, but not predominating, is the student's struggle with the written medium, including a little attention to grammar. There the teacher helps individuals as needed. In addition, when launching the writing, the teacher, without distracting from involvement with the ideas of the topic, can point to certain grammatical usages that need watching. Better still, the teacher will ask for attention to these when the student self-edits the first draft. At other times there can be follow-up, specific instruction, demonstrations, if a wider need is perceived. So what would be included in a minimal intelligible school grammar?

A Minimal Intelligible School Grammar: 7 rule-governed areas, imparted across 12 school years

one

Recognition and naming of the main word classes

noun	pronoun	article
verb	adverb	adjective
preposition	conjunction	interjection

two

Recognition of the four formations above word level

phrase	clause	sentence	paragraph

three

A sentence needs a subject and its verb

Lacking either, a non-sentence or fragment results. However, a skilful 'verbless sentence' is acceptable, its context implying an omitted verb.

These are the only aspects of grammar writers K-12-Professional need to know. They are learnt with little difficulty by students/teachers and are sufficient in discussion of slips that arise day by day in class writing.

four

A verb must agree in number with its subject

Agreement is usually obvious when verb and subject are close together but not when they are widely separated in a long sentence.

five

Tense / Time

This needs to be consistent.

six

Subject and object forms of pronouns need special care

Identification is vital to the use of I / we / she / he /they for *subjects*, and me / us / her / him / them for *objects*.

seven

Both active and passive verbs have value

In most situations, the active form is more forceful, but the passive form has a few uses.

Adapted from an article in *The Education Network* (8/9, 1996), the journal of the Australian Education Network (AEN)

References

Atwell, Nancie (1987) *In the Middle*, Portsmouth: Boynton/Cook.

Barnes, Douglas (1973) *Language in the Classroom*, Milton Keynes: Open University Press.

Crowhurst, Marion (1994) *Language and Learning Across the Curriculum*, Scarborough: Allyn and Bacon Canada.

Elley, W B, et al (1976) "The Role of Grammar in a Secondary School English Curriculum", *Research in the Teaching of English* 10 (1), Spring, pp 5-21.

Goodman, Kenneth (1986) *What's Whole in Whole Language*, Portsmouth, NJ: Heinemann.

Harris, Roland (1965) "The Only Disturbing Feature" in *The Use of English*, 16 (3), pp 197-202.

Loban, Walter (1976) *Language Development, K-12* Urbana: NCTE.

MacKay, D (1968) "Language Standards and Attitudes: A Response" in Marckwardt, A (ed) *Language and Language Learning*, Champaign, Ill: NCTE.

Sawyer, Wayne and Bernhardt, Sandra (1986) "Textbooks for English: 7-10", *English Curriculum Paper #2*, Sydney: NSW Department of Education, Directorate of Studies (June).

Smedley, Don (1983) *Teaching the Basic Skills*, London: Methuen.

Wilkinson, Andrew (1986) *The Quality of Writing*, Milton Keynes: Open University Press.

Functional Grammar

Tina Sharpe and Julie Thompson

The explicit teaching of grammar in the classroom has again become a focus of political and educational debate in the '90s. Lying behind this debate is the question of what we actually mean by the word *grammar*. In this short overview we will discuss the various grammars of English and look in detail at aspects of the particular grammar which has attracted much interest and debate over the last decade: functional grammar, or more accurately, systemic functional grammar.

What Are The Different Grammars?

TRADITIONAL GRAMMAR

Since Greek and Roman times, there have been many attempts to write down the rules governing languages as systems. This endeavour has generated a number of different grammars. Best known is what has come to be referred to as Traditional Grammar. This grammar is based on Latin grammatical forms and focuses on classifying words into classes such as 'noun', verb, 'adjective', 'pronoun'. The classroom application of this kind of analysis focuses on the application of rules for sentence-level analysis and perceptions of correct usage.

The primary focus of teachers working with this model has evolved into helping students to use language in the way that is considered 'correct'. However, some problems associated with traditional grammar result from trying to adapt a framework designed to describe the rules of Latin, to English – a language which works differently. For example, the condemnation in English associated with beginning a sentence with a conjunction, ending a sentence with a preposition, or splitting an infinitive are all based on Latin grammatical structures and are not always necessarily appropriate in certain circumstances in English. *Who did you go with?* is more appropriate in contemporary English than *With whom did you go?* which may be more 'correct' according to the rules of Latin.

Not only are these structures considered wrong, they have sometimes been taken as markers of an uneducated user of the standard English language. The study of traditional grammar has been used as a kind of social and educational gatekeeper. In the classroom, the tendency has been to focus on parsing and analysis for its own sake as a kind of mental exercise. This kind of approach to grammar began to fall into disrepute during the 1970s.

FORMAL GRAMMAR
Formal or structural grammars are other approaches to describing how language works. These are psychologically based models of language and they too focus on language as a set of class-based rules. They focus on the rules of how words of various classes can be combined and concentrate more on what it is possible to say rather than what makes sense. In Chomsky's famous example, it is possible grammatically to say, *Invisible green ideas sleep furiously*, but it makes no sense semantically.

The formal models of grammar explain why this sentence is accurate but not why it is meaningless. The best-known proponent of this type of grammar is Noam Chomsky, who sees this as a tool for linguists rather than for classroom teachers.

FUNCTIONAL GRAMMAR
A third type of grammar is a functional one which has attracted much interest from academics and classroom teachers alike. Devised by M A K Halliday to provide a systematic and socially anchored description of English, it was further developed by linguists such as Hasan, Martin and Matthieson. It systematically describes how language works but, in doing so, relates the patterns of words, sentences and whole texts to the meanings and social purposes intended by the writer or speaker. As the name suggests, a functional approach allows its users to analyse not only whether a text is grammatically correct but also whether it is socially appropriate and achieves its intended purposes.

The advantage of drawing on a functional grammar is the way it allows careful examination of how individual words and sentences are used to create meaning as part of a whole text. It allows for understanding of how word choice in one sentence relates to and builds on to the way the whole text conveys meaning.

Although re-emerging interest in grammar may be politically motivated by 'falling literacy standards', English teachers often express the view that the teaching of grammar of itself is useful and valuable. In addition, both teachers and students feel the need to be able to discuss in detail the way language is working to create different meanings in different contexts. To do this, a common, shared systematic way of describing the way language works is needed – a language with which to talk about language, a shared metalanguage.

So, while any grammar will provide such a metalanguage, choosing to use a grammar which can look beyond sentence level not only enables a description of the pattern of words in phrases and sentences but also provides an explicit picture of how they fit into the way the whole text works. Such a metalanguage allows teachers and students to look at a 'successful' text and talk about how and why it is successful, and it provides a set of tools for assisting students to analyse, evaluate and thus improve their own writing.

WHAT EXACTLY IS THE FUNCTIONAL MODEL OF LANGUAGE?

The functional model of language is concerned with grammatical choices which are deliberately made with awareness by the language user of what the subject matter is (Field), what the roles and relationships are (Tenor) and whether the text is more written-like or spoken-like (Mode). In addition, the model accounts for the predictable and describable patterns of text organisation which allow the text to achieve its meaning and social purpose and are shared by the language users in a community (Text-types or Genres). The model incudes a systematic grammatical framework which incorporates both functional and class-based analysis. In addition, it accounts for how each aspect of the grammar provides the language user with a resource which relates directly to either Field, Tenor or Mode. It also allows for connections to be made between the text organisation, or stages of the text-type, and the use of aspects of the grammar.

In this short article it will not be possible to examine how a functional grammatical analysis can provide specific information about each of these influences on the text. We will simply exemplify three aspects of the grammar in relation to the narrative text-type and illustrate briefly how they can inform a student's understanding of how this particular text-type has been constructed. The skills involved in this analysis can be used with any text across the curriculum by teachers and students to improve both reading and writing. The terminology used here will, for the most part, be that adopted by the general educational community through syllabus development, with the more technically accurate label given in brackets.

Research into the application of this model for the secondary English classroom has been undertaken by Rothery and Steglin as part of the *Write it Right* classroom research project. They identified three major categories of text-types used in the discipline of English, ie: 'story', 'response', 'factual'. Each category can be further refined to reveal a number of sub-text-types.

Teachers and students find an understanding of these text-types a useful starting point to support their reading and writing. In addition, it is even more useful for them to use an explicit metalanguage to describe the language patterns or grammar of these text-types.

Using excerpts from the picture book *The Sign of the Sea Horse: A Tale of Greed and High Adventure in Two Acts* by Graeme Base, we will illustrate briefly how knowledge of the stages of the text, and the associated grammatical choices, allows the student to account for the success of the text. As the focus of this article is the grammar associated with the functional model of language, we will examine three aspects of the grammar – verb types, noun groups and sentence beginnings.

The Sign of the Sea Horse is written in the **form** of a **melodrama** in two acts and includes a prelude and an epilogue. It uses the **narrative text-type**. The characters all live in a marine environment and each has classic characteristics consistent with melodrama – for example, the hapless female, Pearl, and the gallant hero, Bert.

In the classroom, a first analysis would establish the purpose of the text, ie: to entertain and pass on social values. Students would then be asked to note the structure of the text. They would be looking for how the author has deliberately and creatively manipulated the predictable and simple structure of the narrative text-type (orientation, complication, evaluation, resolution, coda) to create a complex and sophisticated chain of events, in different settings which enhance the story.

VERB TYPES

In many traditional classrooms, students have been taught that verbs are 'doing words'. Functional grammar distinguishes a number of verb (process) types: action (material), thinking/feeling (mental), saying (verbal) and being/having (relational). These describe the function that the verb is performing in the particular sentence and becomes useful when students need to focus closely on why certain verbs are effective in a sentence.

For example, in examining the complication stage of the narrative to analyse how the author creates action and a sense of movement in a text, the teacher would draw the students' attention to the verb choice and would highlight the deliberate use of action verbs within this stage. For example:

And through the splintered timbers **crashed** *a massive, orange claw.*
It **smashed** *the door to smithereens, then* **disappeared** *from sight.*

The choice of strong action verbs propels the scene forward, building a sense of excitement until the anticlimax of the disappearance. As the class moves to analysing the next stage of the text, students will be using the same skills to identify text similarities and differences in the patterns of verb usage.

In contrast, as the author moves into the evaluation stage, which is the stage where the characters reflect on their thoughts and feelings in relation to the events, different verb types are used to explore inner responses – for example:

A cornered Shark **is** dangerous, as any Catfish **knows**,
And Finny quickly **realised** this scene could come to blows.

These verbs are from the two types of verbs: thinking/feeling (mental) and being/having (relational). This information is useful to the writer of a narrative because the evaluation stage adds depth to a narrative and engages the reader as they come to understand the inner thoughts and feelings of the characters. It is also the evaluation stage of a narrative in which the text's message is most clearly visible.

Teachers and students armed with this part of the metalanguage can explicitly analyse the deliberate effect of verb choice on the reader. Similarly, they can use their knowledge of this resource to identify where and how the author has constructed the message of the text. Students who have purposefully looked for the verbs of being and thinking/feeling to locate the message can, in turn, also use them in their own analysis of the text to ensure that they interpret rather than retell the story.

THE NOUN GROUP

When analysing the structure of a narrative, the teacher might focus on how, in the orientation stage, a detailed picture of the world of the narrative is being created. Here nouns, adjectives and phrases are combined to form noun groups, which create strong images of the characters and setting. Grammatical analysis of the way a noun group is constructed assists students to use this resource to its full potential in their own writing and to unpack how the description has been created in an analysis of a text.

One of the most useful constituents of the noun group for students to focus on, is the distinction that functional grammar makes between different types of adjectives – the most common being describing adjectives and classifying adjectives. (For example, in the noun group, *the menacing tiger shark, menacing* would be analysed as a describing adjective and *tiger* as a classifying adjective.)

In an example from *Sign of the Seahorse,*

*In a feat of wondrous strength, Bert raised **his mighty claw***

Graeme Base has used a describing adjective. This is in contrast to a technical work on crabs which would have been far more likely to refer to the claw as *a jointed claw*. In that case, the technical author would be using a classifying adjective because the purpose of the writing is different. Students of English need to understand that a limited number of classifying adjectives in a narrative lend credibility to a description, but overuse of them makes the description far too technical for a narrative. Conversely, in scientific writing the use of describing adjectives weakens the scientific validity of the writing.

SENTENCE BEGINNINGS (THEME)

English teachers have always taught that varying sentence beginnings is important for successful writing. However, technical understanding of the grammatical patterns of different types of sentence beginnings can give students active control over their writing and also a powerful tool for analysis. Functional grammar provides us with a means of understanding that the first elements of a clause carry particular significance for the reader. Take, for example, the quotation already examined above:

In a feat of wondrous strength, Bert raised his might claw.

Had the author chosen to say *Bert raised his mighty claw in a feat of wondrous strength*, the emphasis on *the feat of wondrous strength* would not have been as strong. Students need to know that they can influence the impact their writing has on the reader by carefully choosing which element to put first. Note, when a reader finds an element in the first position that is unexpected, additional attention is drawn to it. So, by not placing *Bert*, the subject of the sentence, in its expected initial position, the impact of the use of the opening position is maximised.

Explicit teaching of the impact of different sentence beginnings helps students to both deliberately, rather than randomly, craft the variation in their own sentence beginnings and to critically evaluate their own and others'. Technically, functional grammar calls this first element *Theme* because of the way the element influences the 'flavour' of the clause.

A Final Word

In this brief overview we have attempted to provide a context and rationale for the explicit teaching of grammar in the English classroom. It is our experience that the grammar associated with the Functional Model of Language provides us with a shared metalanguage and explicit tools to assist students in critiquing and creating text, by allowing for the recognition of patterns at sentence, paragraph, stage and whole-text level. This article merely flags some of the grammatical resources useful in the study of English. We recommend that you seek out other information and resources, some of which are listed below.

References

Base, G (1992) *The Sign of the Sea Horse: A Tale of Greed and High Adventure in Two Acts*, Viking.
Cusworth, R (1994) *What is a Functional Model of Language?* PETA Pen No 95.
Halliday, M A K (1985) *An Introduction to Functional Grammar*, London: Edward Arnold.
Martin, J and Rothery, J (1993) "Grammar: Making Meaning in Writing" in *The Powers of Literacy: A Genre Approach to Teaching Writing*, edited Cope, B and Kalantzis, M, New York, London and Philadelphia: The Falmer Press.
Williams, G (1993) *Using Systemic Grammar in Teaching Young Learners: An Introduction in Literacy, Learning and Teaching: Language as Social Practice in the Primary School*, edited Unsworth, L, Melbourne: Macmillan.
Disadvantaged Schools Project (1994) *Write it Right: Exploring Literacy in School English*, Metropolitan East Region, NSW Department of School Education.

Additional Suggested Reading

Butt, D, Fahey, R, Phinks, S, and Yallop, C (1995) *Using Functional Grammar: An Explorer's Guide to Functional Grammar*, NCELTR.

Collerson, J (1994) *English grammar: A Functional Approach*, PETA.

Collerson, J (1997) *Grammar in Teaching*, PETA.

Derewianka, B (1990) *Exploring How Texts Work*, PETA.

Eggins, S (1994) *An Introduction to Systemic Functional Linguistics*, Pinter.

Gerot, L and Wignell, P (1994) *Making Sense of Functional Grammar*, AEE, Cameray.

Kalantzis, M and Wignell, P (1988) *Explain, Argue, Discuss: Writing for Essays and Exams*, Common Ground Press.

CD-ROM (1997) *Literacy for Learning: Years 5-8*, NPDP, NSW.

Sharp, T and Thompson, J (1993) *Accessing Learning: Language and Literacy Development in Key Learning Areas*, CEO, Sydney.

Applications: Language and Media

Mass Media Activities

Eva Gold

For our purposes, the definition of media is limited to print journalism, television, film, radio. These activities examine the function of the media and the role they play in building our perceptions of society and the world. While its intervention between events, institutions and the audience is designed to appear natural, it is the purpose of some of these activities to draw attention to the ways in which meaning is created through the processes of construction by the media.

✦ A *broad overview of the effect of the media in our lives* can be gained by documenting the extent of media penetration. Consider our access to a wealth of music, information, recreational games, imagined worlds. Invite students to choose one of these resources/products for investigation over a week. Construct a survey that examines such factors as:

⬧ how much of the resources each student receives (hours per day);

⬧ the different media through which the resources are received (self created, books, television etc);

⬧ the student's level of awareness of and participation in the reception (distracted, active involvement or generation);

⬧ the different genres of presentation (news report, interview, encyclopaedia entry, orchestral symphony, rap, heavy metal, advertising jingle).

✦ Are there substantial differences in media behaviour within the class? In which areas? And what do these depend on? What statements can be made about these students' demographic?

✦ How might students change one of the media products in their survey to suit a different audience? Brainstorm a range of audiences and make the necessary adaptations to the product for each type of audience.

This activity can be enlarged to a more specific analysis of the *significance of audience to different media products.* Students could find examples of a single media product such as an advertisement for chocolate or report of an event (opening of theme park) and compare and contrast them in terms of purpose, the relationship between writer/presenter and audience (how can they tell?) and the social/economical assumptions that are present. Students can now construct their own items directed at different audiences. Some possible audience features might be male/female, child/adult, general/specialised interest.

✦ Media products do not merely reflect the nature of the audience, they also define it. *How do magazines or advertisements construct social roles and attitudes* such as gender, childhood or taste? You could choose a media product directed at a specific audience and consider it in terms of who is speaking and who is silent. Who is active and who passive? What do these relationships suggest about social roles? Who is excluded? What attitudes/interests/needs remain unacknowledged. In what ways might these exclusions be important?

✦ *Understanding the role of visuals in media:* Pictures are integral to the meaning of any media text. Visual images do not merely illustrate the verbal component of a media text. Because they allow multiple interpretations, it is the image that often determines the focus of the verbal content but is the verbal text that defines a particular meaning of the visual and develops its connotative potential.

Students can understand this concept quite easily by taking any photograph of the kind distributed by press agencies, placing them into different media with a range of audiences (eg, news report, women's magazine, sports report, children's program) and writing the surrounding text.

This exercise has comic potential by taking significant news images and giving them facetious captions or inventing entirely erroneous but plausible stories.

So What Is News?

Look at the front page of any newspaper or view/listen to the summary update of the news bulletin and consider the following:

✦ How do they fulfil the criteria of newsworthiness? (Are the items recent? How are they relevant to the audience? Are they negative? Do they deal with the rich and famous? How do they fulfil the audience's preconceptions?)

✦ By looking at the rest of the paper or listening to/viewing the full news bulletin, find items that are of historical or social significance that were not considered worthy for front page treatment. Why? Can you suggest the extent to which news reporting shapes our view of events and society?

Compare and contrast the front page of tabloid and broadsheet newspapers and news updates on commercial and public broadcasters:

- ✦ Does their content/emphasis differ?
- ✦ Are there differences in style? What are they?
- ✦ Can you readily see the difference between reportage and commentary? How? Has the distinction between fact and interpretation been blurred? (If students have difficulty with this exercise, reproduce a news story with key expressions marked and invite them to replace them with other choices that are more or less colourful.)
- ✦ To what extent is the purpose to inform or to persuade or to entertain?
- ✦ Which seems to have the most authority? What makes you think so? Why have you chosen these criteria to make your judgement?

I read it in the papers so it must be true

It is sometimes suggested that tabloid newspapers are a more honest brand of journalism as their sensationalism invites readers to be sceptical and constantly question the truth of the text. Broadsheets, on the other hand, give the appearance of objectivity and so invite readers to accept their version of events so becoming compliant rather than resistant readers. Do you think this is a valid argument?

Current Affairs Programs – The Stories Behind the News

It is quite fruitful to tape segments of current affairs programs and consider them in terms of narrative or dramatic conflict. The structural components of these stories depend on simplification through clarification into binary oppositions such as "victim" and "villain" or "little Aussie battler" and "massive exploitative global corporation". Often these stories echo traditional mythic, literary or folk tales such as fall-of-hero-figure, dream-come-true, clash-of-giants, etc. Students could consider such questions:

- ✦ What is the essential conflict?
- ✦ In what ways are the antagonists made to appear wrong and in what ways right?
- ✦ Whose position is the viewer invited to support?
- ✦ Can you think of a well known story or situation that is similar?
- ✦ If you wanted to present a different view of the story, what kinds of questions might you explore?

Video Clips

Video clips are useful resources for the analysis of media products because of their brevity, concentration of filmic techniques and 'coolness' factor. For the purpose of analysis it is helpful to begin by separating the sound and the visuals. When listening to the music, consider such questions as:

- What is the situation outlined in the song?
- What mood is developed?
- What words or phrases are easily grasped?

Now look at the visuals:

- How much emphasis is there on the artist's (s') performance?
- Is there a succession of images which offer an interpretation of the meaning of the song? How? Through narrative? Metaphor? Symbol? All of the above?
- How is colour used? Movement? Style of custom/set?
- What generic shifts such as animation, montage etc, are used and to what effect?
- How has the editing of visuals extended the emotional scope of the song?
- How do the visuals and audio interrelate to develop the meaning and impact of the video clip?

Creative extension . . .

- Take any piece of music that you believe will make an effective video clip and create a storyboard of images to accompany it. If you have the resources, film it.

The Popular Television Series

It can be interesting to view these in terms of their context and consider such questions as:

- Why has this channel chosen to screen the series? (What image of itself is it projecting? What kind of audience is it attempting to attract?)
- Why has it scheduled the program at this time slot? What is the intended audience? Does this differ from the real audience?
- What advertisements support the screening of this program? How do the nature of the advertisements influence the image of the program? How do the advertisements shape the nature of the audience?

One can also adapt imaginative recreation tasks to the exploration of the meanings of a television series or episode such as:

- Creating a history or future for any characters to give reasons for, or effects of, their actions/traits.
- Creating a 'spin-off' episode or series outline which centralises a minor character and marginalises the main character(s) so that the events/attitudes etc can be viewed from different perspectives.
- Viewing events etc from the point of view of the villains through dramatic monologue or creation of an episode.
- Recast characters into different narrative genres to highlight generic features and assumptions underlying the values of the program.
- Create a dialogue or episode in which characters from one program encounter characters from another. This activity can have a variety of

purposes from articulating and challenging the values implied by certain programs to simply exploring the bizarre as a creative and intellectual exercise.

(These activities have been adapted from Jenkins, H (1992) *Textual Poachers*, New York: Routledge, quoted in Storey, J (1996) *Cultural Studies and the Study of Popular Culture: Theories and Methods*, Athens: University of Georgia Press.)

Language Study

Ken Watson

Metaphor

Students often leave school with the idea that metaphor and simile are language devices peculiar to poetry. But metaphor is a vital ingredient of everyday conversation, and one of the most important ways in which the language grows. Our language is littered with dead metaphors: a *ladder* in a stocking; the *neck* of a bottle; the *brow* of the hill; a cheque that *bounced;* a *dry* book. As David Crystal points out,

> We argue with each other using the terms of battle (she attacked my views; he defended himself ; I won the argument). We talk about countries as if they were people (America's been a good friend to them; France and her neighbours). We discuss economics in terms of human health (oil is our lifeline; an ailing economy).
>
> David Crystal – The Cambridge Encyclopedia of the English Language (p421)

Overworked metaphors that do not 'die', however, simply add to the store of clichés that clutter the language.

Perhaps the best starting point for a study of metaphor is to direct students to the sporting pages of newspapers, which are full of metaphorical language, and then have them listen for metaphors in everyday conversation. This example from the sporting pages is taken from a description of an Australian Rules game by Martin Flanagan:

> . . . Cransberg seemed untouched by the general hurly burly and kept flitting in and out of the game like a graceful, long-legged water bird. . . . In the final minute, with the ball wedged in the Collingwood goal mouth, bodies ricocheted into the packs like electrons attempting to split the atom.

Australians seem to be especially inventive when it comes to striking metaphors and similes, eg. "flash as a rat with a gold tooth"; "as useless as a dunny with a glass door"; "a rooster one day, a feather duster the next". When Mr Keating was Prime Minister, he described the Leader of the

Opposition as " a shiver looking for a spine to run up". G A Wilkes's *Exploring Australian English* (Sydney: ABC , revised edition, 1993) is full of amusing examples of Australian speech.

Metaphor plays an important role in structuring the way we think about the world. Think of the ways in which metaphors about schooling have shaped public thinking about education: schooling as a race; schools as factories with inputs and outputs.

The Language of Propaganda and Politics

An important area of language study is the language of propaganda: the attempt to pin unfavourable labels on opponents (*commo, fascist*); the constant resort to stereotypes (*the Jew, the Communist*); the use of clichés (*Business is business*) and slogans (*Ein Volk, ein Reich, ein Fuhrer!*).

Allied to such study is an analysis of the language of politics, and elections come about so frequently in Australia that every senior class ought to be able to undertake such a study at election time. When analysing political speeches and advertisements, some questions that students should ask themselves include:

1. What attention-getting techniques are used?
2. What attempts are made to establish positive associations (eg., with the family, patriotism etc.)?
3. What fears are played on?
4. Are attempts made to create a sense of urgency?
5. Are there gaps in logic? sweeping generalisations? one-sided arguments?
6. Is there an over-reliance on slogans, key words, symbols?

NB: Further language activities are to be found on pages 56, 100, 117, 163 and 262.

Section VII: Assessment

26 Assessment in English

Neil E Béchervaise

Introduction

Systems which rely on continuous assessment and use grades for attitude put the purpose of judgement and social control above that of enhancing student development   (Johnston, 1987:15)

Traditional summative assessment procedures leading to over-simplification in the reporting process have reduced the credibility of English teachers in the public perception. Political and media-driven campaigns to identify and apparently improve literacy levels from unstated base levels have provided apparent support for this view.

As schools continue their move toward outcomes-based, criterion-referenced assessment, the need to emphasise diagnostic and formative assessment to support teaching methods, resources selection and achievement profiling becomes more urgent. This chapter identifies a range of assessment and reporting procedures available to English teachers and argues that their implementation is an essential suport for current practice.

The Assessment Debate

Debates about the form, frequency and reporting of student learning have a strong tendency to degenerate into special pleading on behalf of particular interest groups. In both Canada and America, where residents pay local taxes to elect and employ regional School Boards and teachers, to determine text selection and to administer schools, the special pleading (and differing ability to pay) leads to substantial differences in the effectiveness of schooling across the country. As a consequence, the United States takes data from mass administration of centrally produced objective tests as the single most meaningful indicator of school quality, teacher effectiveness and student learning (Berlak, 1986).

The process of large-scale testing generates a public confidence based in what is presented as a scientific certainty. By the same argument, 2 million lemmings pouring over a cliff cannot be wrong. By the same argument, literacy testing at Year 3 level is becoming universal in Australia though the state education systems are unaligned, the aims of the courses are developed independently and the tests are generated, administered and reported differently in each state. That this national testing trend appears set to include Years 5, 7 and 9 suggests that we believe the testing to be a more potent tool in establishing education than the learning process itself.

The purpose for this chapter, however, is not to debate the strengths and weaknesses of various assessment procedures. It is to recognise a more substantial truth:

> While the purpose of school education is seen to be the passing of formal tests and examinations, the control of assessment will remain tantamount to the control of curriculum.

Movements away from formal testing procedures are usually met with cries of falling standards and decline in academic rigour. In consequence, rather than evaluating the effectiveness of its Year 12 exit examination, the Higher School Certificate, as an effective assessment of the intentions of its education curriculum, the current New South Wales government held the examination sacrosanct while it reviewed the curriculum. The changes proposed have raised little media debate. Subsequent complaints from interest groups representing students who wished a more appropriate training for entry to the work-force, who did not wish to enter tertiary education institutions, or who found the syllabus range too narrowing for their interests, remain effectively unheard by the vested interest groups who control the education system through their electoral power.

In a similar vein, the governmental review of the Victorian Certificate of Education expressed concern at the separate inclusion of school performance in the reporting of results and proposed a move back to more centralised testing. Commonwealth moves to establish national literacy testing procedures – following earlier governmental initiatives to establish agreed outcomes from the educational process – have met with equally conservative responses.

So what is the purpose of assessment – whether in school or from beyond? Is it intended to measure student performance, teacher performance, learning appropriateness, public desire or national security priorities?

The Purposes of Assessment

Assessment fulfils three major functions:

+ *diagnosis* of problems needing remedy or shortcomings to be addressed;
+ *formative feedback* used to improve, modify or extend the initial work;
+ *summative feedback* to establish the quality of the product presented.

While summative assessment focuses on student work as a final product, diagnostic and formative assessment procedures focus on refinement or extension of a process represented by the work-in-progress. Large-scale testing programs are necessarily summative though some, like the ELLA (English Language and Literacy Assessment) in NSW claim diagnostic authority.

> *If we want to assess in ways which encourage students to reflect on their own work, we must be careful that we are not in such a hurry that we try to squeeze assessments out of them before they have reflected on the specifics of their experience.* (Johnston, 1987:16)

Donald Graves' approach, now commonly referred to as *process writing*, assumes that every piece of student writing is a work-in-progress. In taking this approach, Graves presumes that the work is intrinsically useful, that it has a purpose, that there is an identifiable audience for the work and that the student-as-artist/artisan has a desire to create the most effective product for the purpose intended.

In his concentration on process, Graves' work is supportive of a dynamic process in which growth towards excellence is the fundamental objective of education. His approach supports the student, at whatever stage of development, and works towards the achievement of outcomes which are presumed to be shared between all parties to the educational process. Arnold (1996) repeats Applebee's (1981) claims that this affective involvement in the development of the work represents the only realistic assessment of what they term 'authentic' writing. In this context, the work process itself provides a powerful indicator for the establishment of a formative assessment base.

The shared approach to education was identified by people such as Dixon, Britton, Barnes, Rosen and Moffett and, later, by Arnold, Wilkinson, et al into the '90s. It has developed largely in recognition of the tendency for English educators to claim the address of a full palette of communicative skills while summatively assessing writing products (essay writing in particular) as an almost singular means of determining student learning (Britton, et al, 1975).

Current understanding of assessment (eg Masters and Forster [1996 a, b], Broadfoot, [1991], McGregor and Meiers, [1991]) strongly supports the views propounded by Johnston (1987) in his still excellent work *Assessing English* (which much of this chapter necessarily supports). "To learn to control the medium they also must reflect, conceptualise and experiment" (Johnston, 1987, p105).

Criterion-Referenced Assessment

While some English teachers still insist that they assess on the basis of an innate understanding of what constitutes excellent performance for a student at a given level, research strongly suggests that most have a highly developed set of assessment criteria which they apply to the task. In recent years, these have been elaborated as *learning outcomes*. The resulting outcomes have been published as exhaustive lists which have met with stern resistance in some areas (eg Little, 1992) and applauded in others. More commonly, they have alerted English teachers to the complexity of the task they undertake when they enter the assessment process.

Learning outcomes are the criteria which students are expected to be able to demonstrate in a specific assessment task.

They are descriptors of behaviour which students are expected to display when they submit work for assessment. More importantly, however, they are descriptors of behaviour which students are expected to have mastered if they are to be considered competent communicators. As a consequence, the list of criteria to be displayed in an oral presentation differs markedly from that to be displayed in a written work.

Our expectations of a well-crafted letter to the editor are substantially different from our expectations of a verbal summary of the newspaper article which inspired the letter. The difference between written and spoken forms appears to be obvious but when the reflective nature of the one is compared with the compressed, emotive nature of the other, necessary differences in assessment criteria become more obvious.

The following example of an assessment task suggests some of the criteria which might be used for its assessment. The work sample following the task indicates that a clear statement of expected criteria would have clarified the demands of the task and made the assessment task less difficult than this response will demand.

Murgha High School

Lord of the Flies   Year 10

Assignment

Using your understanding of the events which led to the close of the story, write the report sent by the senior Naval Officer to his superior describing what he discovered when he landed on the island.

Present your report in a form appropriate to the audience.

Royal Navy

Incident Report

Reporting Officer: Captain Murray Grey
Date: 14 May, 1957
Incident: Discovery of boys on Island K234

Report

✱ After landing to investigate a bushfire on island K234, we were confronted with a group of poorly clad and filthy schoolchildren.

---

* The child named Ralph appeared to be running for his life from the main group led by a youth named Jack.

* The main group carried spears and were painted like primitives.

* Subsequent interviews determined that the main group were attempting to bring Ralph to justice for killing one of their group named Simon.

* Investigation established the remains of a mutilated youth decomposing beside a tidal pool.

* The youth named Ralph denies the charge, blaming the group for murdering Simon.

* Ralph claims that Simon was killed when he tried to reveal the truth about a dead pilot. The body of the pilot was found hanging from the shrouds of his parachute in a tree.

* Ralph then claims that another boy, whom the group call Piggy, was also killed by the group. Again, the interview with Jack and twin brothers in the group clearly indicate that Ralph is the real killer.

* Under the rules of martial law imposed at the Dartmouth Conference, the youth, Ralph, was summarily executed on the beach and buried there.

* The island has fresh water and is habitable for extended periods so should be redefined in the Survival Orders Manual.

* The remainder of the group were landed into the care of our Consul General in Manilla on 25th April, 1957.

Report ends

The response, in several senses, meets the implicit demand of the assessment task. It is evidently written in the form of a report. It outlines events as they might have unravelled upon examination of the boys. It establishes the coherence of the group under Jack's leadership. It identifies what are probably the most horrific features of the island occupation for all of the boys. It provides a summary adult response appropriate to wartime and unsympathetic with either the subtleties of adolescent male development or with behaviour outside wartime naval regulations. To this extent, the response meets the implied criteria of the exercise but it is unlikely that the teacher who set the assignment had this fictionalised response in mind. As a consequence, it seems likely that the student will be disappointed at the assessment and perhaps even mystified at what he/she could do to satisfy the teacher.

The development of clear criteria need not, however, be a teacher-directed or a syllabus-determined exercise:

When English teachers avoid grades and marks, and involve students in assessing their own work, then the students are more motivated to improve their writing than are students who continuously receive grades and marks.
(Johnston, 1987:1)

The following extract from a Year 9 student writing journal suggests a shared intention in the process of developing a story:

Draft 2: After we talked about writing an interesting opening to grab the reader, I began to think about who would read this story. I decided that it could be published in a magazine that would be read by girls who were interested in surfing maybe. [I couldn't think of a magazine like that so I looked at some of the magazines in the library.] It wouldn't fit in a surf magazine because the readers would be older so I tried to write a story for something like 'Girlfriend'. I looked at the opening of their articles and tried to write for that audience so the words are fairly simple and the sentences are short and very descriptive and it brings in girls and surf from the beginning – like a newspaper story in a pyramid.

The reflection of the author suggests that discussion of the first draft opening was sufficient to establish that the story needed an audience. Stylistic and narrative structural details follow from the clear identification of audience reading needs and demands.

It seems evident that the second draft should display the features identified by the author – that these should become the criteria for further formative assessment. It seems clear too that a sample audience of girls from the class might be engaged as second draft readers to suggest whether the story is achieving its intended purpose and whether the girls feel that the style is appropriate to the magazine identified. The teacher may not, indeed, be involved in the second, or subsequent, draft conferences.

The criteria for assessment become dependent upon the intention of the work being assessed. The developmental nature of the writing process established in the example above suggests that the criteria for assessment might, themselves, be developed as the intention of the work is refined. At the point at which summative assessment is finally applied, the criteria may have grown from a collaboration between the student, the teacher and peers as potential audience.

Outcomes and Objectives

It takes little experience for most of us to realise that we will never write a concerto like Beethoven, that we will never write with the simplicity of

Basho, that we will never speak with the poignancy of Syu San Ju or the emotive depth of Nelson Mandela. We recognise a distinct difference between our objectives as musicians, writers, artists and orators and the outcomes we personally achieve. Similarly, we recognise that our objectives as English educators are often markedly variant from the outcomes achieved by our students.

Teaching objectives describe the intention of the teacher in relation to particular goals or aims identified in the syllabus.

Outcomes describe the intended, observable achieve- ment of the students as a result of teaching.

Not uncommonly, it is my intention to bring students to an understanding that literature describes, comments on and suggests responses to what I might call 'the human condition'. This, at least, is one of my principal objectives in teaching literature. More observably, my students may: report orally on their enjoyment of the story; write about how they feel parts of the story are reflected in the experience of their sister or mother or friend and develop play scripts, film scenarios or storyboards to show how they would translate a particular sequence to another medium. These observable outcomes point towards my having achieved my objective for particular students though none can show me, undeniably, that it is so.

The identification of outcomes at national and state levels has presented English teachers with a bewilderingly comprehensive set of criteria for the assessment of a very wide range of skills. From a classroom teacher's viewpoint, the lists of outcomes are exhaustive and exhausting. Despite this, the lists remain incomplete. Arnold's (1991) 'magic in the brain' remains hidden behind the lists. The sparkle which separates capable from great writing, exciting from interesting speaking, breath-taking from tedious negotiation of an art form is missing from the lists. Yet these remain the objectives of every English teacher. They remain the objectives behind our every effort to educate students as active respondents and creators, as competent communicators.

The Roles of Assessment

While it remains tempting to argue that the school demands a summative assessment or that society only understands percentages, the truth remains elsewhere. While parents appear to expect rank orders and numerical or other gradings, the effect of the reporting procedure which confirms this identified desire is far from satisfying. The following reports for a Year 8 student display a range of reporting options.

Conforming to the perceived demands of the school and society, this traditional report provides a grade, a ranking and a comment on Diana's achievement after a year in the English classroom. Whether the teacher knows Diana is, fortunately, not an issue. The question of what Diana might do to improve her grade could, however, perplex her.

The number of students at the Year level (124) suggests that Diana is in one Year 8 class (8T) and that there are others – probably another four or five. Why she is a 'satisfactory' student when she is among the top ten per cent at her year level is not revealed. Possibly she is performing at about the middle of her own class and the comment is written on the basis of class rather than grade level. The report does not reveal very much of use to Diana, her parents or the society which is presumed to be demanding it.

An alternative report, shown below, establishes the criteria used to determine performance at Murgha High School. Diana and her parents will be able to discuss the range of tasks undertaken during the year and an outside observer will be able to identify the tasks on which, it is reported, Diana has performed successfully. How Diana might work to improve her assessed grade cannot be clear because the range of abilities required to complete each task successfully is unidentified. More problematically, perhaps, the grading on each task appears to have been added as if the effect of success on one criterion can be added to success on each of the others to generate a meaningful single mark summary of Diana's achievement over a whole school year.

Murgha High School
English

Diana Vassilios   Year 8T 1997
Grade: 73%
For success in year 8 English, students are expected to have:
✳ presented a prepared 3 minute speech
✳ read at least one novel
✳ written an essay on one of the books they have read
✳ drafted and written stories, poems and plays
✳ presented group devised plays
Comment: Diana has satisfied the requirements
                    of year 8 English

By the late '80s in Australia, the movement towards writing criterion-referenced achievement profiles for students was gaining momentum. The following report demonstrates one example of a student profile in subject English.

Murgha High School
English

Diana Vassilios   Year _8T_ 1997

Profile: Diana began the year with weaknesses in her grammatical structuring of written sentences, her punctuation and spelling. During the year she has worked to overcome these difficulties. She has also overcome her apparent reluctance to draft and discuss work before final submission.

Diana has presented a very entertaining talk on her Uncle's role in developing tartan paint to a whole class audience, read an average of four novels each term and written several thoughtful essays about the way characters respond to each other in science fiction.

Diana has developed a portfolio of plays, stories, poems and illustrated work which she has shared with her peers. In addition, she helped her writing group perform a short play on the theme of 'Friendship'.

While paragraphing in essays and use of orthodox punctuation still need close attention, Diana has clearly satisfied the requirements of year 8 English. She has already developed a number of the work patterns and skills she will need for success in English next year.

In the student profile, Diana is assessed according to her entry ability and behaviour and against identifiable performance criteria. Her development, her achievement on the identified criteria and the extent to which she has satisfied the requirements for success at the Year level are summarised. The summative grade has been replaced with a description of what Diana can already do and what she needs to do to ensure continued success. The positive tone and diagnostic/formative nature of the profile allow her to identify continuing problems, target areas for future work, celebrate her achievement with her parents and feel confident that she is moving along a continuum towards success as an English student.

The student profile of the Year 8 English student provided by the third report card appears to be a far cry from the initial report card. It informs both parents and society of the achievements of Diana, the student, and it provides a basis for discussion of identified areas requiring further work. The Year 9 teacher who accepts Diana into her class can immediately identify areas which should be focused on and areas in which Diana is already developing confidently.

Gathering Data for Profile Assessment

The argument that a student profile takes more time to write than the initial grade/rank/comment report is undoubtedly true. Nevertheless, the information which must be gathered to write the report remains unchanged.

For English teachers, already burdened with a plethora of 'marking', the argument against further work rightly attracts a sympathetic hearing. Fortunately, the use of the computer to store diagnostic and formative commentary throughout the year, as the 'marking' is completed, is a powerful tool.

Printouts of criterion-referenced assessments for drafts and final 'published' works alike provide a powerful data base for parent/teacher interviews, for interim reports and as a focus for discussion of student progress with students themselves.

Assessment commentary sorted according to reading, writing, speaking, listening and viewing inevitably provides a comprehensive record of student progress. It also provides powerful evidence in support of summative assessment statements. Both content acquisition and skills development are recorded but, in addition, affective development becomes part of the profile. The deep learning approaches which have been shown to substantiate long-term language development (eg Palincsar and Brown, 1984) are shown to be valued and the role of the teacher as facilitator is amplified.

The development of a spreadsheet to collect data for each student is an essential beginning of year task but the establishment of a mark book is equally time consuming and less useful at reporting season.

One of the most powerful arguments in support of student profiling, perhaps, remains the extent to which it establishes teacher professionalism. Through both formal and informal assessment procedures, English teachers develop a comprehensive knowledge of their students' writing, speaking and thinking abilities. They become aware of the feelings and thoughts, the communicative strengths and weaknesses and the breadth of personal experience of their students. That they should reduce this to a single number, a few words and a ranking is a belittling exercise in self-deprecation.

More significantly, to return to the beginning: if, as English educators, we continue to permit simplistic political and media notions of literacy to drive the curriculum then the control of assessment will, most certainly, be identified as control of curriculum. When we adopt more student-centred assessment procedures, our roles as English educators will be strengthened and confirmed in practice.

It is not possible to develop criteria for achievement in communicative excellence which neglect changes to the way we teach. We cannot record the development of student talk without having provided the regular opportunity for various forms of talk within a conscious learning environment. We cannot report the development of student's writing across the available genres, without having modelled the genres, having provided opportunities to experiment with the genres on the way to facility and having provided examples of the genres as displayed by experts. In brief, the development of sound assessment procedures is necessarily predicated on the development of sound teaching practices. If our assessment reflects student outcomes as a consequence of our teaching then it equally reflects the quality of our teaching and the resources we bring to bear on the educative process.

References

Adams, A (1974) *Every English Teacher*, Oxford: Oxford University Press.

Applebee, A (1981) *Writing in the Secondary School: English and the Content Areas*, Urbana, Illinois: NCTE.

Arnold, R (1996) "Writing Development: Psychodynamic Principles and Practices" In Watson, K (1996) *English Teaching in Perspective*, Rozelle: St Clair.

Barnes, D, Britton, J and Rosen, H (1969) *Language, the Learner and the School*, Harmondsworth: Penguin.

Berlak, H (1985) "Testing in a Democracy", *Educational Leadership*, XLIII, October, 16-17.

Britton, J, Burgess, T, Martin, N, McLeod, A and Rosen, H (1975) *The Development of Writing Abilities (11-18)*, London: Macmillan.

Broadfoot, P (1991) "Assessment: Keeping Students Fit for Education" in *Assessment: a Celebration of Learning*, Australian Curriculum Studies Association: Belconnen, ACT .

Dixon, J (1967) *Growth Through English*, Huddersfield: NATE.

Holbrook, D (1961) *English for Maturity*, Cambridge: Cambridge University Press.

Johnston, B (1987) *Assessing English*, Buckingham: Open University Press.

Little, G (1992) "The Value-Added Child" in Sawyer, W (ed) (1992) *Outcomes and Incomes*, Springwood: Australian Education Network Inc.

Masters, G and Forster, M (1996a) *Portfolios*, Melbourne: Australian Council for Educational Research.

Masters, G and Forster, M (1996b) *Developmental Assessment*, Melbourne: Australian Council for Educational Research.

Maclure, M, Phillips, T and Wilkinson, A (1988) *Oracy Matters*, Buckingham: Open University Press.

McGregor, R and Meiers, M (1991) *Telling the Whole Story*, Hawthorn: ACER.

Moffett, J (1968) *Teaching the Universe of Discourse*, Boston: Houghton Mifflin.

Murray, D M (1982) *Learning by Teaching*, Montclair, New Jersey: Boynton Cook.

Palincsar, A S and Brown, A L (1984) "Reciprocal Teaching of Comprehension – Fostering and Comprehension – Monitoring Activities" *Cognition and Instruction*, 1 (2), 117-175.

Wilkinson, A (1991) "Talking Sense: The Assessment of Talk", in Booth, D and Thornley-Hall, C *The Talk Curriculum*, Ontario: Pembroke.

Section VIII:
Aboriginal
Perspectives

26 Approaches to Teaching Aboriginal Perspectives in the Classroom

Nancy Burridge

It is important to note that the comments and views expressed in this paper are those of a non-Aboriginal person who has gained experience in indigenous issues largely through working with Aboriginal people in an atmosphere of shared learning. The terms 'Aboriginal' and 'indigenous' are deliberately interchanged throughout the text. The term 'Aboriginal peoples' has been used rather than 'Aboriginal and Torres Strait Islander peoples' because the author has based her comments on her work with Aboriginal communities, mostly in New South Wales.

The intention of this short chapter is to touch on some of the issues related to the teaching of an Aboriginal perspective in the curriculum, and also to give some insights into established methodologies of teaching Aboriginal children. The comments are couched in general terms as they apply not only to the English classroom, but to all other subjects.

If there is one essential point which needs to be made it is the need to involve the local indigenous community in matters associated with the teaching of Aboriginal culture and Aboriginal students.

Largely as a result of a number of important national reviews of Aboriginal education in the last twenty-five years – reviews which confirmed the low level of achievement of Aboriginal children in mainstream schools – there has been a significant shift in the mindset of educationists towards the teaching of Aboriginal culture and history and the teaching of Aboriginal students. These reviews culminated in the release of the National Aboriginal

Education Policy in 1989 and in the introduction of their own Aboriginal Education Policies by the various states.

A further impetus to improve educational attainment for Aboriginal people came from the recommendations of the *Aboriginal Deaths in Custody Royal Commission* in 1991. One of its recommendations (No 295) clearly set out the need for pre-service teacher training courses to include units which incorporated Aboriginal viewpoints on social, cultural and historical matters and for Aboriginal people to be involved in the training courses both at student teacher and at inservice level.

In general, all of these policy documents see education as the conduit for Aboriginal people to gain some equality of opportunity in society as well as a way of building greater knowledge and understanding of Aboriginal culture for all students. They acknowledge that mainstream schooling appears to be failing Aboriginal students and that the deficit is in the system not in the individual.

Some considerations in the Implementation of an Aboriginal Perspective in the Curriculum

What Will be Taught and by Whom?

It is of great importance to the success of a curriculum unit incorporating Aboriginal issues that there is a level of commitment to the teaching of such a unit by individual classroom teachers. This might be a highly charged comment, but the teaching of Aboriginal culture and history in the context of any subject in schools carries more than just an educational responsibility in the traditional sense. This expanded responsibility focuses on the teacher's ability to foster in students an understanding of Aboriginal culture and Aboriginal history as well as the capacity to challenge preconceived notions of Aboriginal people. Challenging these notions is very difficult, particularly if a teacher is young and the attitudes are entrenched. That is not to say that controversial issues should not be debated, or that one should paint a rosy picture of the Aboriginal life, past and present. However, great skill and sensitivity are needed to ensure that a balanced debate occurs. For example, issues such as high alcohol consumption and the resultant negative media images of Aboriginal people need to be debated because they are ever present in the minds of individuals. However, such images can be countered by simple national statistics which show that indigenous people as a group drink far less than non-indigenous people.

This commitment by the teacher extends to the need to network with Aboriginal people; to gain their confidence and involve them in the design and teaching of courses and units. The process of involving Aboriginal people requires its own set of skills and sensitivities which can only be developed through contact with Aboriginal people.

What will be taught is largely determined by the structure of the syllabus. Most English-based activities involve discussion of Aboriginal life stories and the experiences of indigenous peoples as a result of European invasion. Much of the writing of Aboriginal authors centres on issues of Aboriginality. The words of Mudrooroo, Sally Morgan and Archie Weller are such examples. It is interesting to note that for many of these authors their own indigenous identity has been publicly called into question – mainly by non-Aboriginal people who still adhere to the old notion of categorising Aboriginal people by 'blood line' (see below).

In designing a unit of work on indigenous experiences it is important to note that Aboriginal communities are very regionalised and the differences between one language group (or nation) and another must be acknowledged. Consultation with the local Aboriginal communities is essential to establish what is appropriate to be taught about that community and what sites can be visited. Wherever possible, Aboriginal educators should be brought in when teaching about cultural matters, particularly if it is to do with ceremonies and secret/sacred sites, stores or objects. The underlying principle here is one of respect for the protocols of a culture different from the mainstream.

The Need for Appropriate Resources

Apart from the usual constraints of lack of funding in resourcing any curriculum unit, there are other considerations when choosing resources for a unit on Aboriginal history and culture. A sound policy is to avoid resources which are ethnocentric, which present Aboriginal peoples as monolithic ('the Aborigines'), and which have not had their content overseen or approved by a known Aboriginal educator or a member of the local Aboriginal community, such as an elder.

Junior high school textbooks, by their very nature as generalist texts, have been the greatest offenders in reinforcing stereotypical images of Aboriginal people. There still exist, on some library shelves, examples of what are now seen as blatantly racist textbooks. More recent textbooks can still offend, but more subtly. They offend through the often unconscious use of paternalistic and ethnocentric text which evaluates Aboriginal culture from a western perspective. Most Aboriginal education units have a 'checklist' of items which are used to evaluate good resources.

Consultation With the Aboriginal Community

Aboriginal people are the custodians of their culture. They understand the intricacies of their laws and lore. They can express their own world view and tell it like it is or was, and by right they are the ones who should be consulted and involved in the teaching process.

The main premise the points below present is one of giving Aboriginal people the time and space to become involved in the school's activities. This might be difficult in a tight school schedule but the rewards are worth the extra input of time.

✦ Consultation must be a two-way process; it is not a power relationship. It is a learning process for all participants, requiring negotiation, flexibility and open minds.

✦ Always acknowledge the work done by Aboriginal people and pay for their services at the accepted rate. Historically, Aboriginal communities have had unfortunate experiences with researchers (for example, anthropologists) who have merely utilised their community for scientific observations, paying little heed to cultural sensitivities.

✦ Many Aboriginal people have had negative experiences of schooling. Teachers need to rebuild trust between school and home.

✦ Be conscious of the way you use language. Avoid bureaucratic language and jargon.

✦ When seeking to make contact with a community, if possible work through an Aboriginal person of that community who is trusted by them.

✦ Be aware of the pressures on resources in Aboriginal communities. Have realistic expectations about what people can do.

✦ Above all, be flexible and adapt to circumstances.

What Terminology is Appropriate When Teaching Aboriginal Perspectives and Who Decides?

Historically, much of the terminology used to describe Aboriginal culture and peoples has had western anthropological or western socio-cultural frames of reference. Terms were often used to codify Aboriginality and to reduce human beings to mere objects of scientific study.

While one must acknowledge that there is no uniform policy on appropriate terminology acceptable to all, it is important to understand that there are terms which are seen as generally unacceptable to Aboriginal people and may cause offence. Teachers should be aware of what is, and what is not, acceptable in the local community.

It should also be noted that while it may be acceptable for Aboriginal people to use various terms amongst themselves to refer to one another, it is not necessarily appropriate for non-Aboriginal people to use those terms in that context. Sensitive judgment is needed.

Terms such as 'half-caste', 'quarter-caste' and 'octoroon' were used to define Aboriginal people in terms of 'blood line' and skin colour in what was, in essence, an official policy of 'breeding out' Aboriginality. Even today, this practice has not changed, as Mick Dodson comments:

The obsession with distinctions between the offensively named 'full bloods' and hybrids, or 'real' and 'unauthentic' Aborigines, continues to be imposed on us today. There would be few urban Aboriginal people who have not been labelled as culturally bereft, 'fake' or 'part-Aborigine', and then expected to authenticate their Aboriginality in terms of percentages of blood or clichéd 'traditional' experiences. (Dodson, 1994)

Terms such as 'primitive', 'simple', 'savage', 'stone age' are definitely not acceptable except perhaps in their historical contexts as mentioned above. When referring to different groups, terms such as 'clan' or 'language group' or 'nation' are preferred. But even these terms are ethnocentric in that they reflect western world views of progress and civilisation, implying that to be different is to be inferior. They fail to come to grips with the complex organisational structures associated with Aboriginal societies, their spirituality and the depth of understanding Aboriginal people have of their environment.

Aboriginal people may traverse the boundaries of 'traditional' and 'contemporary' on an everyday basis in their value systems and their world views. To label 'traditional' Aborigines, living in the 'outback', as the 'real' Aborigines is to again misconstrue the concept of Aboriginality. Similarly, it is preferable to speak of 'the Dreaming' when referring to Aboriginal creation stories (not 'myths' or 'legends'), rather than 'the Dreamtime'. 'Dreamtime' implies a time in the distant past, unreal and removed, rather than what the Dreaming is – a dynamic, ongoing spiritual expression of the relationship between Aboriginal people and their links with the world around them. (Hollingsworth, 1991)

What are the Considerations When Teaching Aboriginal Children?

Catering for individual differences in mixed-ability classrooms has been the mainstay of educational programs for many years. The ethnic diversity in our classrooms has added the cultural dimension to our appreciation of these differences.

Our level of understanding of the cultural differences between Aboriginal and non-Aboriginal Australians is crucial to the design of programs which should reflect and value these differences. Yet, balance is needed so that an 'us' and 'them' mentality does not emerge. The differences should be highlighted and explained as valuable contributors to a common Australian heritage which we all share.

Educational theorists such as Merody Malin and Stephen Harris (Harris and Malin, 1994) maintain that there is a distinctive 'Aboriginal Pedagogy' which can work to facilitate Aboriginal student learning. Research conducted with young urban Aboriginal students has established strong arguments for the recognition that there are distinct learning styles which pertain to Aboriginal students and these reflect the cultural differences as exemplified in the value system, the extended familial structures, the roles Aboriginal children play within those structures, and the co-operative (rather than competitive) nature of Aboriginal communities. Learning in traditional Aboriginal communities was holistic, it occurred within everyday life, unlike the English model which is much more compartmentalised.

It is claimed that these differing 'world views' impact heavily on students' behaviour in the highly structured environment of the mainstream classroom. What is often perceived by teachers as inattentiveness and misbehaviour may well be an expression of the greater autonomy given to Aboriginal children by their parents as well as a desire to learn in a communal atmosphere rather than an individual one. Research into learning styles has made some claims that Aboriginal children learn experientially. Without wanting to generalise, many children are seen as kinaesthetic learners: they much prefer to learn by doing and interacting with their peers. The concept of Shaming should also be understood by teachers. Aboriginal students do not like to be singled out from their group to perform tasks or show mastery of skills – this can be seen as a real 'Shame job' by many. These perceived differences has led some educationists to categorise these differences into 'cultural comparison' lists.

While these generalised cultural comparisons lists may be useful to give a broad sweep of understanding of the differences between indigenous and 'western' cultures, there are dangers in giving them too much importance. Kevin Keeffe (1992) challenges the value of these lists.

> Unfortunately, . . . the elements they select are not common, not universal, not essential and not enduring.   (Keeffe, 1992, p75)

These cultural comparisons lists, by their very nature, generalise about cultures, and in this way they merely become another instrument of stereo- typing. The assumption that there is one Aboriginal society negates all our knowledge about the regional diversity of Aboriginal communities. The short, point-form structure of these comparisons hardly provides for detailed understanding of Aboriginal society in any case. And more importantly, the danger is that these lists will be taken as holy writ by some teachers. Students will then be asked to copy them into their exercise books and to learn them for exams.

Differing 'world views' between indigenous communities and non-Aboriginal communities definitely exist. In general, indigenous peoples have an outlook far more enmeshed in spirituality, familial bonds and human emotional understandings which transcend the boundaries of rationality or scientific thinking. These elements, however, cannot be conveyed in structured lists of identifiable attributes of Aboriginality.

How Accepting Are We of Aboriginal English in Our Classrooms?

Great strides have been made in the acceptance of Aboriginal English in the classroom. Aboriginal education units in a number of states have produced a number of excellent publications (for example, *Langwij Comes to School* produced by DEET in 1995), encouraging the use of language in context, and many states now have endorsed Aboriginal English and 'Creole' as variants of English. Teachers are now more readily accepting of the fact that the language of the home and the playground is just as valid and real as the standard English encouraged in our classrooms. Each has a place and a part to play in the educative process and we need to value both the vernacular and the standard English in their appropriate contexts.

Aboriginal English combines the speech patterns of standard English with words and speech patterns of the local Aboriginal language. Its intensity of usage and its variance from standard English differs from community to community. It is a valid form of expression (as is ethnic English) and has a place in the classroom. Teachers should learn to value and utilise it to gain the confidence of Aboriginal children as it is the mode in which some children will learn best. It is useful sometimes to use Aboriginal language to break the ice with an Aboriginal student or to get the essence of a point across. It is a valid and dynamic form of expression in creative writing.

This of course is not to deny the importance of teaching children standard English and Aboriginal children are no exception. Education is about empowerment. Learning the language structure of the dominant culture enables Aboriginal students to gain access to the opportunities offered within that society without negating the values of their own culture. We need to teach children that each form of expression is valid and appropriate in its cultural and social context. But first we have to get this message across to the teachers.

Conclusion

In summary, introducing an Aboriginal perspective into a mainstream subject such as English can be a very rewarding challenge. But it will take time and persistence to remove the obstacles which will undoubtedly emerge. Aboriginal culture can teach us much about our relationship with our environment, about ourselves and our own sense of spirituality. If we take the time to value, appreciate and learn from the wisdom of a culture far more ancient than the current dominant, western model, and we allow it to contribute to our sense of identity as a people, we will be far richer for the experience. A quotation from *Wisdom of the Elders* illustrates this more eloquently:

> But if Western science does not need the Native Mind, the human mind and, in particular, the Western mind and society do. We will always need the Native Mind's vibrant images of a living natural world that can penetrate to the deepest and most heartfelt (what science calls "irrational" or "intuitive") realms of human understanding. We need the

Native Mind's bold assurance that while much of the universe is accessible to human sensibilities, it possesses dimensions that may remain forever beyond human logic and reason, and that cosmic forces of mystery, chaos, and uncertainty are eternal. Perhaps more than anything else we need the glimmer of hope for the kind of future that indigenous nature-wisdom foreshadows – by its historic precedent of sustaining a longterm ecological equilibrium, despite occasional lapses.

(Knudtson and Suzuki, 1992)

References

Dodson, M (1994) "The End in the Beginning: Re(de)finding Aboriginality", *Australian Aboriginal Studies* 1994 No 1.

Harkins, J (1994) *Bridging Two Worlds: Aboriginal English and Cross-Cultural Understanding,* Brisbane: Queensland University Press.

Hollingsworth, D (1991) *Guidelines for Non Racist Language Use in Aboriginal Studies,* Aboriginal Studies Conference Papers.

Hudsmith, P (1992) "Culturally Responsive Pedagogy in Urban Classrooms", *The Aboriginal Child at School* Vol 20 No 3, pp3-12.

Keeffe, K (1992) *From the Centre to the City: Aboriginal Education, Culture and Power,* Canberra: Aboriginal Studies Press.

Knudtson, D and Suzuki, D (1992) *Wisdom of the Elders,* Sydney: Allen and Unwin.

Malin, M, Harris, S (1994) *Aboriginal Kids in Urban Classrooms,* Wentworth Falls, NSW: Social Science Press.

Mudrooroo (1997) *The Indigenous Literature of Australia: Milli Milli Wangha,* Melbourne: Hyland House.

Contributors

Peter Adams has taught in a number of metropolitan and country schools in South Australia over the last twenty years. His book, *At the Far Reach of Their Capacities*, was published by the Australian Association for the Teaching of English in 1996.

Roslyn Arnold is Associate Professor and Head of School in the Faculty of Education, University of Sydney. She is the author of *Writing Development: Magic in the Brain* (1991), and has recently published a volume of poetry, *Mirror the Wind* (1997).

Gillian Barnsley is a Senior Lecturer in English Education at the Burwood Campus (formerly Rusden) of Deakin University. Her recent publications include the *Information Problems: Using Computers to Process Solutions* package, (Macmillan, Melbourne 1997) in which she takes a cross-curricular approach to the implementation of the technology framework at secondary level.

David Baxter began teaching at Oxley High School, Tamworth, NSW in 1975, becoming Head Teacher there in 1988 and then North West Regional Consultant in 1994-95. He is currently a Lecturer in English Education at the University of New England, Armidale, NSW.

Neil Béchervaise, Senior Lecturer in Education at the University of Sydney, had a thirty-year career in secondary classrooms in Australia and Canada before moving into teacher education. He is a prolific writer on secondary English, with research interests in early reading development, change management, gifted and multicultural education, assessment and the uses of technology in education.

Nancy Burridge is currently Director of the Institute of Aboriginal Studies and Research at Macquarie University. She has been a teacher of history in secondary schools and more recently has been involved in teacher education.

Brenton Doecke is a Senior Lecturer in the Faculty of Education at Monash University. He is currently Editor of *English in Australia*, the journal of the Australian Association for the Teaching of English.

Cal Durrant is a Senior Lecturer in the Department of Curriculum Studies and the Co-ordinator of Studies in English and Media Education at the University of New England. He has published widely on aspects of English Curriculum.

Margaret Gill is an Associate Professor in the Faculty of Education, Monash University. She has researched, taught and published in the fields of English curriculum change, the politics of literacy and issues relating to teacher professional standards and professional development.

Eva Gold has been a classroom practitioner for many years. She is actively involved in English teacher professional development and has contributed to *Instant English, Word and Image* and *Timeless Truths* (all St Clair Press).

John Hughes is Senior Lecturer in Educational Drama and Chair of the Arts Education Academic Unit at the Faculty of Education, University of Sydney.

Michael Kindler taught languages, teacher-librarianship and English from 1976 to 1993 in high schools in Western Sydney. From 1994 to 1996 he lectured at the Univesity of Western Sydney and is now lecturing at Macquarie University.

Douglas McClenaghan teaches at Viewbank Secondary College in Melbourne. He is the co-author of *Thoughtworks, Mindworks and Englishworks 2*, all published by Cambridge University Press, and has written numerous articles and reviews.

Barbara McLean has taught and lectured in the area of multicultural education and ESL for many years. She is currently a Lecturer at Macquarie University.

Jackie Manuel lectures in English Education at the University of Western Sydney, Macarthur. Her publications include four textbooks for senior secondary English.

Ray Misson is Senior Lecturer in Language and Literacy Education and Associate Dean (Preservice Programs) in the Faculty of Education at the University of Melbourne. He has written extensively on popular culture, critical literacy, and on literary and cultural theory in relation to teaching English in secondary schools.

Diana Mitchell is President of the Michigan Council of Teachers of English (USA) and co-Director of a National Writing Project site. She is co-author (with Stephen Tchudi) of *Exploring and Teaching the English Language Arts* (4th edition).

Wendy Morgan is a Senior Lecturer in Language and Literacy Education at Queensland University of Technology. Her publications include a text for senior secondary students based on post-structuralist theories of texts, reading, culture and politics, called *Ned Kelly Reconstructed* (Cambridge, 1994) and *Critical Literacy in the Classroom: The Art of the Possible* (Routledge, 1997).

Robin Peel is Subject Leader for English at the University of Plymouth. He is currently working with Annette Patterson and Jeanne Gerlach on a book on perceptions of English to be published by Routledge later this year.

Paul Richardson is a Senior Lecturer in Education at Monash University, Gippsland Campus. He has a special interest in literacy education.

Wayne Sawyer lectures in English Education at the University of Western Sydney Nepean and was formerly a Head Teacher of English in Sydney's western suburbs. He is the author of a number of books on secondary English teaching, including *English Teaching from A to Z* (with Anthony Adams and Ken Watson) for Open University Press.

Tina Sharpe is a part-time consultant and **Julie Thompson** is the Director of Professional Development for the Association of Independent Schools (NSW). They are co-authors of a range of literary professional development courses, including *Accessing Learning In English* and *Accessing Critical Literacy and the Media*.

John Stephens is an Associate Professor in English at Macquarie University, where he teaches mainly children's literature and discourse analysis. He is the author of four books and many articles, including studies of film, television and picture books.

Jack Thomson was Senior Lecturer in English in Education at Charles Sturt University at Bathurst. Since his retirement he has worked as a Visiting Research Fellow at Edith Cowan University in Perth and as a visiting lecturer in six cities in Pakistan. He has also been a consulting editor for the Cambridge University series *Englishworks* for Years 7-10, and has just completed a research report for the NSW Department of Training and Education Co-ordination on literacy education in NSW preservice teacher education institutions.

Ernie Tucker is an education consultant in children's literature, drawing on his long experience in teaching high school English, heading an English department, teaching at Macquarie University and being leading teacher at Newtown High School of the Performing Arts.

R D (Bob) Walshe has been a significant figure in the teaching of writing and has played a key role in the growth of the Primary English Teaching Association and the Australian Education Network. A tireless campaigner on environmental issues, he founded the Sutherland Shire Environment Centre in Sydney.

Ken Watson, formerly Senior Lecturer in Education at the University of Sydney, had twenty years' experience as a high school teacher and has been a visiting lecturer at the universities of Cambridge, Michigan State, British Columbia and New York. He has written and edited many books, including *English Teaching in Perspective* and *English Teaching from A to Z*.